THE WICKED + ƎИIVIᗡ ƎHT

OLD IS THE NEW NEW

This volume collects the Specials which we published during the run of *The Wicked + The Divine*. They were released between the main arcs, with guest artists joining us. They're primarily historical Specials, each of which explores the end of one of the previous pantheons. They were released in an order which was aimed to juxtapose with the just-released single issues, so we could introduce a concept in the arc, and then the historical story that comes after it tells you something else.

We planned to publish them towards the end of our run in a single volume, and so knew that in a collected edition they'd have to serve a different purpose. They've been rearranged chronologically, which highlights their connective elements as a narrative. *Mothering Invention* gave a lot about what Ananke has been up to, and by arranging them like this, you'll see a lot more.

The two other Specials are a Christmas Annual (which shows some scenes we'd wished we'd have a chance to show before now) and The Funnies (which is the end-of-term party). They've been put at the end, but can be read whenever.

However, in case any of you want to recreate the actual single-issue reading experience, this is where you should insert them...

You should read 1873AD after the end of *Rising Action* (ie after issue 22).

You should read 455AD after the end of *Imperial Phase (Part I)* (ie after issue 28).

You should read 1923AD and the Christmas Annual after *Imperial Phase (Part II)* (ie after issue 33).

You should read 1373AD and The Funnies after *Mothering Invention* (ie after issue 39).

Have fun. See you shortly with our final arc, *"Okay"*.

|⌐! MᶜK

Kieron and Jamie

455AD

THE WICKED + THE DIVINE

VOL. 8, OLD IS THE NEW NEW

GILLEN

MᶜKELVIE

WILSON

COWLES

THE WICKED + THE DIVINE

CREATED BY
KIERON GILLEN AND JAMIE MCKELVIE

CLAYTON COWLES
LETTERER

SERGIO SERRANO
DESIGNER

CHRISSY WILLIAMS
EDITOR

KATIE WEST
EXECUTIVE ASSISTANT

HISTORICAL SPECIALS

KIERON GILLEN
WRITER

ANDRÉ ARAÚJO
455AD ARTIST

MATTHEW WILSON
455AD & 1373AD COLOURIST

DEE CUNNIFFE
455AD & 1373AD FLATTER

RYAN KELLY
1373AD ARTIST

STEPHANIE HANS
1831AD ARTIST

AUD KOCH
1923AD ARTIST

CHRISTMAS ANNUAL

STORIES BY
KIERON GILLEN

'SUMER LOVING'
INKS BY **KRIS ANKA & JEN BARTEL**
FLATS BY **DEE CUNNIFFE**
COLOUR BY **MATTHEW WILSON**

'IF YOU'RE FELINE SINISTER'
INKS BY **RACHEL STOTT**
FLATS BY **LUDWIG OLIMBA**
COLOUR BY **TAMRA BONVILLAIN**

'HITCHED'
INKS BY **CHYNNA CLUGSTON FLORES**
FLATS BY **LUDWIG OLIMBA & BRANDON DANIELS**
COLOUR BY **TAMRA BONVILLAIN**

'DECOMPOSITION'
INKS BY **EMMA VIECELI**
FLATS BY **DEE CUNNIFFE**
COLOUR BY **MATTHEW WILSON**

'STOLEN MOMENT'
INKS BY **RACHEL STOTT**
FLATS BY **DEE CUNNIFFE**
COLOUR BY **MATTHEW WILSON**

'TOXIC COMMUNITY'
INKS BY **CARLA SPEED MCNEIL**
FLATS BY **FERNANDO ARGÜELLO**
COLOUR BY **TAMRA BONVILLAIN**

'UH-HUH-HUH'
INKS BY **EMMA VIECELI**
FLATS BY **DEE CUNNIFFE**
COLOUR BY **MATTHEW WILSON**

THE FUNNIES

'THE WICKED + THE CANINE'
STORY BY **KIERON GILLEN**
INKS & COLOUR BY **ERICA HENDERSON**
FLATS BY **JUAN CASTRO**

'THE WICKER + THE DIVINE'
STORY & ART BY **LIZZ LUNNEY**

'THE LOST GOD'
STORY & ART BY **CHIP ZDARSKY**
FLATS BY **BECKA KINZIE**

'GENTLE ANNIE VS. THE WORLD'
STORY BY **CHRISSY WILLIAMS**
INKS BY **CLAYTON COWLES**
COLOUR BY **DEE CUNNIFFE**

'MAKING A DIFFERENCE'
STORY BY **ROMESH RANGANATHAN**
INKS BY **JULIA MADRIGAL**
COLOUR BY **DEE CUNNIFFE**

'5 THINGS EVERYONE WHO'S LIVED WITH SAKHMET WILL UNDERSTAND'
STORY & ART BY **HAMISH STEELE**

'13 GO MAD IN WILTSHIRE'
STORY & ART BY **KITTY CURRAN & LARISSA ZAGERIS**

'GUILTY PLEASURE SONG'
STORY BY **KATE LETH**
ART BY **MARGAUX SALTEL**

'SECRET ORIGIN'
STORY BY **KIERON GILLEN**
INKS BY **JAMIE MCKELVIE**
FLATS BY **DEE CUNNIFFE**
COLOUR BY **MATTHEW WILSON**

THE WICKED + THE DIVINE, VOL. 8, OLD IS THE NEW NEW
First printing. March 2019.
ISBN: 978-1-5343-0880-0
Published by Image Comics Inc.
Office of publication: 2701 NW Vaughn St., Suite 780, Portland, OR 97210.

For information regarding the CPSIA on this printed material call: 203-595-3636.
Representation: Law Offices of Harris M. Miller II, P.C. (rights.inquiries@gmail.com).

This book was designed by Sergio Serrano, based on a design by Hannah Donovan and Jamie McKelvie, and set into type by Sergio Serrano in Edmonton, Canada. The text face is Gotham, designed and issued by Hoefler & Co. in 2000. The paper is Liberty 60 matte.

IMAGE COMICS, INC.
Robert Kirkman, CHIEF OPERATING OFFICER
Erik Larsen, CHIEF FINANCIAL OFFICER
Todd McFarlane, PRESIDENT
Marc Silvestri, CHIEF EXECUTIVE OFFICER
Jim Valentino, VICE PRESIDENT
Eric Stephenson, PUBLISHER / CHIEF CREATIVE OFFICER
Corey Hart, DIRECTOR OF SALES
Jeff Boison, DIRECTOR OF PUBLISHING PLANNING & BOOK TRADE SALES
Chris Ross, DIRECTOR OF DIGITAL SALES
Jeff Stang, DIRECTOR OF SPECIALTY SALES
Kat Salazar, DIRECTOR OF PR & MARKETING
Drew Gill, ART DIRECTOR
Heather Doornink, PRODUCTION DIRECTOR
Nicole Lapalme, CONTROLLER
www.imagecomics.com

GILLEN M^cKELVIE WILSON COWLES

THE WICKED + DIVINE THE

VOL. 8, OLD IS THE NEW NEW

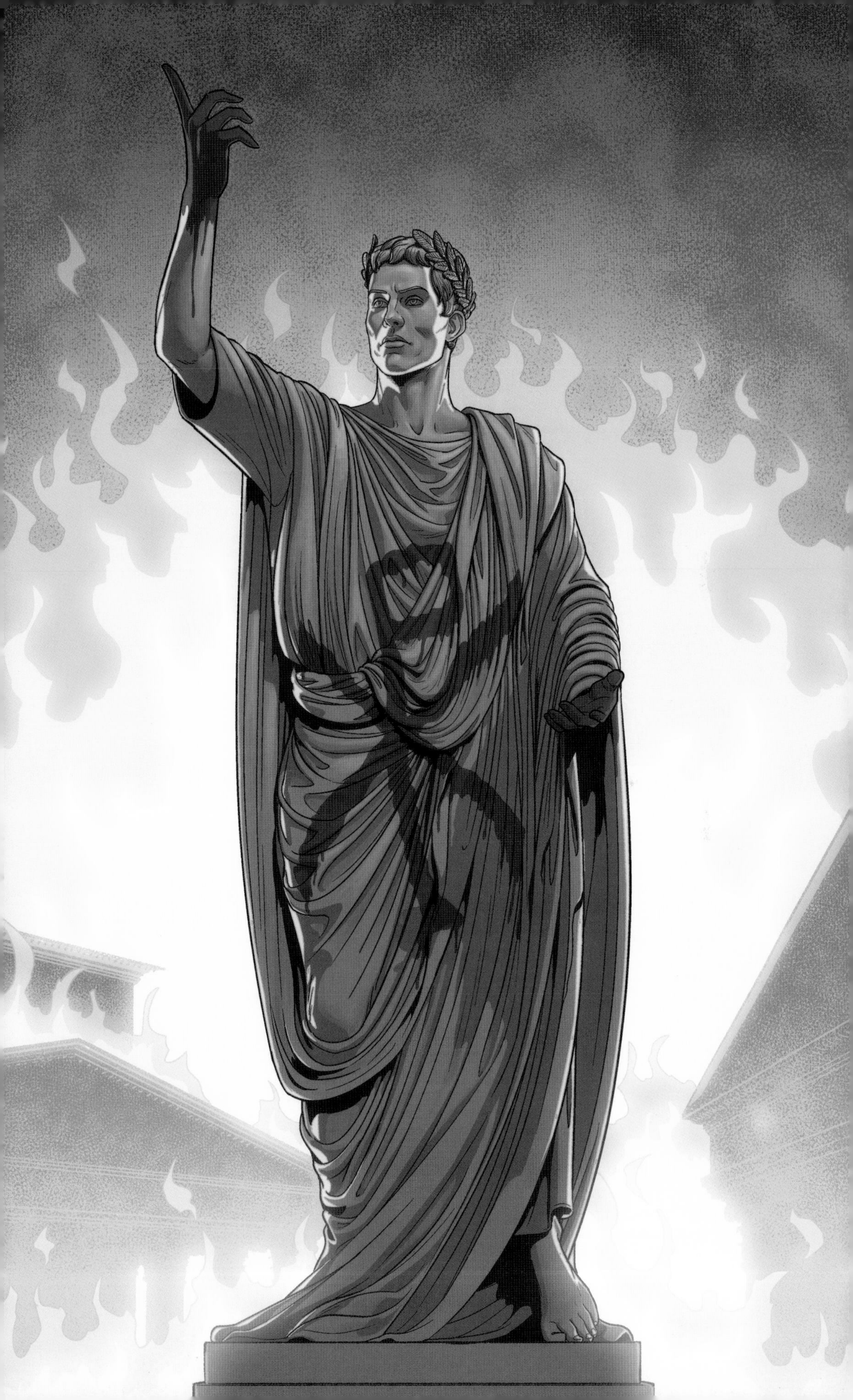

THE
WICKED
+
THE DIVINE

Every ninety years twelve gods return as young people. They are loved.
They are hated. In two years, they are all dead.

The year is 455. It's happening now. It's happening again.

This is the year when the Vandal army sacked Rome, presaging the final
collapse of the Western Roman Empire.

Or so history would have us believe.

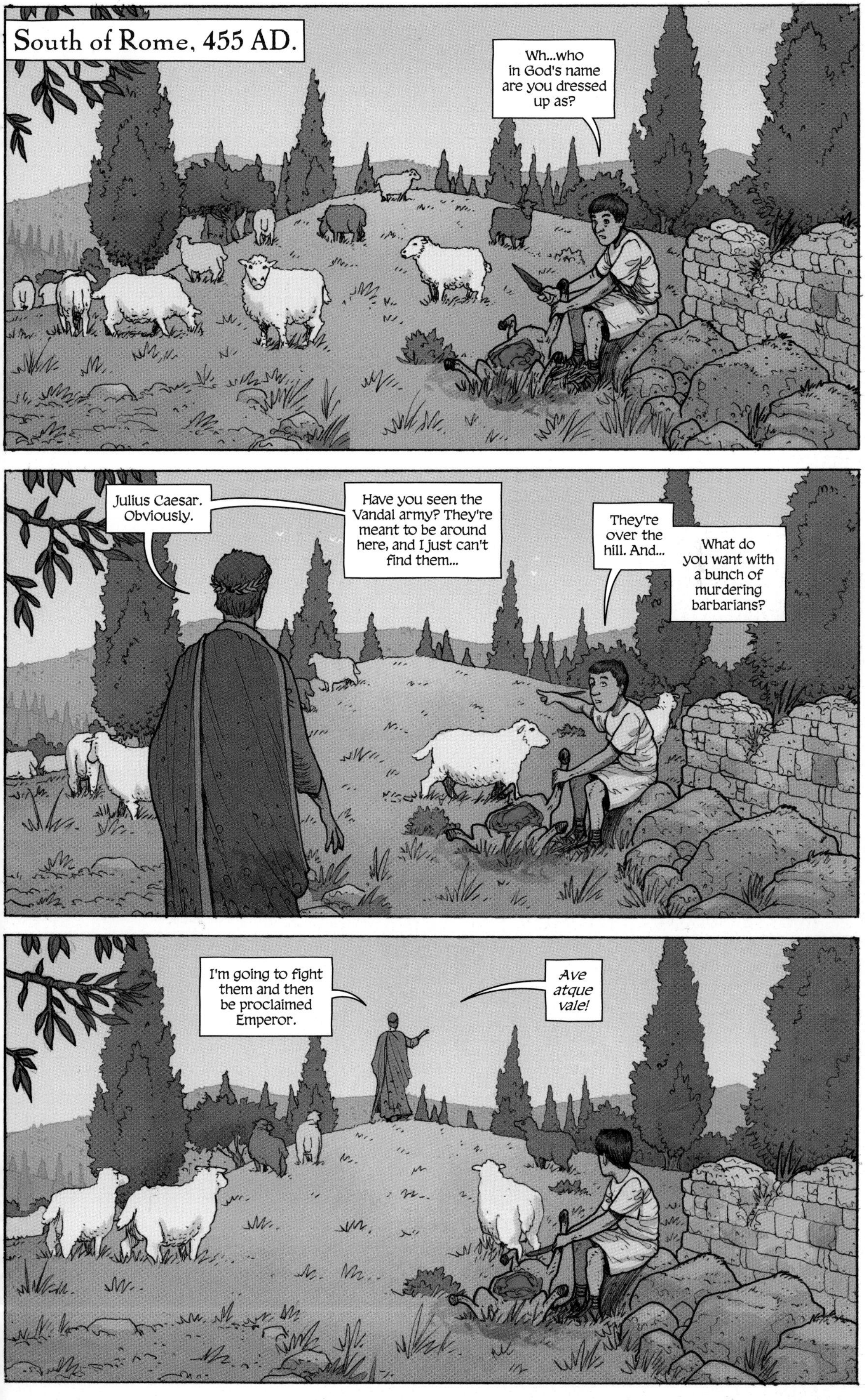
South of Rome, 455 AD.
Wh...who in God's name are you dressed up as?
Julius Caesar. Obviously.
Have you seen the Vandal army? They're meant to be around here, and I just can't find them...
They're over the hill. And...
What do you want with a bunch of murdering barbarians?
I'm going to fight them and then be proclaimed Emperor.
Ave atque vale!

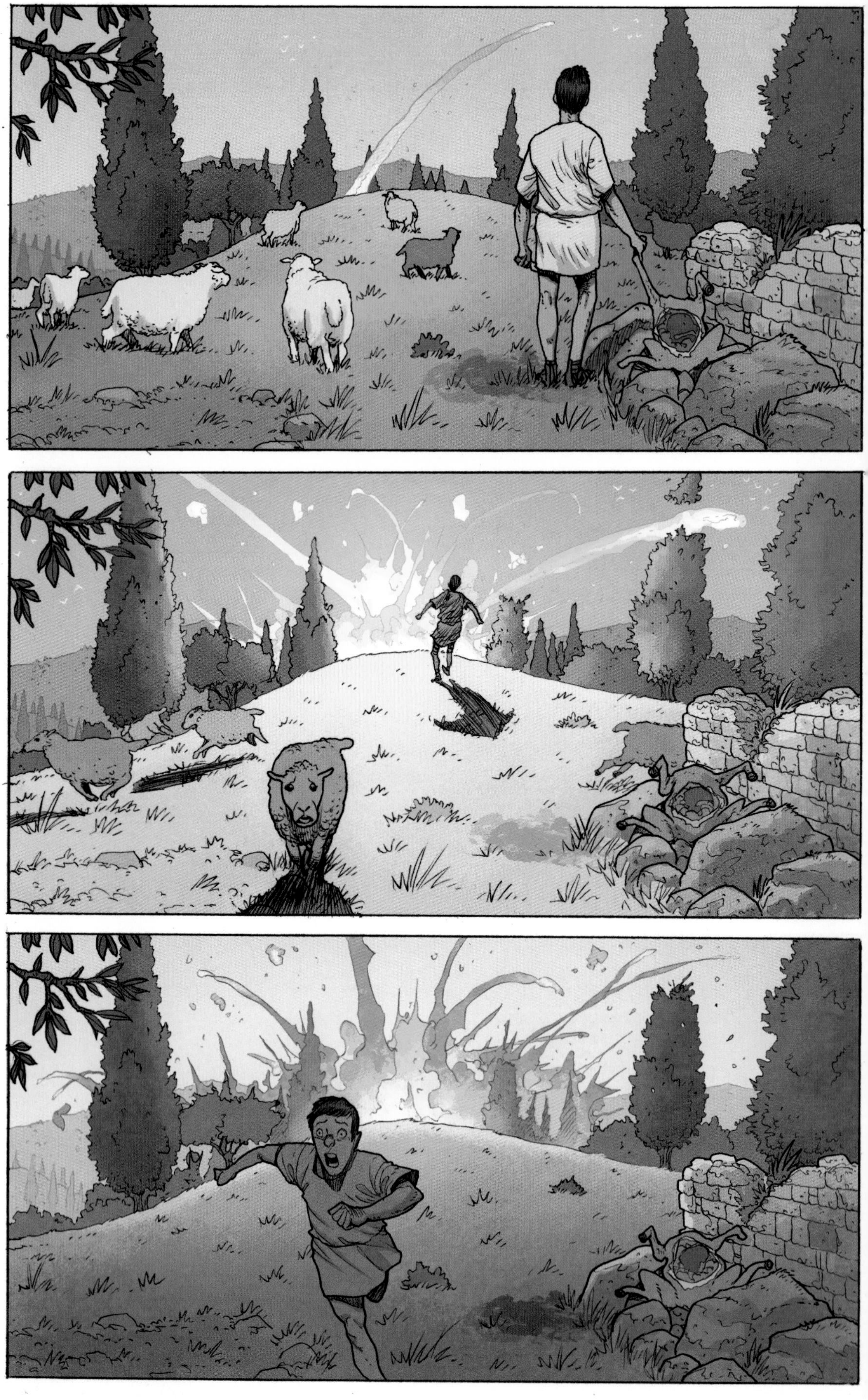

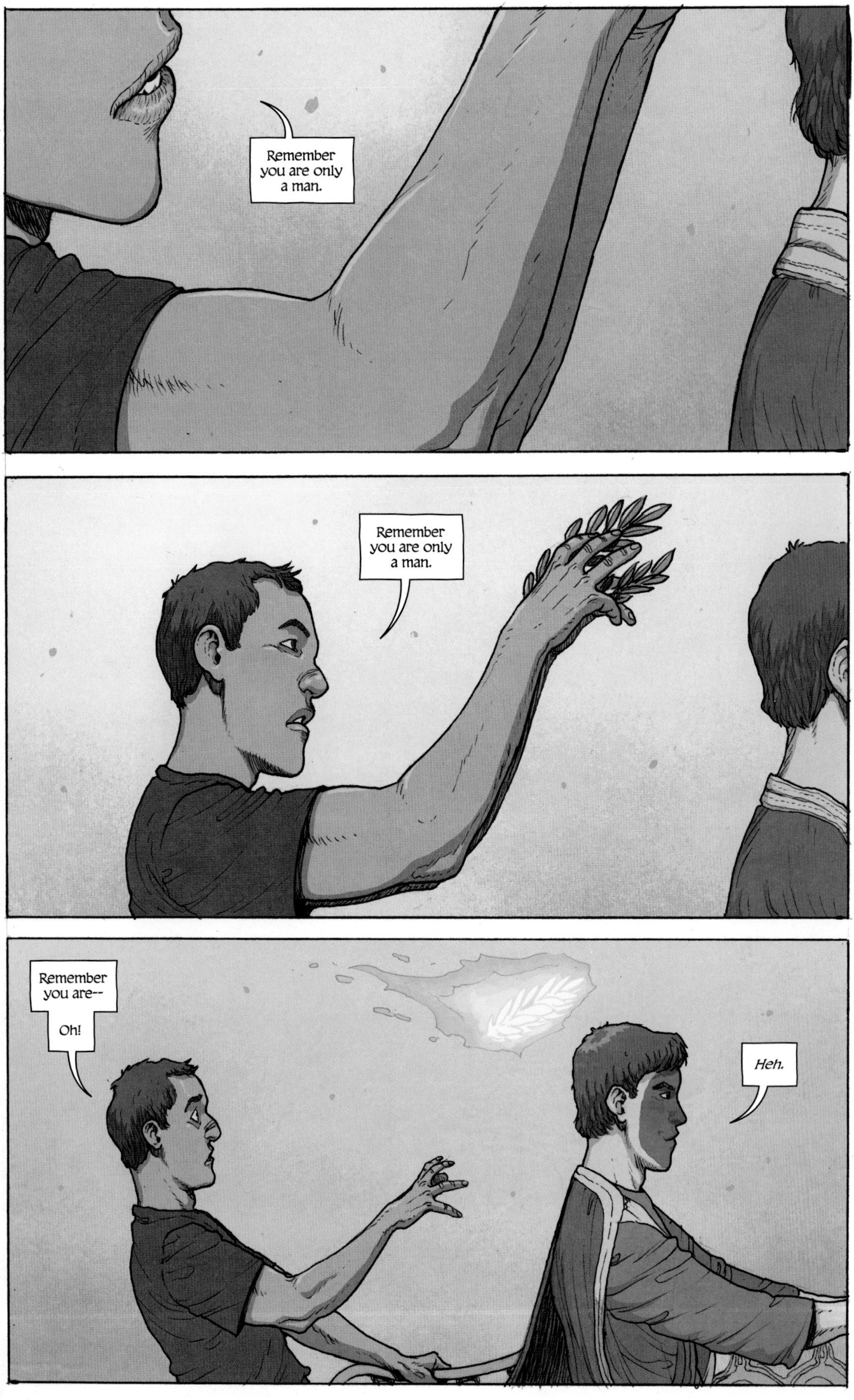
Remember you are only a man.
Remember you are only a man.
Remember you are--
Oh!
Heh.

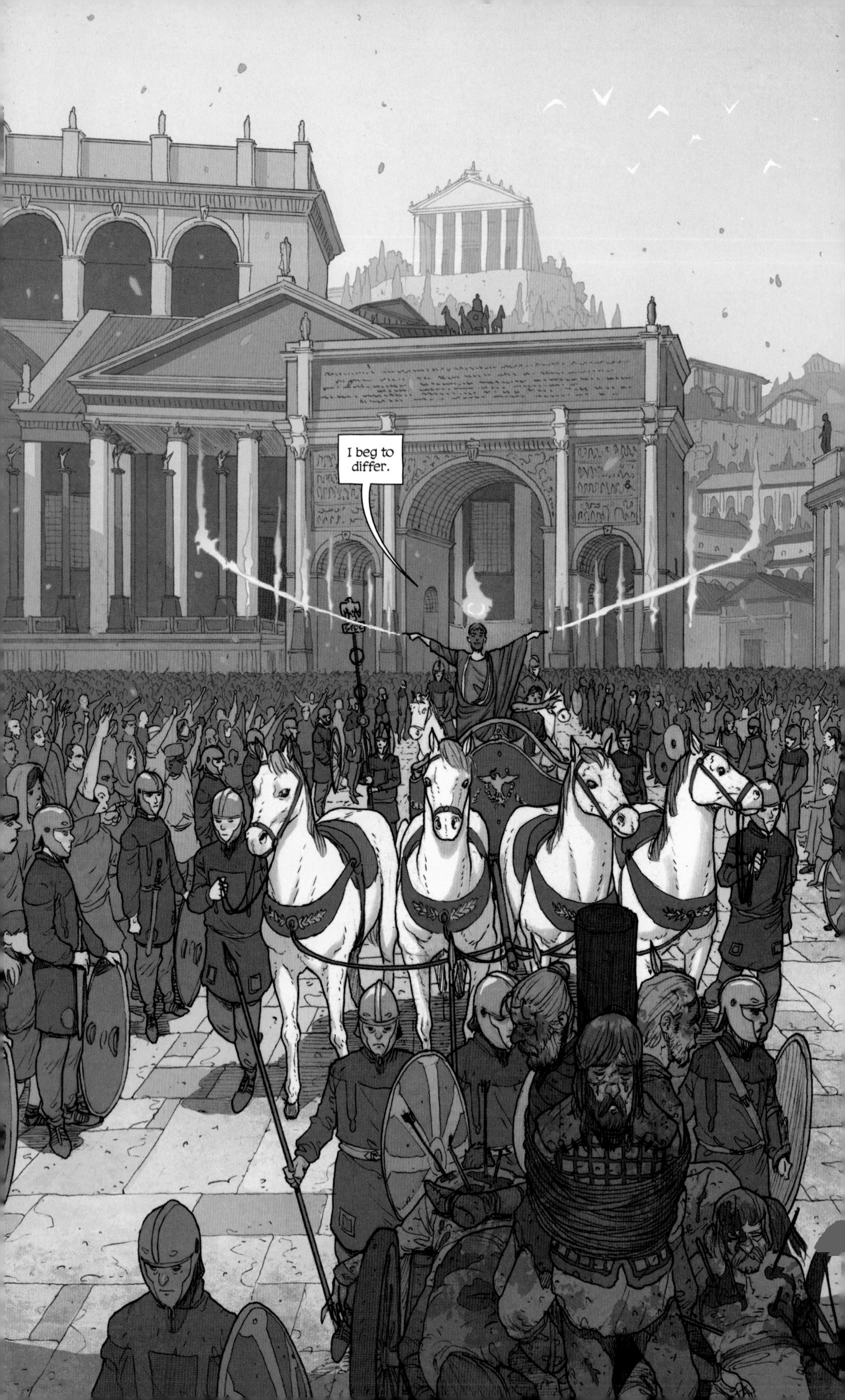
I beg to differ.

IMPERIAL PHASE

2 AUGUST 455

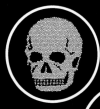

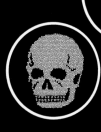

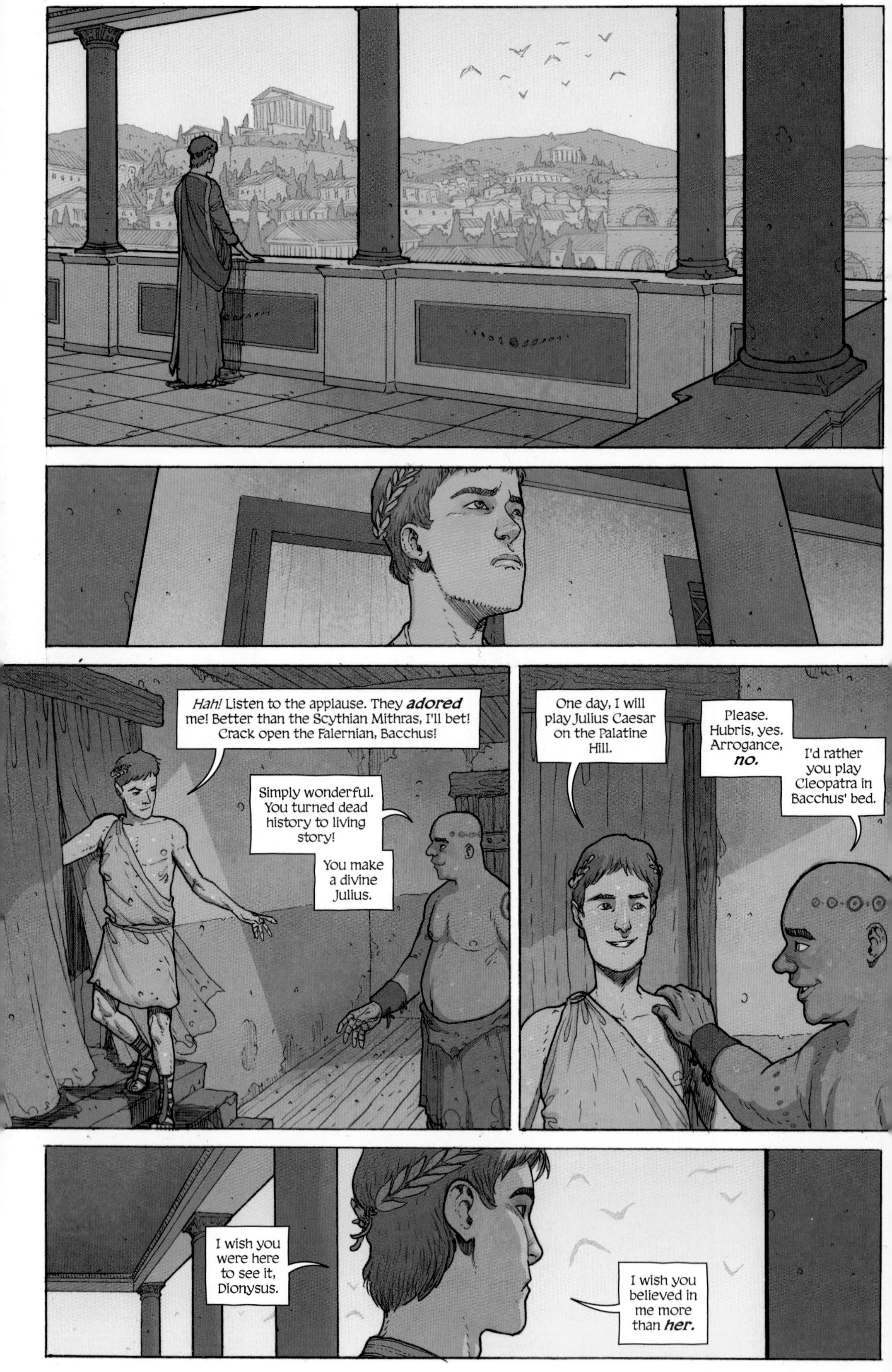
Hah! Listen to the applause. They ***adored*** me! Better than the Scythian Mithras, I'll bet! Crack open the Falernian, Bacchus!
Simply wonderful. You turned dead history to living story!
You make a divine Julius.
One day, I will play Julius Caesar on the Palatine Hill.
Please. Hubris, yes. Arrogance, ***no.***
I'd rather you play Cleopatra in Bacchus' bed.
I wish you were here to see it, Dionysus.
I wish you believed in me more than ***her.***

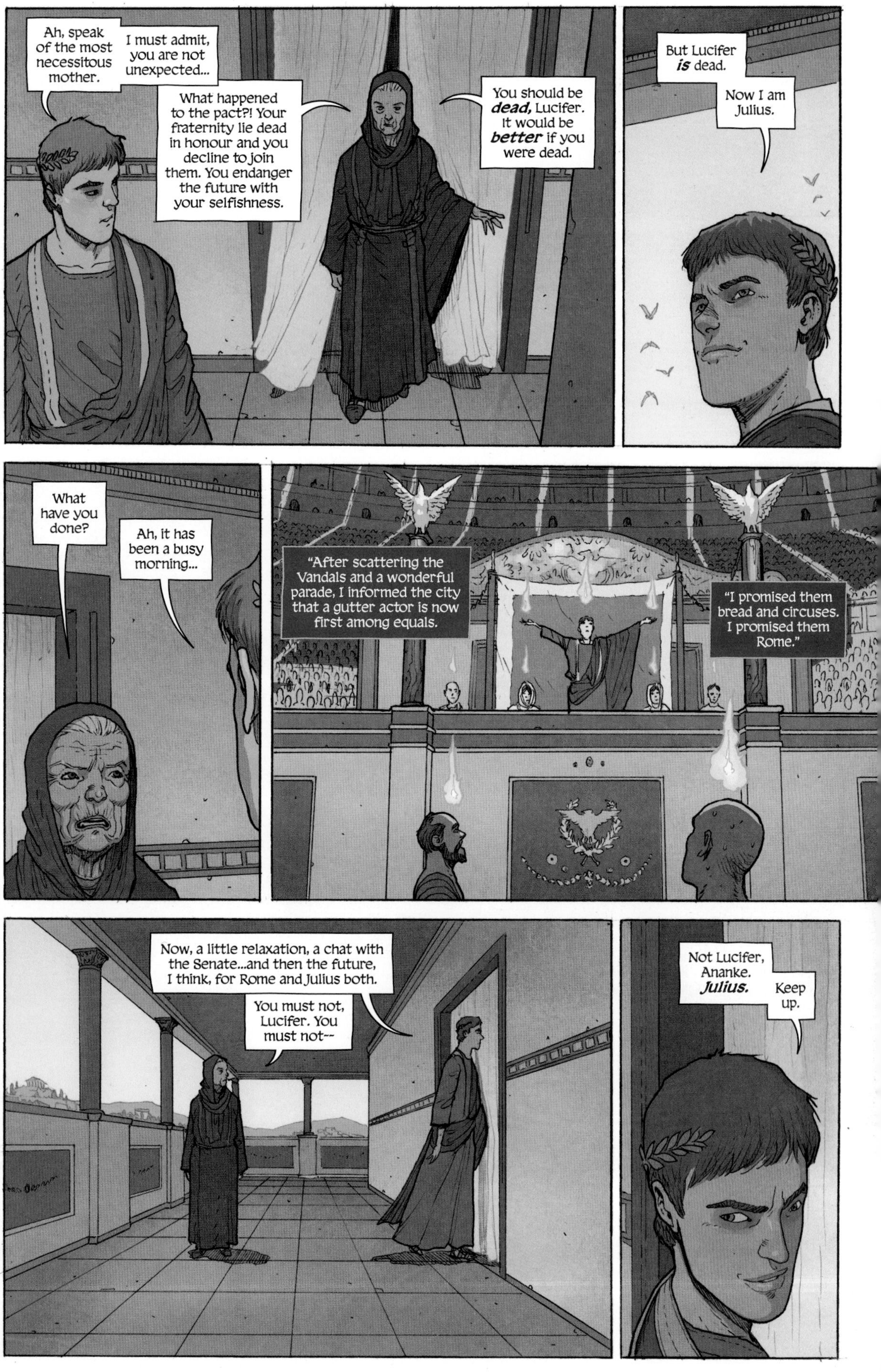
Ah, speak of the most necessitous mother.
I must admit, you are not unexpected...
What happened to the pact?! Your fraternity lie dead in honour and you decline to join them. You endanger the future with your selfishness.
You should be *dead,* Lucifer. It would be *better* if you were dead.
But Lucifer *is* dead.
Now I am Julius.
What have you done?
Ah, it has been a busy morning...
"After scattering the Vandals and a wonderful parade, I informed the city that a gutter actor is now first among equals.
"I promised them bread and circuses. I promised them Rome."
Now, a little relaxation, a chat with the Senate...and then the future, I think, for Rome and Julius both.
You must not, Lucifer. You must not--
Not Lucifer, Ananke. *Julius.*
Keep up.

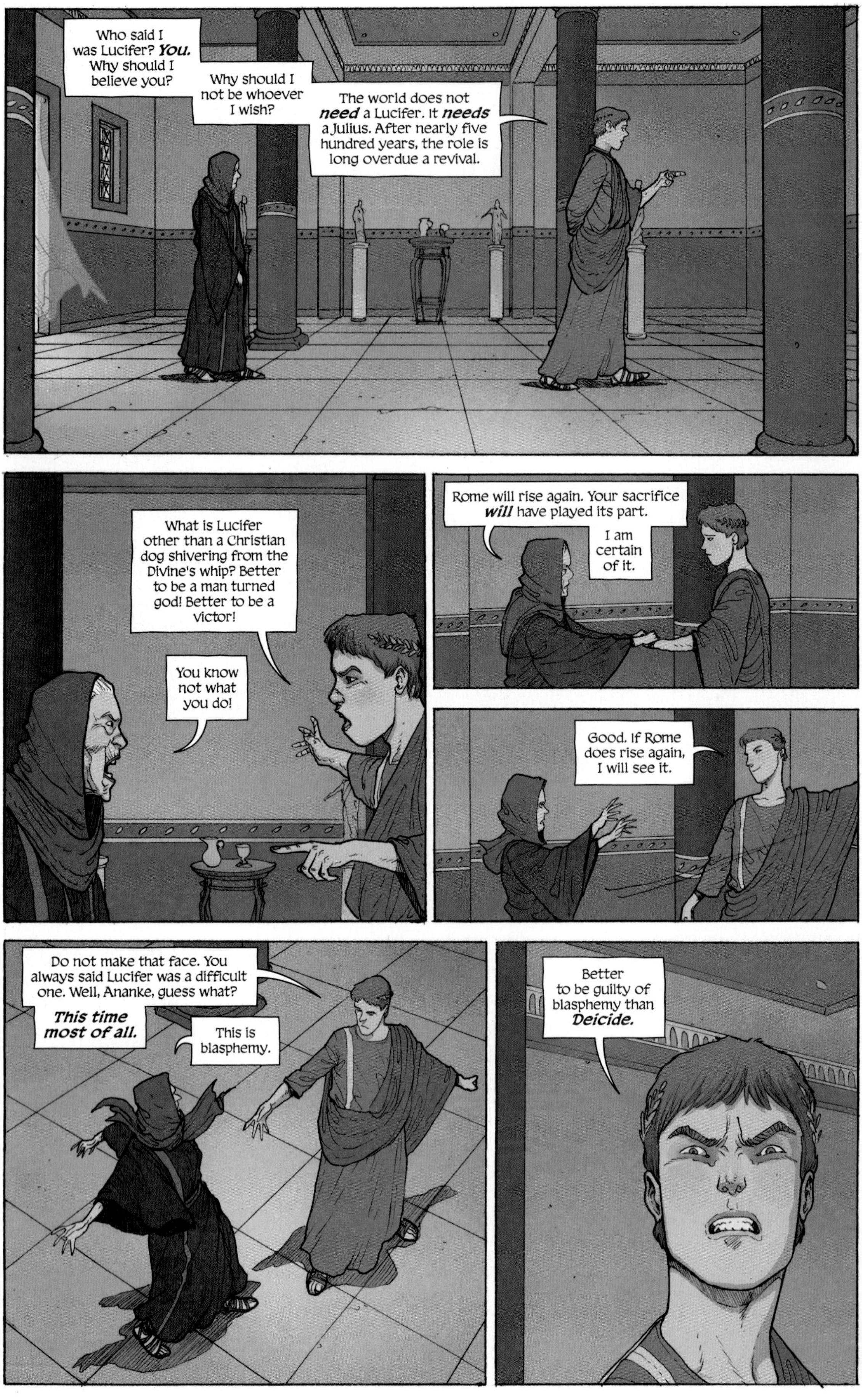
Who said I was Lucifer? You. Why should I believe you?
Why should I not be whoever I wish?
The world does not need a Lucifer. It needs a Julius. After nearly five hundred years, the role is long overdue a revival.
What is Lucifer other than a Christian dog shivering from the Divine's whip? Better to be a man turned god! Better to be a victor!
You know not what you do!
Rome will rise again. Your sacrifice will have played its part.
I am certain of it.
Good. If Rome does rise again, I will see it.
Do not make that face. You always said Lucifer was a difficult one. Well, Ananke, guess what?
This time most of all.
This is blasphemy.
Better to be guilty of blasphemy than Deicide.

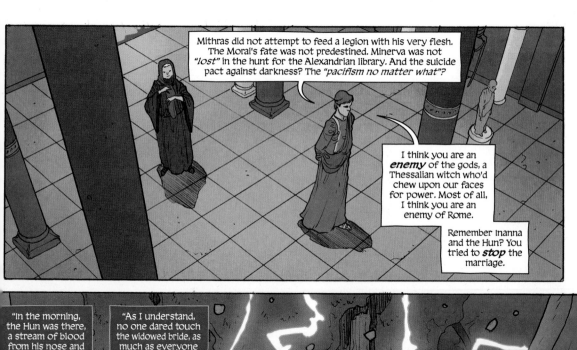

Mithras did not attempt to feed a legion with his very flesh. The Morai's fate was not predestined. Minerva was not *"lost"* in the hunt for the Alexandrian library. And the suicide pact against darkness? The *"pacifism no matter what"*?

I think you are an *enemy* of the gods, a Thessalian witch who'd chew upon our faces for power. Most of all, I think you are an enemy of Rome.

Remember Inanna and the Hun? You tried to *stop* the marriage.

"In the morning, the Hun was there, a stream of blood from his nose and a smile on his face.

"As I understand, no one dared touch the widowed bride, as much as everyone wanted to.

"Attila was dead, and the Empire spared. Inanna would not make war, but she would make love knowing the Scourge of God would not survive it..."

Now, the Vandals come to Rome...

Well, Lucifer is no Inanna. War it is!

I thought it was *"Julius"*, Lucifer.

Yes...

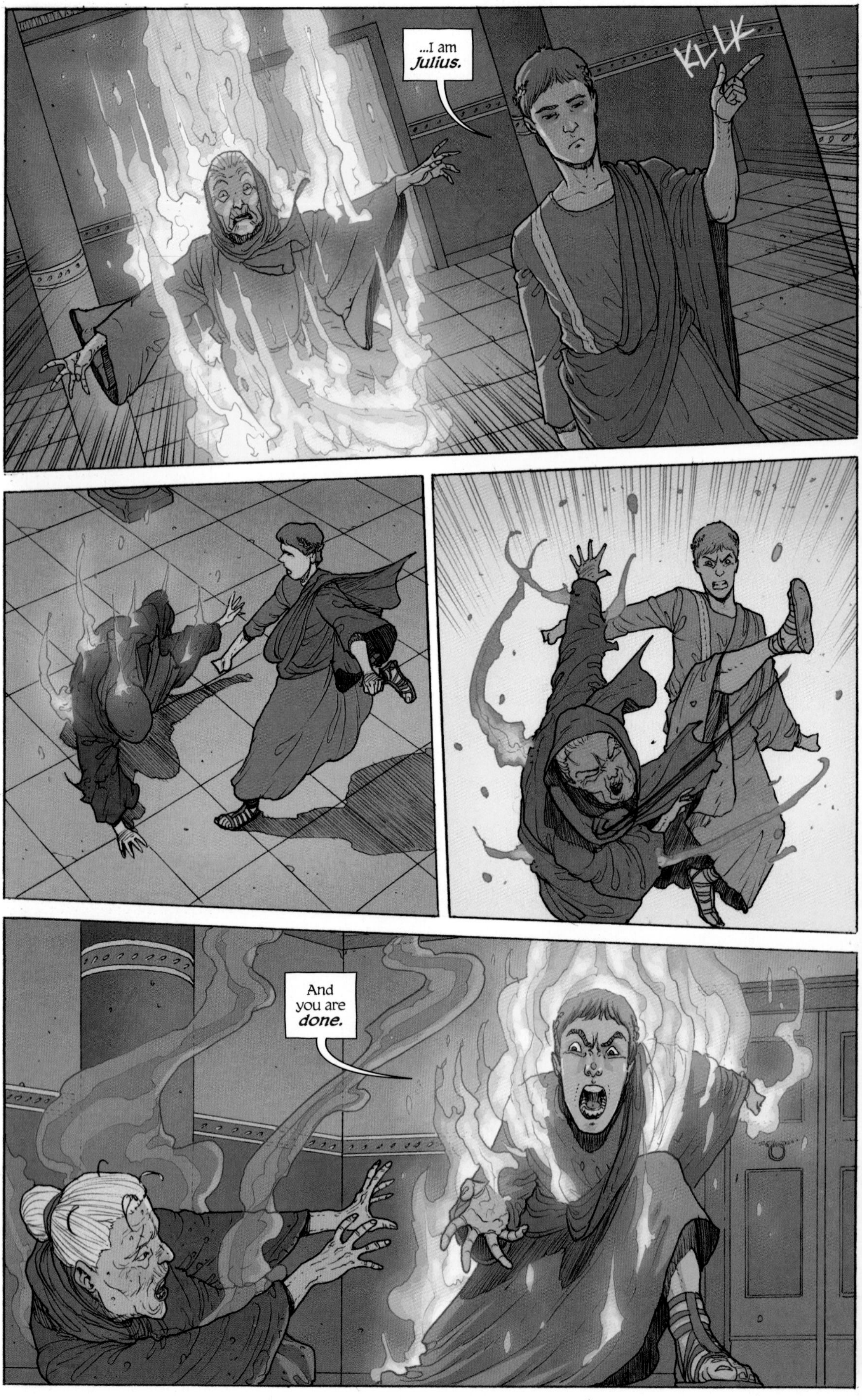

...I am *Julius.*
KLIK
And you are *done.*

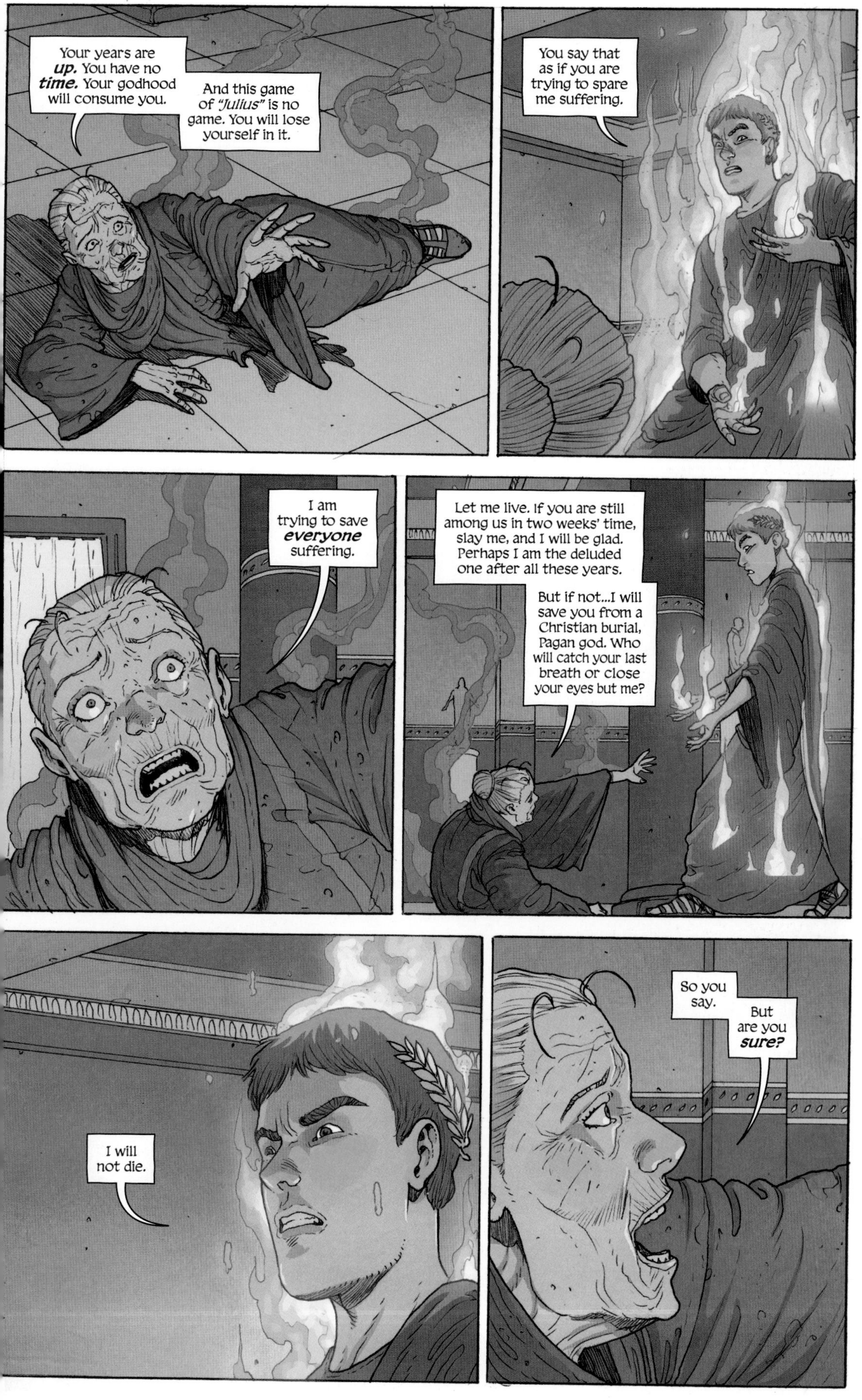
Your years are *up.* You have no *time.* Your godhood will consume you.
And this game of *"Julius"* is no game. You will lose yourself in it.
You say that as if you are trying to spare me suffering.
I am trying to save *everyone* suffering.
Let me live. If you are still among us in two weeks' time, slay me, and I will be glad. Perhaps I am the deluded one after all these years.
But if not...I will save you from a Christian burial, Pagan god. Who will catch your last breath or close your eyes but me?
I will not die.
So you say.
But are you *sure?*

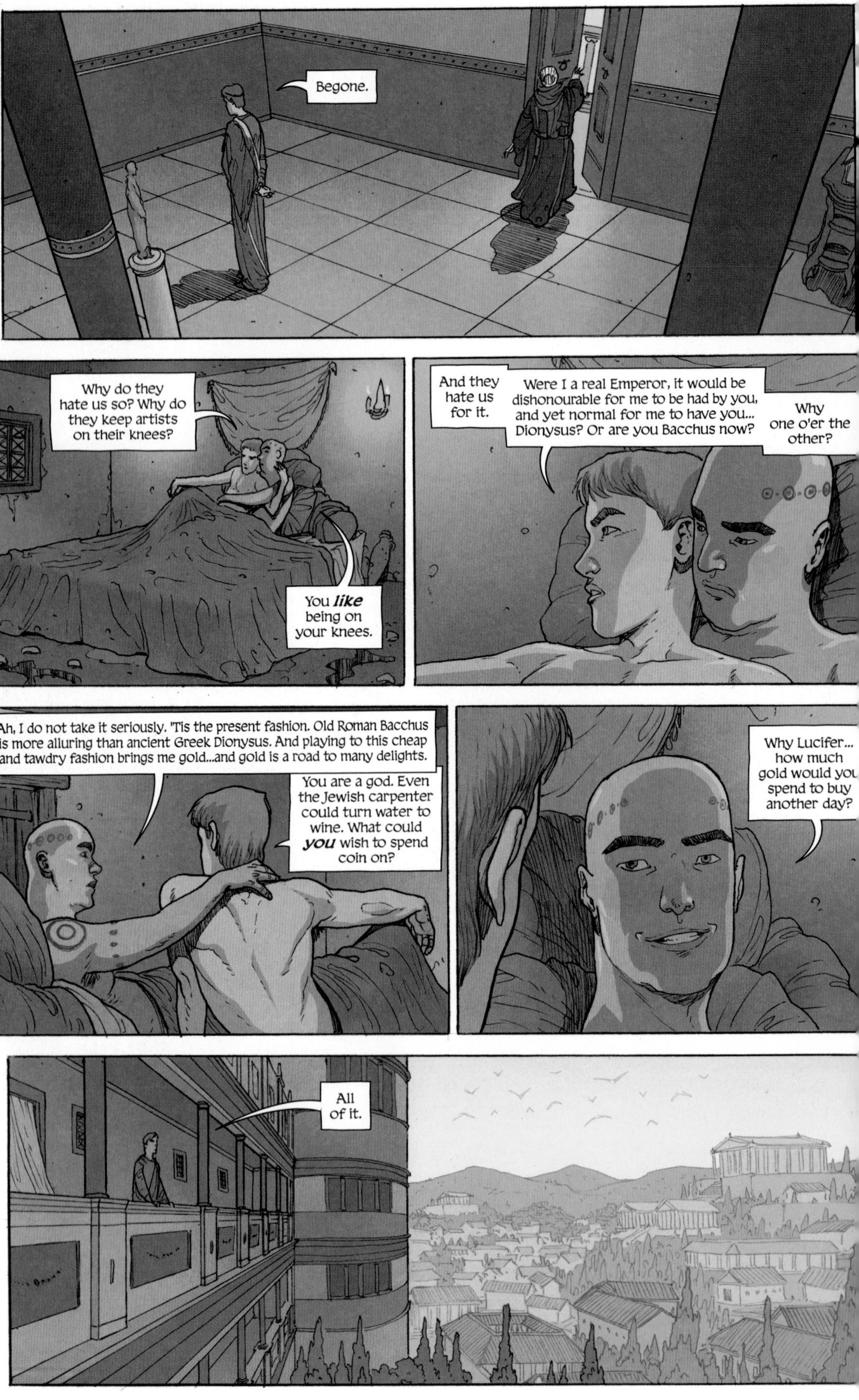
Begone.
Why do they hate us so? Why do they keep artists on their knees?
You like being on your knees.
And they hate us for it.
Were I a real Emperor, it would be dishonourable for me to be had by you, and yet normal for me to have you... Dionysus? Or are you Bacchus now?
Why one o'er the other?
Ah, I do not take it seriously. 'Tis the present fashion. Old Roman Bacchus is more alluring than ancient Greek Dionysus. And playing to this cheap and tawdry fashion brings me gold...and gold is a road to many delights.
You are a god. Even the Jewish carpenter could turn water to wine. What could you wish to spend coin on?
Why Lucifer... how much gold would you spend to buy another day?
All of it.

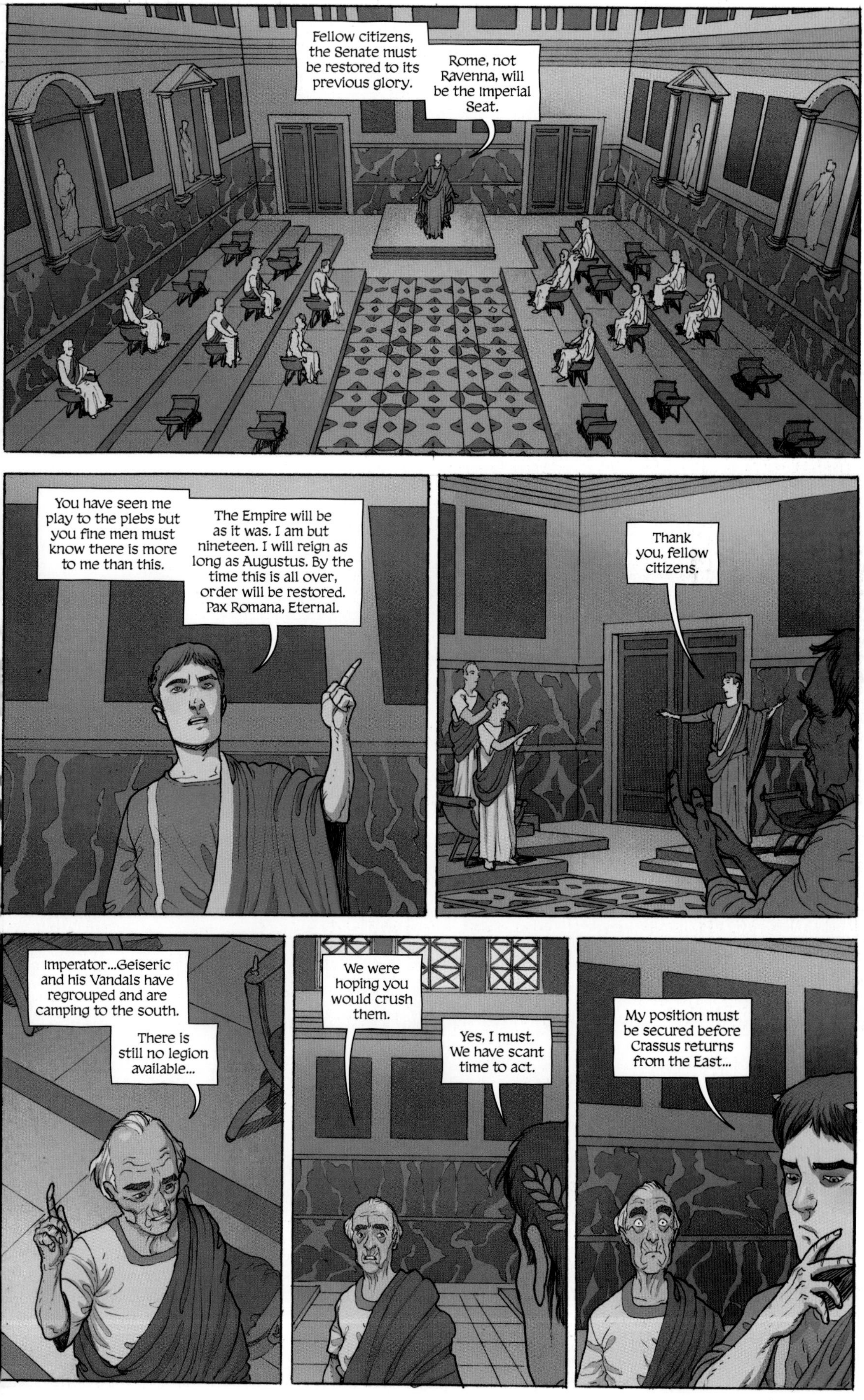
Fellow citizens, the Senate must be restored to its previous glory.
Rome, not Ravenna, will be the Imperial Seat.
You have seen me play to the plebs but you fine men must know there is more to me than this.
The Empire will be as it was. I am but nineteen. I will reign as long as Augustus. By the time this is all over, order will be restored. Pax Romana, Eternal.
Thank you, fellow citizens.
Imperator...Geiseric and his Vandals have regrouped and are camping to the south.
There is still no legion available...
We were hoping you would crush them.
Yes, I must. We have scant time to act.
My position must be secured before Crassus returns from the East...

B-But...Crassus is dead. He was destroyed by the Parthians.

Crassus is dead?

He was a great Roman. He will be missed.

We must honour his name. Our triumvirate made this city great...

As you wish, Imperator. It does well for you...to acclaim... your rival.

Good. Our first step should be...

Wait.

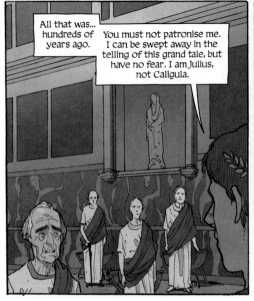

All that was... hundreds of years ago.

You must not patronise me. I can be swept away in the telling of this grand tale, but have no fear. I am Julius, not Caligula.

I must be a *good* Emperor.

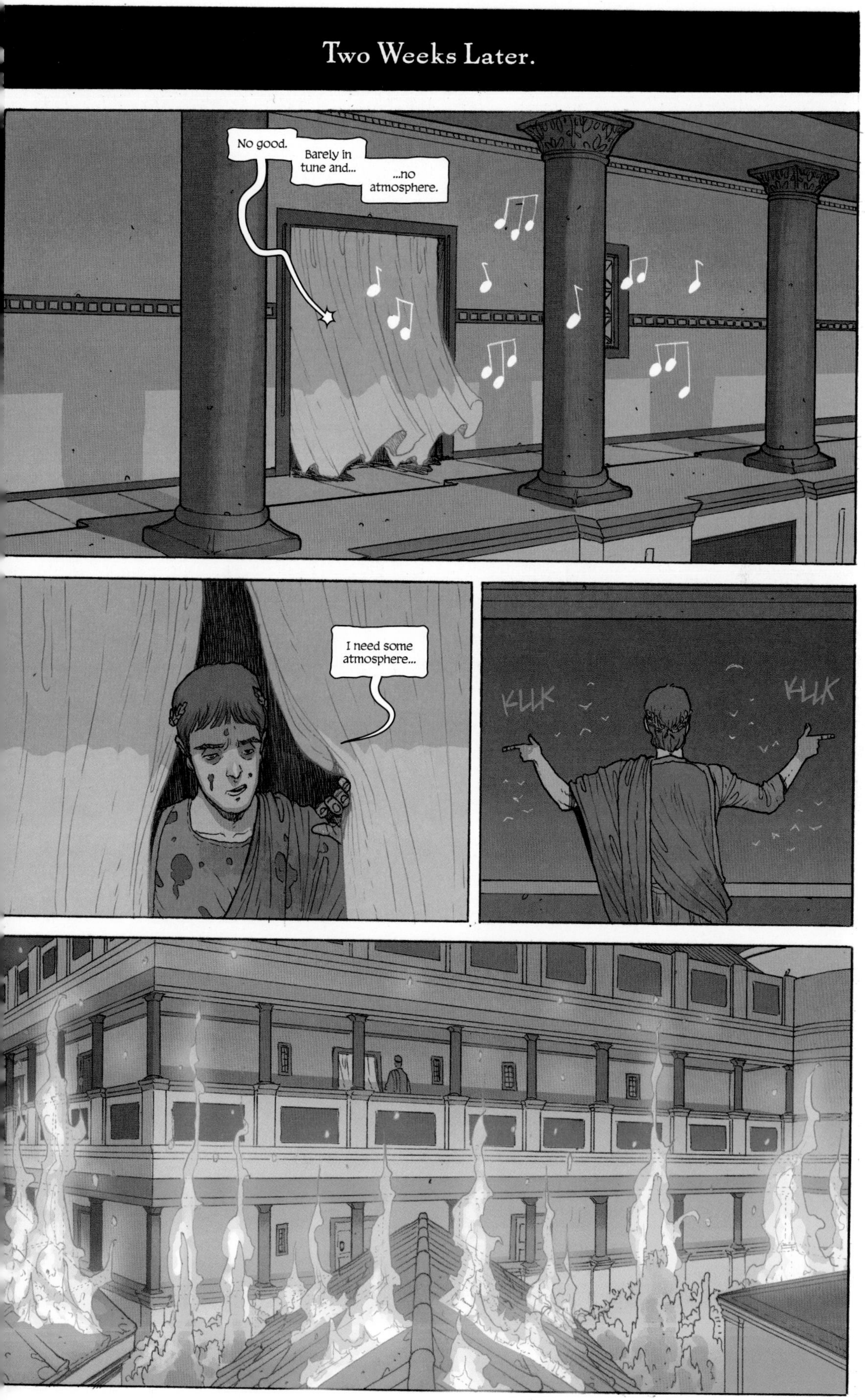
Two Weeks Later.
No good.
Barely in tune and...
...no atmosphere.
I need some atmosphere...
KLIK
KLIK

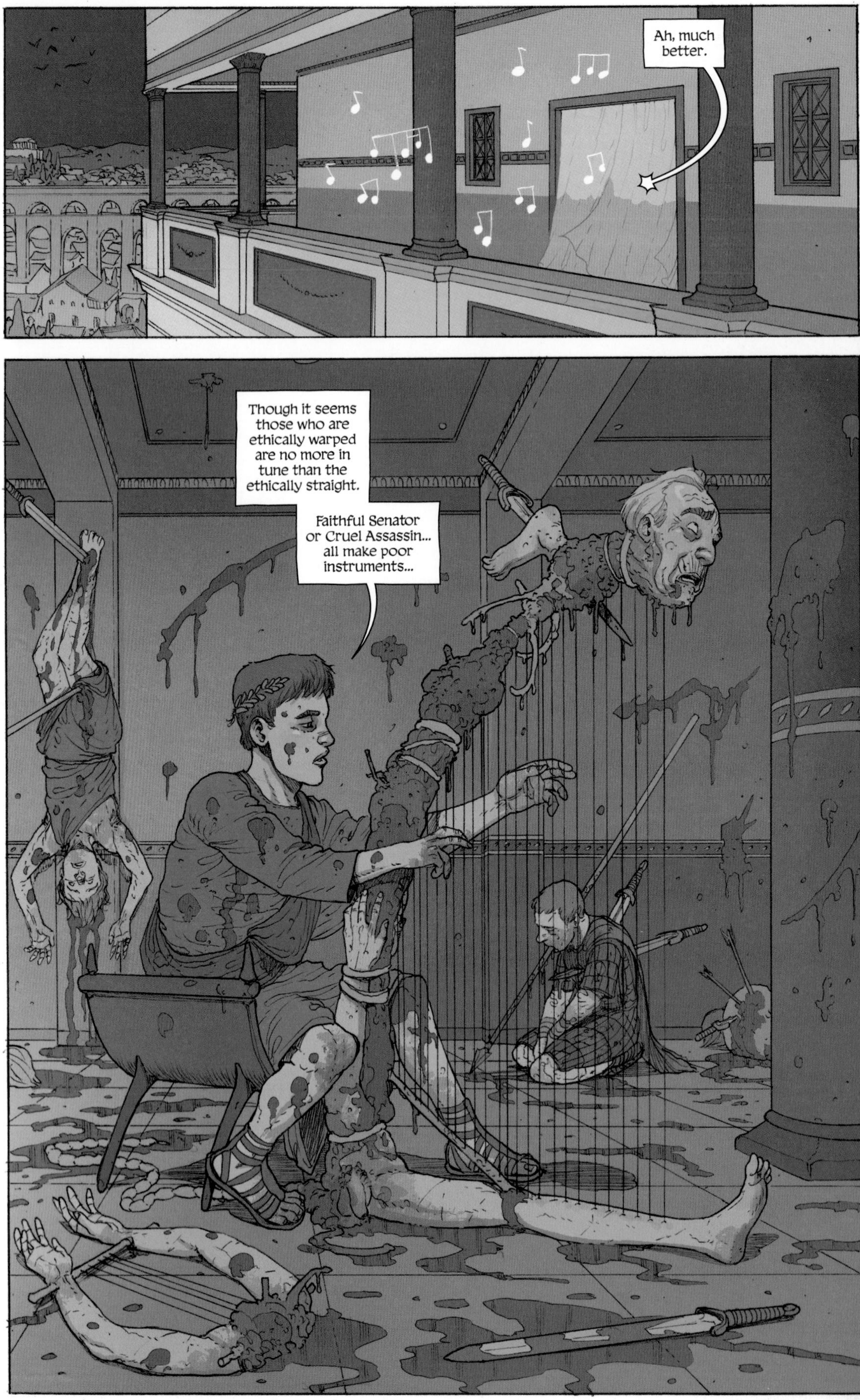
Ah, much better.
Though it seems those who are ethically warped are no more in tune than the ethically straight.
Faithful Senator or Cruel Assassin... all make poor instruments...

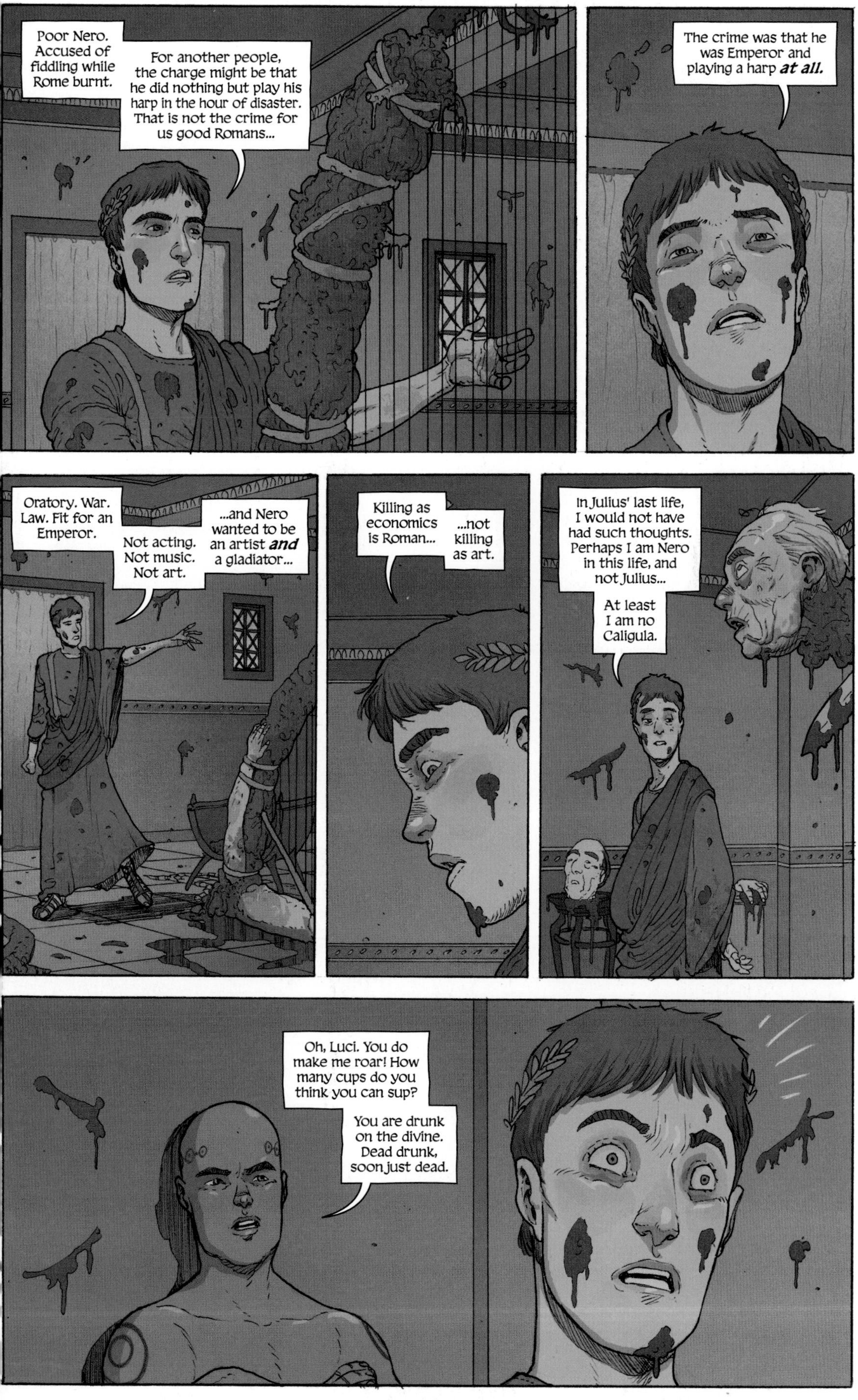
Poor Nero. Accused of fiddling while Rome burnt.
For another people, the charge might be that he did nothing but play his harp in the hour of disaster. That is not the crime for us good Romans...
The crime was that he was Emperor and playing a harp ***at all.***
Oratory. War. Law. Fit for an Emperor.
Not acting. Not music. Not art.
...and Nero wanted to be an artist ***and*** a gladiator...
Killing as economics is Roman...
...not killing as art.
In Julius' last life, I would not have had such thoughts. Perhaps I am Nero in this life, and not Julius...
At least I am no Caligula.
Oh, Luci. You do make me roar! How many cups do you think you can sup?
You are drunk on the divine. Dead drunk, soon just dead.

Dionysus? Bacchus?

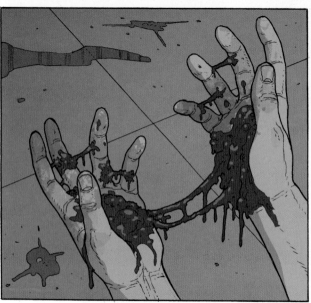

This is... unacceptable.

I need to talk to Father.

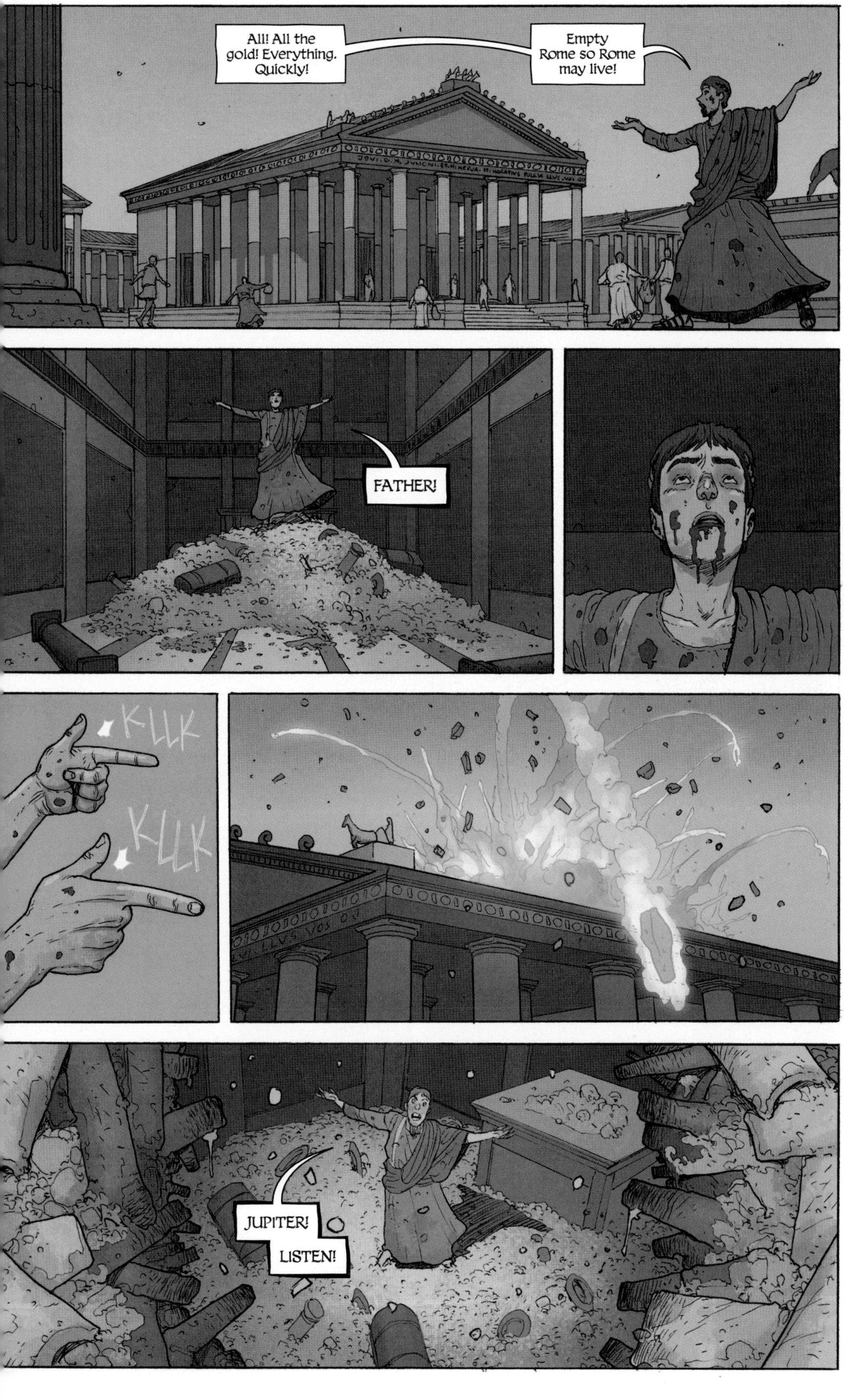
All! All the gold! Everything. Quickly!
Empty Rome so Rome may live!
FATHER!
KLLK
KLLK
JUPITER!
LISTEN!

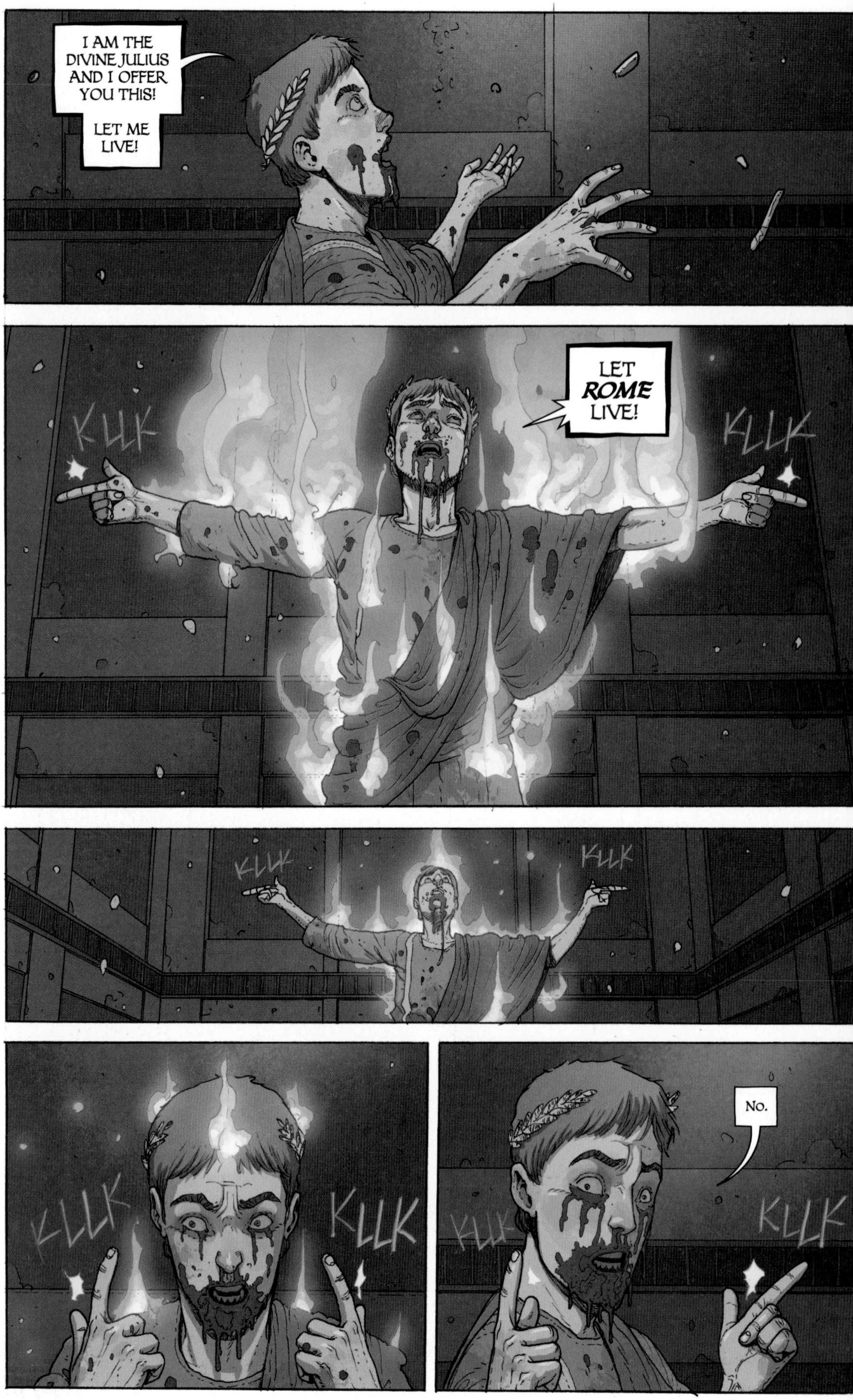
I AM THE DIVINE JULIUS AND I OFFER YOU THIS!
LET ME LIVE!
LET ROME LIVE!
KLLK
KLLK
KLLK
KLLK
KLLK
KLLK
No.
KLLK
KLLK

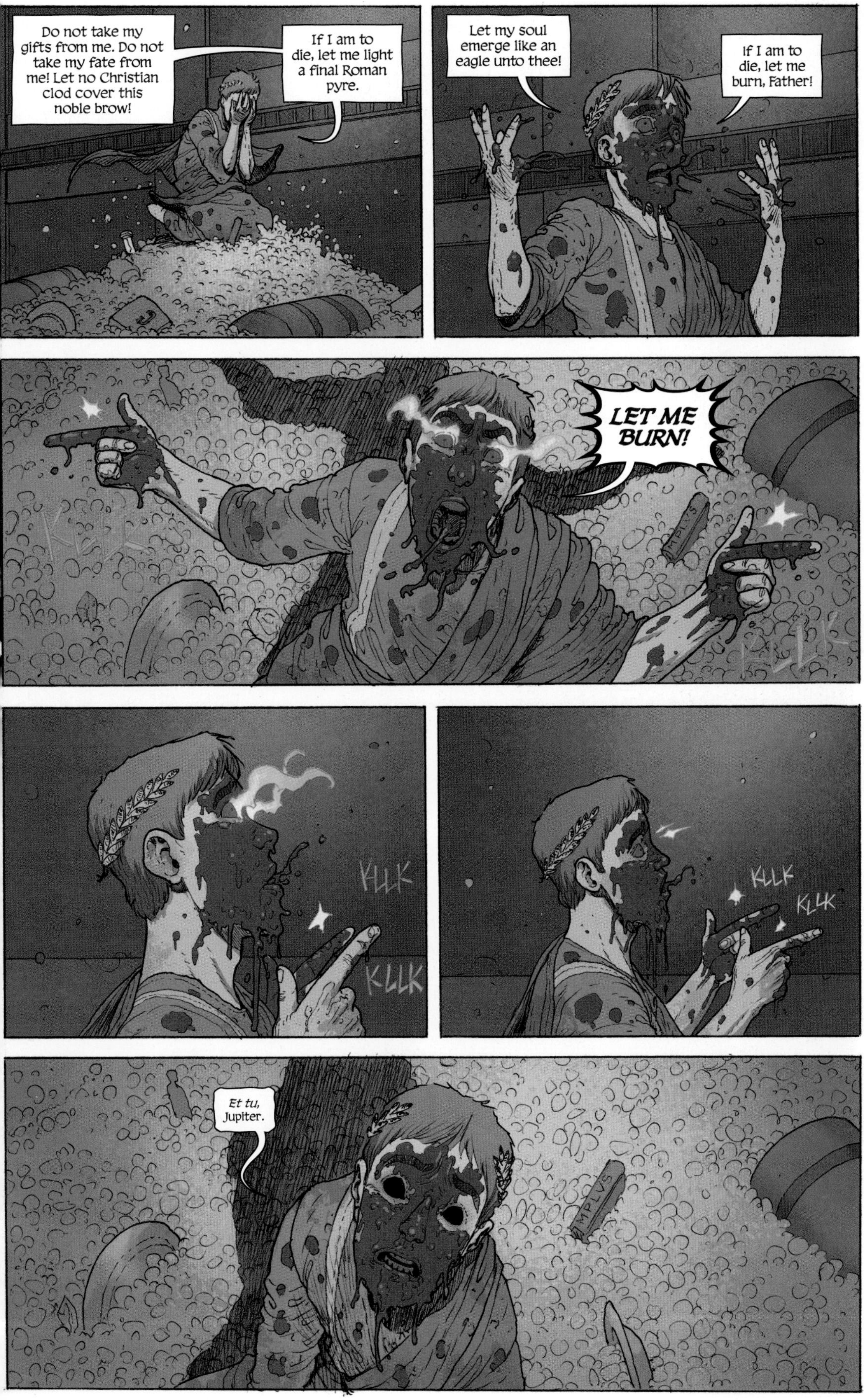

Do not take my gifts from me. Do not take my fate from me! Let no Christian clod cover this noble brow!
If I am to die, let me light a final Roman pyre.
Let my soul emerge like an eagle unto thee!
If I am to die, let me burn, Father!
LET ME BURN!
KLLK
KLLK
MPLVS
KLLK
KLLK
KLLK
KLLK
Et tu, Jupiter.
MPLVS

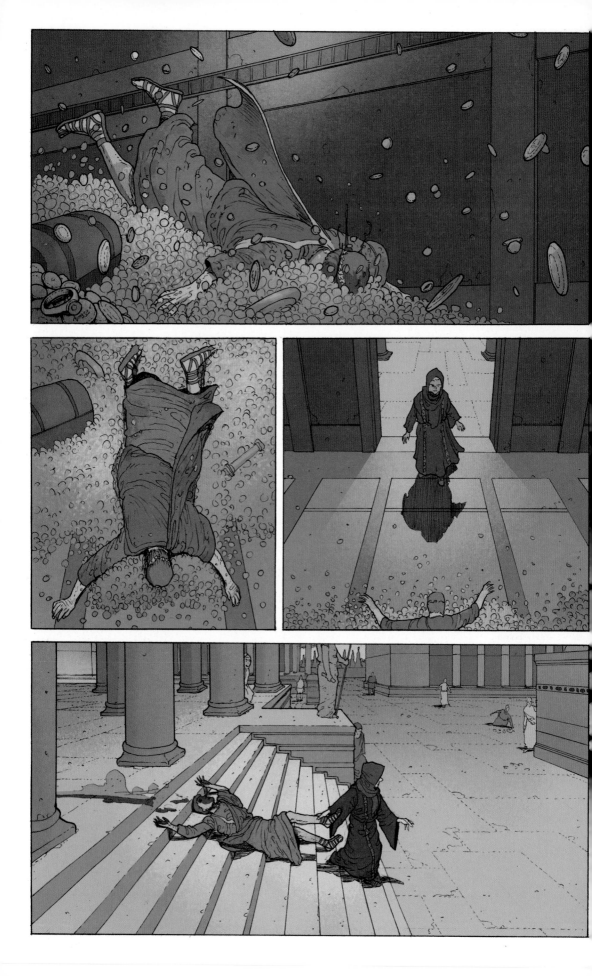

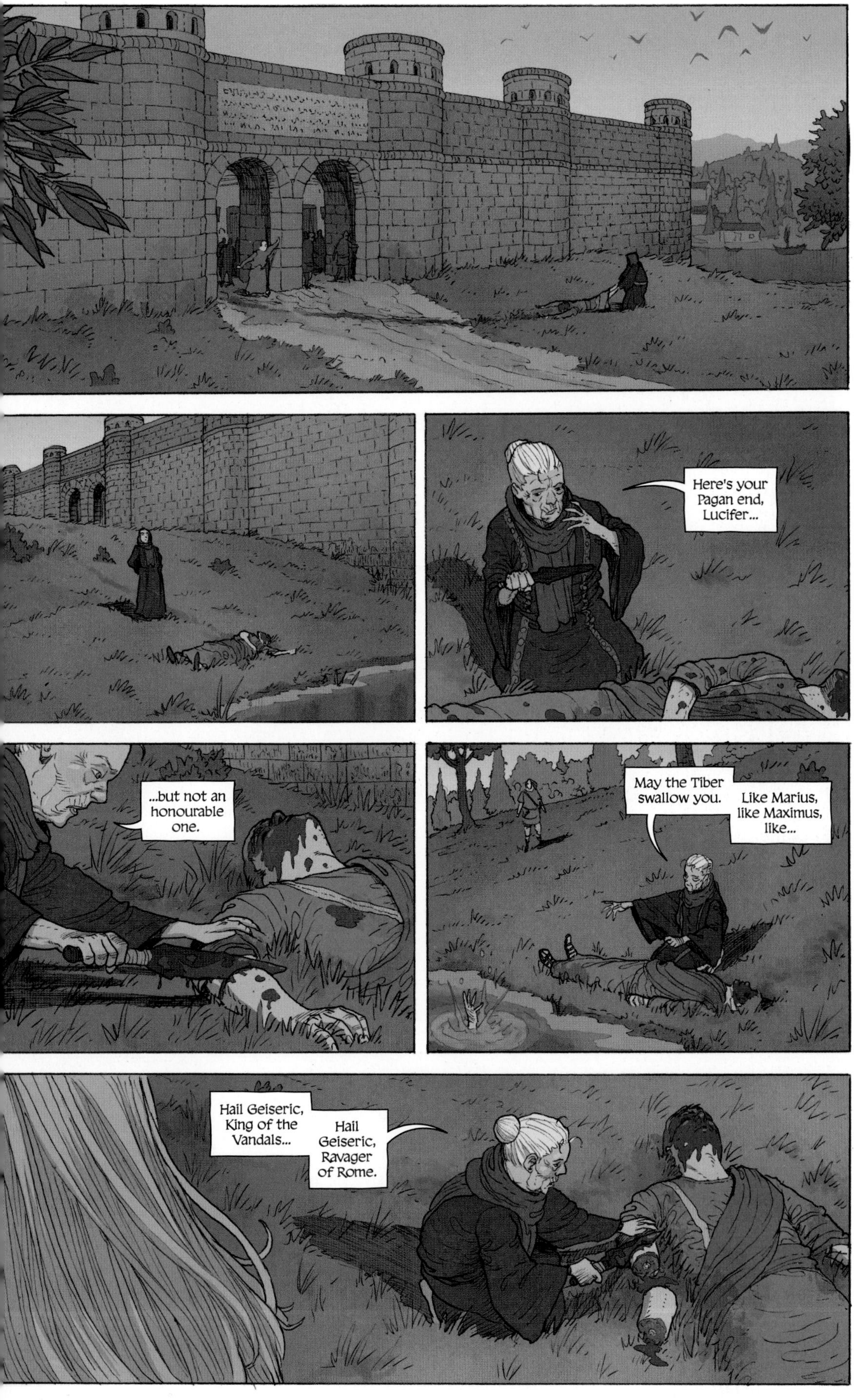
Here's your Pagan end, Lucifer...
...but not an honourable one.
May the Tiber swallow you.
Like Marius, like Maximus, like...
Hail Geiseric, King of the Vandals...
Hail Geiseric, Ravager of Rome.

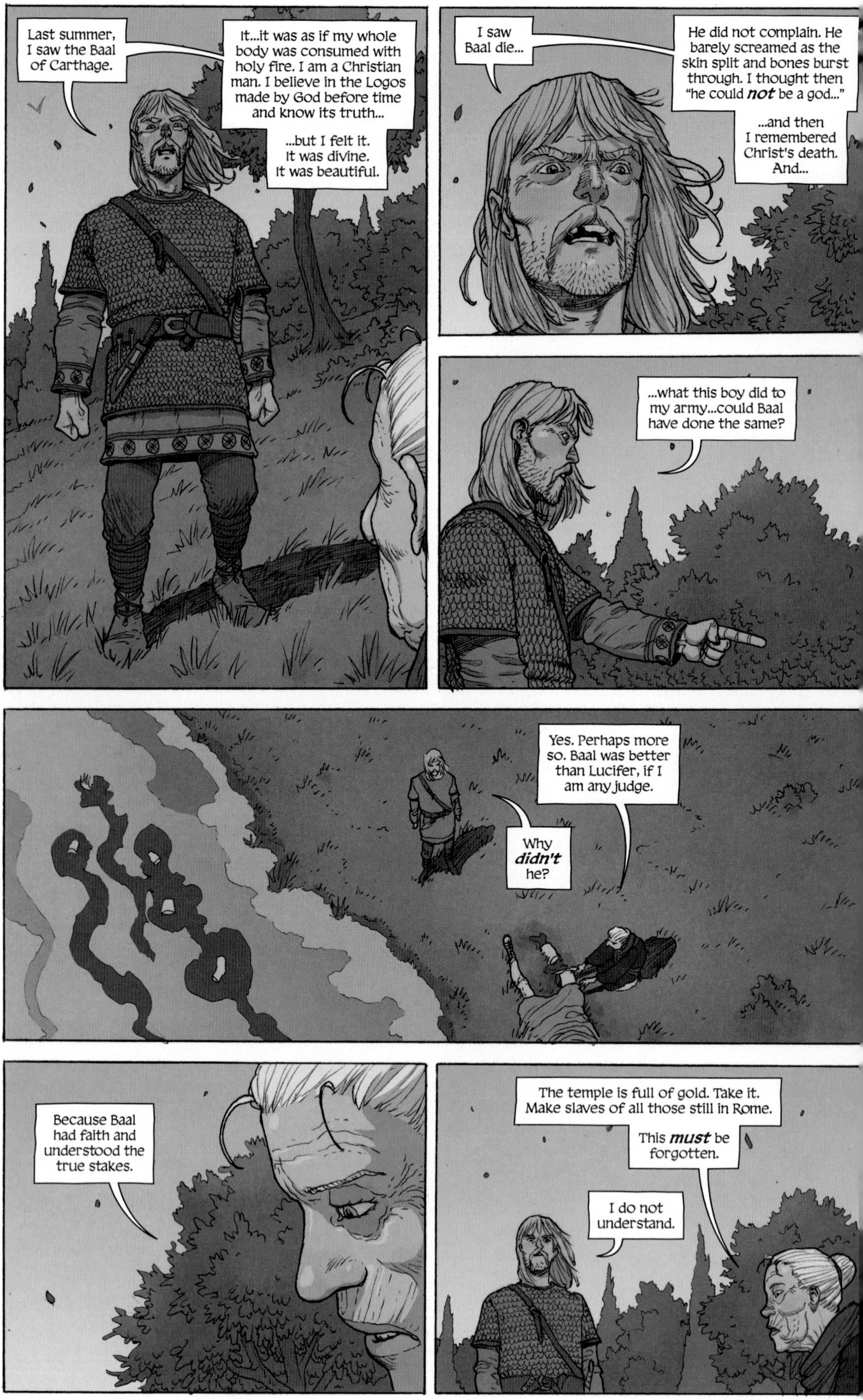
Last summer, I saw the Baal of Carthage.
It...it was as if my whole body was consumed with holy fire. I am a Christian man. I believe in the Logos made by God before time and know its truth...
...but I felt it. It was divine. It was beautiful.
I saw Baal die...
He did not complain. He barely screamed as the skin split and bones burst through. I thought then "he could *not* be a god..."
...and then I remembered Christ's death. And...
...what this boy did to my army...could Baal have done the same?
Yes. Perhaps more so. Baal was better than Lucifer, if I am any judge.
Why *didn't* he?
Because Baal had faith and understood the true stakes.
The temple is full of gold. Take it. Make slaves of all those still in Rome.
This *must* be forgotten.
I do not understand.

Once upon a time, Sulla was the first to march on Rome with Roman arms.

He spent the remainder of his life trying to ensure no other would repeat it. Everything he did, he did to save the Republic.

He failed to understand the only lesson he was truly teaching is that once you have shown something can be done, it will be done again.

In ninety years the children will return. If they know **this** is an option, one, maybe two, maybe **all** will repeat it.

Which means that in your children's children's time, we all risk being rendered into dust...

There will be no Empire, no Vandals, no **man.**

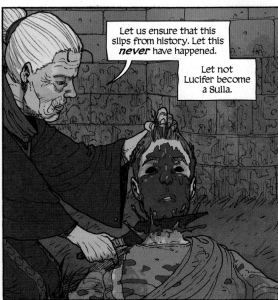

Let us ensure that this slips from history. Let this **never** have happened.

Let not Lucifer become a Sulla.

Perhaps by then, instead of Germanic hands merely guiding it, a **Vandal** will sit upon the throne.

I understand your son has made a profitable marriage into the Imperial family. A good step towards a new Germanic empire...

Do you whisper anything other than what I wish to hear?

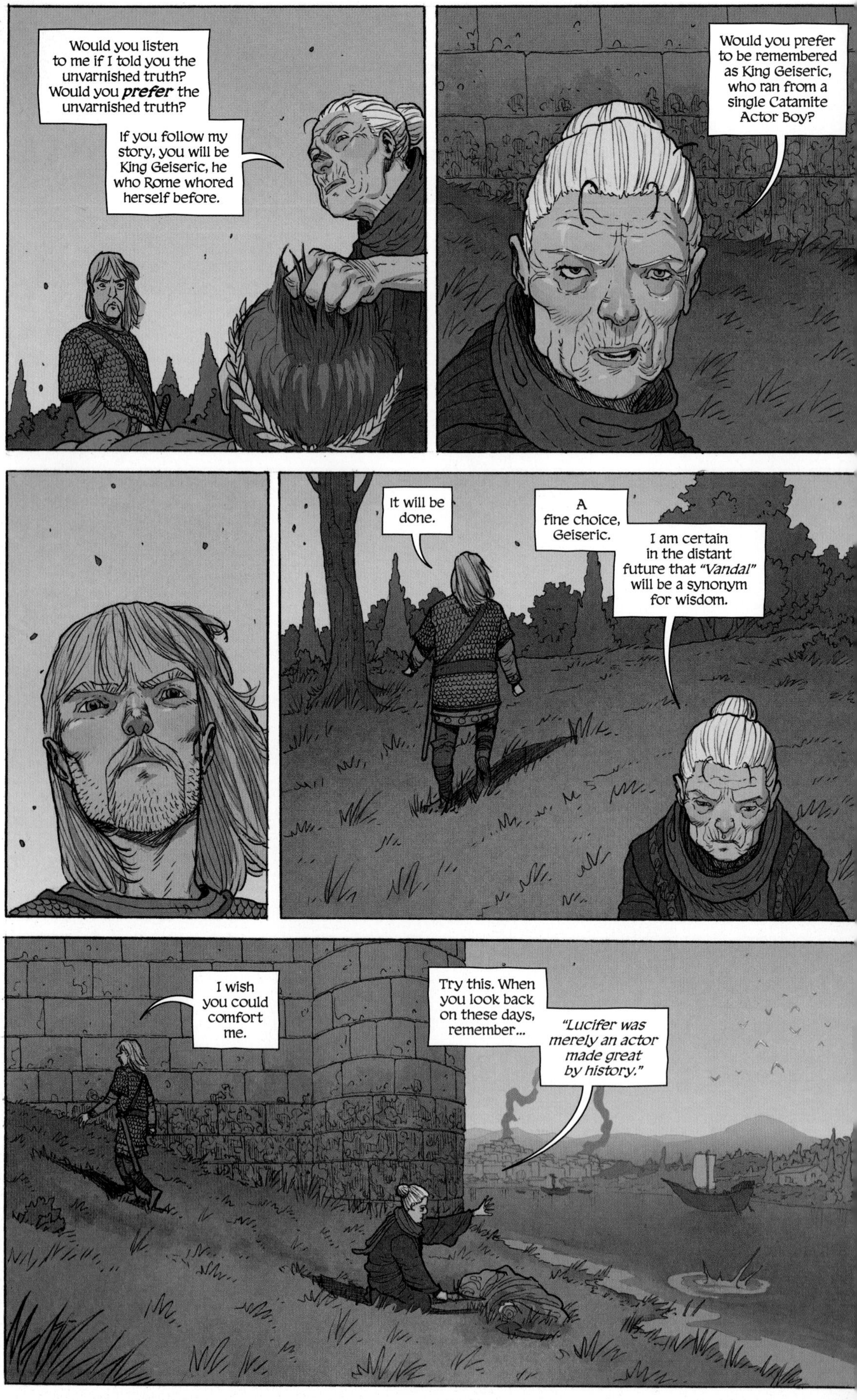
Would you listen to me if I told you the unvarnished truth? Would you *prefer* the unvarnished truth?
If you follow my story, you will be King Geiseric, he who Rome whored herself before.
Would you prefer to be remembered as King Geiseric, who ran from a single Catamite Actor Boy?
It will be done.
A fine choice, Geiseric.
I am certain in the distant future that *"Vandal"* will be a synonym for wisdom.
I wish you could comfort me.
Try this. When you look back on these days, remember...
"Lucifer was merely an actor made great by history."

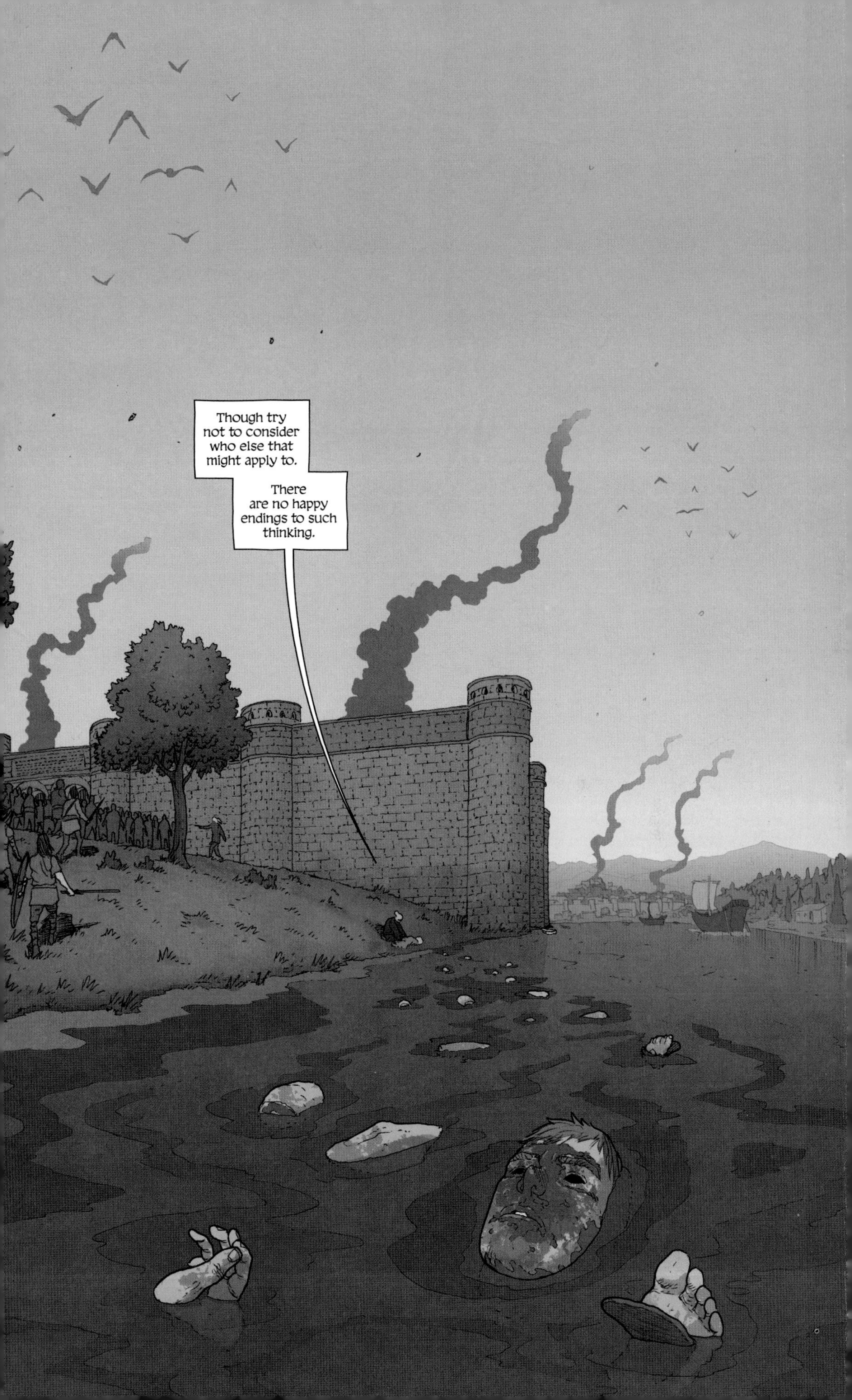
Though try not to consider who else that might apply to.
There are no happy endings to such thinking.

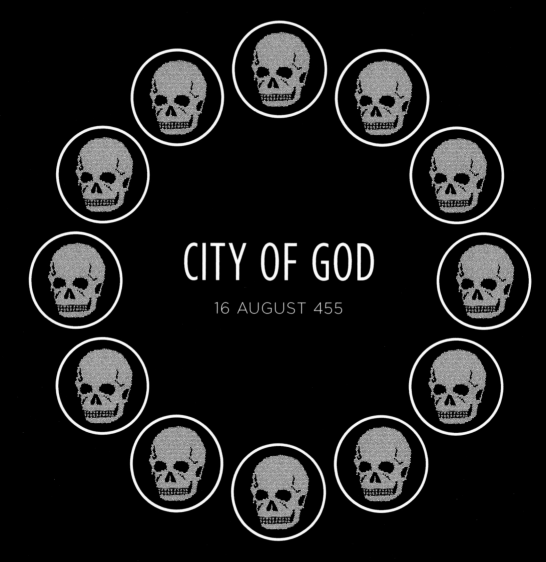

CITY OF GOD

16 AUGUST 455

THE
WICKED
+
ƎNIΛID
THE

1373AD

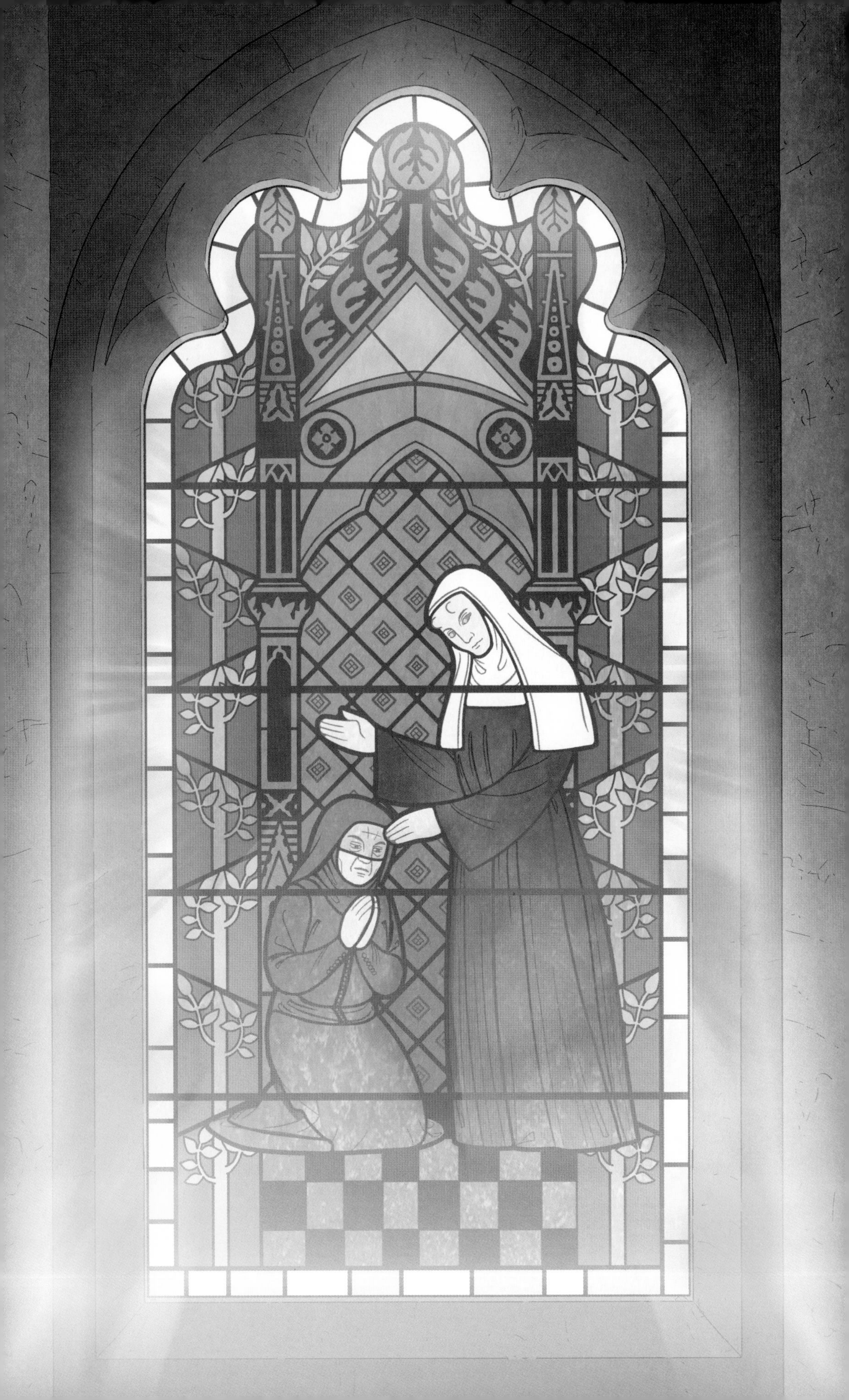

THE WICKED
+
THE DIVINE

Every ninety years twelve gods return as young people. They are loved.
They are hated. In two years, they are all dead.

The year is 1373. It's happening now. It's happening again.

It's twenty-two years since the Black Death devastated Europe.
It is thought to be the greatest natural disaster of all time.

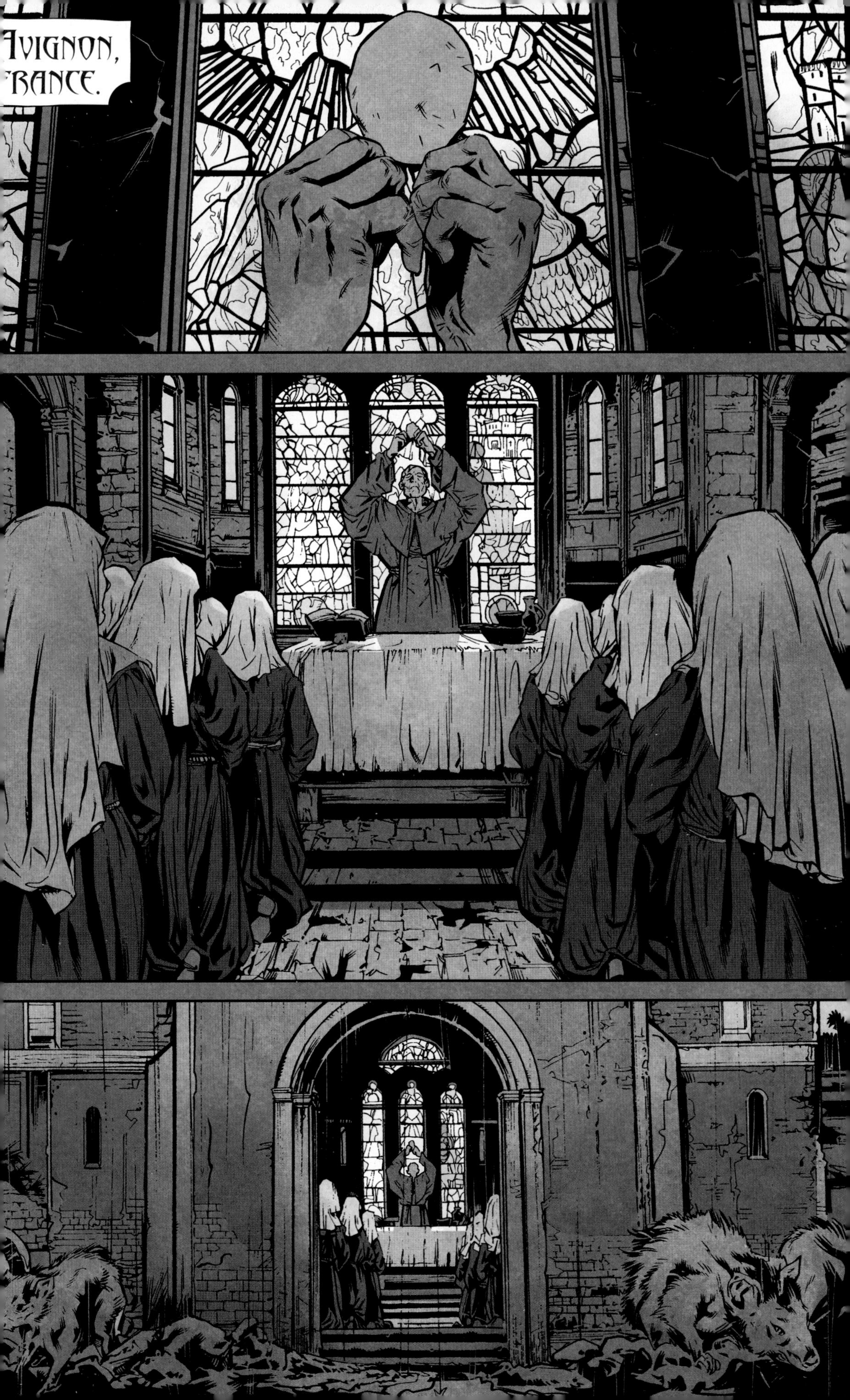
AVIGNON,
FRANCE.

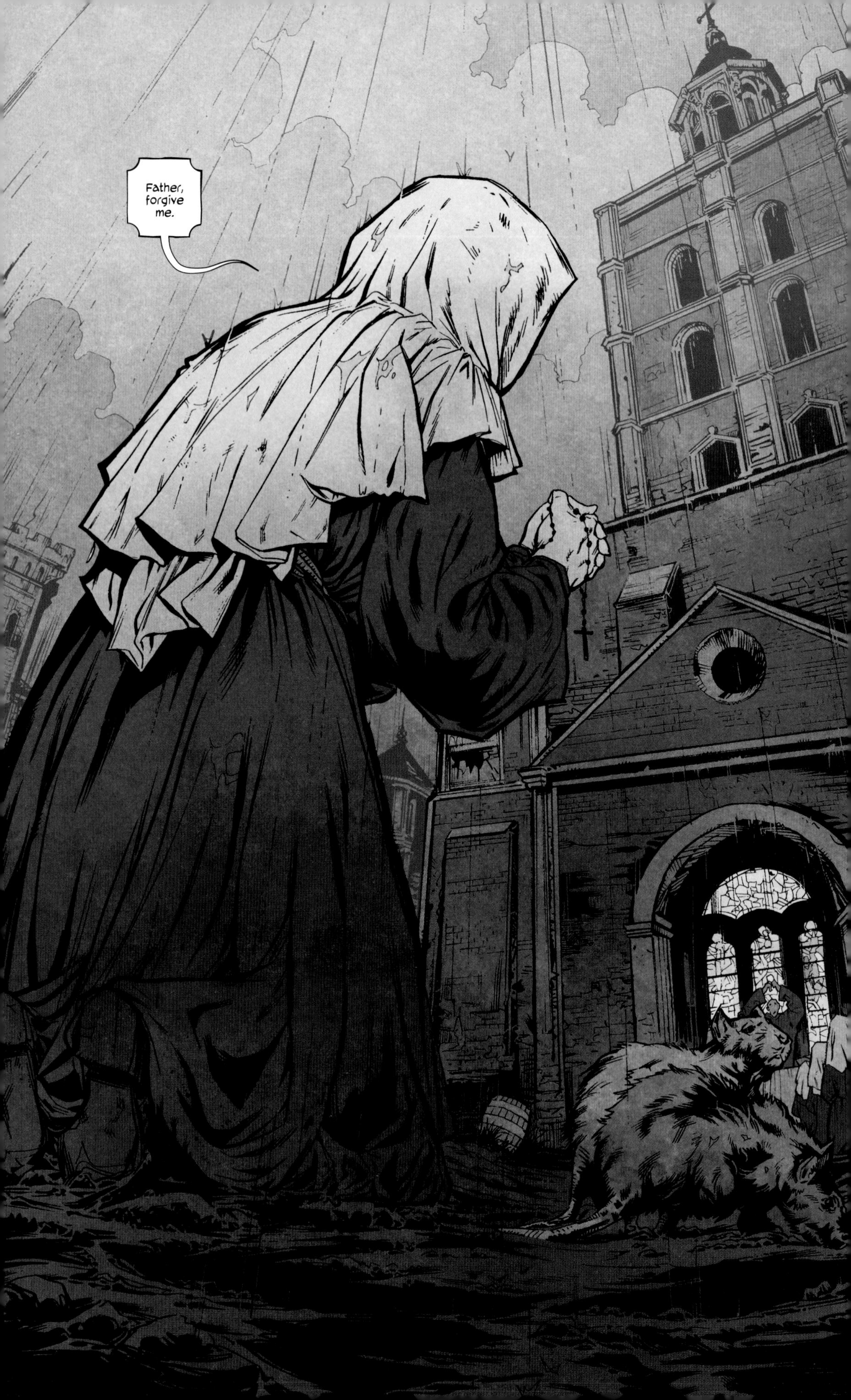
Father, forgive me.

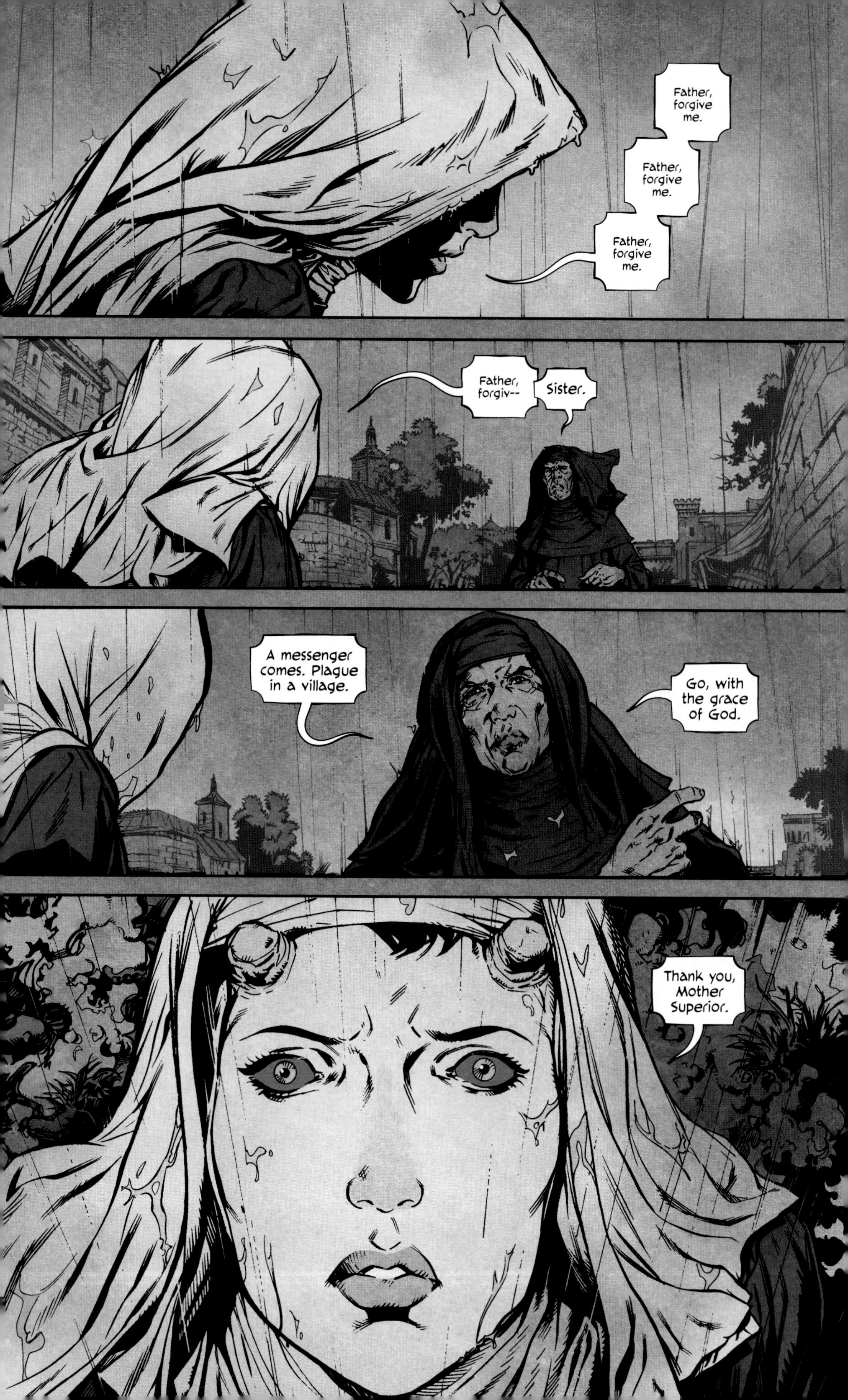
Father, forgive me.
Father, forgive me.
Father, forgive me.
Father, forgiv--
Sister.
A messenger comes. Plague in a village.
Go, with the grace of God.
Thank you, Mother Superior.

WE ALL
FALL DOWN

28 FEBRUARY 1373

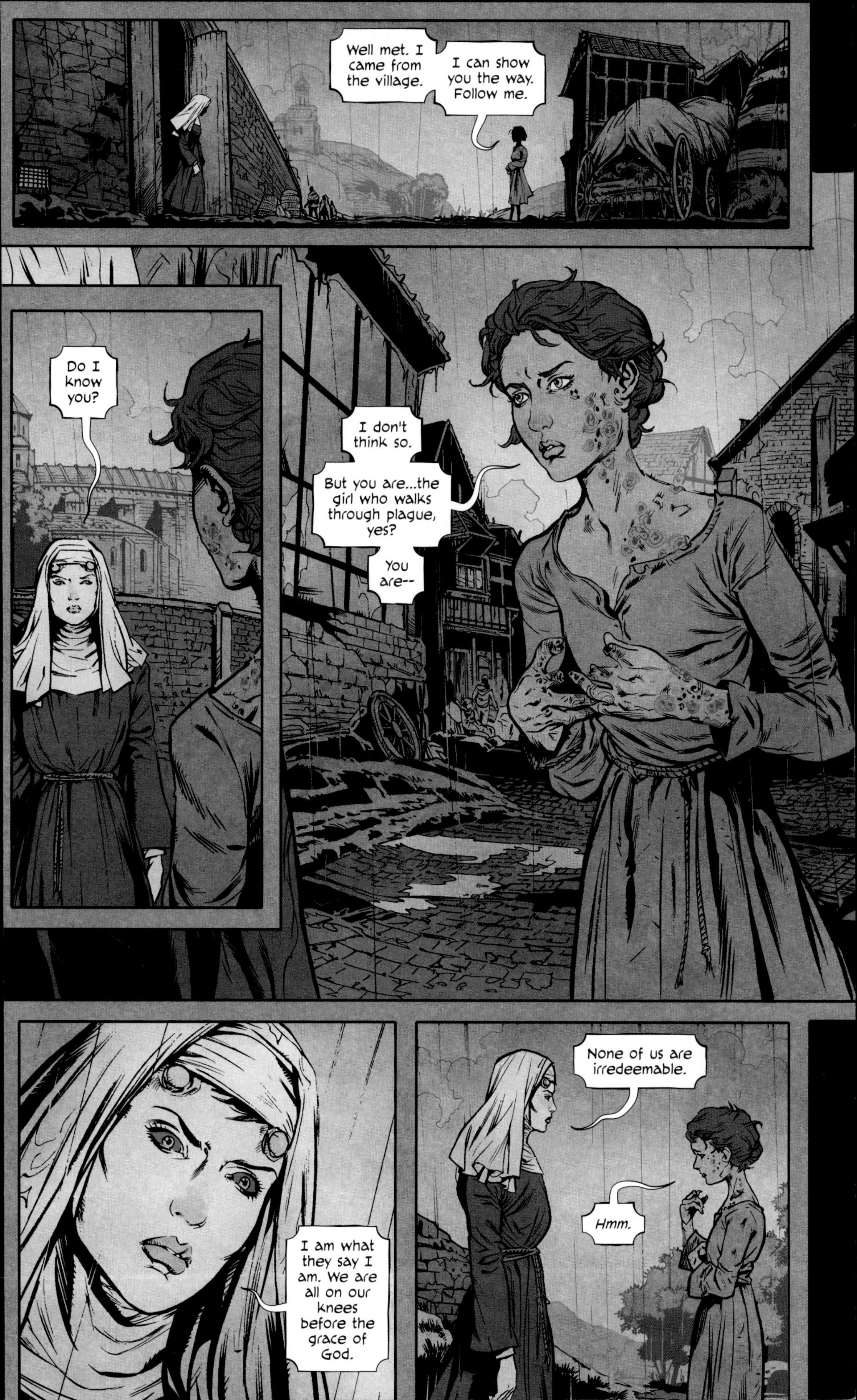
Well met. I came from the village.
I can show you the way. Follow me.
Do I know you?
I don't think so.
But you are...the girl who walks through plague, yes?
You are--
I am what they say I am. We are all on our knees before the grace of God.
None of us are irredeemable.
Hmm.

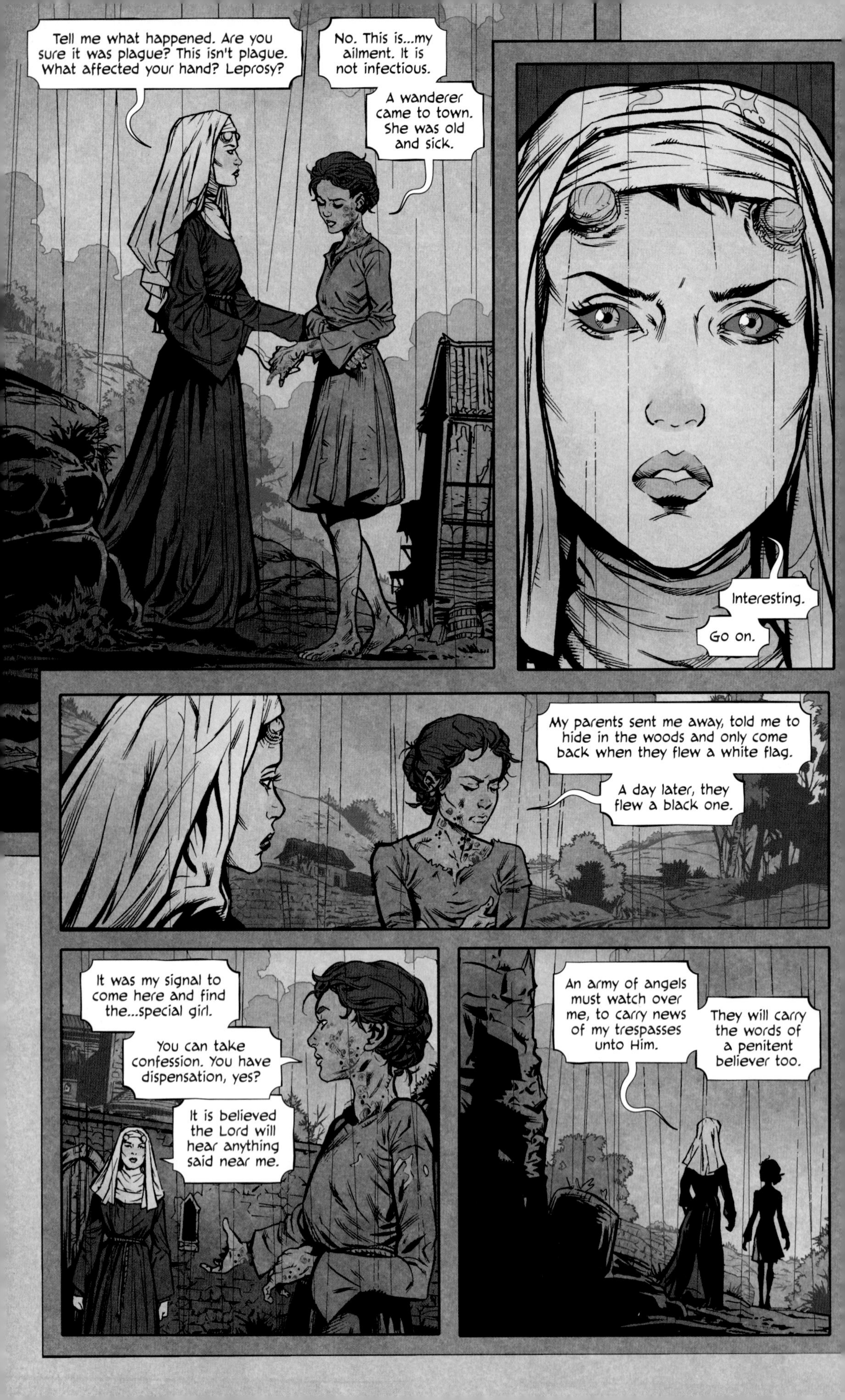

Tell me what happened. Are you sure it was plague? This isn't plague. What affected your hand? Leprosy?
No. This is...my ailment. It is not infectious.
A wanderer came to town. She was old and sick.
Interesting.
Go on.
My parents sent me away, told me to hide in the woods and only come back when they flew a white flag.
A day later, they flew a black one.
It was my signal to come here and find the...special girl.
You can take confession. You have dispensation, yes?
It is believed the Lord will hear anything said near me.
An army of angels must watch over me, to carry news of my trespasses unto Him.
They will carry the words of a penitent believer too.

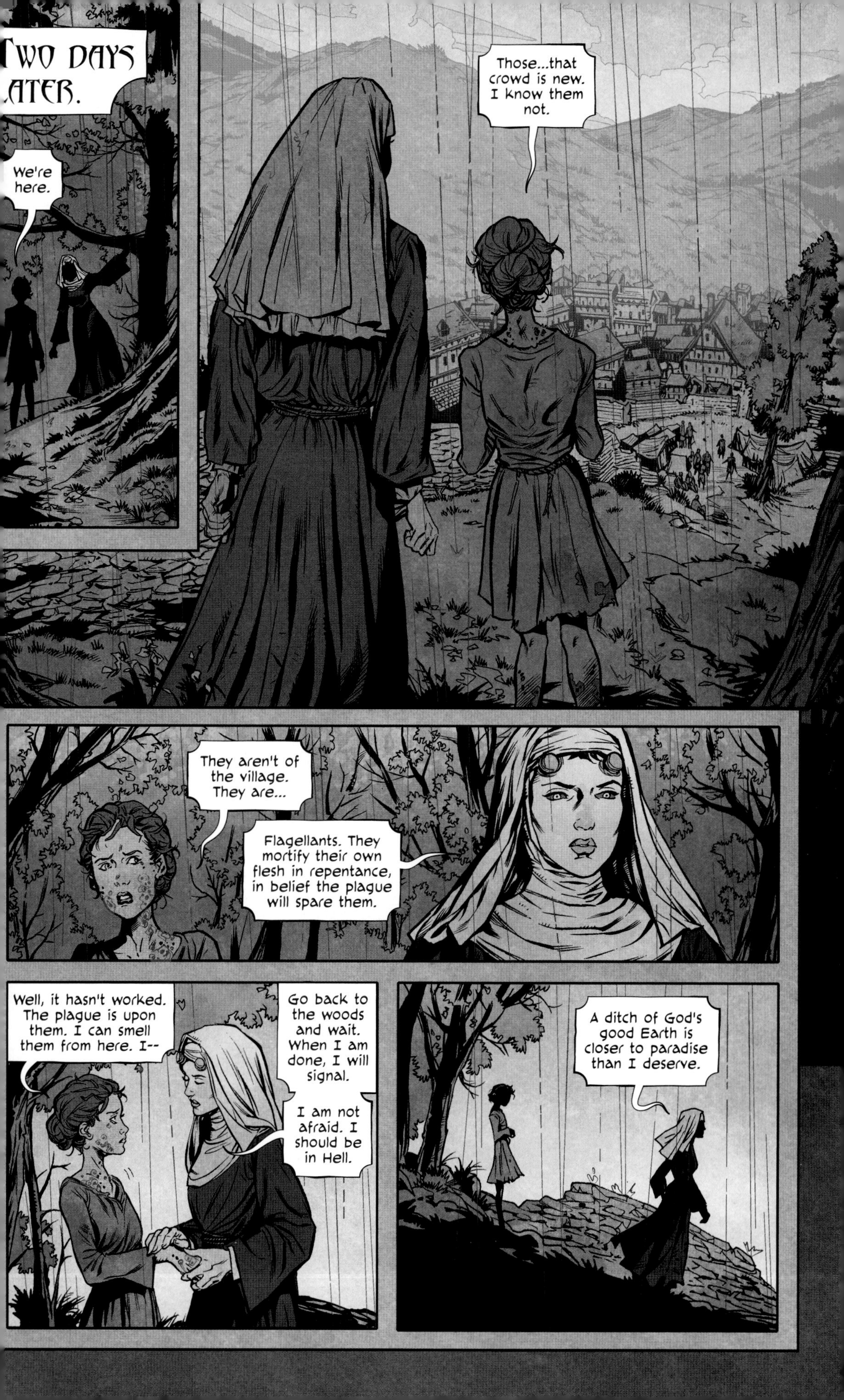
TWO DAYS LATER.
We're here.
Those...that crowd is new. I know them not.
They aren't of the village. They are...
Flagellants. They mortify their own flesh in repentance, in belief the plague will spare them.
Well, it hasn't worked. The plague is upon them. I can smell them from here. I--
Go back to the woods and wait. When I am done, I will signal.
I am not afraid. I should be in Hell.
A ditch of God's good Earth is closer to paradise than I deserve.

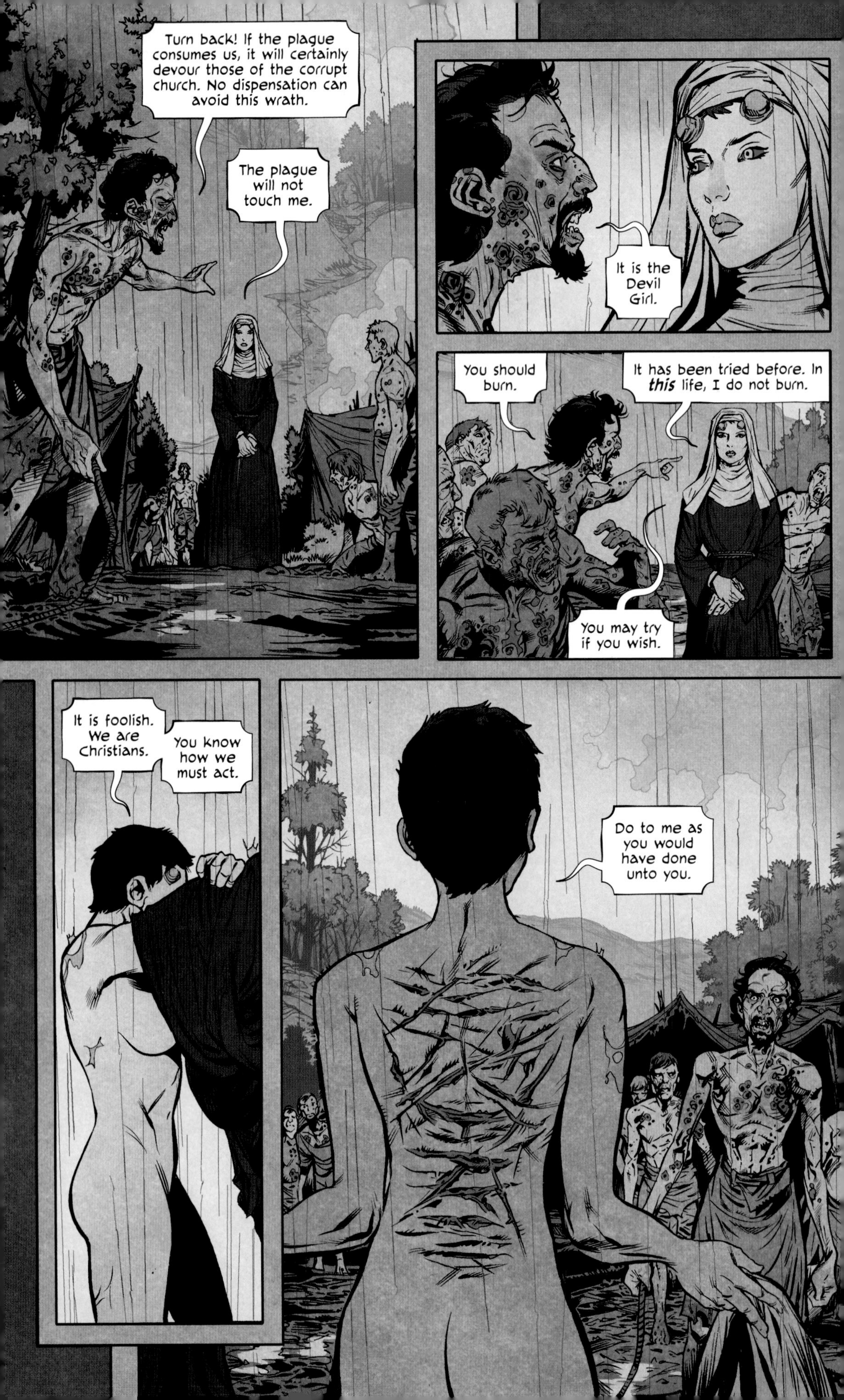

Turn back! If the plague consumes us, it will certainly devour those of the corrupt church. No dispensation can avoid this wrath.
The plague will not touch me.
It is the Devil Girl.
You should burn.
It has been tried before. In *this* life, I do not burn.
You may try if you wish.
It is foolish. We are Christians.
You know how we must act.
Do to me as you would have done unto you.

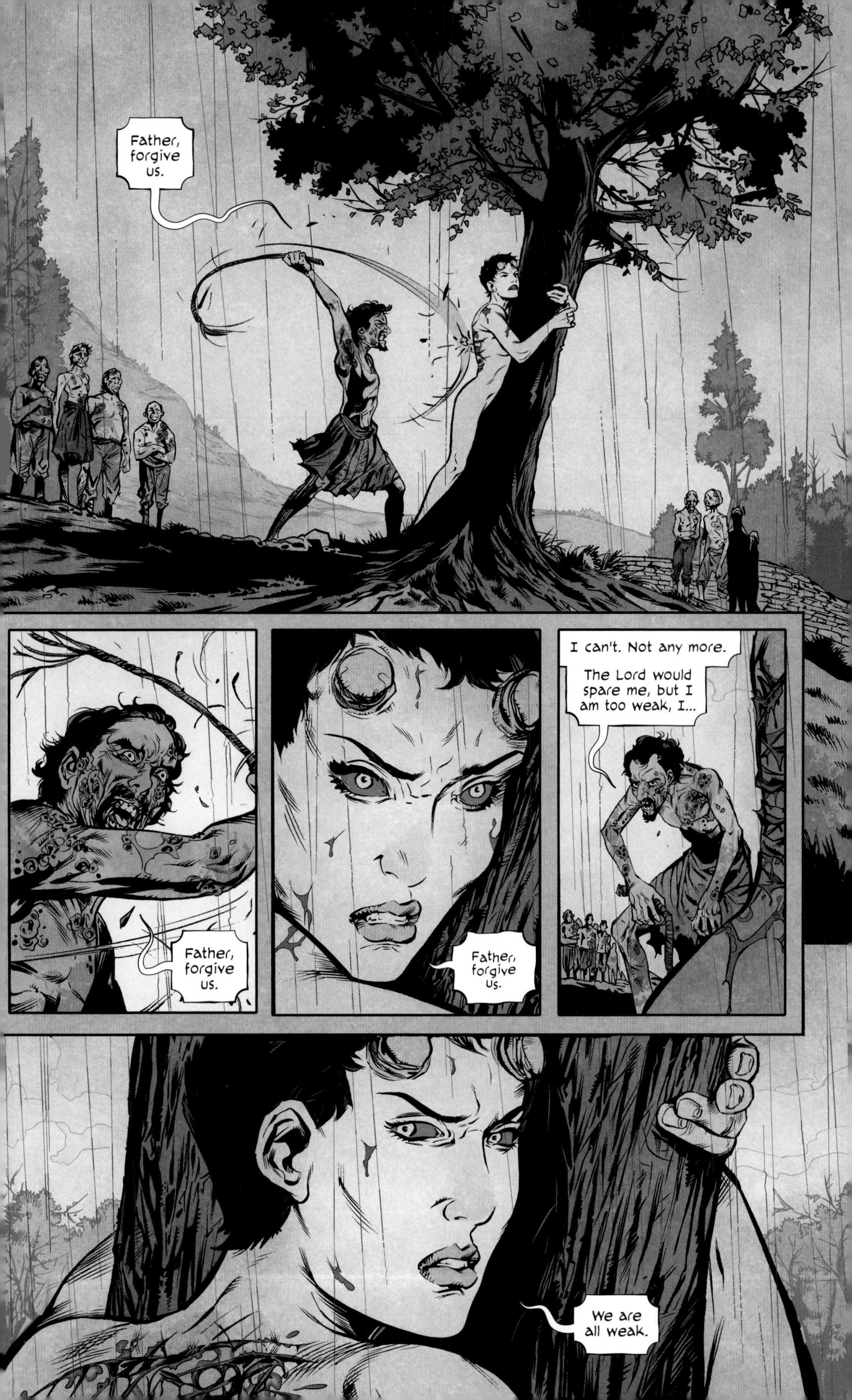
Father, forgive us.
Father, forgive us.
Father, forgive us.
I can't. Not any more.
The Lord would spare me, but I am too weak, I...
We are all weak.

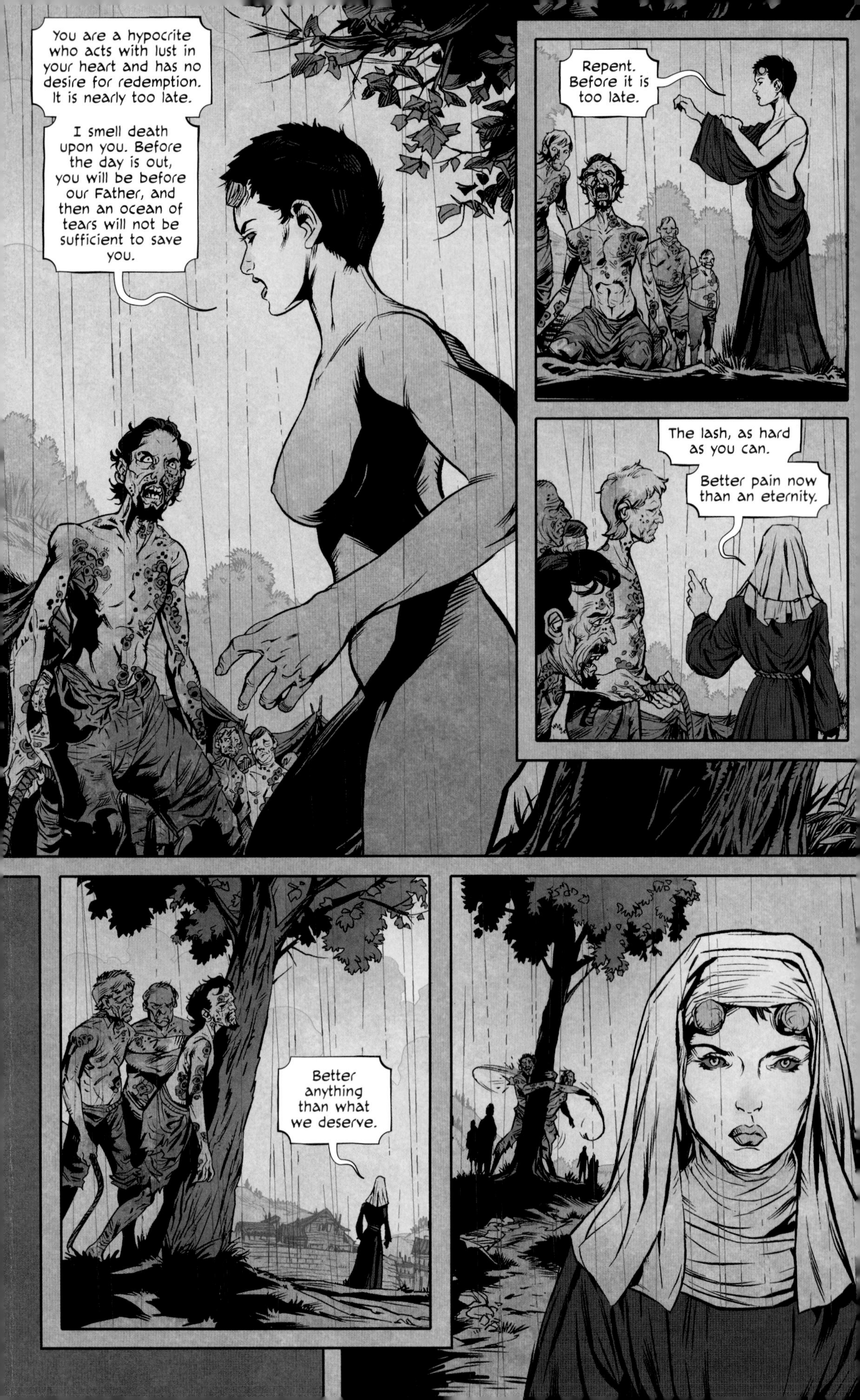
You are a hypocrite who acts with lust in your heart and has no desire for redemption. It is nearly too late.
I smell death upon you. Before the day is out, you will be before our Father, and then an ocean of tears will not be sufficient to save you.
Repent. Before it is too late.
The lash, as hard as you can.
Better pain now than an eternity.
Better anything than what we deserve.

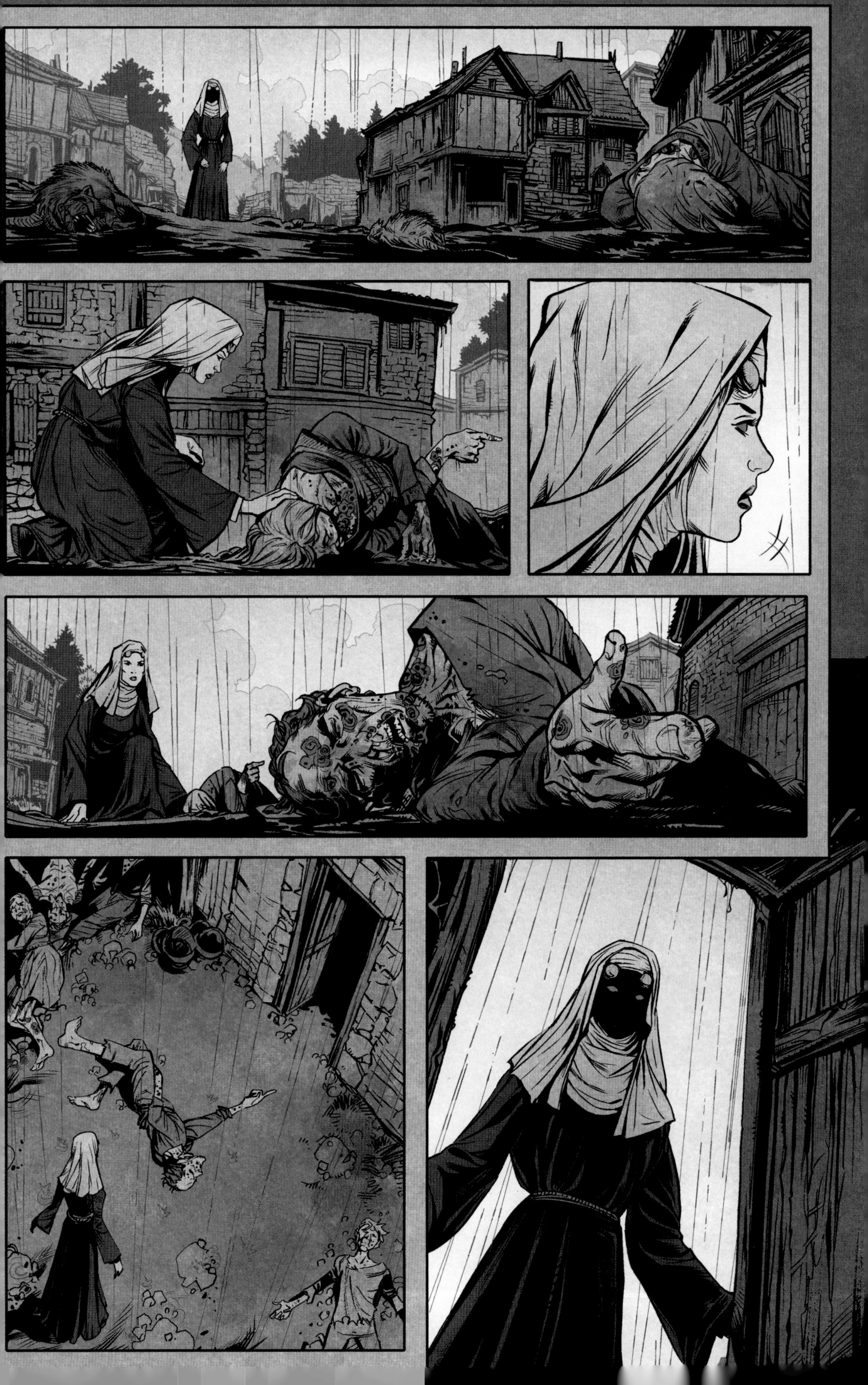

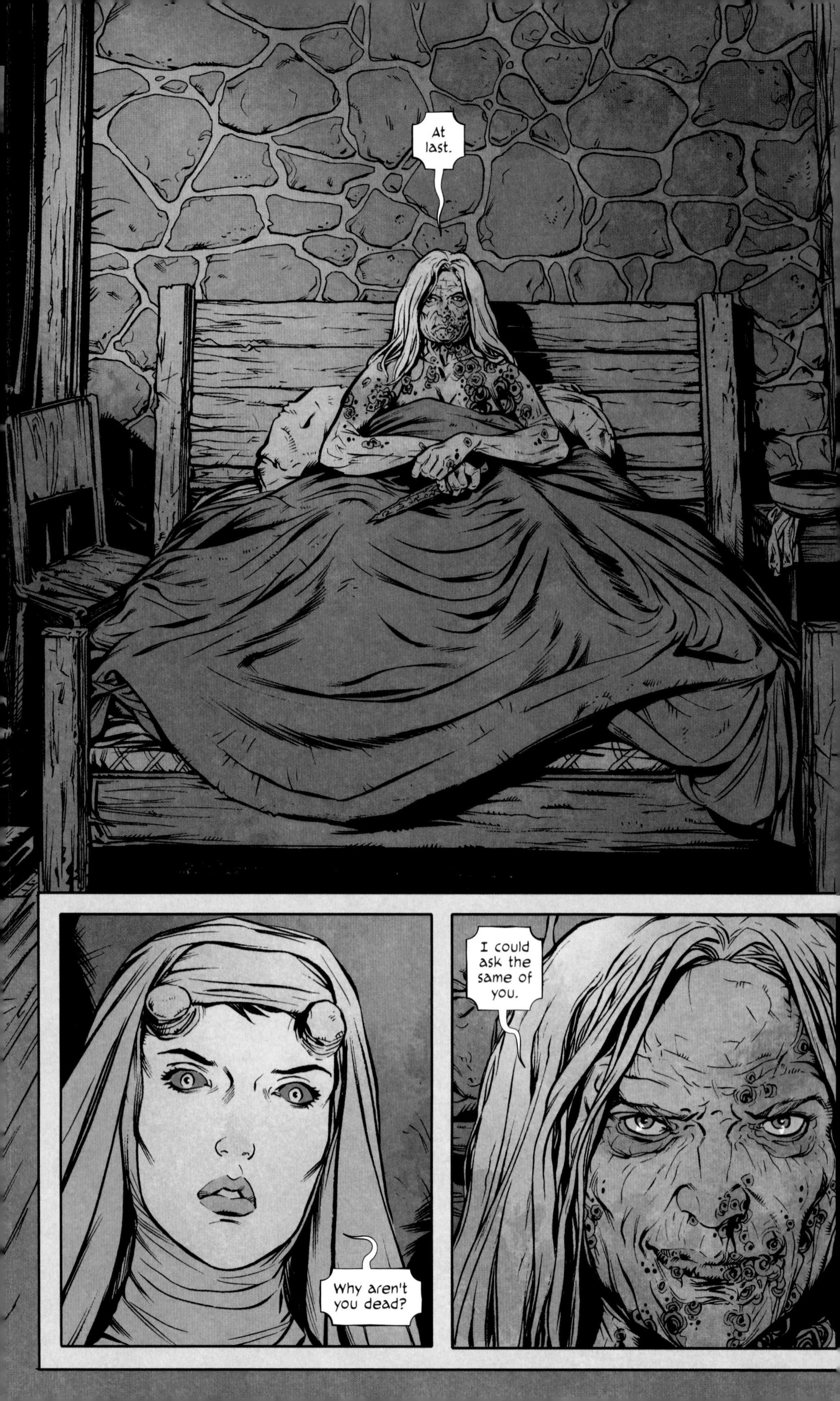
At last.
Why aren't you dead?
I could ask the same of you.

You had your two years. You should be mad by now, your powers out of control.

But you remain, while your peers are gone. I am confused.

They were false gods. I have pity for them.

I am the true Adversary. I know my fate.

Has...one from the pantheons ever lingered before?

Not regularly. Not as long as this. Of course, by definition, rare things happen but rarely...

How do you feel...?

Death is close. Every night there are dreams.

I will return to my Father for a second judgement soon enough.

I will kneel before the throne and pray the harrowing of Hell may save demons too...

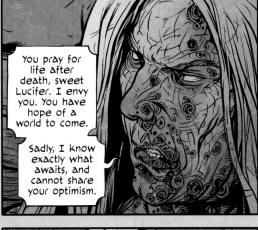

You pray for life after death, sweet Lucifer. I envy you. You have hope of a world to come.

Sadly, I know exactly what awaits, and cannot share your optimism.

Father will forgive you.

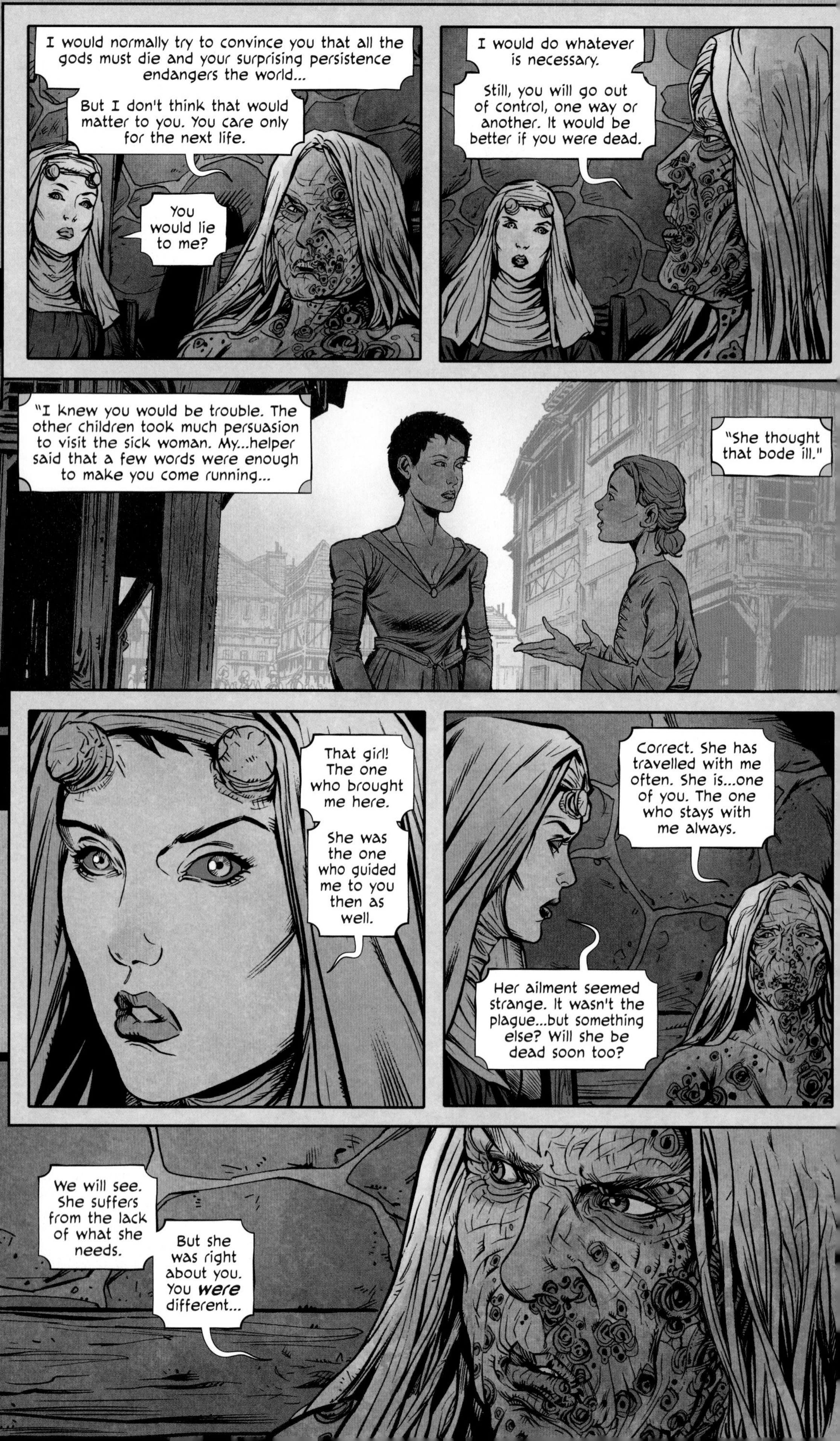
I would normally try to convince you that all the gods must die and your surprising persistence endangers the world...
But I don't think that would matter to you. You care only for the next life.
You would lie to me?
I would do whatever is necessary.
Still, you will go out of control, one way or another. It would be better if you were dead.
"I knew you would be trouble. The other children took much persuasion to visit the sick woman. My...helper said that a few words were enough to make you come running...
"She thought that bode ill."
That girl! The one who brought me here.
She was the one who guided me to you then as well.
Correct. She has travelled with me often. She is...one of you. The one who stays with me always.
Her ailment seemed strange. It wasn't the plague...but something else? Will she be dead soon too?
We will see. She suffers from the lack of what she needs.
But she was right about you. You *were* different...

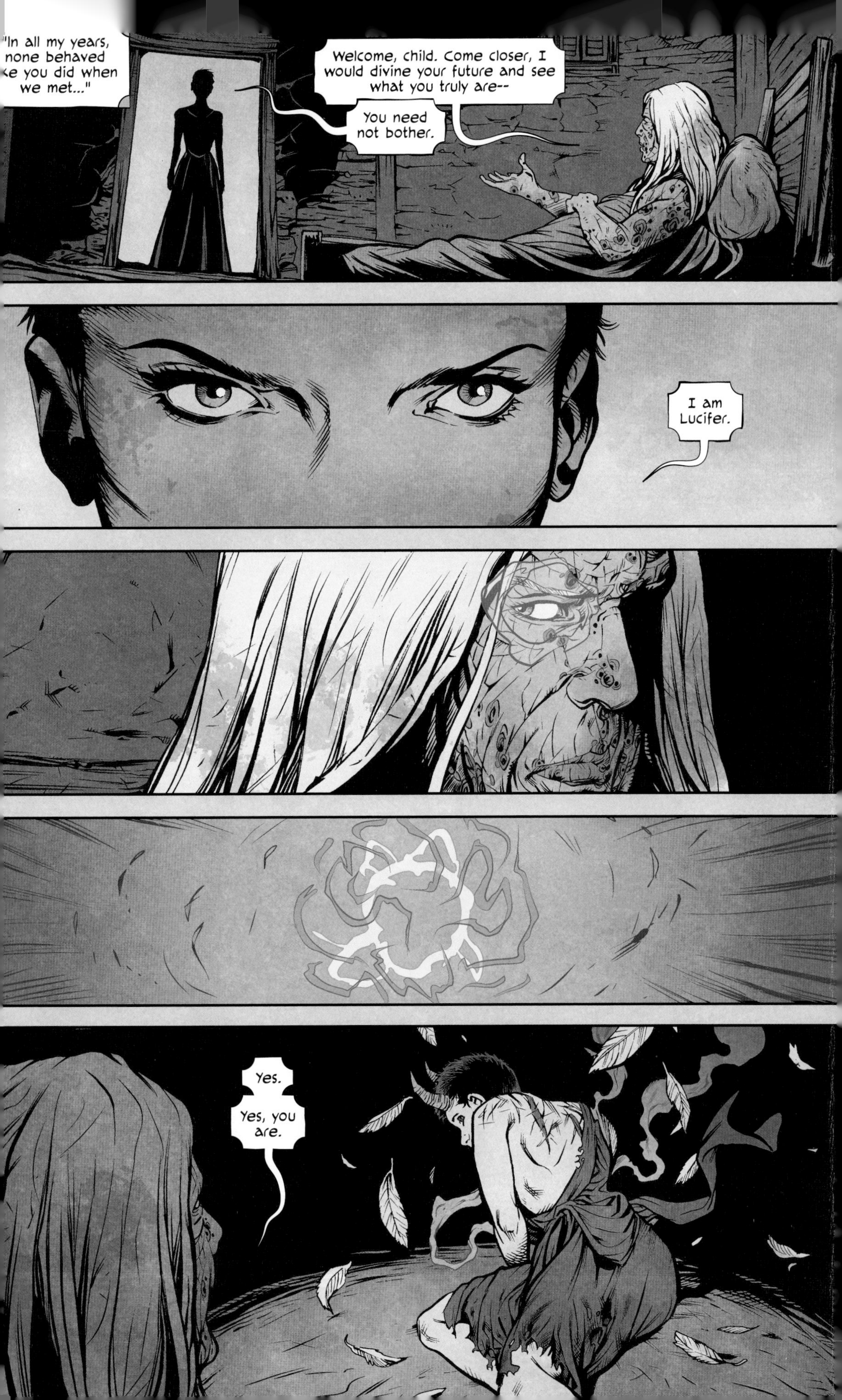
"In all my years, none behaved ke you did when we met..."
Welcome, child. Come closer, I would divine your future and see what you truly are--
You need not bother.
I am Lucifer.
Yes.
Yes, you are.

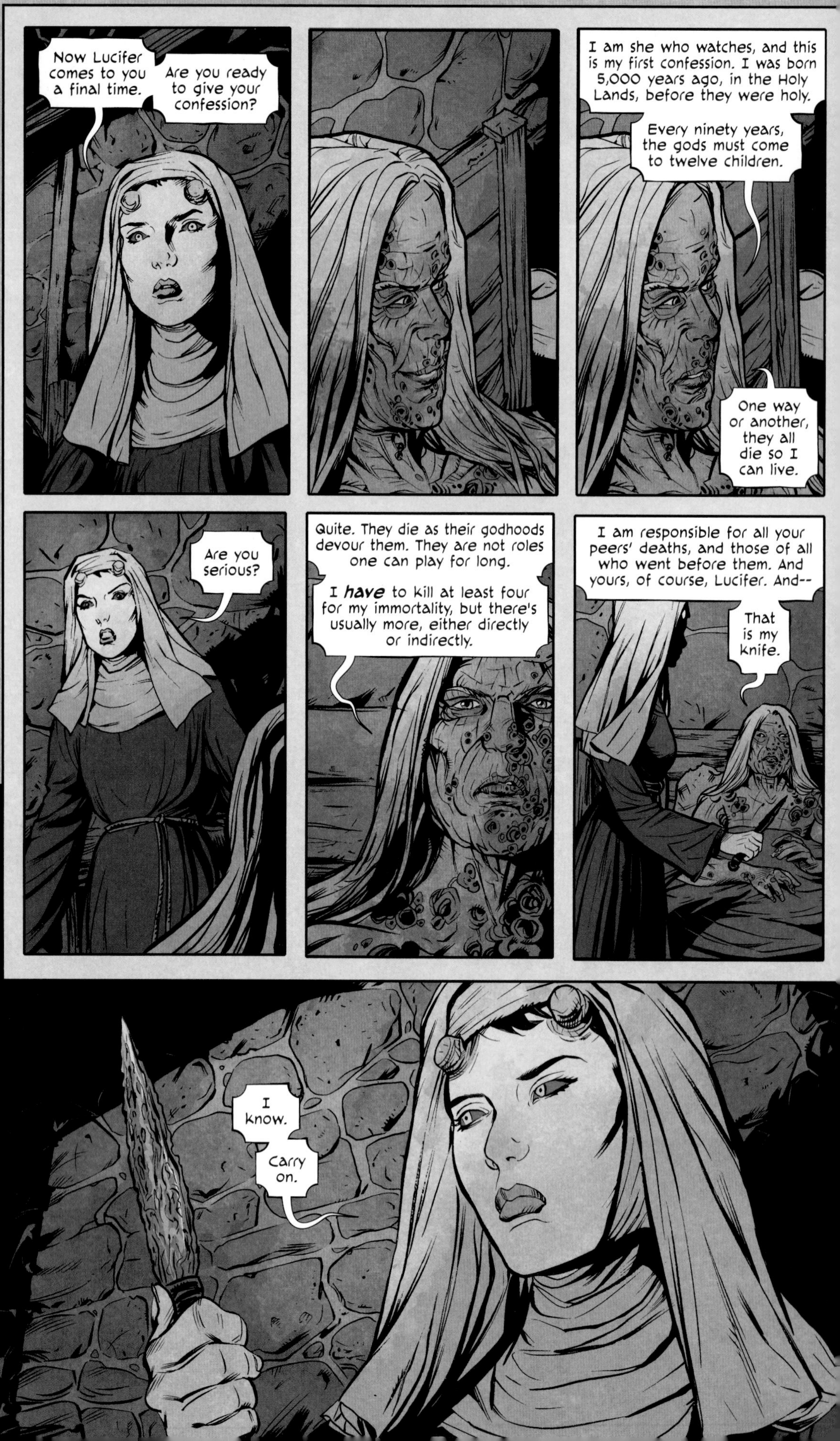

Now Lucifer comes to you a final time.
Are you ready to give your confession?
I am she who watches, and this is my first confession. I was born 5,000 years ago, in the Holy Lands, before they were holy.
Every ninety years, the gods must come to twelve children.
One way or another, they all die so I can live.
Are you serious?
Quite. They die as their godhoods devour them. They are not roles one can play for long.
I *have* to kill at least four for my immortality, but there's usually more, either directly or indirectly.
I am responsible for all your peers' deaths, and those of all who went before them. And yours, of course, Lucifer. And--
That is my knife.
I know.
Carry on.

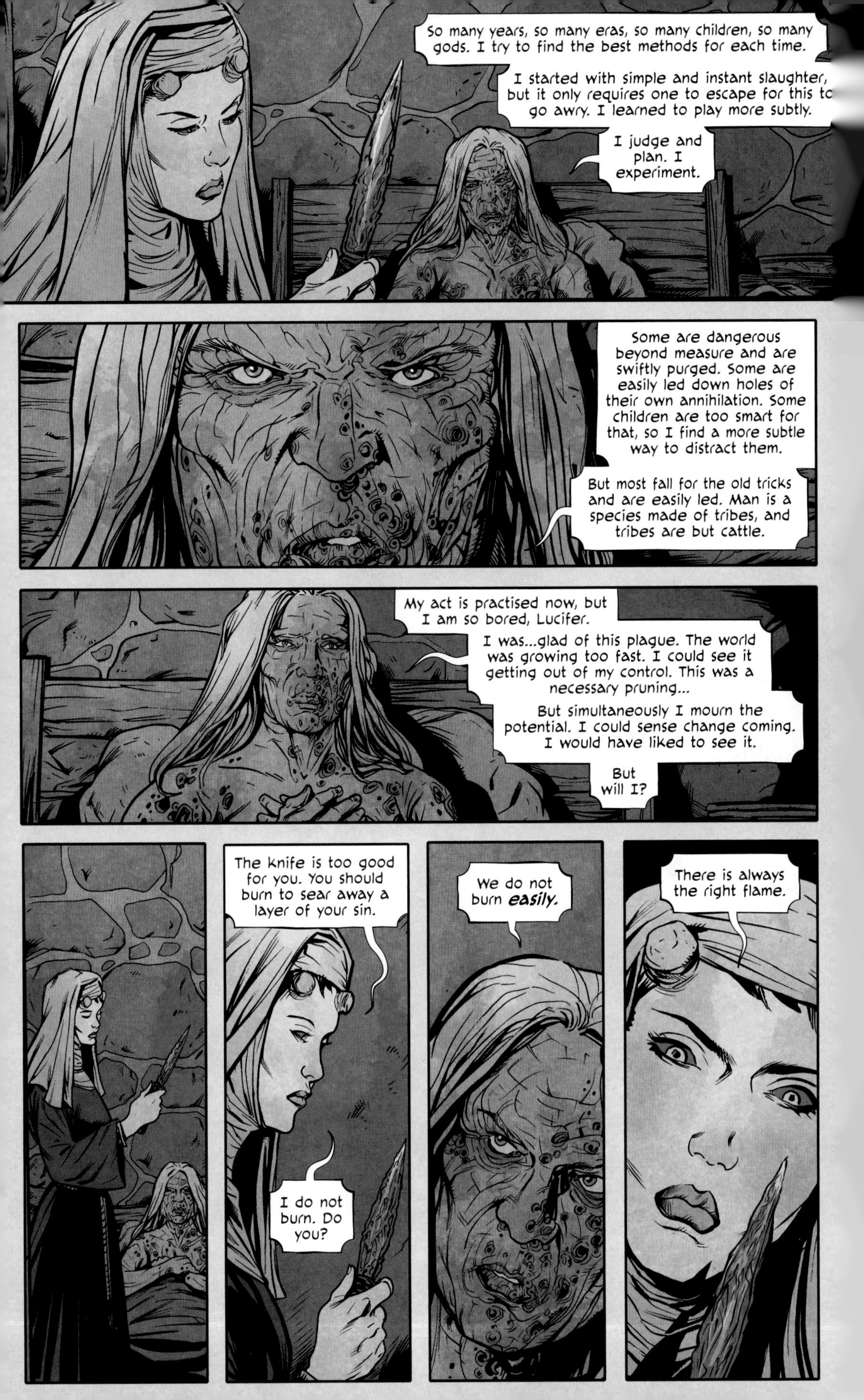
So many years, so many eras, so many children, so many gods. I try to find the best methods for each time.
I started with simple and instant slaughter, but it only requires one to escape for this to go awry. I learned to play more subtly.
I judge and plan. I experiment.
Some are dangerous beyond measure and are swiftly purged. Some are easily led down holes of their own annihilation. Some children are too smart for that, so I find a more subtle way to distract them.
But most fall for the old tricks and are easily led. Man is a species made of tribes, and tribes are but cattle.
My act is practised now, but I am so bored, Lucifer.
I was...glad of this plague. The world was growing too fast. I could see it getting out of my control. This was a necessary pruning...
But simultaneously I mourn the potential. I could sense change coming. I would have liked to see it.
But will I?
The knife is too good for you. You should burn to sear away a layer of your sin.
I do not burn. Do you?
We do not burn *easily.*
There is always the right flame.

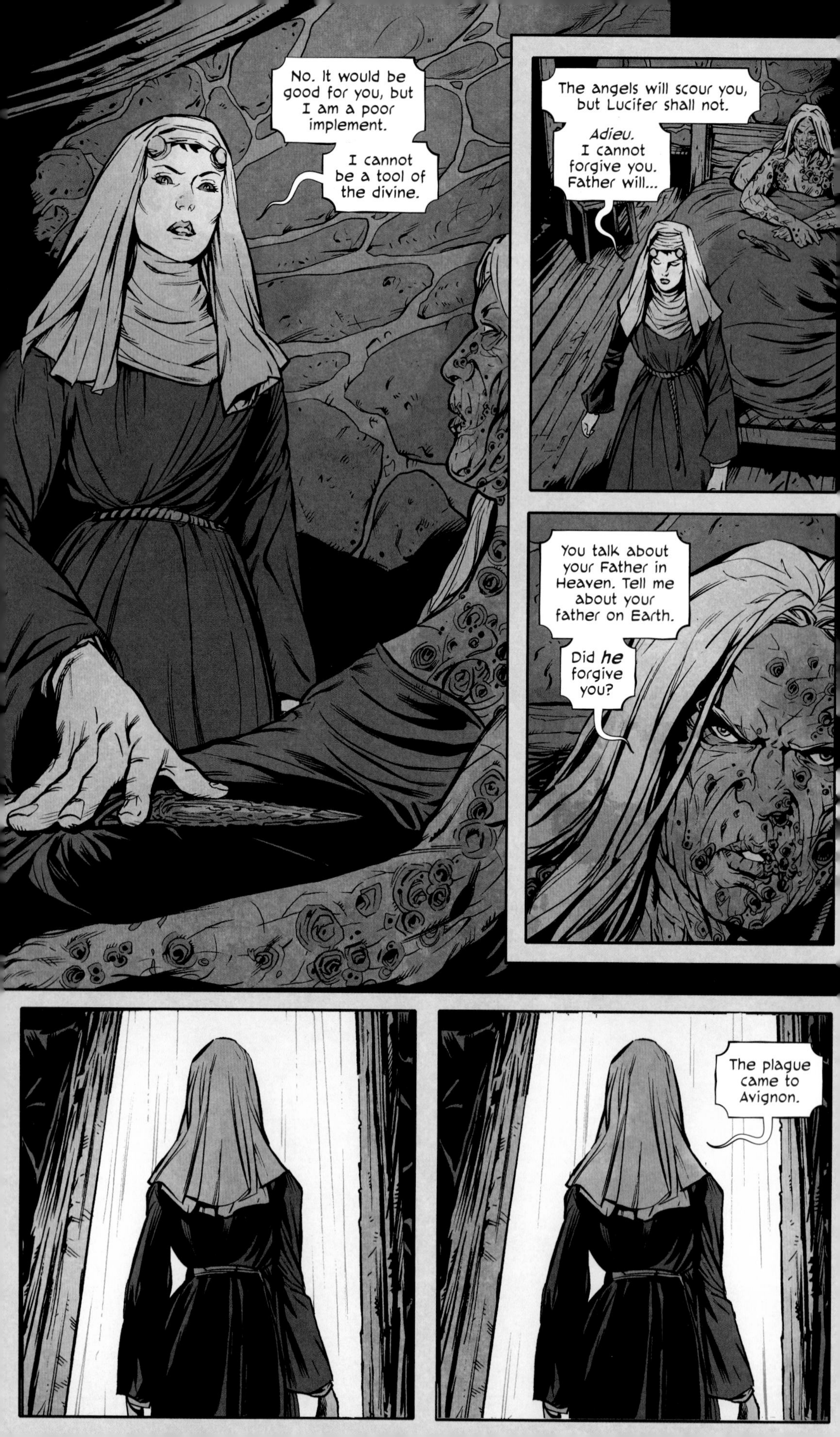
No. It would be good for you, but I am a poor implement.
I cannot be a tool of the divine.
The angels will scour you, but Lucifer shall not.
Adieu. I cannot forgive you. Father will...
You talk about your Father in Heaven. Tell me about your father on Earth.
Did ***he*** forgive you?
The plague came to Avignon.

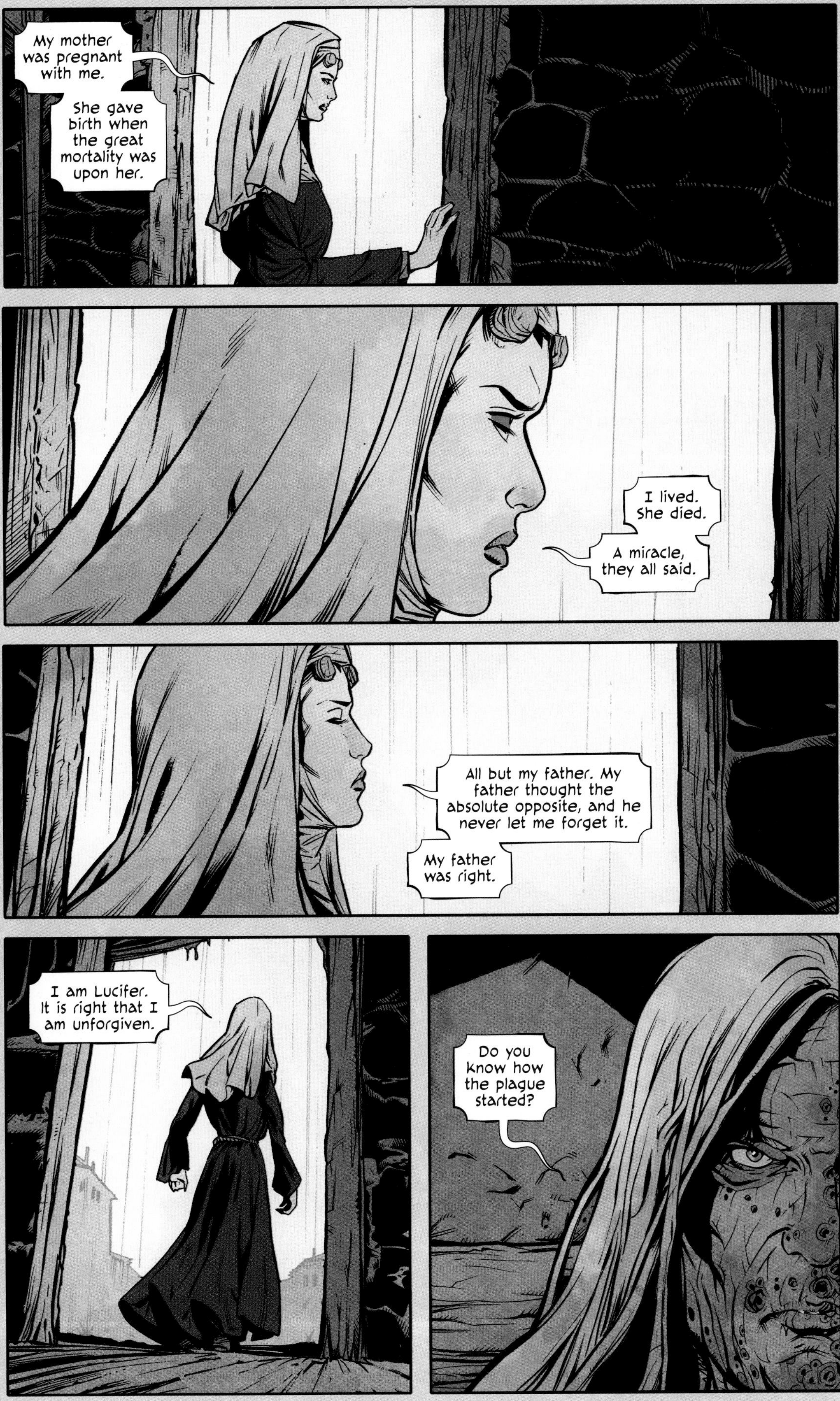

My mother was pregnant with me.
She gave birth when the great mortality was upon her.
I lived. She died.
A miracle, they all said.
All but my father. My father thought the absolute opposite, and he never let me forget it.
My father was right.
I am Lucifer. It is right that I am unforgiven.
Do you know how the plague started?

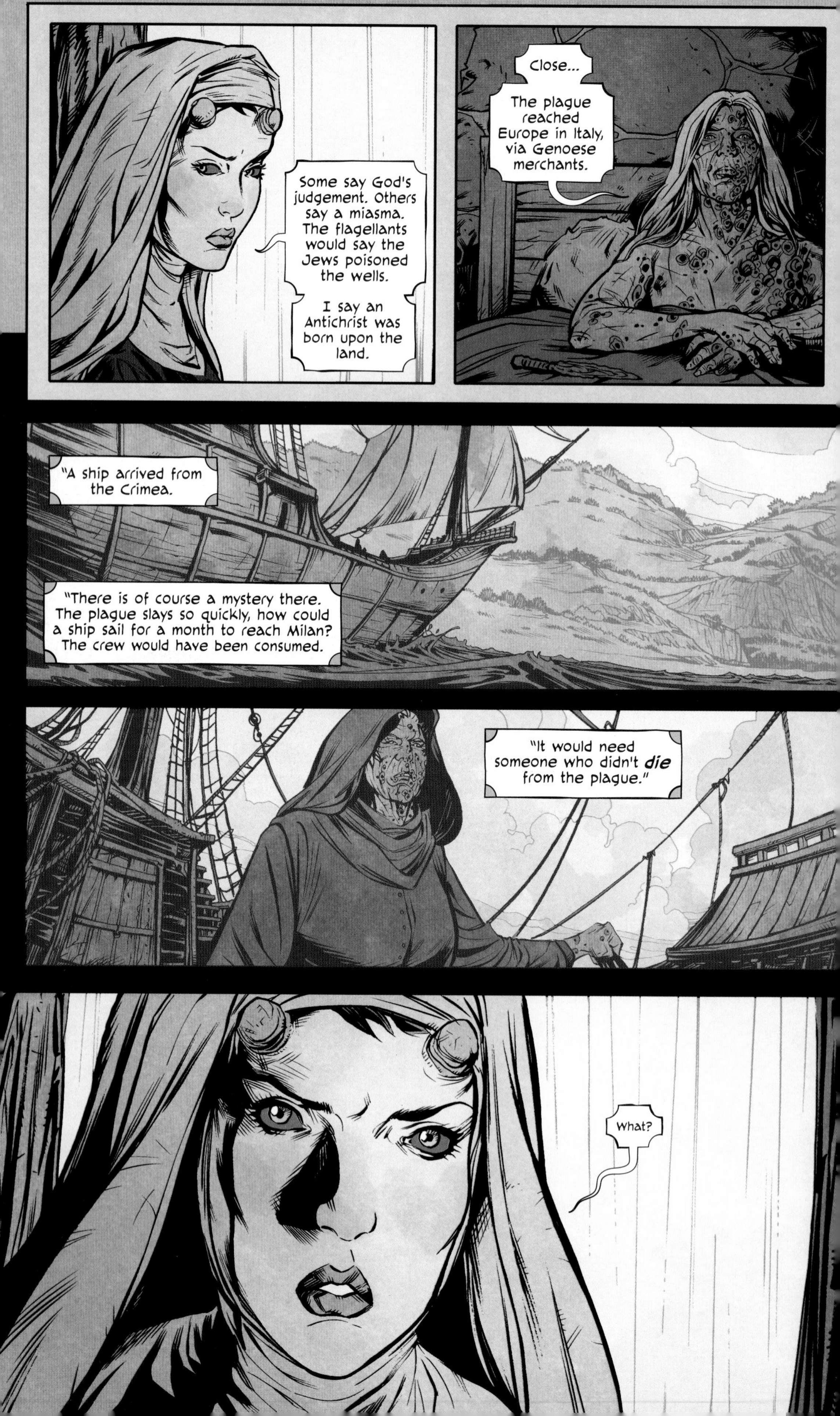
Some say God's judgement. Others say a miasma. The flagellants would say the Jews poisoned the wells.
I say an Antichrist was born upon the land.
Close...
The plague reached Europe in Italy, via Genoese merchants.
"A ship arrived from the Crimea.
"There is of course a mystery there. The plague slays so quickly, how could a ship sail for a month to reach Milan? The crew would have been consumed.
"It would need someone who didn't *die* from the plague."
What?

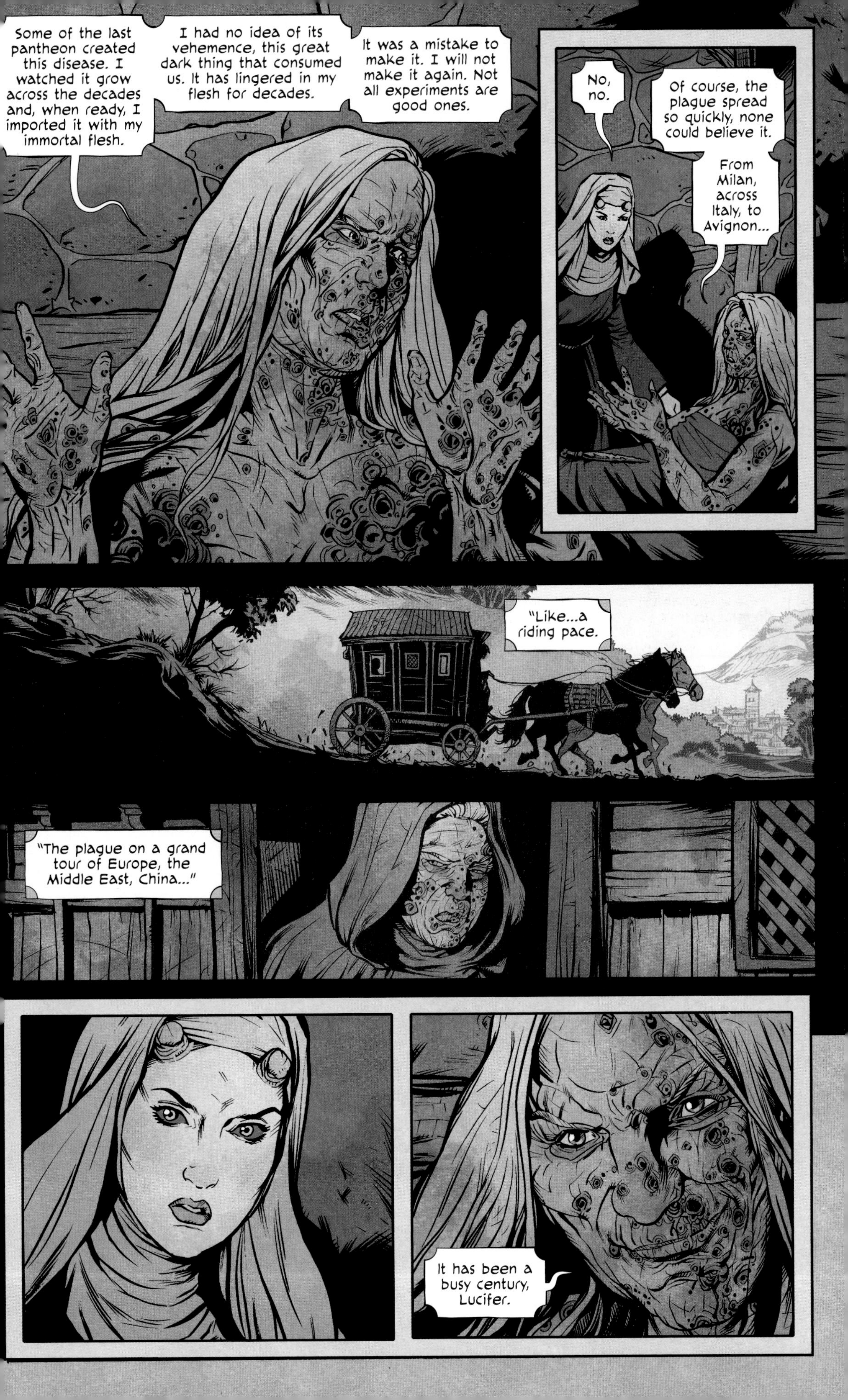
Some of the last pantheon created this disease. I watched it grow across the decades and, when ready, I imported it with my immortal flesh.
I had no idea of its vehemence, this great dark thing that consumed us. It has lingered in my flesh for decades.
It was a mistake to make it. I will not make it again. Not all experiments are good ones.
No, no.
Of course, the plague spread so quickly, none could believe it.
From Milan, across Italy, to Avignon...
"Like...a riding pace.
"The plague on a grand tour of Europe, the Middle East, China..."
It has been a busy century, Lucifer.

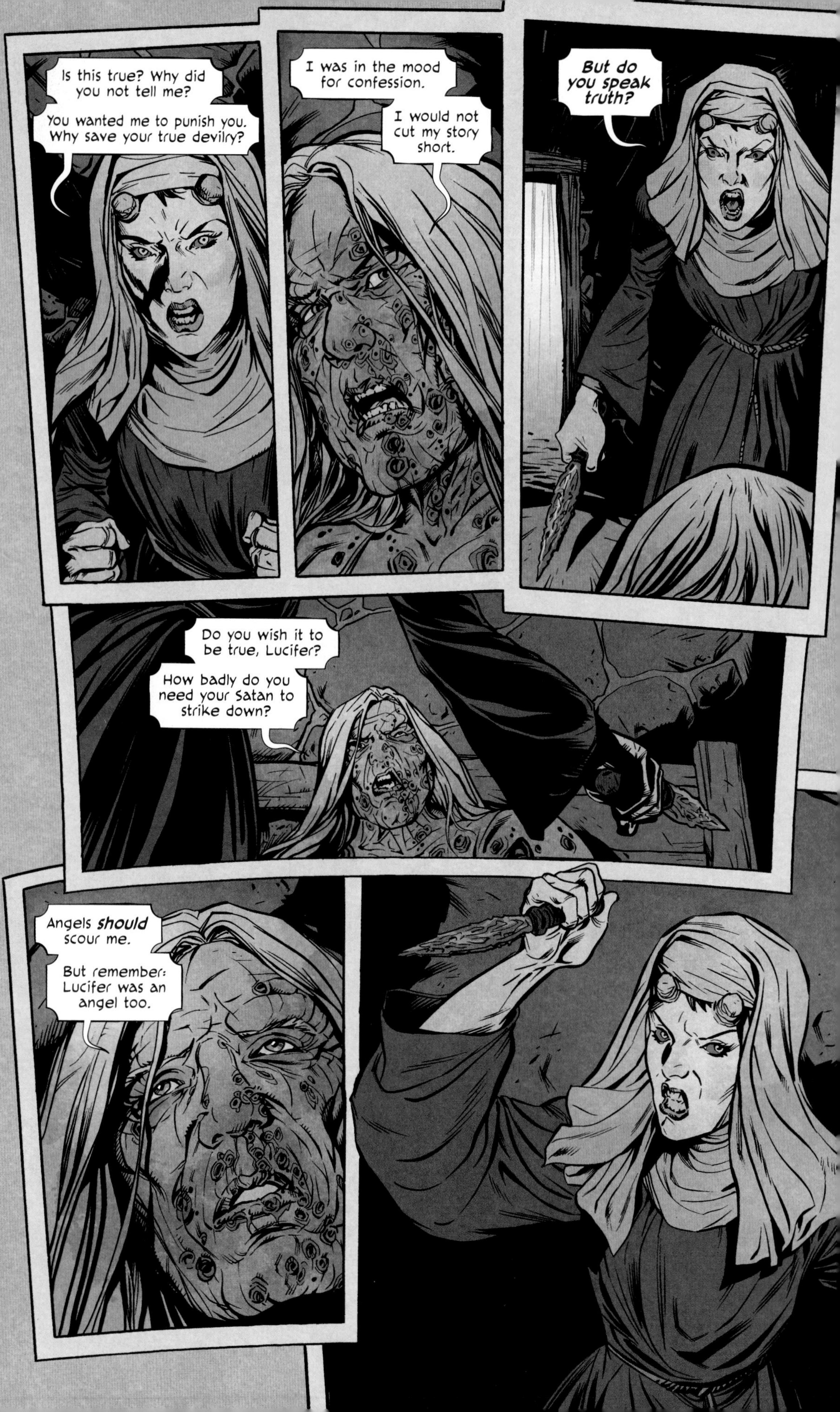

Is this true? Why did you not tell me?
You wanted me to punish you. Why save your true devilry?
I was in the mood for confession.
I would not cut my story short.
But do you speak truth?
Do you wish it to be true, Lucifer?
How badly do you need your Satan to strike down?
Angels should scour me.
But remember: Lucifer was an angel too.

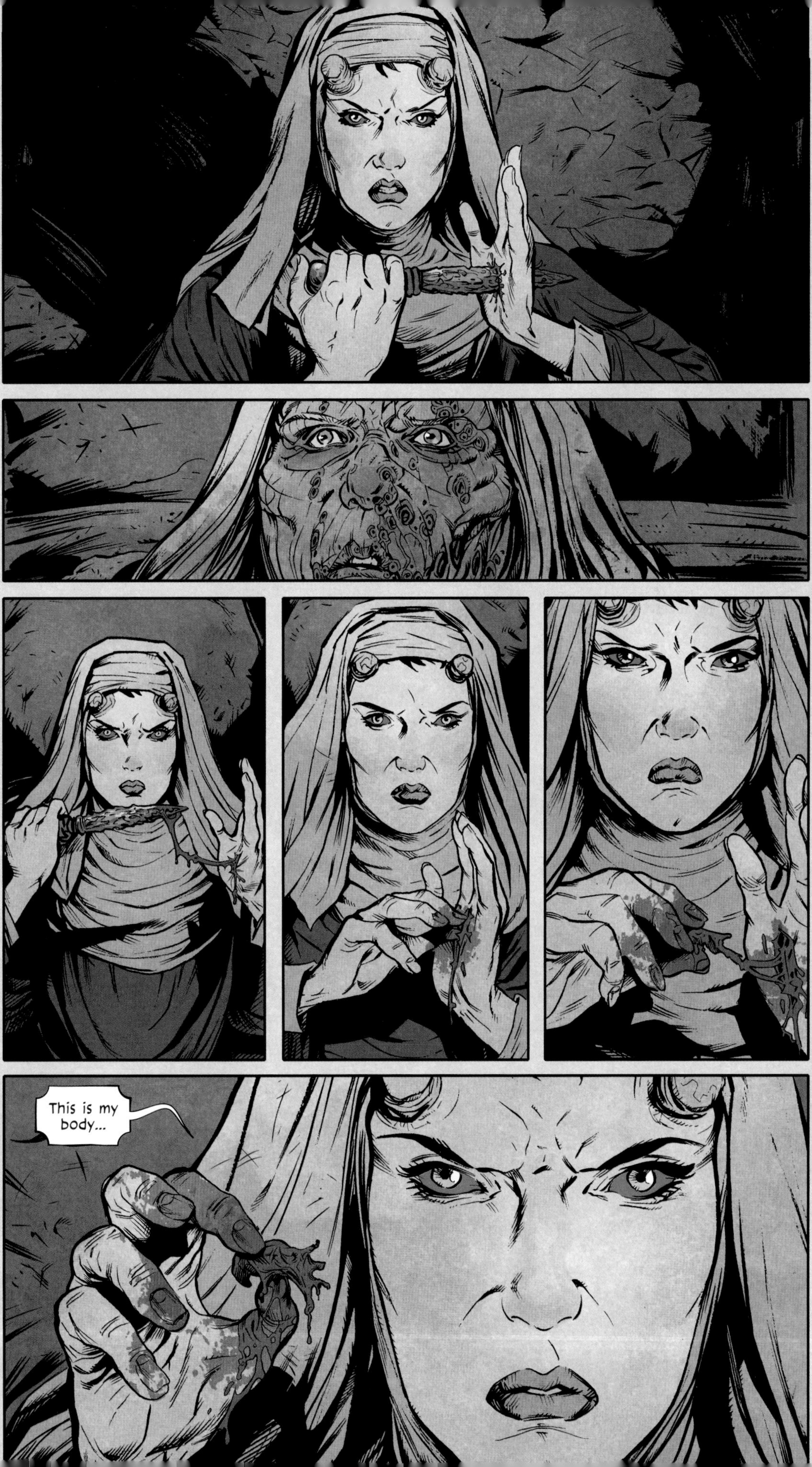
This is my body...

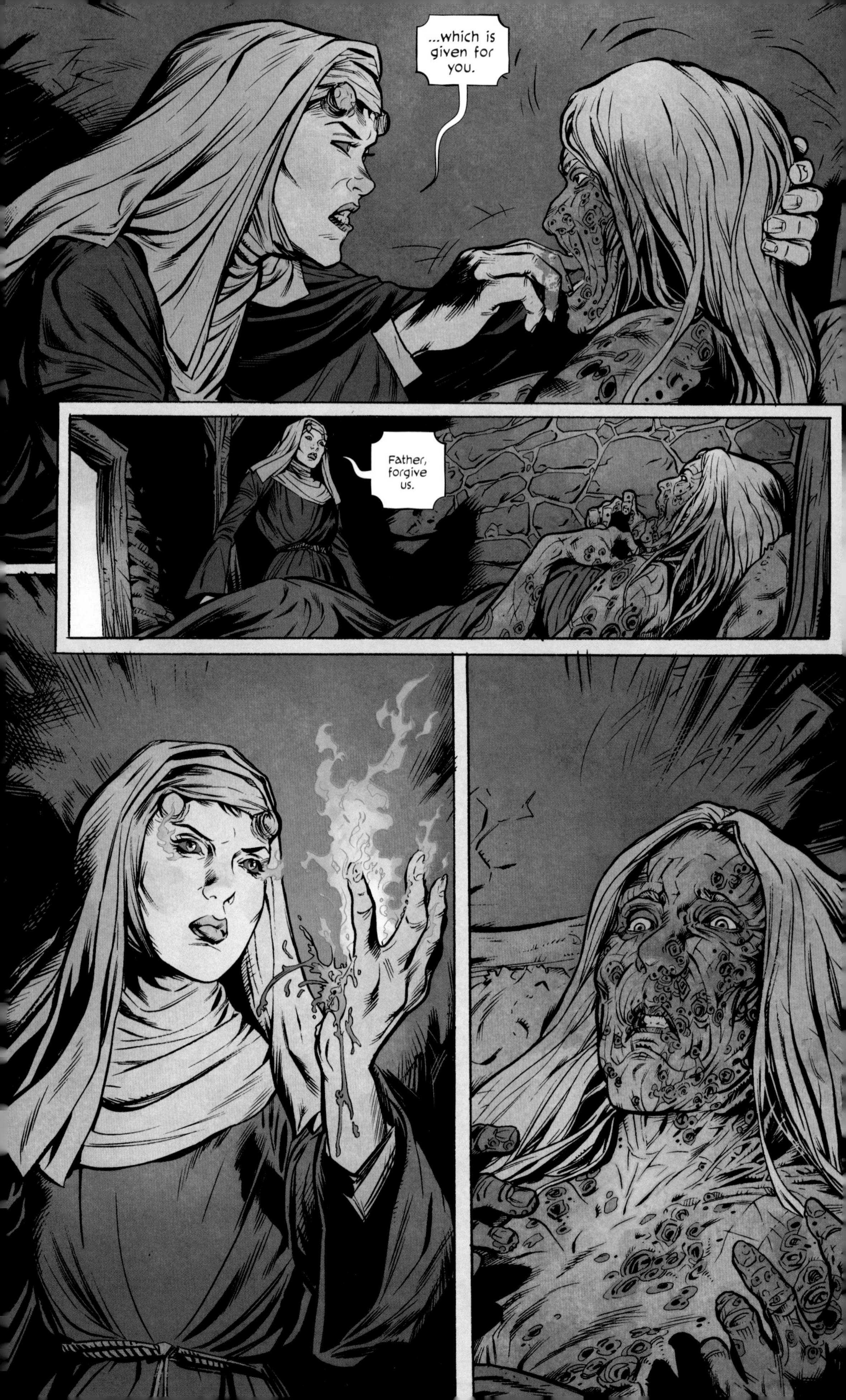
...which is given for you.
Father, forgive us.

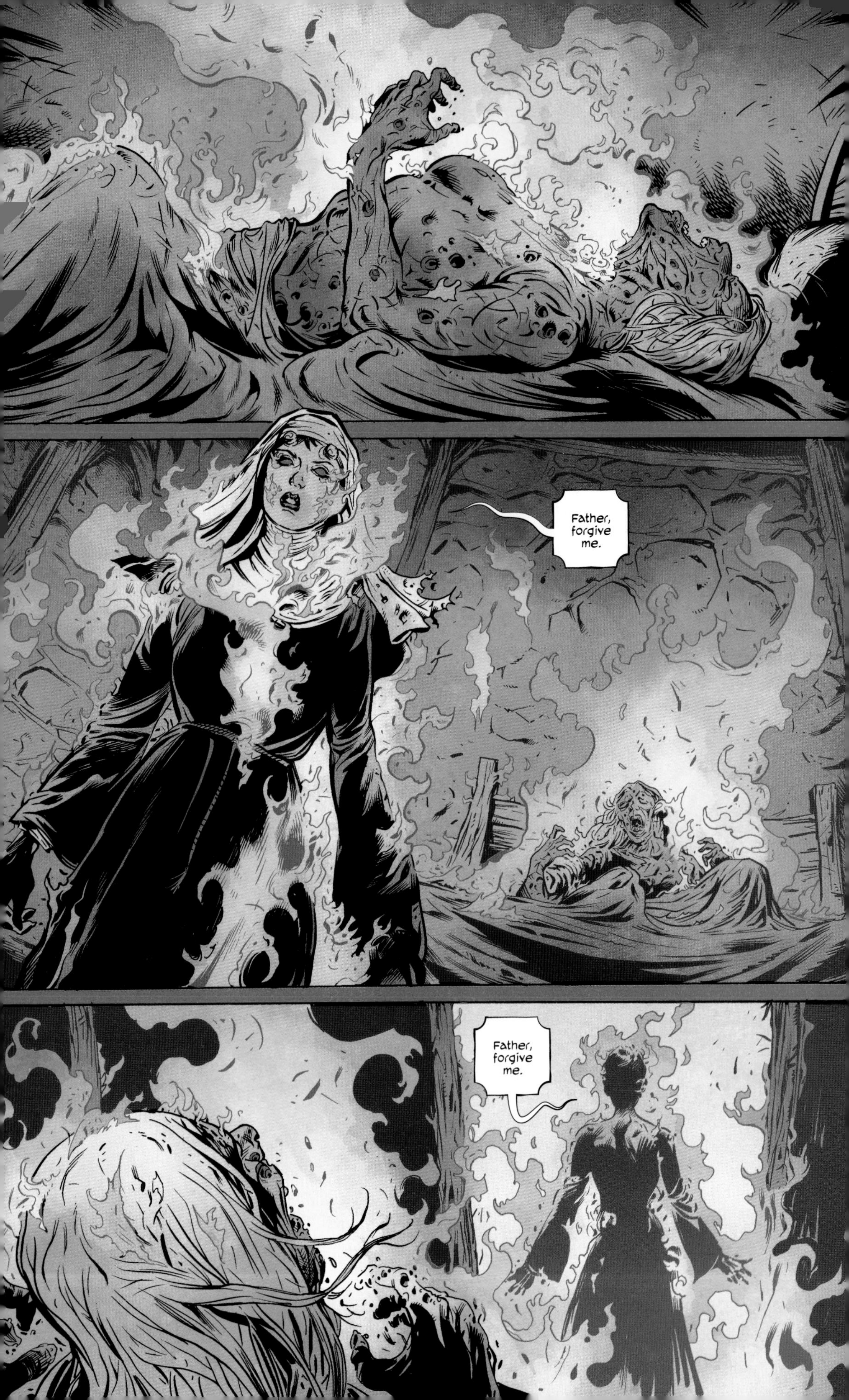

Father, forgive me.
Father, forgive me.

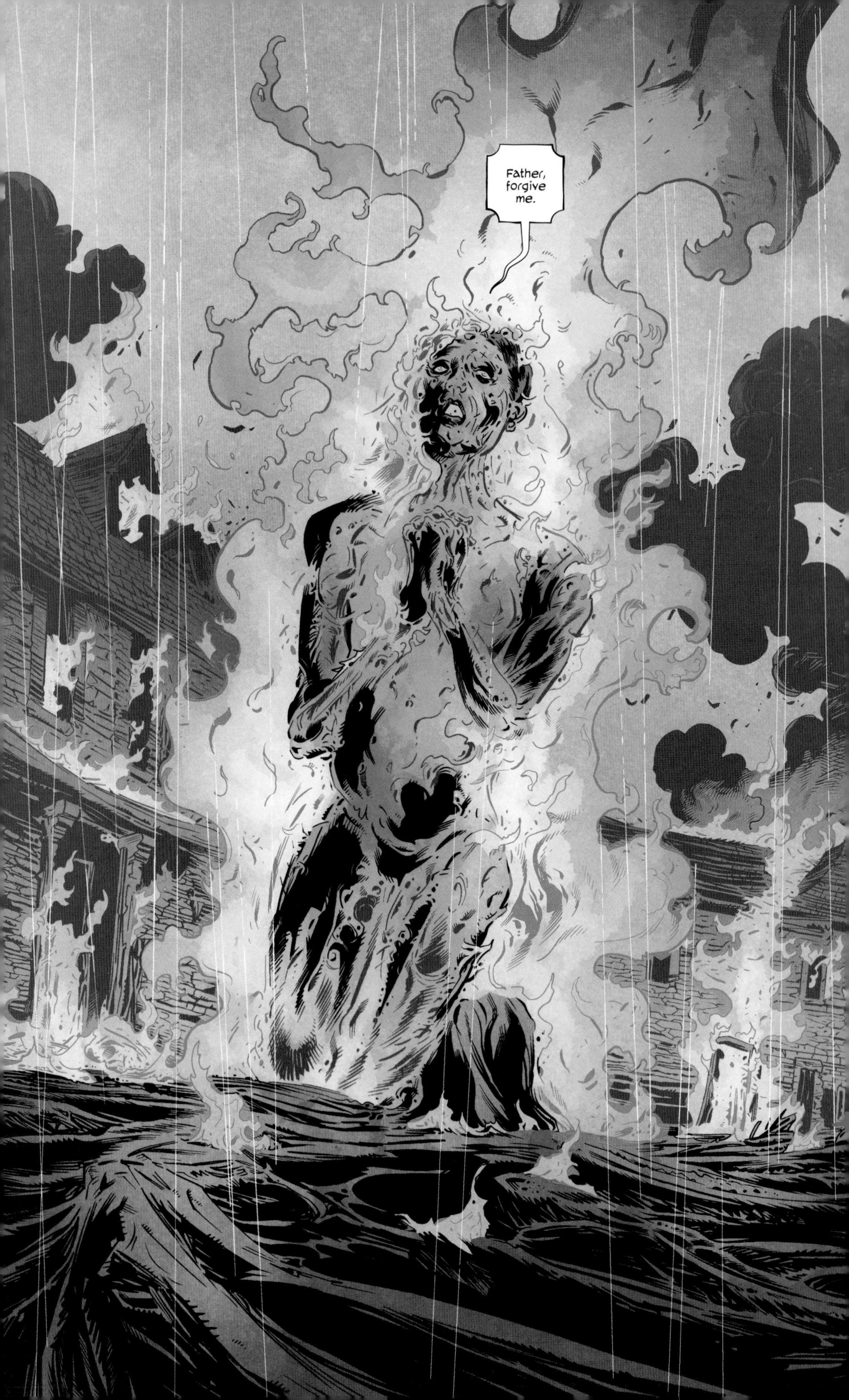
Father, forgive me.

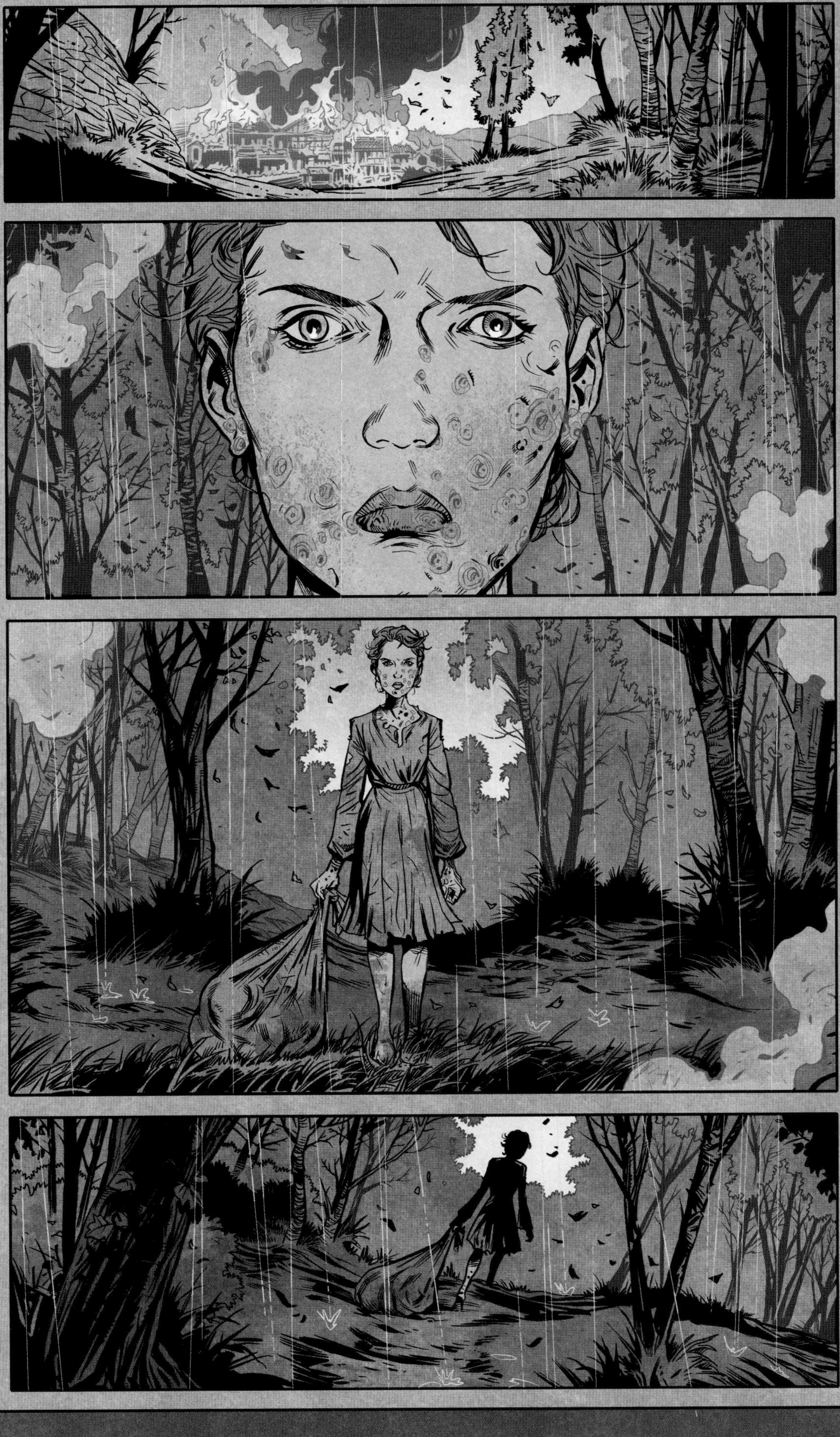

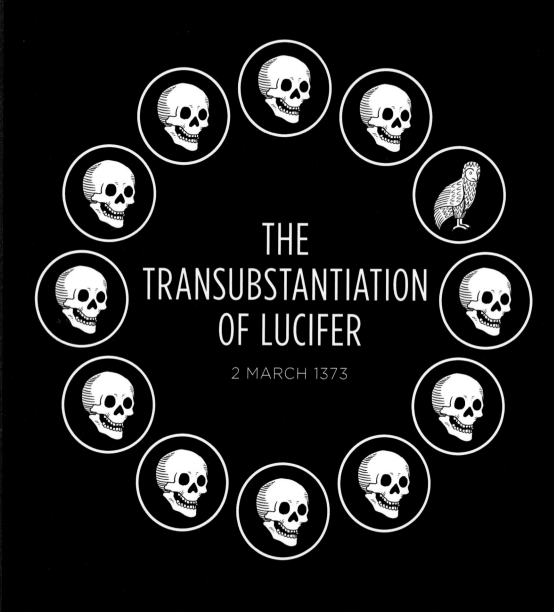

THE
TRANSUBSTANTIATION
OF LUCIFER

2 MARCH 1373

THE
WICKED
+
ƎNIVIꓷ
ƎHꓕ

1831AD

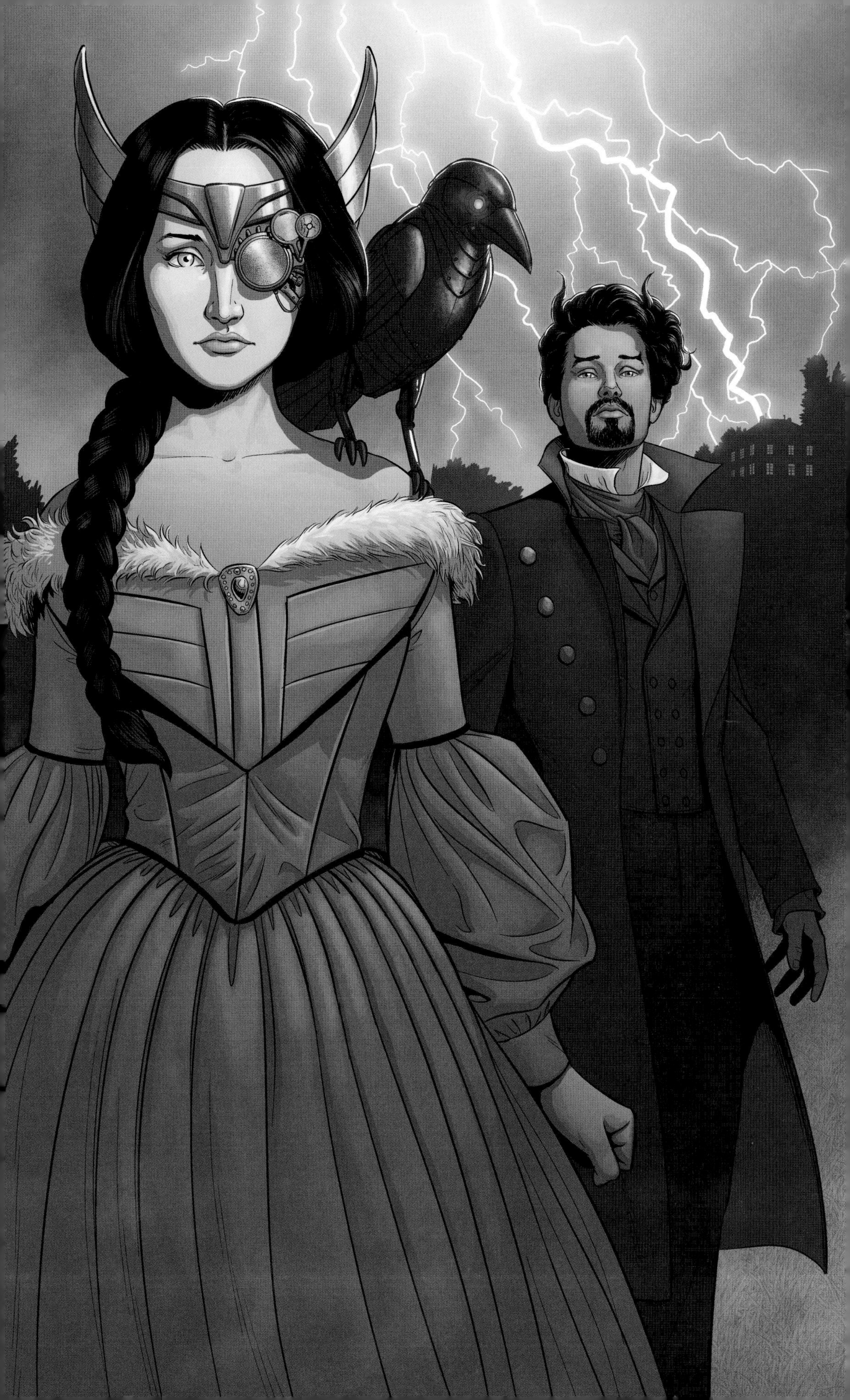

THE WICKED + THE DIVINE

Every ninety years twelve gods return as young people. They are loved. They are hated. In two years, they are all dead.

The year is 1831. It's happening now. It's happening again.

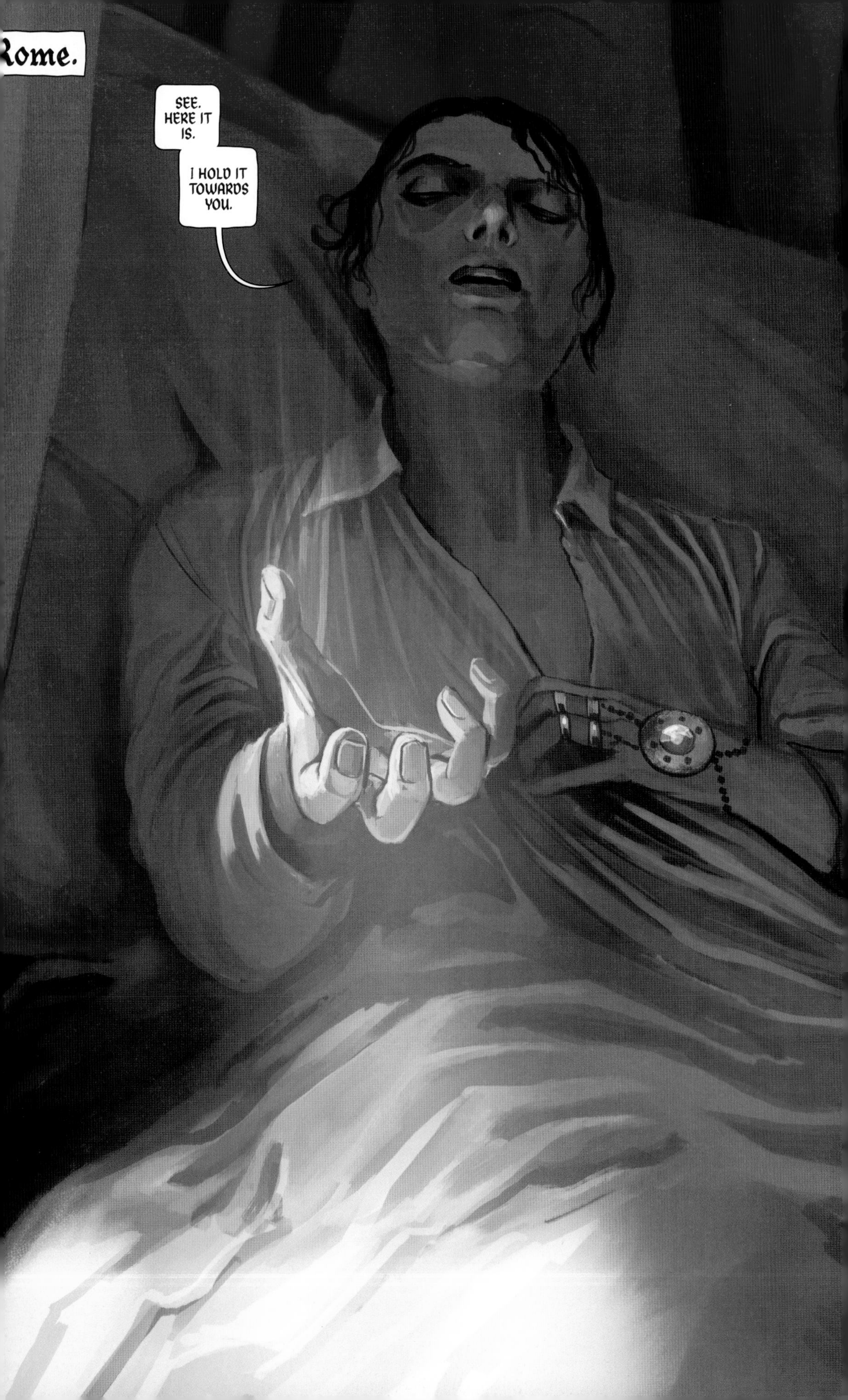
Rome.
SEE. HERE IT IS.
I HOLD IT TOWARDS YOU.

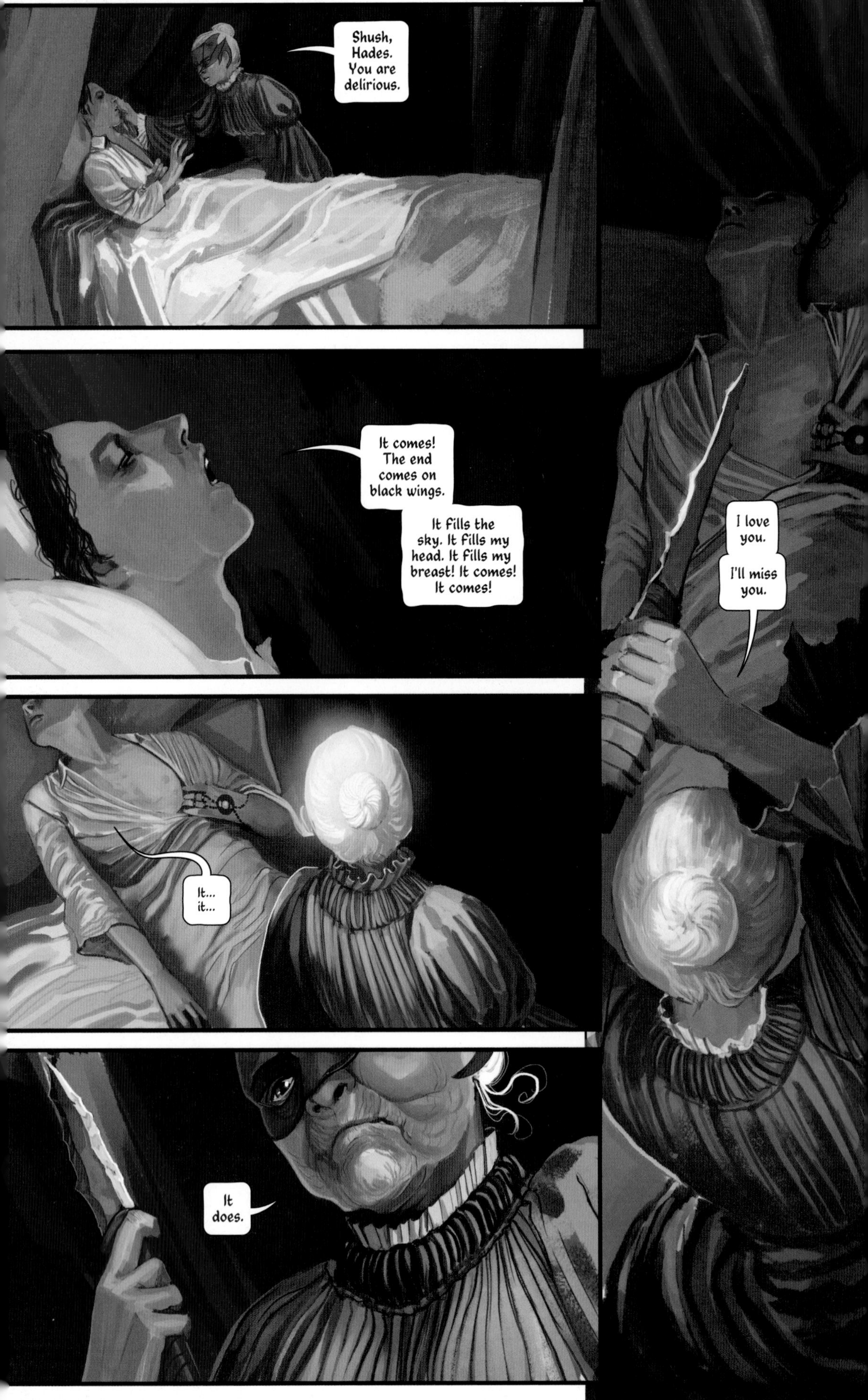
Shush, Hades. You are delirious.
It comes! The end comes on black wings.
It fills the sky. It fills my head. It fills my breast! It comes! It comes!
It... it...
It does.
I love you.
I'll miss you.

MODERN
ROMANCE

11 MARCH 1831

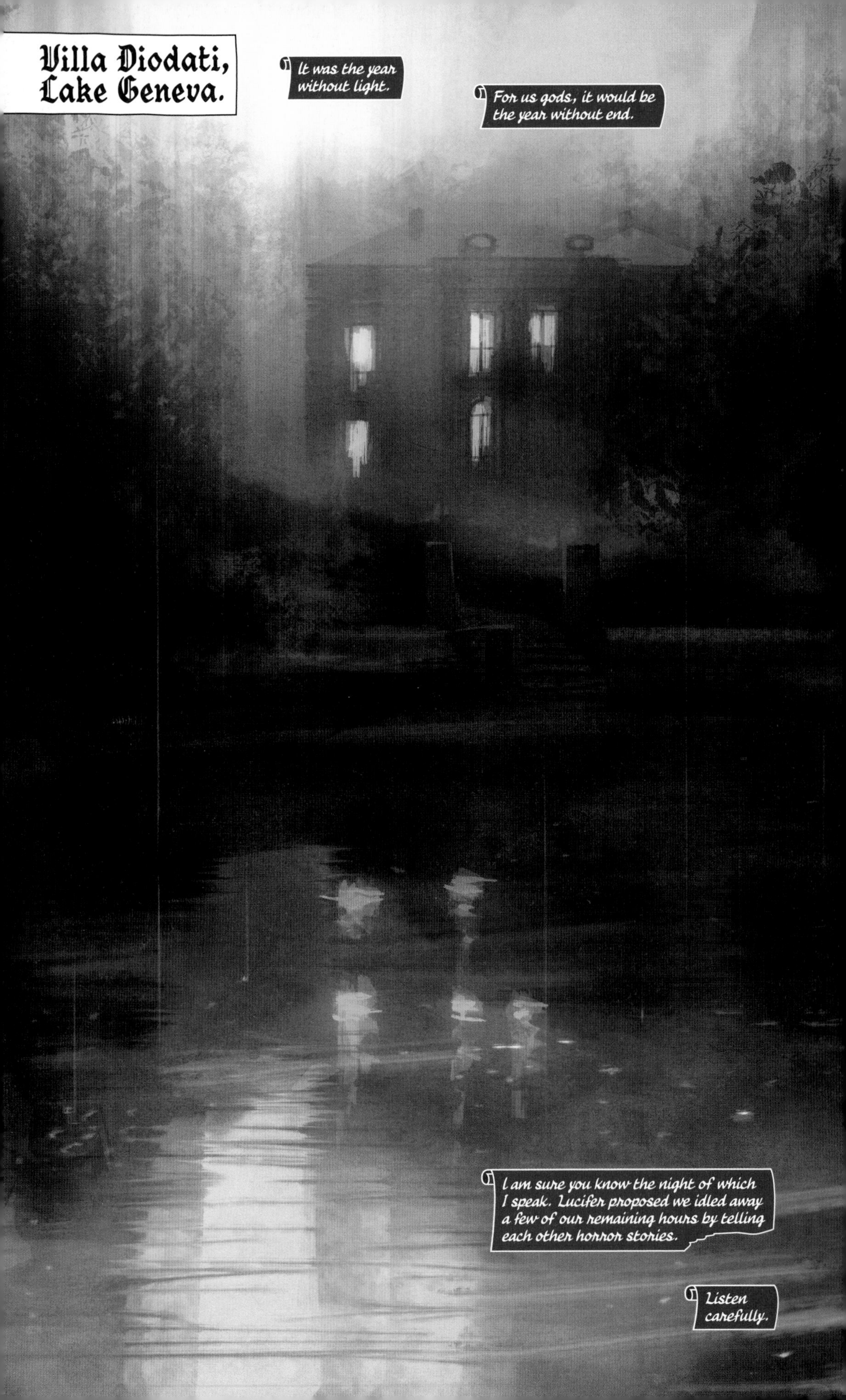
Villa Diodati, Lake Geneva.
It was the year without light.
For us gods, it would be the year without end.
I am sure you know the night of which I speak. Lucifer proposed we idled away a few of our remaining hours by telling each other horror stories.
Listen carefully.

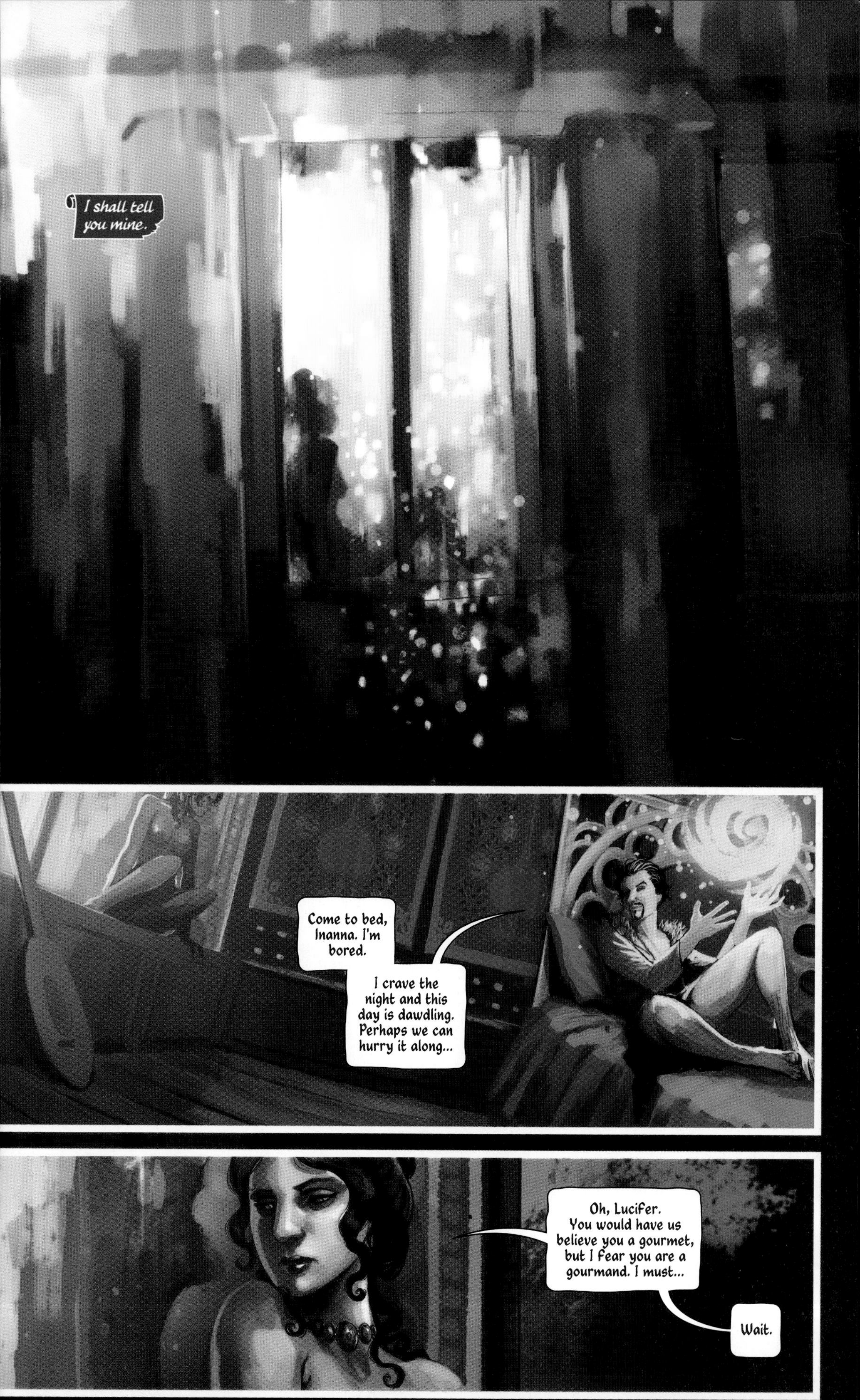
I shall tell you mine.
Come to bed, Inanna. I'm bored.
I crave the night and this day is dawdling. Perhaps we can hurry it along...
Oh, Lucifer. You would have us believe you a gourmet, but I fear you are a gourmand. I must...
Wait.

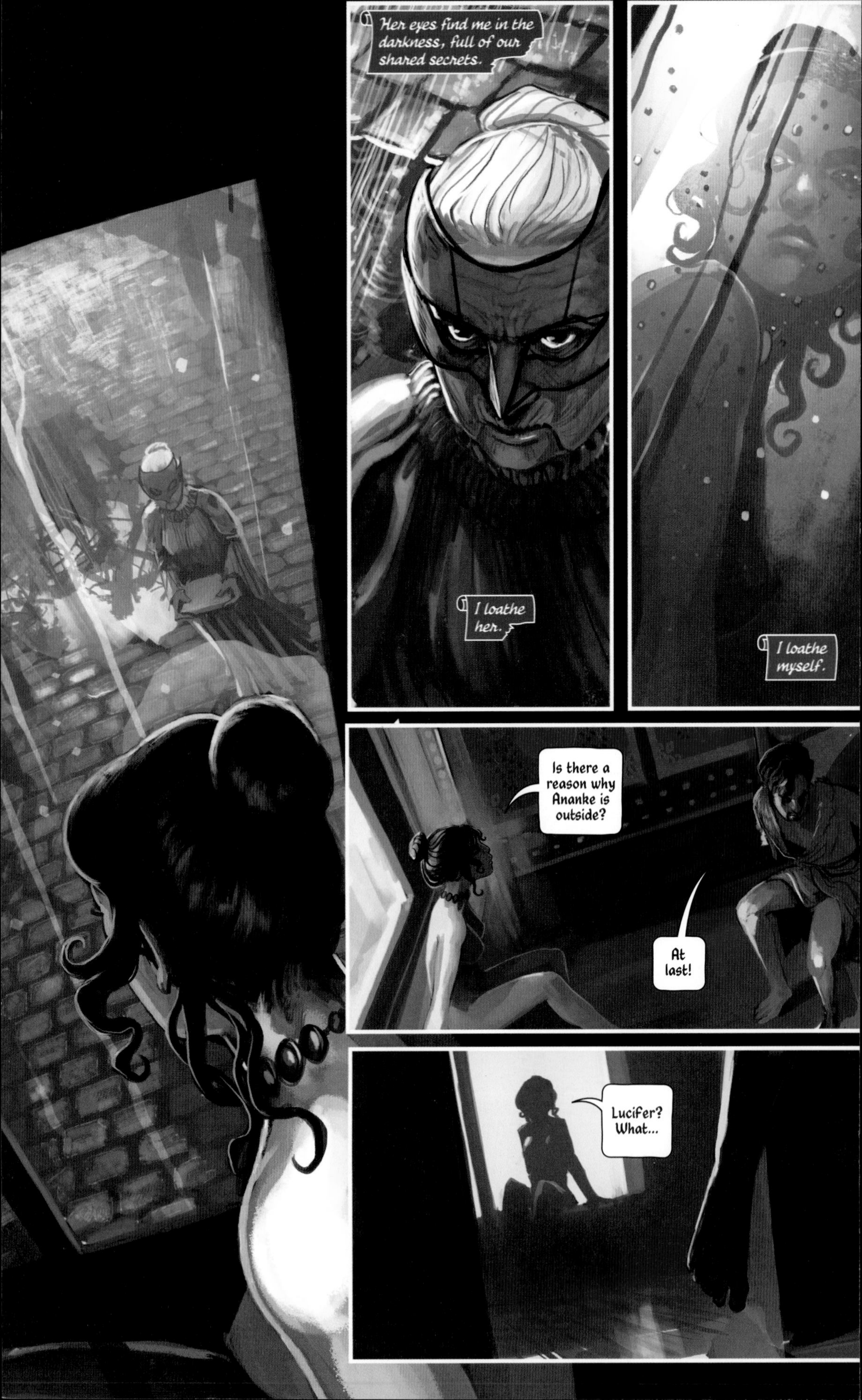

Her eyes find me in the darkness, full of our shared secrets.
I loathe her.
I loathe myself.
Is there a reason why Ananke is outside?
At last!
Lucifer? What...

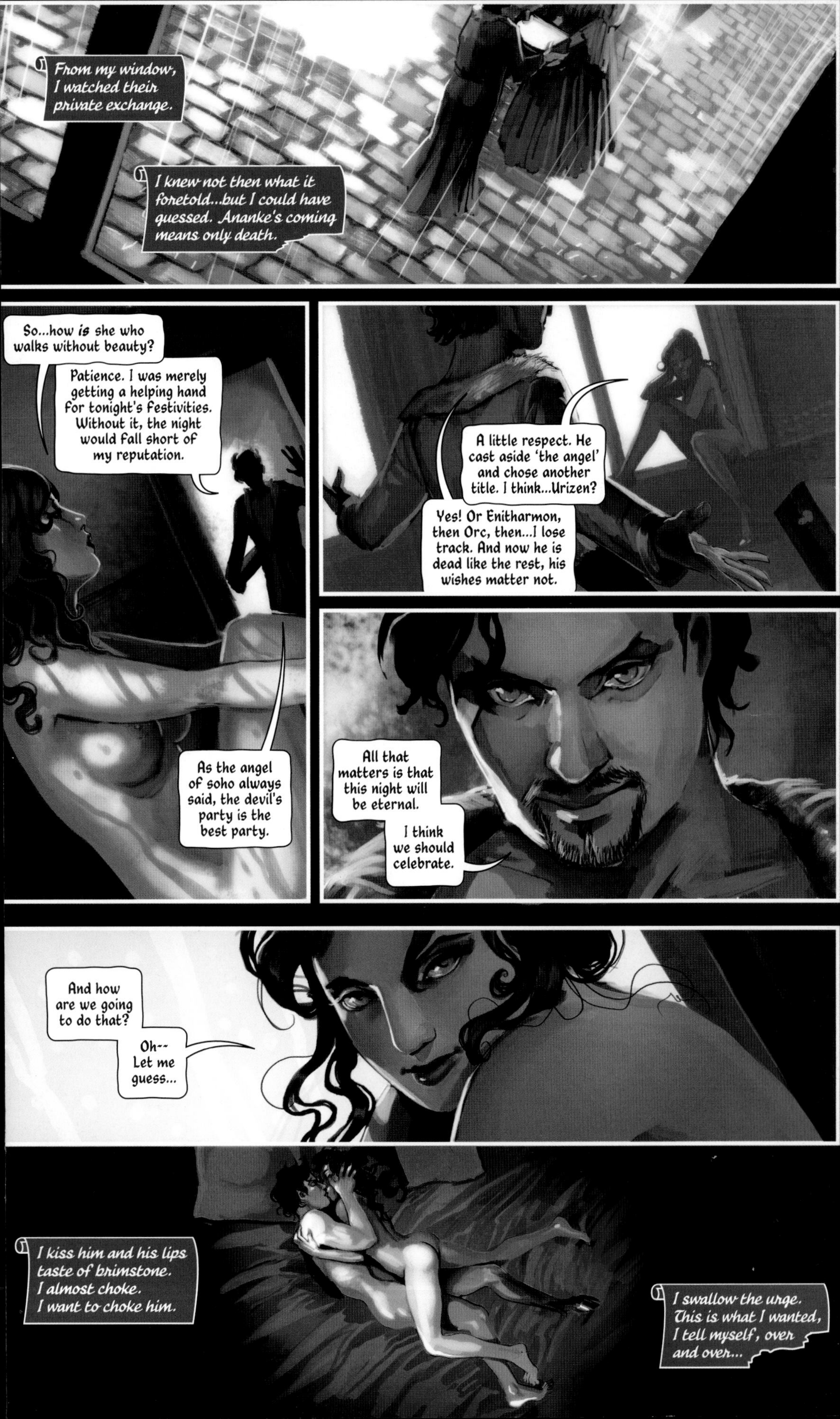

From my window, I watched their private exchange.
I knew not then what it foretold...but I could have guessed. Ananke's coming means only death.
So...how *is* she who walks without beauty?
Patience. I was merely getting a helping hand for tonight's festivities. Without it, the night would fall short of my reputation.
As the angel of soho always said, the devil's party is the best party.
A little respect. He cast aside 'the angel' and chose another title. I think...Urizen?
Yes! Or Enitharmon, then Orc, then...I lose track. And now he is dead like the rest, his wishes matter not.
All that matters is that this night will be eternal.
I think we should celebrate.
And how are we going to do that?
Oh-- Let me guess...
I kiss him and his lips taste of brimstone. I almost choke. I want to choke him.
I swallow the urge. This is what I wanted, I tell myself, over and over...

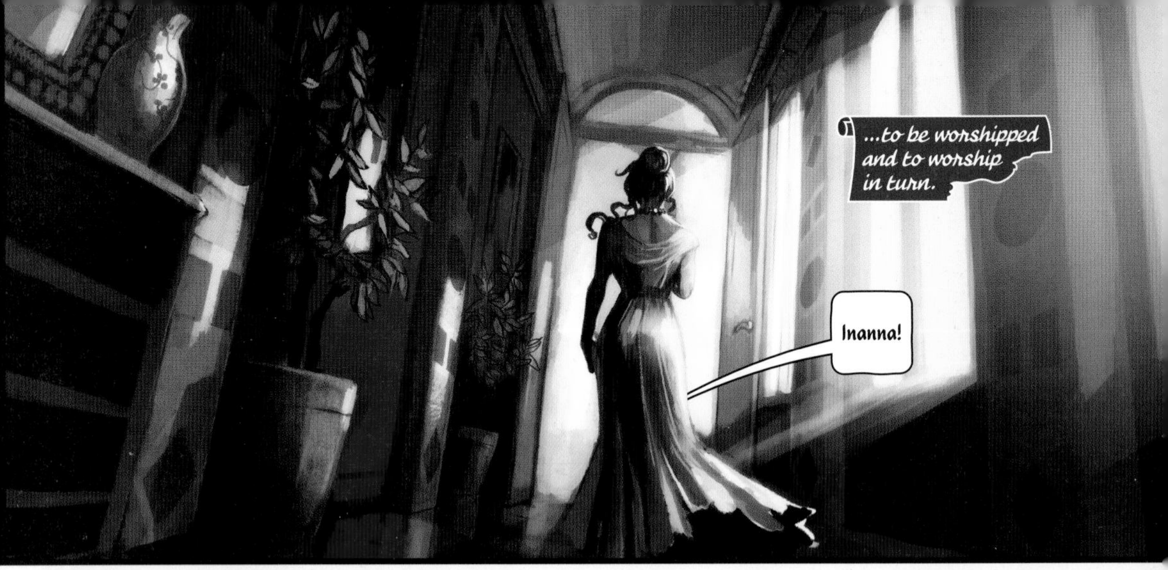
...to be worshipped and to worship in turn.
Inanna!

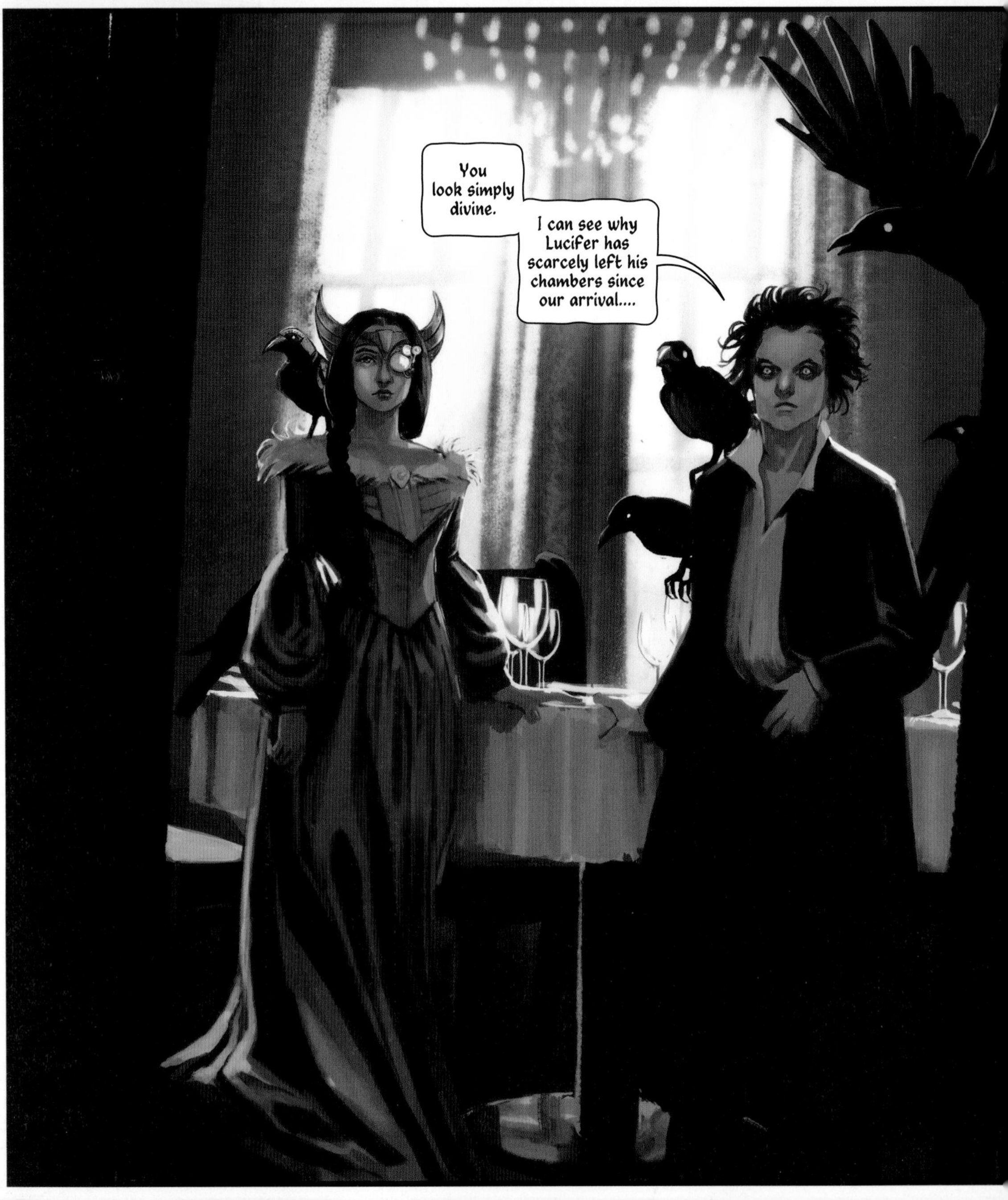
You look simply divine.
I can see why Lucifer has scarcely left his chambers since our arrival....

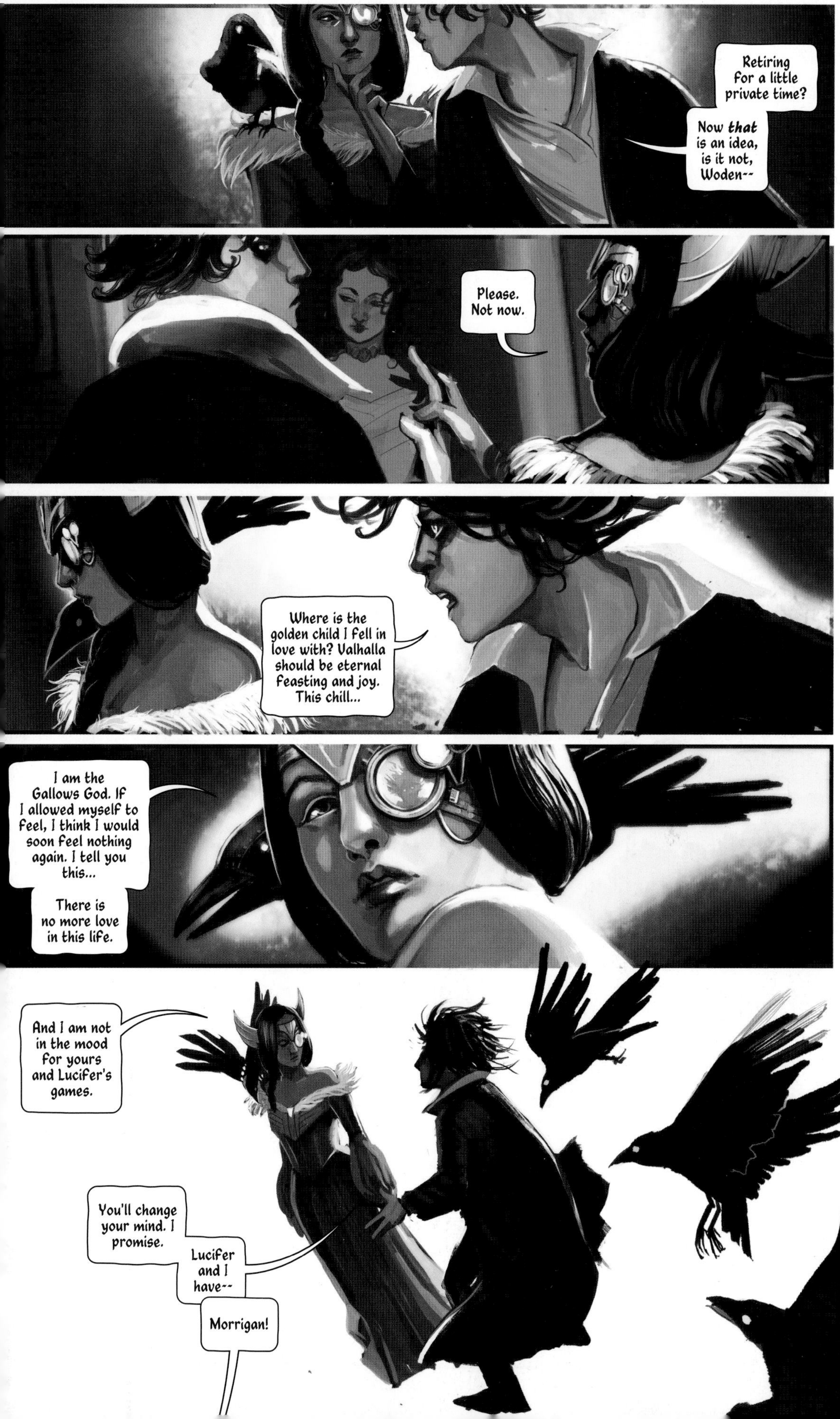
Retiring for a little private time?
Now *that* is an idea, is it not, Woden--
Please. Not now.
Where is the golden child I fell in love with? Valhalla should be eternal feasting and joy. This chill...
I am the Gallows God. If I allowed myself to feel, I think I would soon feel nothing again. I tell you this...
There is no more love in this life.
And I am not in the mood for yours and Lucifer's games.
You'll change your mind. I promise.
Lucifer and I have--
Morrigan!

Your tongue flaps like your birds. It is not yet quite the hour.

Be rid of your pets! Let us eat, drink and try to curdle every drop of blood in our bodies...

What do you have there, Lucifer?

A twist for my tale. Or *our* tale, really...

And speaking of which...

...does anyone wish to begin the amusements? Perhaps Inanna?

I'm sure that mind can find something suitably dark...

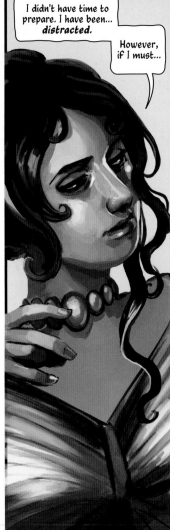

I didn't have time to prepare. I have been... *distracted.*

However, if I must...

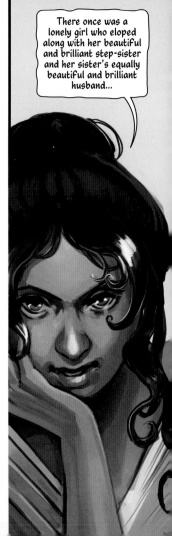

There once was a lonely girl who eloped along with her beautiful and brilliant step-sister and her sister's equally beautiful and brilliant husband...

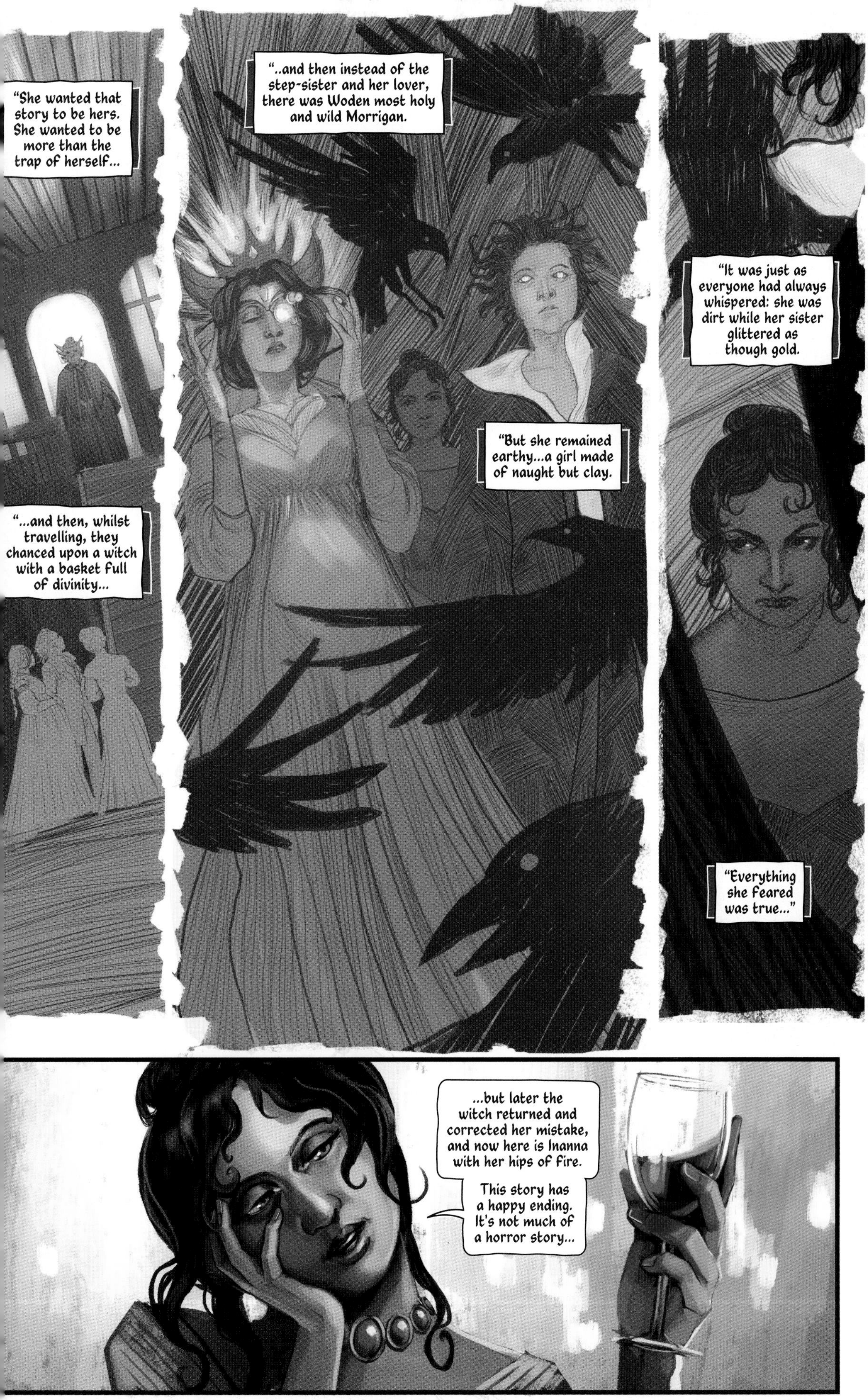
"She wanted that story to be hers. She wanted to be more than the trap of herself...
"...and then, whilst travelling, they chanced upon a witch with a basket full of divinity...
"..and then instead of the step-sister and her lover, there was Woden most holy and wild Morrigan.
"But she remained earthy...a girl made of naught but clay.
"It was just as everyone had always whispered: she was dirt while her sister glittered as though gold.
"Everything she feared was true..."
...but later the witch returned and corrected her mistake, and now here is Inanna with her hips of fire.
This story has a happy ending. It's not much of a horror story...

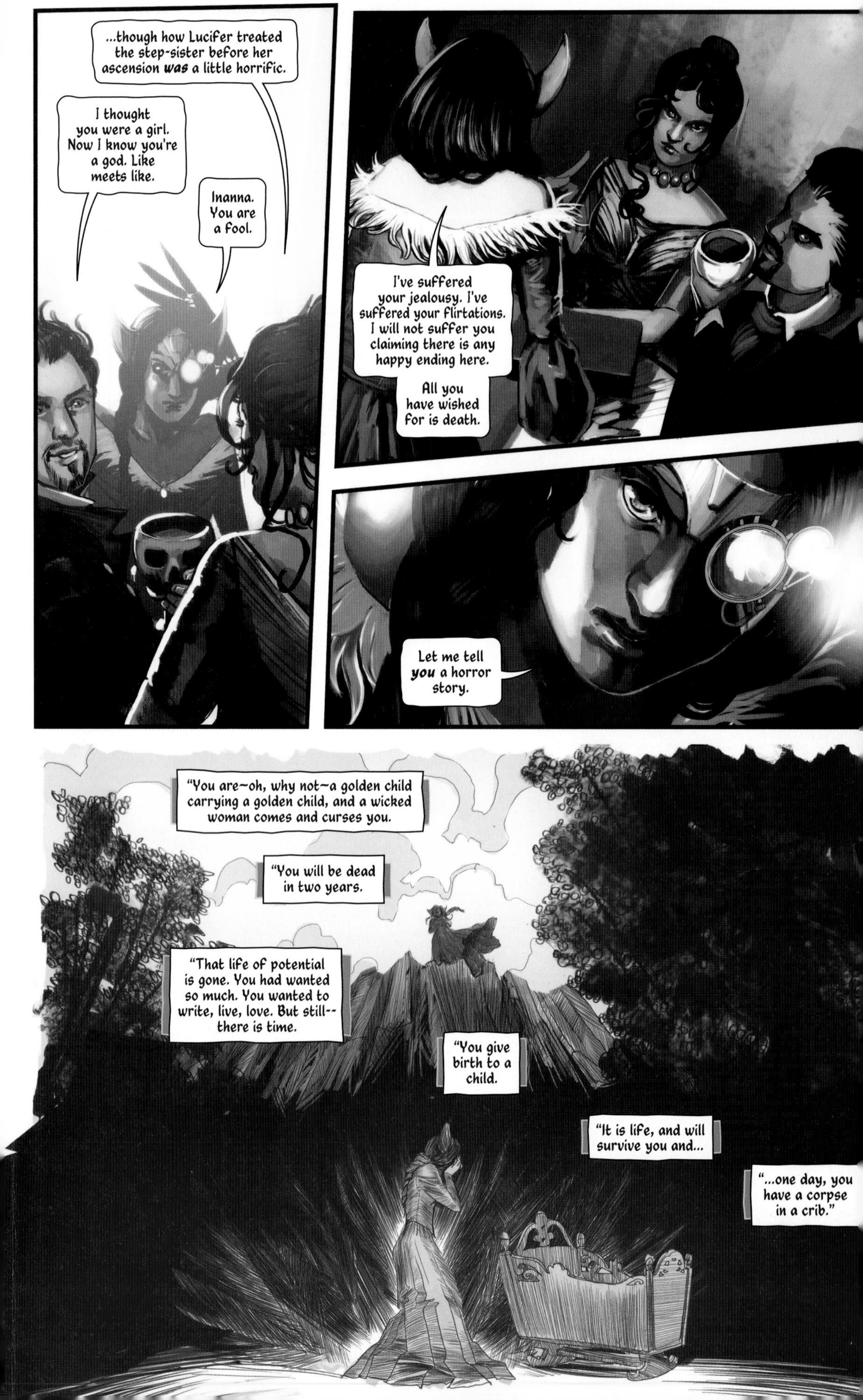
...though how Lucifer treated the step-sister before her ascension *was* a little horrific.
I thought you were a girl. Now I know you're a god. Like meets like.
Inanna. You are a fool.
I've suffered your jealousy. I've suffered your flirtations. I will not suffer you claiming there is any happy ending here.
All you have wished for is death.
Let me tell *you* a horror story.
"You are—oh, why not—a golden child carrying a golden child, and a wicked woman comes and curses you.
"You will be dead in two years.
"That life of potential is gone. You had wanted so much. You wanted to write, live, love. But still--there is time.
"You give birth to a child.
"It is life, and will survive you and...
"...one day, you have a corpse in a crib."

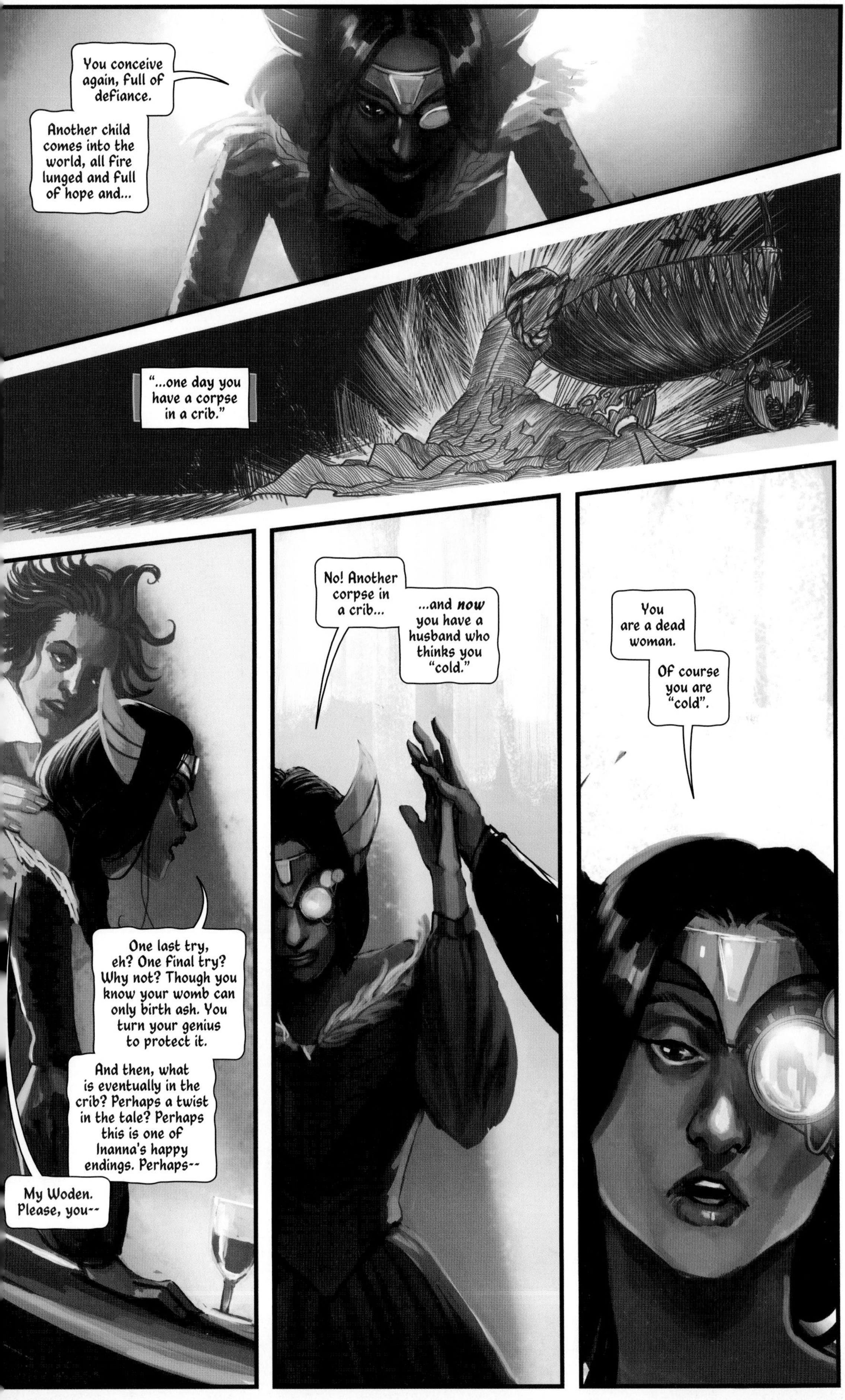
You conceive again, full of defiance.
Another child comes into the world, all fire lunged and full of hope and...
"...one day you have a corpse in a crib."
One last try, eh? One final try? Why not? Though you know your womb can only birth ash. You turn your genius to protect it.
And then, what is eventually in the crib? Perhaps a twist in the tale? Perhaps this is one of Inanna's happy endings. Perhaps--
My Woden. Please, you--
No! Another corpse in a crib...
...and *now* you have a husband who thinks you "cold."
You are a dead woman.
Of course you are "cold".

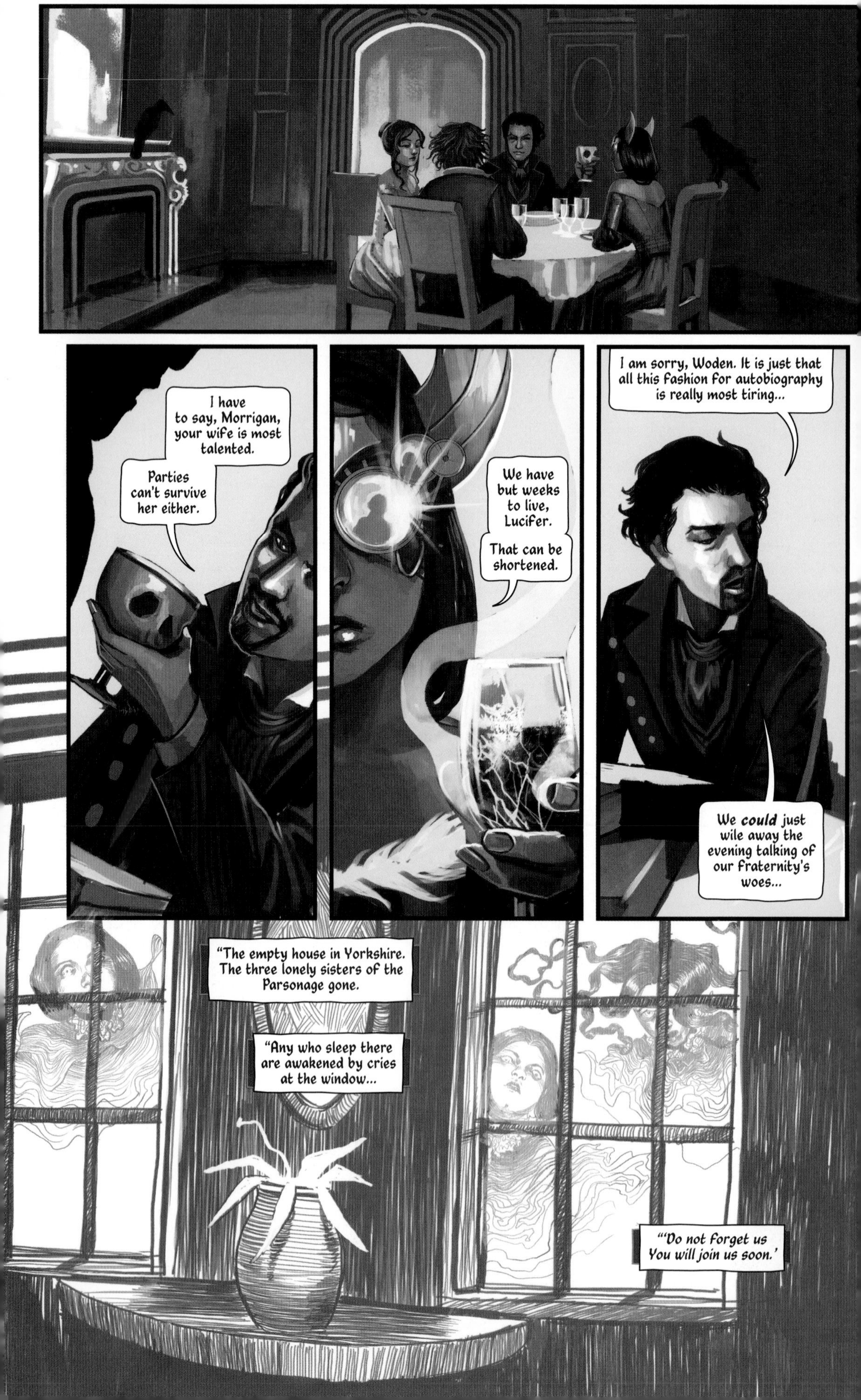
I have to say, Morrigan, your wife is most talented.
Parties can't survive her either.
We have but weeks to live, Lucifer.
That can be shortened.
I am sorry, Woden. It is just that all this fashion for autobiography is really most tiring...
We **could** just wile away the evening talking of our fraternity's woes...
"The empty house in Yorkshire. The three lonely sisters of the Parsonage gone.
"Any who sleep there are awakened by cries at the window...
"'Do not forget us You will join us soon.'

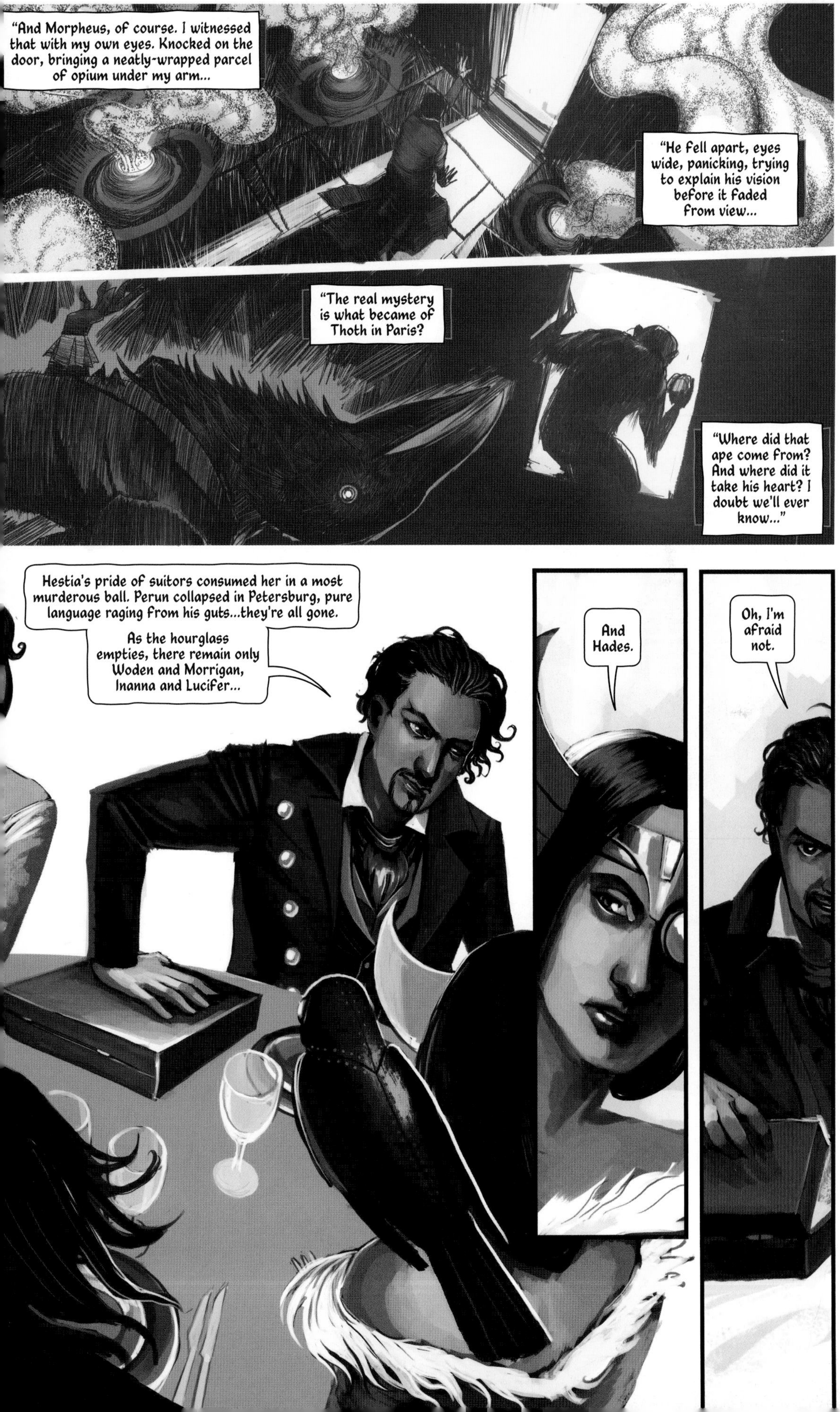
"And Morpheus, of course. I witnessed that with my own eyes. Knocked on the door, bringing a neatly-wrapped parcel of opium under my arm...
"He fell apart, eyes wide, panicking, trying to explain his vision before it faded from view...
"The real mystery is what became of Thoth in Paris?
"Where did that ape come from? And where did it take his heart? I doubt we'll ever know..."
Hestia's pride of suitors consumed her in a most murderous ball. Perun collapsed in Petersburg, pure language raging from his guts...they're all gone.
As the hourglass empties, there remain only Woden and Morrigan, Inanna and Lucifer...
And Hades.
Oh, I'm afraid not.

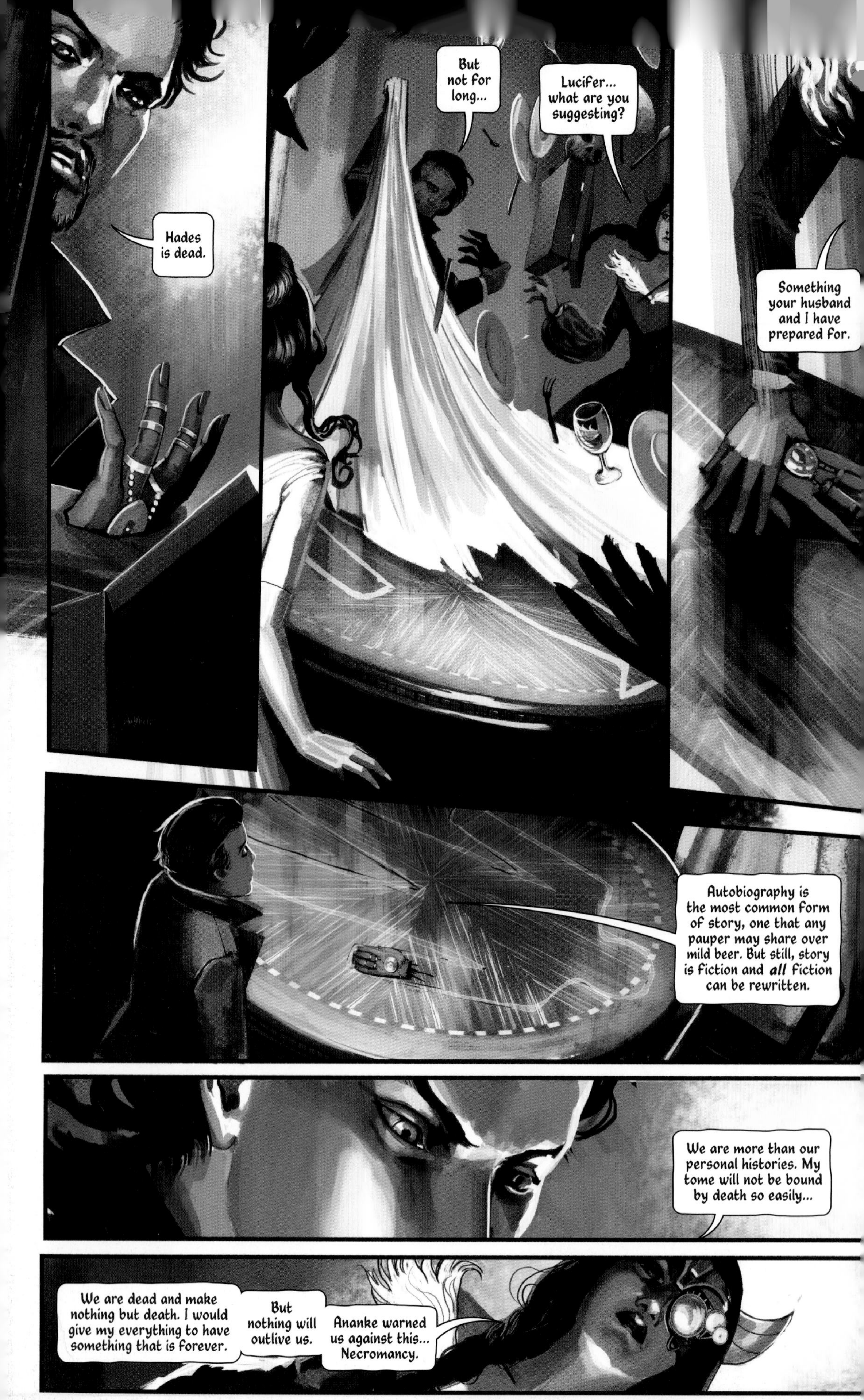
Hades is dead.
But not for long...
Lucifer... what are you suggesting?
Something your husband and I have prepared for.
Autobiography is the most common form of story, one that any pauper may share over mild beer. But still, story is fiction and *all* fiction can be rewritten.
We are more than our personal histories. My tome will not be bound by death so easily...
We are dead and make nothing but death. I would give my everything to have something that is forever.
But nothing will outlive us.
Ananke warned us against this... Necromancy.

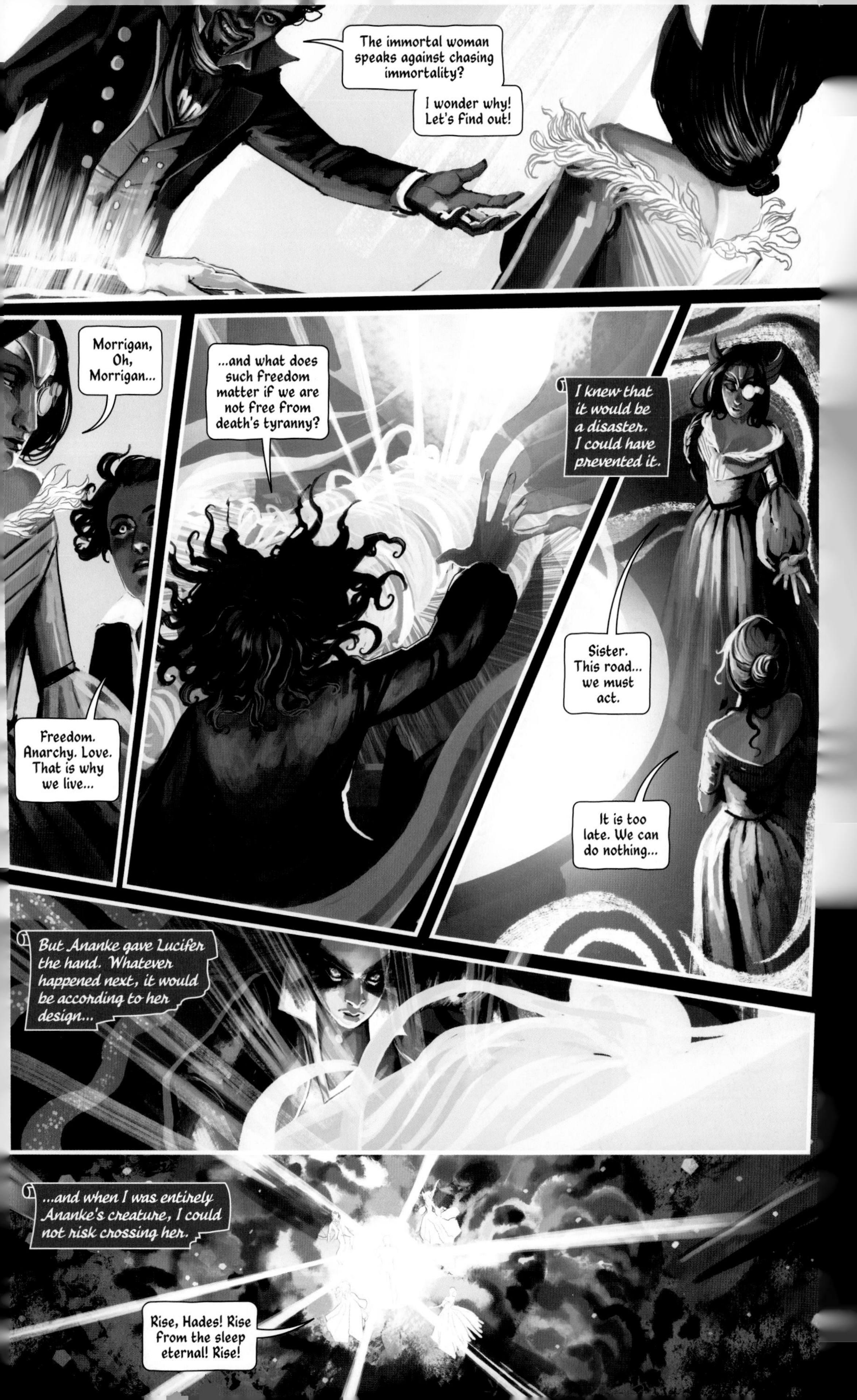
The immortal woman speaks against chasing immortality?
I wonder why! Let's find out!
Morrigan, Oh, Morrigan...
Freedom. Anarchy. Love. That is why we live...
...and what does such freedom matter if we are not free from death's tyranny?
I knew that it would be a disaster. I could have prevented it.
Sister. This road... we must act.
It is too late. We can do nothing...
But Ananke gave Lucifer the hand. Whatever happened next, it would be according to her design...
...and when I was entirely Ananke's creature, I could not risk crossing her.
Rise, Hades! Rise from the sleep eternal! Rise!

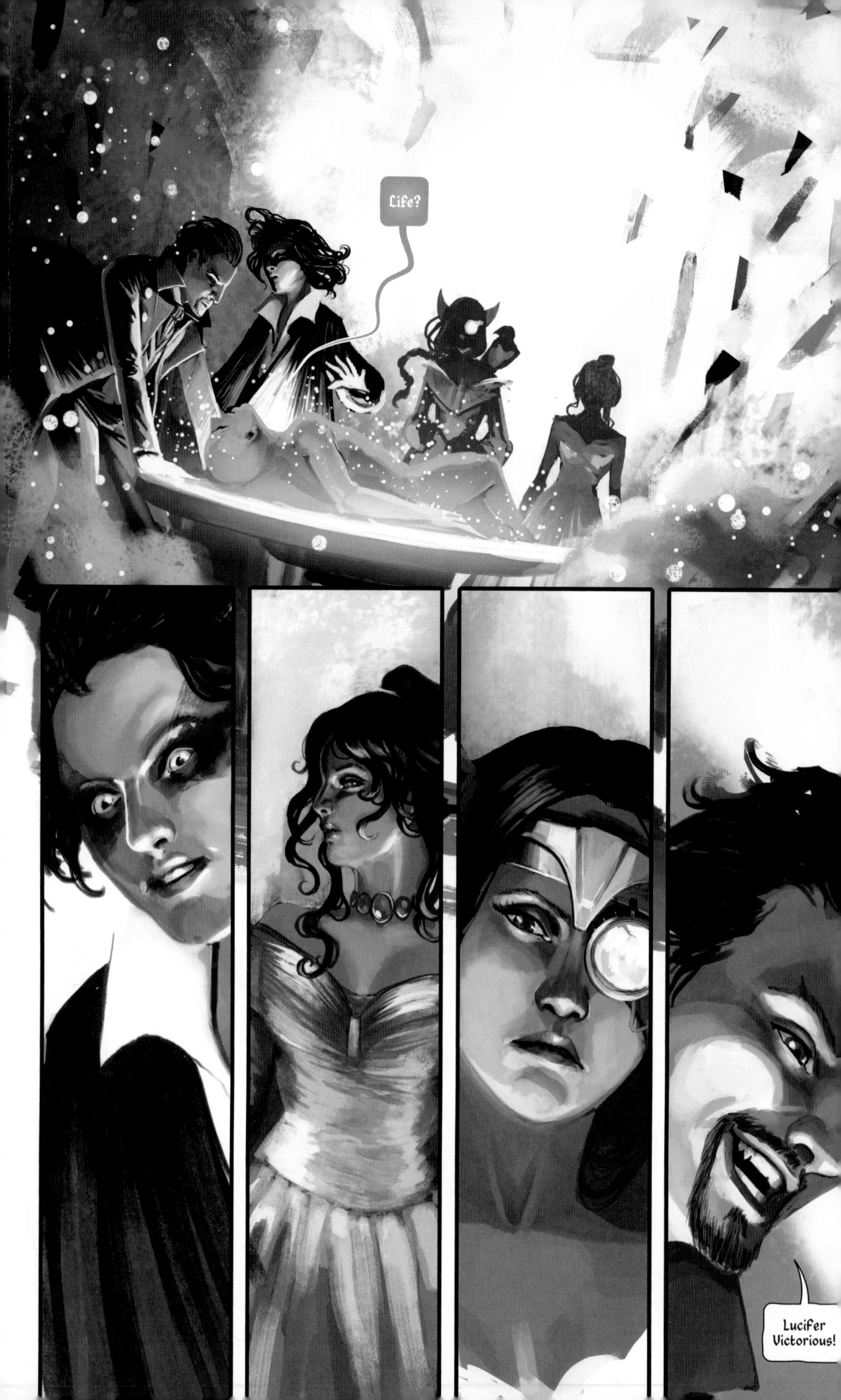

Life?
Lucifer Victorious!

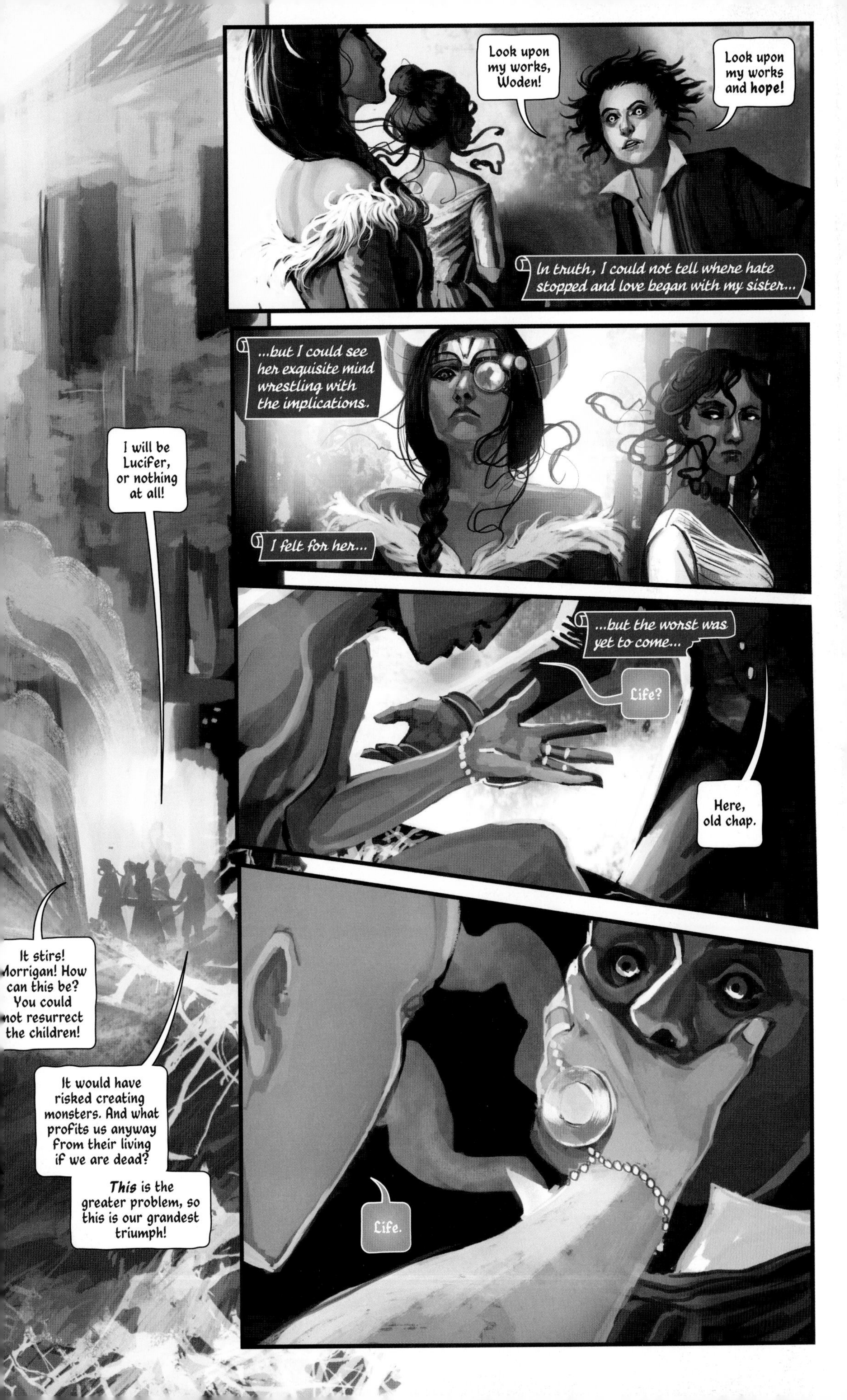

Look upon my works, Woden!
Look upon my works and hope!
In truth, I could not tell where hate stopped and love began with my sister...
...but I could see her exquisite mind wrestling with the implications.
I felt for her...
I will be Lucifer, or nothing at all!
...but the worst was yet to come...
Life?
Here, old chap.
It stirs! Morrigan! How can this be? You could not resurrect the children!
It would have risked creating monsters. And what profits us anyway from their living if we are dead?
This is the greater problem, so this is our grandest triumph!
Life.

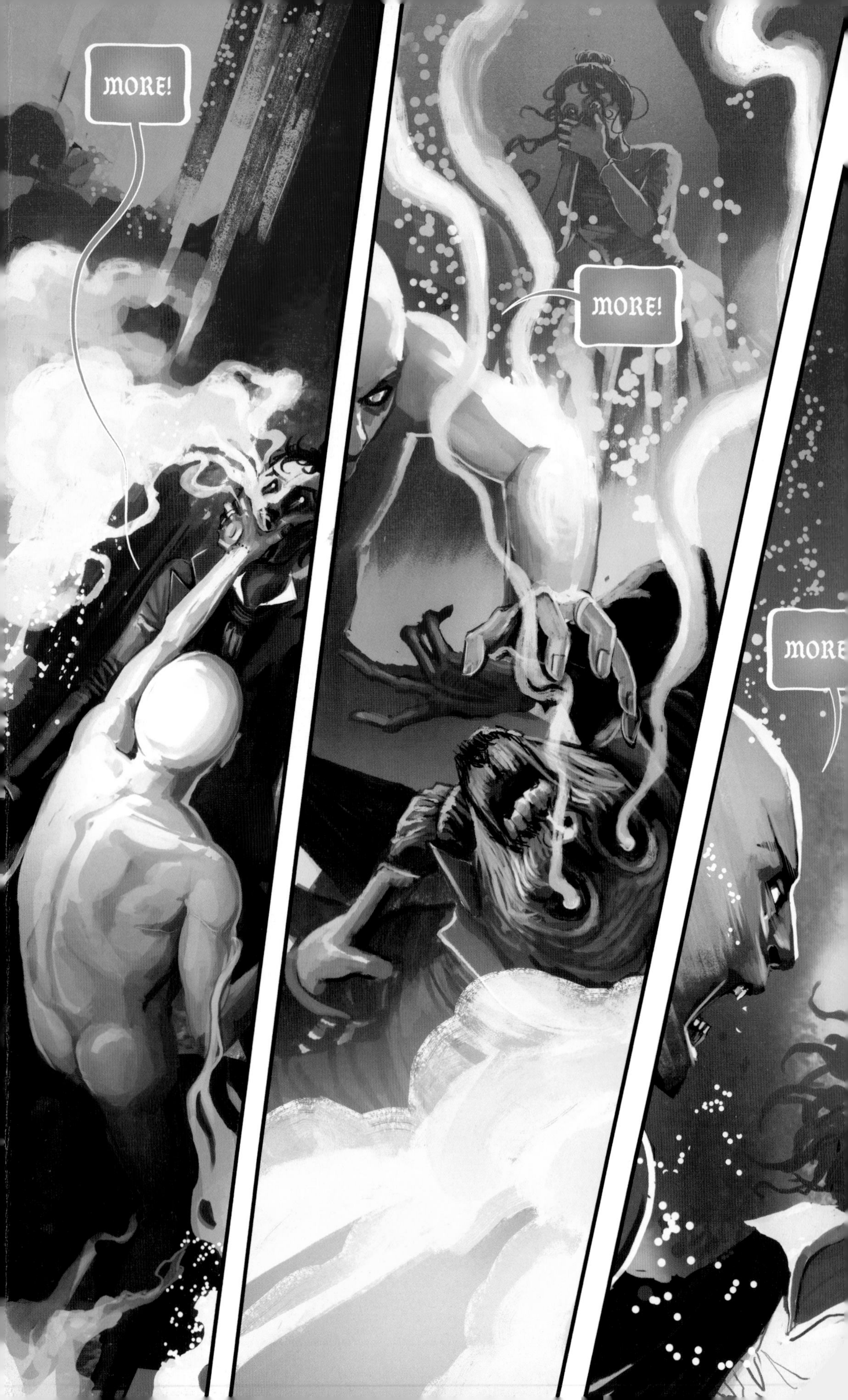
MORE!
MORE!
MORE

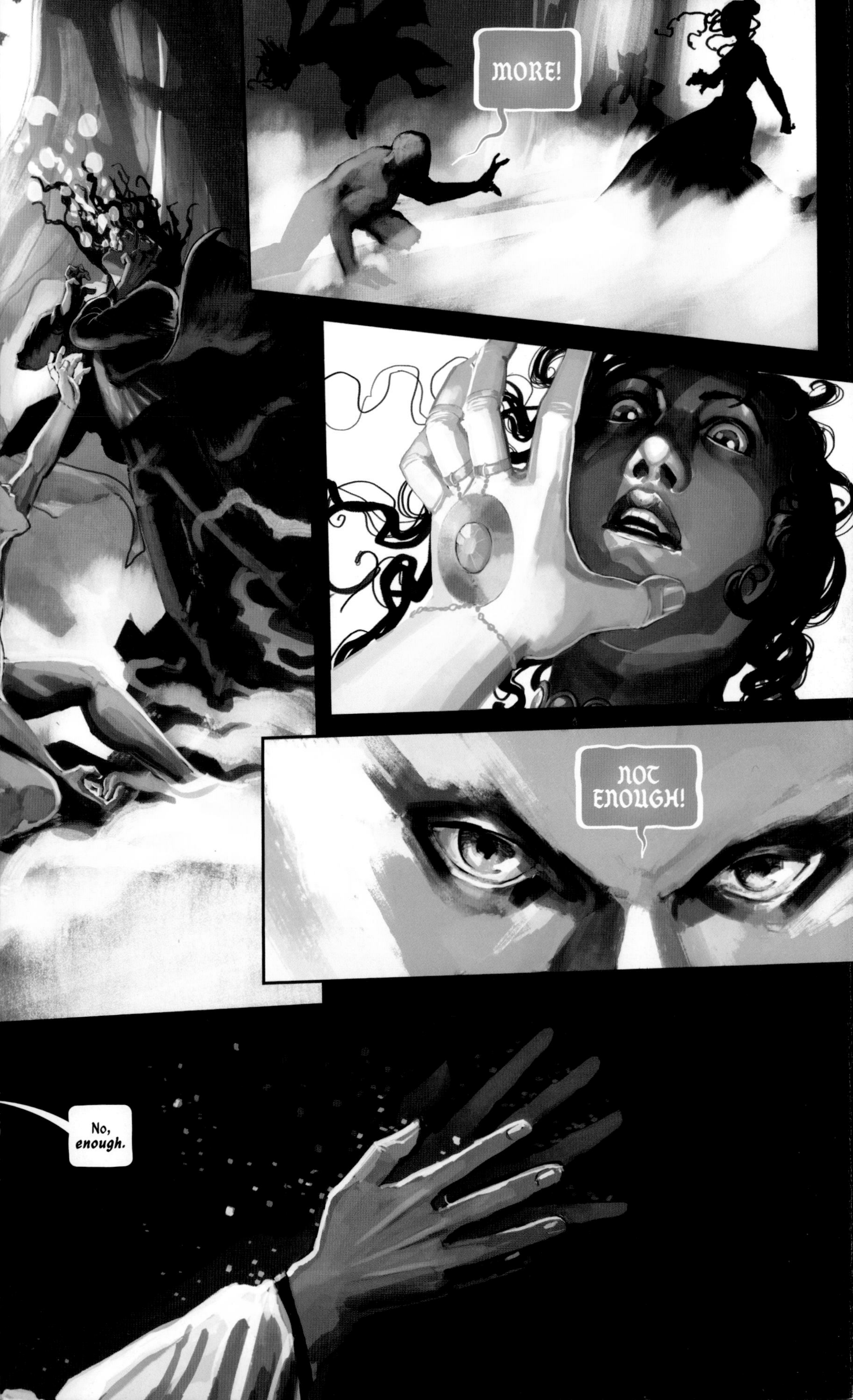
MORE!
NOT ENOUGH!
No, enough.

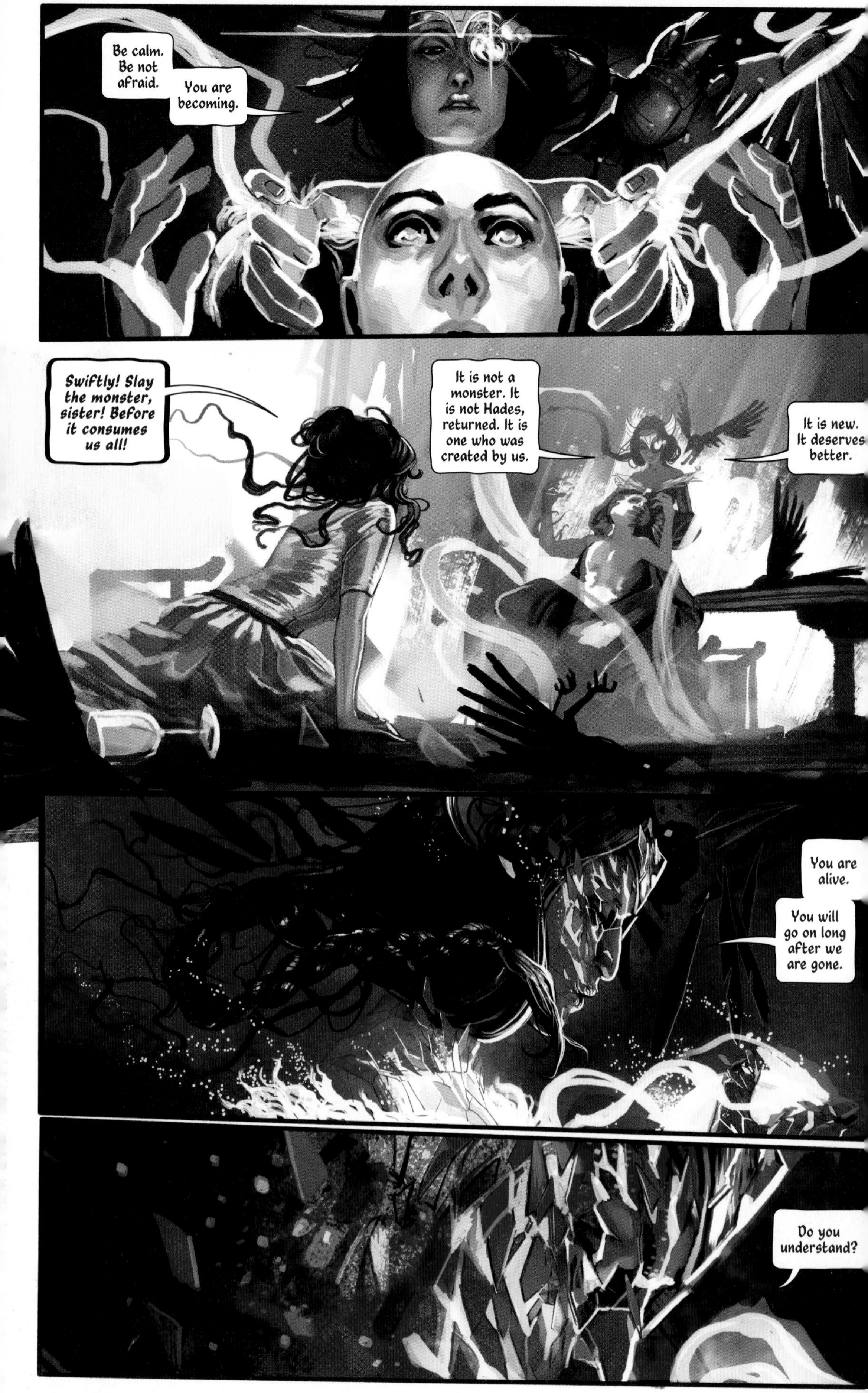
Be calm. Be not afraid.
You are becoming.
Swiftly! Slay the monster, sister! Before it consumes us all!
It is not a monster. It is not Hades, returned. It is one who was created by us.
It is new. It deserves better.
You are alive.
You will go on long after we are gone.
Do you understand?

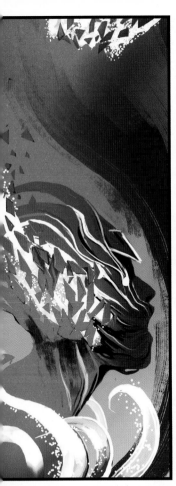

I do.

My sister was gone. The monster remained, a living statue of her likeness.

I watched for many moments, my hand a gag fastened across my mouth.

Eventually, it turned for the frozen lake.

I followed in silence...

...until I could bear the quiet no longer.

STOP!

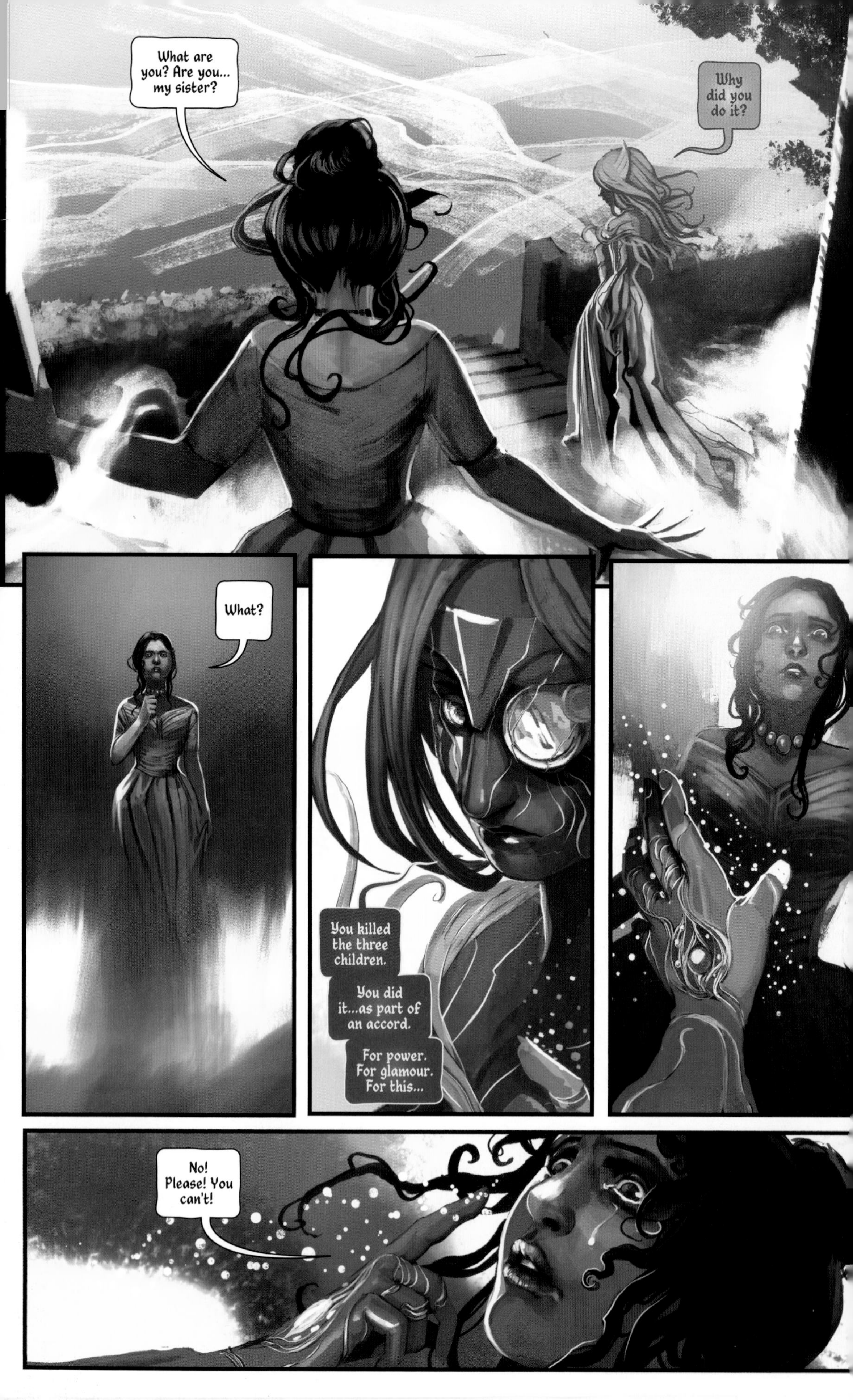
What are you? Are you... my sister?
Why did you do it?
What?
You killed the three children.
You did it...as part of an accord.
For power. For glamour. For this...
No! Please! You can't!

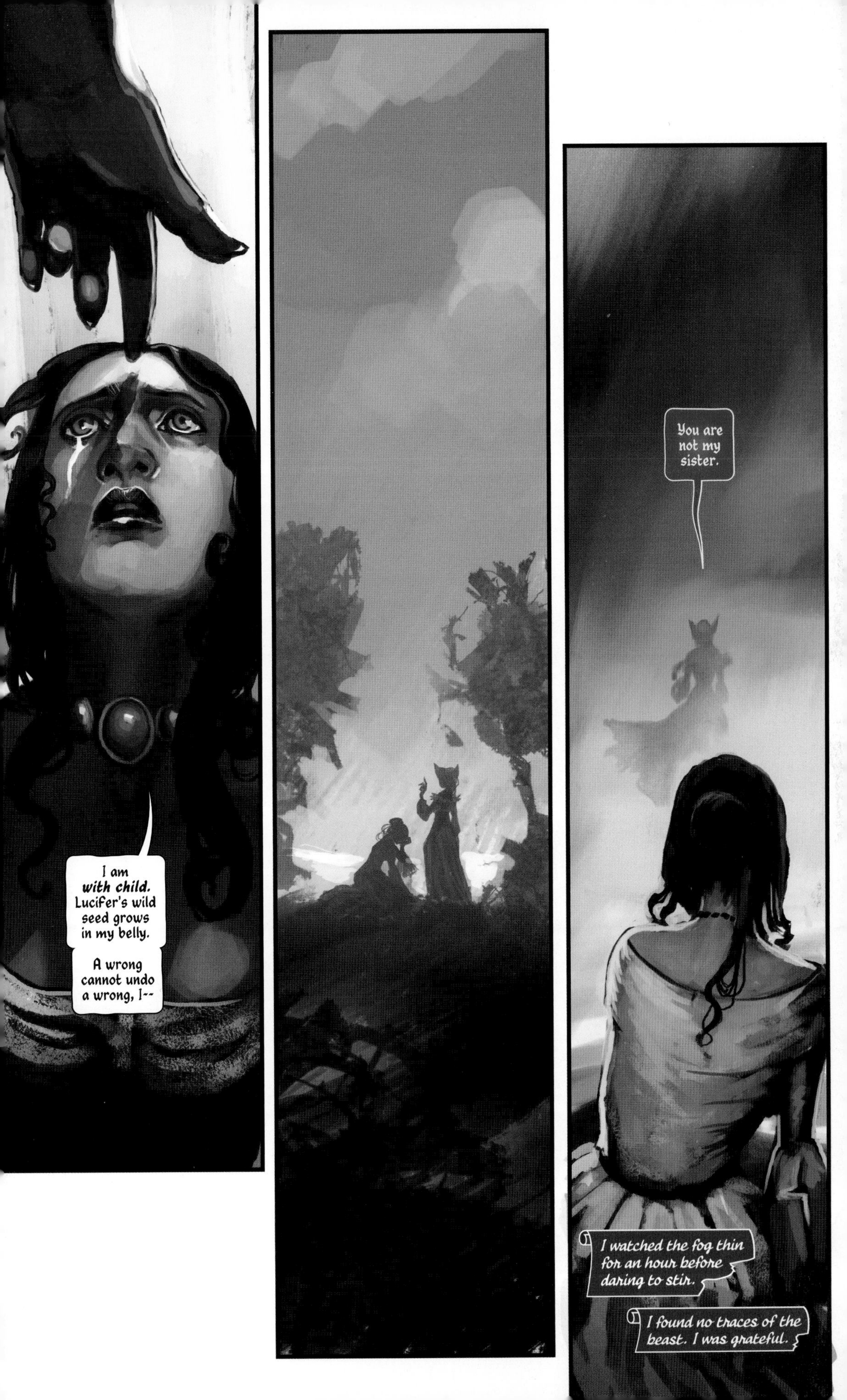
I am *with child.* Lucifer's wild seed grows in my belly.
A wrong cannot undo a wrong, I--
You are not my sister.
I watched the fog thin for an hour before daring to stir.
I found no traces of the beast. I was grateful.

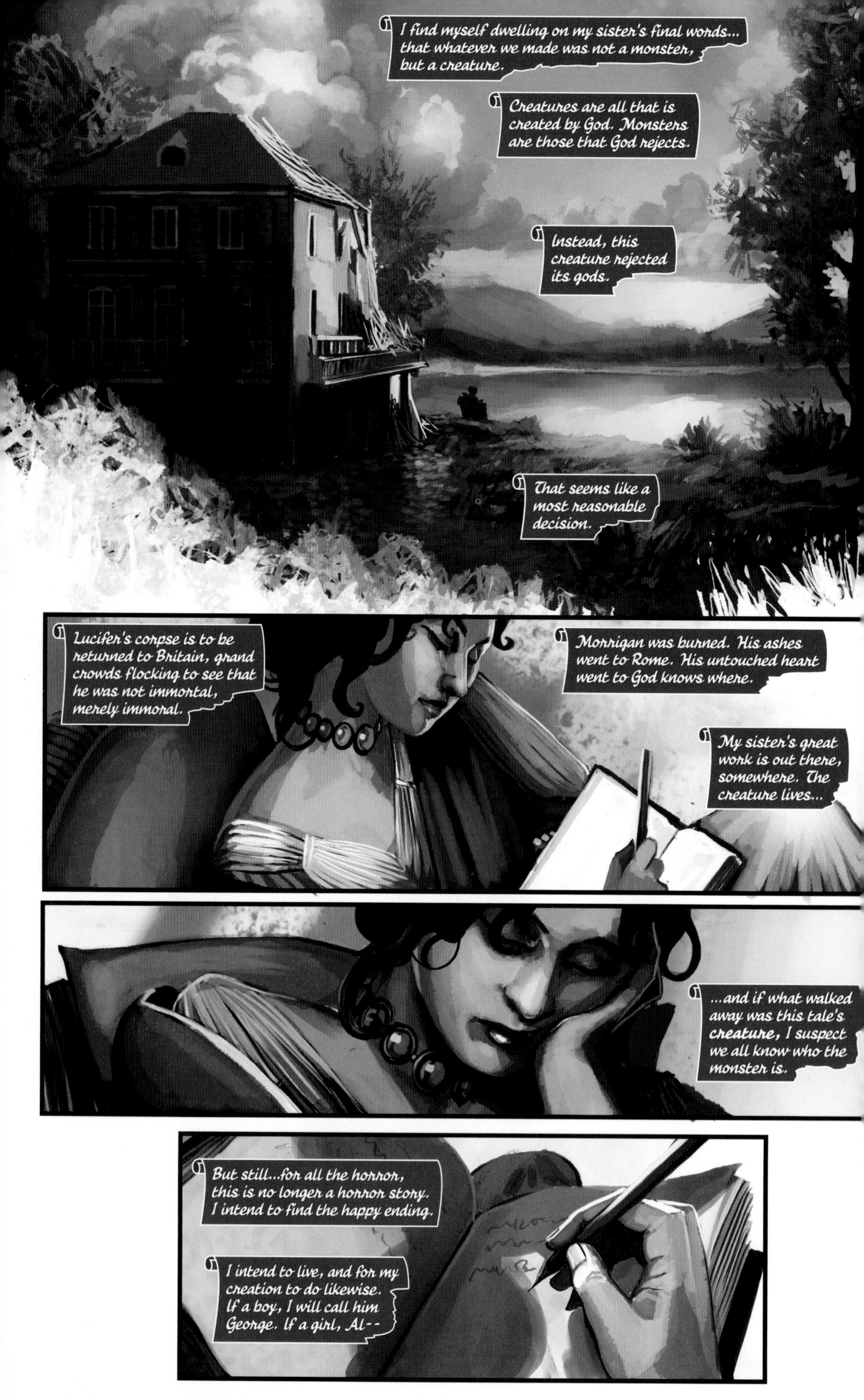
I find myself dwelling on my sister's final words... that whatever we made was not a monster, but a creature.
Creatures are all that is created by God. Monsters are those that God rejects.
Instead, this creature rejected its gods.
That seems like a most reasonable decision.
Lucifer's corpse is to be returned to Britain, grand crowds flocking to see that he was not immortal, merely immoral.
Morrigan was burned. His ashes went to Rome. His untouched heart went to God knows where.
My sister's great work is out there, somewhere. The creature lives...
...and if what walked away was this tale's creature, I suspect we all know who the monster is.
But still...for all the horror, this is no longer a horror story. I intend to find the happy ending.
I intend to live, and for my creation to do likewise. If a boy, I will call him George. If a girl, Al--

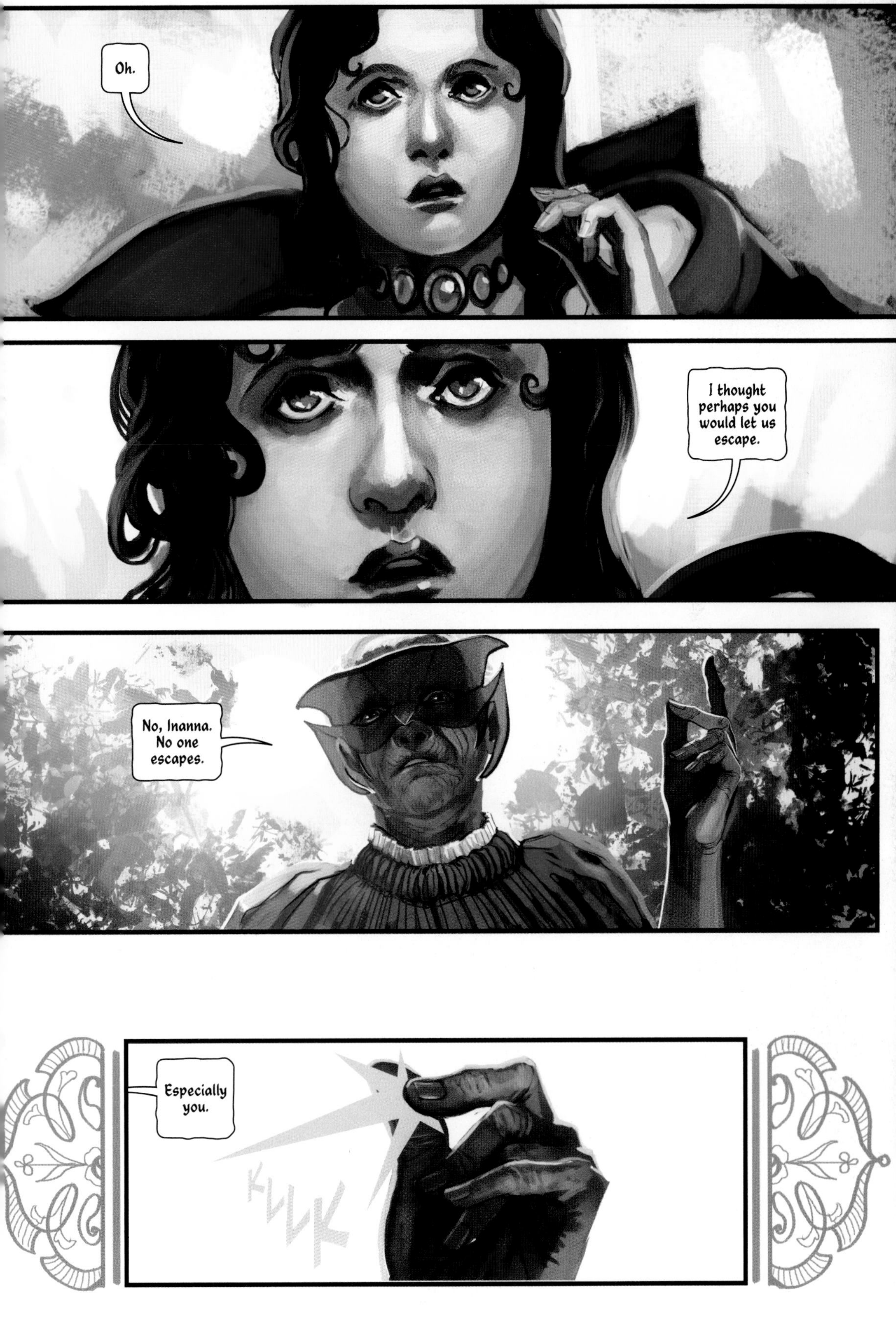
Oh.
I thought perhaps you would let us escape.
No, Inanna. No one escapes.
Especially you.
KLLK

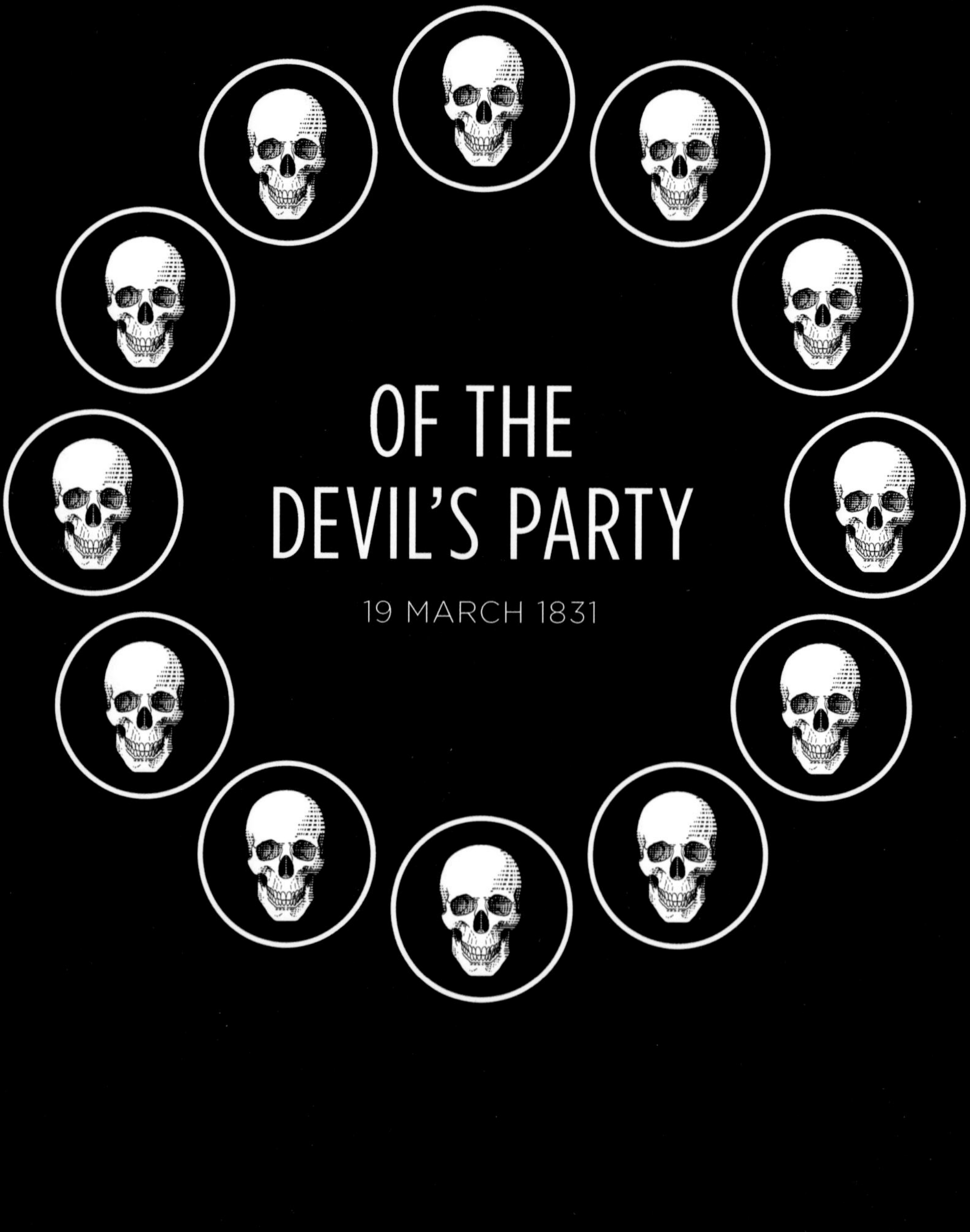

OF THE DEVIL'S PARTY

19 MARCH 1831

THE
WICKED
+
THE DIVINE

1923 AD

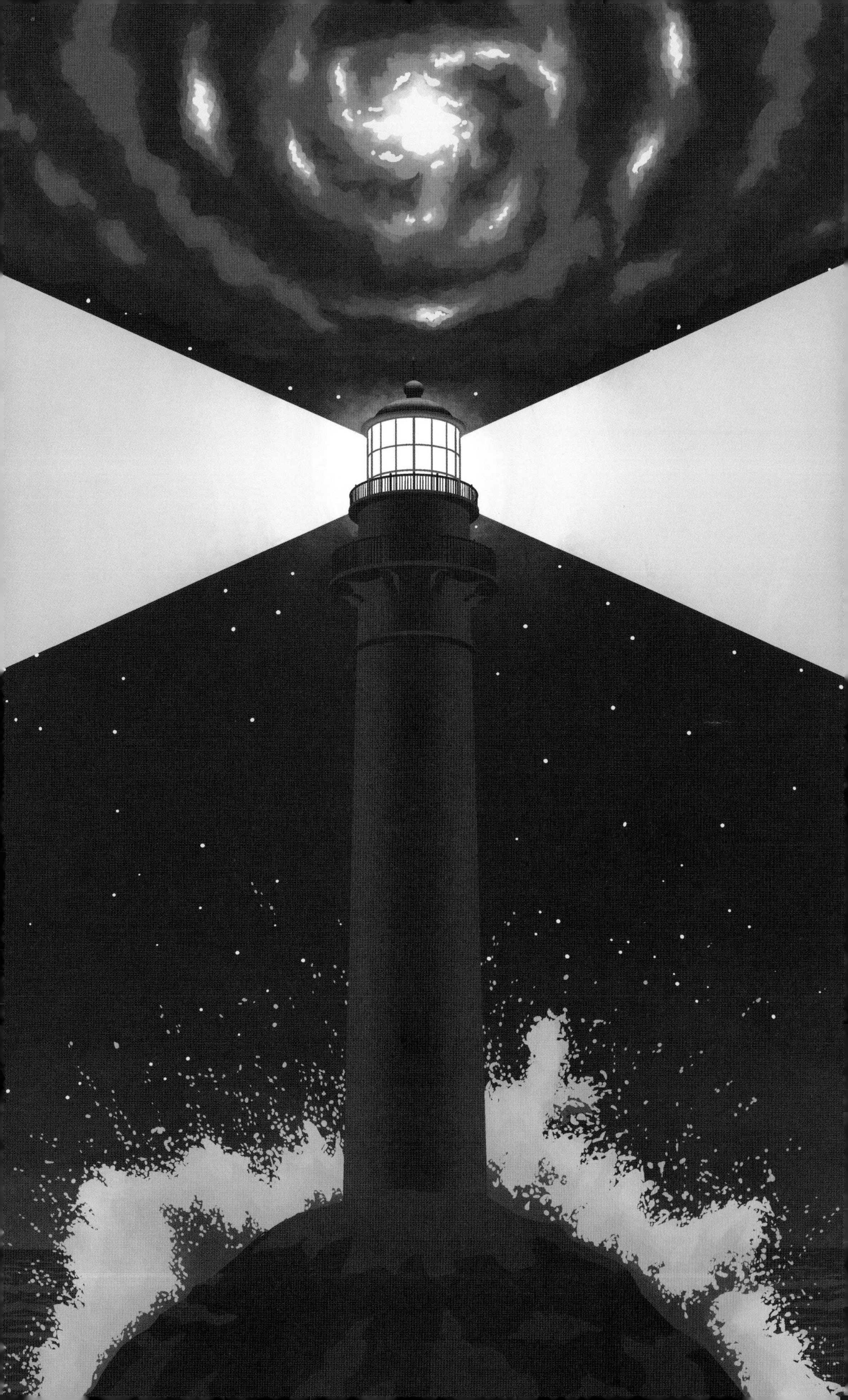

EVERY NINETY YEARS TWELVE GODS RETURN AS YOUNG PEOPLE.
They are loved. They are hated. In two years, they are all dead.

The year is 1923. It's happening now. It's happening again.

BAAL

*Storm god.
Elitist aesthete.*

AMATERASU

*Dramatic screen
goddess of light.*

LUCIFER

*Dapper underworld
god/social climber.*

SUSANOO

*Silver-lightning
storm god.*

THE MORRIGAN

*Underworld and
unconsciousness god.*

NEPTUNE

*Sea god.
Short sentences.*

THE NORNS

*Future, future
and future god.*

SET

*Awfully complicated.
Bloomsbury, London.*

AMON-RA

*Terse and regal
sun god.*

WODEN

*Expressionism and
nationalism god.*

MINERVA

*Irrepressible goddess
of wisdom.*

DIONYSUS

*God of wine
and cubism.*

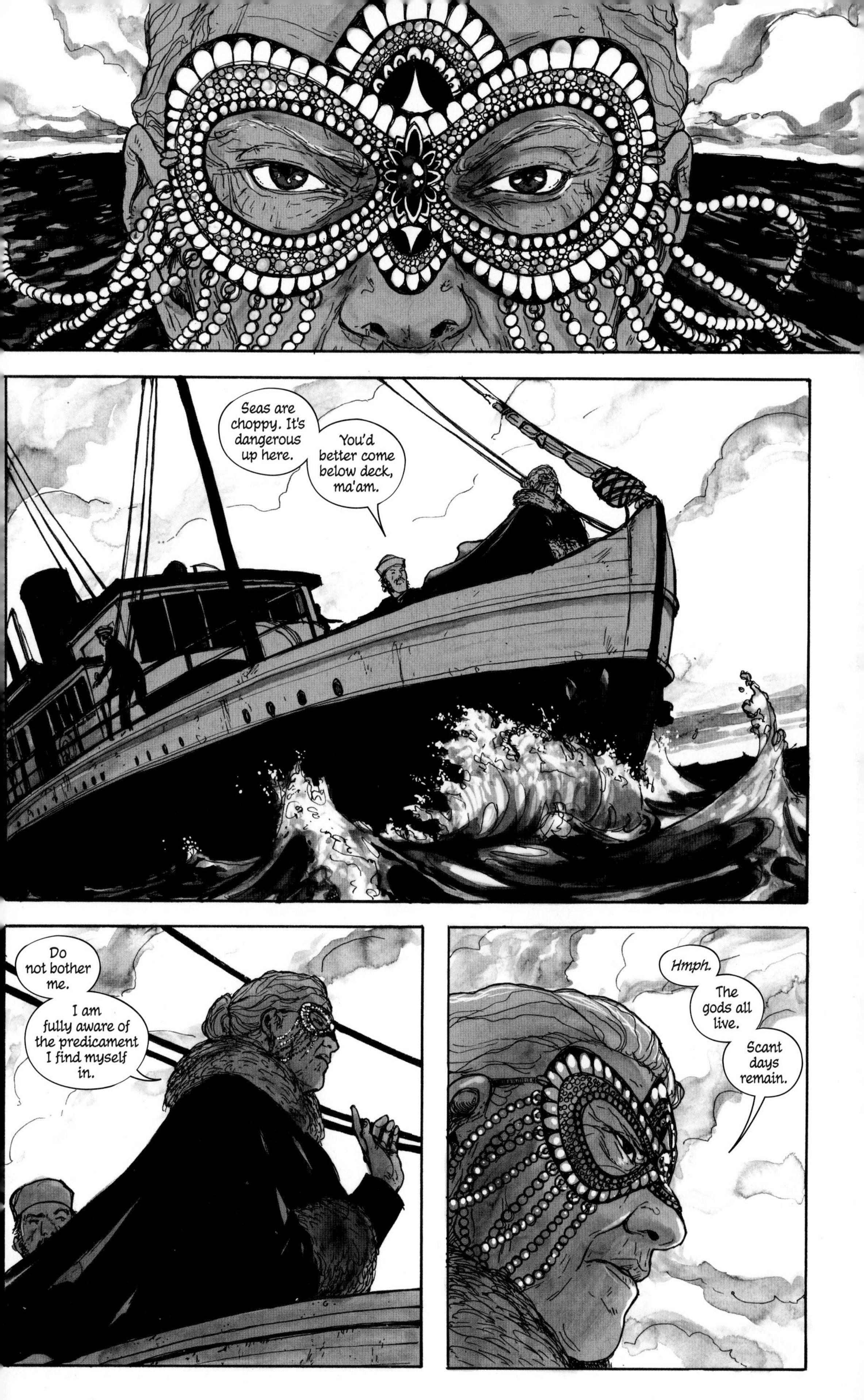
Seas are choppy. It's dangerous up here.
You'd better come below deck, ma'am.
Do not bother me.
I am fully aware of the predicament I find myself in.
Hmph.
The gods all live.
Scant days remain.

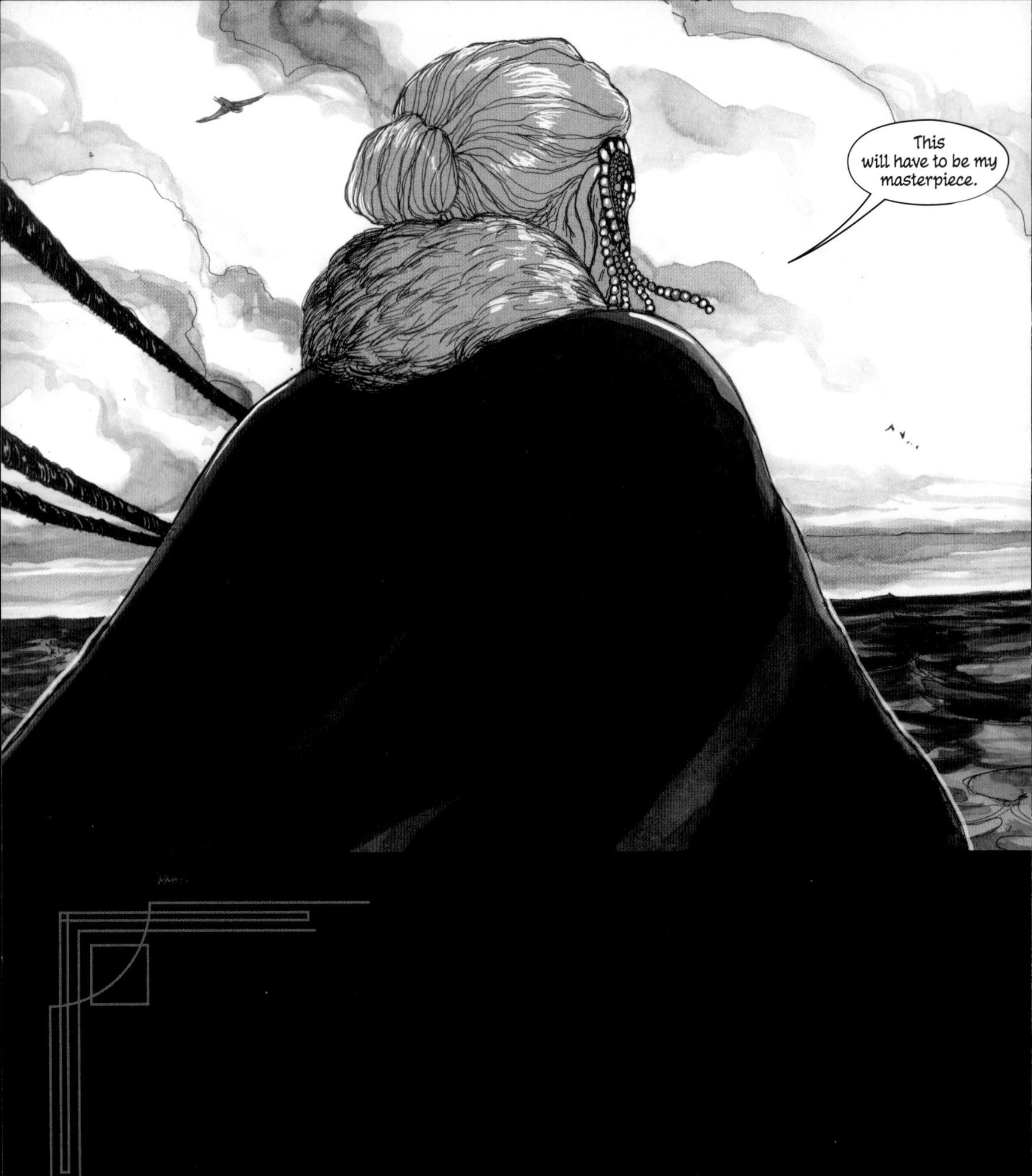
This will have to be my masterpiece.

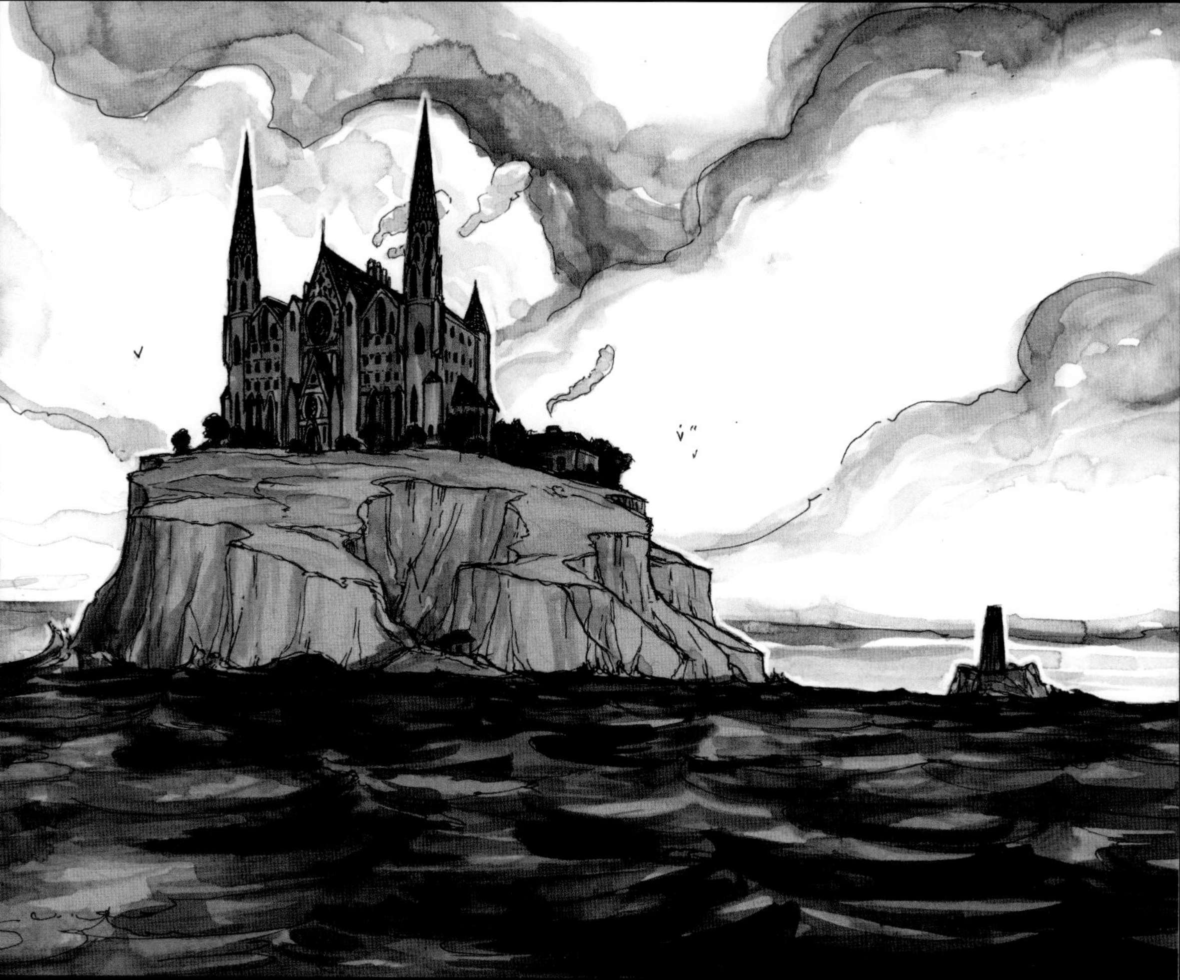

AND THEN THERE WAS ONE...

Kieron Gillen
Aud Koch
Clayton Cowles

1

THE ISLAND LOOKED like a threat, a fist of rock that had forced its way through the waves. The sky was an ink wash, the waters darkly echoing it. Scattered gulls cried lonely warnings, though it was impossible to say whether they were encouraging you to hasten or turn back.

The fishing boat fought against the wind. The island inched closer.

"Hellish," said Neptune, to no one in particular, wrestling with the wheel, enjoying the battle. The Indian god's dark beard was like the sea in miniature, all curls tipped with early white. He didn't smile, even when he was having fun.

"Perhaps that explains why the Devil chose here?" said Dionysus. The tanned Spaniard looked deceptively normal at first, until you stared into his eyes long enough, and caught one of their intermittent explosions of light. He carelessly leaned off the edge of the ship, only his paint-smudged fingertips on the rigging holding him there. "It's not a landscape I'd pick, unless I was in a particularly bleak period. Why here?"

"Perversity," said Neptune. They were close enough to pick out the harbour at the base of the cliffs. A single yacht was already moored. A long curl of a staircase swept up towards the mansion. Nearly there. The approach had reached the point where the wall of rock obscured Lucifer's monstrosity with its twin spires. It was designed to look like horns, but Neptune thought it looked like a sacrilegious crown nestling on the skyline. With only a few weeks' grains of sand in the glass for some of them, everyone considered architecture a

strange use of Lucifer's last months. Perhaps answers awaited, as well as a party.

All had received an invite on paper which ignited, leaving only a smell of brimstone. The gods conversed, either excitedly or dismissively. Scorn or glee didn't change a thing; all agreed to come. They were intrigued. Say what you would about Lucifer—and people always did—the American always did throw the most wonderful parties.

The Norns surfaced from below decks in black-suited triplicate, each holding a section of a newspaper. Three sets of crackling eyes tried to discern the future.

"There's a war ahead," they said together in an artillery barrage of words.

"Can we spare the theatrics?" said Neptune. "One man, one voice. My hangover's killing me."

The Norns considered. Urðr and Skuld nodded towards Verðandi.

"The peace cannot hold." he said. "Germany writhes. The next war will be worse. The skies and the seas and the earth will be filled with new steel..."

"The war is behind us," said Neptune. "It's buried in France."

Neptune was the sort of man who thought the only sins were war, wasted wine and needless adjectives—the latter being a category in which he placed *all* adjectives. He would not be argued with. The Old Man of the pantheon had been sixteen at the Somme, seventeen at Passchendaele, eighteen at Amiens. At twenty-two he would die, along with the rest of them. He had seen the war and, whether there was one or not, he would never see another.

The three students considered a reply, when Dionysus' body fractured.

It is difficult to explain.

He was there for a second, then not. Or *not* not. The euclidean rules shattered and he became something close to the idea of a man, movement and feeling materialised in a vision. Eventually he fell into brightly coloured cubes, before recoalescing on his knees, panting.

It was a novel thing, a reimagining of human flesh. It would have been uncanny had it not happened three times already on their journey from the mainland. The Norns wished they could have sent their 'Little Brother' out to study Dionysus, but they had promised Ananke to save their levitating marvel for the privacy of the island. Still, while they would have liked to examine him, it was purely for their own interests. They didn't need their technological miracle to make a diagnosis.

Dionysus was one of the first gods to return to Earth. If all that Ananke said was true, he would be one of the first gods to depart. His experiments in his form and shape were growing more violent, and had long since escaped his conscious control.

"The future... I've seen it," said Dionysus, recovering.

"What is it?" said the Norns, their cannonade resumed in excitement. Neptune set his eyes on the island. This pain would pass.

Dionysus struggled to find the words. "It is hard to say. It can only be shown," he eventually stuttered out. "It is horrible."

"You think the peace doesn't last?" said Neptune before he snorted to himself, angling the boat on its final approach.

"The Future is coming," said Urðr, "Nothing lasts."

"A brave new world," said Skuld, "though it remains to be seen what manner of people we may find in it."

The sea off to port churned, and from the water emerged a metallic squid, a gothic monstrosity of a submersible. It looked like a futurist sculpture in black glass, dank vapours pouring from vents along its flanks. It spoke of days to come and warned against them simultaneously.

"I like *that*," said Urðr appreciatively.

"It's not so impressive," said Neptune. "I used to have a submarine myself. It was even made to look like a squid. Woden's got no d—— ideas of his own."

"Why did you ever get rid of such a wonderful thing?" said Verðandi.

Neptune patted the wooden wheel of the fishing boat, enjoying the feel of the sea speaking to him through it.

"A god must be many things," said Neptune, "but a man most of all."

MINERVA STRUGGLED WITH the hatch at the top of the submarine. The child's dress was as full of smudges as her make-up, her corkscrew curls bouncing as her head strained with the effort. She gave up her task, took a deep breath, and struggled to get into character.

"Oh golly," she yelped, back in the gloom of the strange ship, "I can't get this blasted thing open."

For a second there was but a smile in the dark, then Morrigan emerged from the blackness, petting a crow. With his old overcoat and eyepatch, he gave the perpetual impression that he had been sleeping rough. The crow cawed. He spoke.

"There, in the shadows of Woden's vessel, a man of night and feathers came to assist the tiny star. Stoic and silent, he stepped around her to turn the greasy handle..." he said, as he grasped what was more of a cog than a handle. It was definitely greasy.

"Thank you for coming, Mr Morrigan," said Minerva. "I don't think I would have enjoyed the trip with the beastly Woden fellow alone."

"*MORRIGAN (softly): Aye,*" said Morrigan, softly, as he twisted the cog three times, "*And Woden may have enjoyed himself too much. Best not to let the likes of him have too much fun.*"

The light fell into the chambers as Morrigan climbed up on deck, offering his hand down to the girl.

"*Morrigan never trusted Woden,*" he said. "*Woden reminded Morrigan of many things: stains in a stout glass, spectres on the dock, the shadow of a raised fist on a wall, blood running, not stopping. Morrigan wouldn't tell the girl that, of course. He wouldn't want to scare her.*"

"You do talk funny!" said Minerva, pulled up into the dusk. She hugged the man's side. "I adore it. It's simply the latest thing!"

She gasped in excitement at the grand sweep of the island above her, before turning her attention to the boats around the dock. A fishing boat was coming in, and an elegant yacht was already tied up. The ships were as expensive as the docks were strange, ridged ebony tentacles intertwining with a tangle of ropes and moorings. Minerva stood on her tiptoes, straining to see who was aboard the approaching craft.

"Oh, there are the Norns and Neptune and Dionysus. How exciting! I haven't seen Mr Neptune in ages!" she said. "Where's everyone else?"

"*Morrigan drew Minerva's attention to Amaterasu's yacht,*" said Morrigan, drawing her attention to the yacht. "*Morrigan would think that implied that Susanoo would also already be here, but wouldn't elaborate why to Minerva.*"

"I should think not! Talking to me about a brother and sister who kiss?" said Minerva with a shiver. "Ugh!"

Minerva continued to wave excitedly towards the boat. As one, the Norns waved back. Minerva appeared delighted, and then a thought appeared to strike her.

"I thought Woden said we would be here first? This ugly vessel was meant to be fast!" said Minerva, pouting.

Woden slunk up the step behind her, his alabaster horror mask of a face finding a deeper scowl. His fists curled into talons beneath his robe, adding to his countenance as a creature straight from a gothic penny dreadful. The girl had the worst habit of saying annoying childish truths just within earshot. He was starting to think she may be doing it on purpose, the precocious little minx.

"No," he said. "I said this ship *could* have beaten them. The Japanese gods arrived last night. Ananke said she would be arriving with the last shipment of supplies yesterday. Those who think themselves so above us will be arriving by airship, in their own good time. I'm sure the untermensch are already swarming over the island."

"*MORRIGAN (angrily): Don't poison the girl's mind with such ideas,*" said Morrigan. "*He refused to even look at the German. He was the sort of god who reminded Morrigan why he preferred the company of mortal men and all the mysteries that lie within them. The journey would soon be over, and Lucifer had promised him Guinness. They say it doesn't travel from Ireland and in his experience that proved true, but he always looked for a chance to be wrong.*"

"Oh, he is such a delight!" Minerva laughed, slapping Morrigan's arm before staring up at the clouds, hands shading her eyes so she could see more clearly. Her yelping subsided momentarily before resuming with greater intensity.

"Look!" she said, finger thrusting upwards. "Set's ship! She's coming! She'll be here in time for supper! Yay!"

BAAL TILTED HIS GLASSES downwards to better let him take in the view of the world below. The champagne he sipped added to the sense that he was an academic dressed for an awards ceremony, his demeanour indicating it was an award he felt sure he would win but that was also beneath him. It was all beneath him, particularly the view. Lucifer's mansion was a monstrosity, its sprawl of a design seeming to believe that a surfeit of features could match the results of good taste by fortuitous accident. Lucifer needed an editor. A good editor is paramount, in this, as all things.

Baal had heard the argument that quantity has a quality of its own, but had long since decided that the quality was "being quite awful".

To be fair, he was uncertain of Set's airship too. It had too much the sense of the modern to it, redeemed only by the long curves of an Egyptian barge in its hull, and the kohl-eyed windows that let him take in the disappointing view. "I always remember Rameses II telling me he'd adore a sky barge," she had said, "and as I was quietly having an affair with his best wife, I promised myself I'd make a sky barge in memory of him." Looking out to the north, Baal found the view much agreeable. That lighthouse past the main island! Quite elegant, with something of the classical to its curves, a sliver of ivory against the dying light...

Back to the home country, thought Baal with a shudder. America, for the last time. Baal had hoped he would never have to look at his homeland again. He left it for a good reason, but at least he returned for one as well.

He was considering the ironies of life when he was disturbed by a tall, sombre black man in a black suit, who stepped out of a sunbeam.

"Baal," said the new arrival, giving a slight nod and a tiny adjustment of his cufflinks.

"Amon-Ra," said Baal, raising his champagne flute in a perfunctory salute.

It was stiff between them, as it always was. Baal couldn't hide his contempt and Amon-Ra wouldn't hide the fact that he saw Baal for the elitist bigot he was. Baal wished

he could like Amon-Ra, but couldn't help but be amused by the pretension of it. 'A Harlem Renaissance.' As if any renaissance could come from the New World? Baal didn't consider himself in opposition to those of other races, even when science suggested them to be generally inferior. Amon-Ra was in no part to blame for his origins or his nature, but Baal had to agree with Set—experiences and one's origins can distemper one, rob one of the requisite cool clarity, make one simply incapable of creating true art. This was a tragedy, yes, but it was still a fact.

Amon-Ra glanced back down the ship. "Where's Set?"

"She's just preparing for her grand entrance. Lucifer wants to impress people, and you know Set wouldn't like to be upstaged," Baal replied, before gesturing downwards. "Have you taken in Lucifer's folly?"

Amon-Ra pressed against the window, peering through the clouds. "Lucifer tries so hard," he said. "He's trying to speak to everyone, and he's saying nothing. That building's singing so many songs he can't carry the d—— tune. I think he..."

He trailed off, then paused. He made the briefest of excuses and disappeared into sunlight.

Baal rushed to the window, looking for the cause of the disturbance.

Three vessels were now at harbour. A string of figures were making their way up the cliff face. A couple, sitting side by side in the grounds, were overlooking the seas. Even at this distance, Baal could see the shimmer of light that was Amon-Ra materialising beside them.

Of course. All artists, great or small, find their own level.

SUSANOO LAY BACK on the sparse grass and wondered: if Lucifer could afford a mansion, then surely he could afford a trifle more grass seed? Perhaps it took too long to grow? The one thing they didn't have

was time. He straightened his plaid waistcoat, ensuring all was as it should be, and hoped it would remain in fashion with their remaining weeks on Earth. He really was rather fond of it. "Fond" was too small a word for the woman beside him. Amaterasu sat on Susanoo's jacket, dressed in a white summer dress in winter. She was never cold. She was always radiant. He thought her beautiful in the fading red sunlight. He thought her beautiful in the moonlight. He thought her beautiful, wherever, whenever. He knew the symptoms of his disease well, and had grown quite fond of them.

He gestured at the falling sun and smiled lopsidedly at his companion. "Before I say 'nice work', is that one of yours or is it *his*?"

She smiled back, and it was as though the sun's path was reversing. "Please, Susanoo," she said. "Don't tease. I'm dreading seeing Amon again. He'll—"

The sunlight coalesced beside them and a kingly man in a black suit stepped out.

"Oh, hello, Amon-Ra," said Susanoo. "We were discussing sunsets. Is a god of the sun a fan? You'd think so."

"Since my baby left me?" said Amon-Ra, pointedly. "No."

Susanoo couldn't have summoned a cloud as thick as Amon-Ra's words.

"You will leave us be," Amaterasu glared.

"I will," said Amon-Ra, glancing between the pair. "You know this is a mistake. He's a fool. You know better."

Amon-Ra always made Susanoo feel stupid, which Susanoo heartily disliked, as opposed to feeling foolish, which was one of Susanoo's favourite things. He had no idea how Amaterasu could like someone as majestic and dramatic as Amon-Ra, whilst still finding time for a buffoon such as himself. On this mystery, as with so many others, she stayed silent, even when her eyes said so much.

Instead, she went in a most unexpected direction.

"Oh!" said Amaterasu. "Lucifer asked a favour. There's still enough sunlight left to reach the mainland and back. They find themselves short of preserves, and breakfast will be unbearable without them."

Amon-Ra considered it. All three knew that Amaterasu could also make the trip. None of them would be rude enough

to mention it. Without further words, Amon-Ra disappeared.

Susanoo looked over at the wet-eyed Amaterasu. Amon-Ra had made her sad. That was unbearable.

"Good to see you," said Susanoo, once Amon-Ra had safely vanished. Susanoo got up and walked backwards, waving theatrically towards the sky. "For a god of the sun, that man always has the blues," said Susanoo, backing towards the cliff edge.

"Susanoo!" said Amaterasu as he approached the drop. Susanoo ignored her, and took the final step that would see him over the edge—which stole a gasp from her—then spun on his heel, landing back safely. Susanoo didn't give away any awareness that he was in mortal danger. Amaterasu's gasp turned to a laugh. Susanoo waggled his eyebrows.

"Oh, my clown," said Amaterasu, fondly... before a sadness returned.

Amon-Ra made her sad, but so did Susanoo. This business with Susanoo was, perhaps, a mistake. As man and woman, they were complete strangers. As gods, they were brother and sister. The desire was unconsummated, but the desire was there.

"I'll see you at dinner," said Amaterasu. "Be good."

"And afterwards?" said Susanoo. She didn't answer, leaving the storm god rocking back and forth on his heel on the cliff edge. He saw that the gods from the newly arrived boats were approaching the mansion, and Amaterasu ran to meet them. She would put on a good show. She always did.

Lucifer's stage awaits, he thought. The cast are all here. At least, almost. He noticed Set's airship making its awkward descent. Of course she'd be the last to arrive. He remembered how Amaterasu described it: "The airship seems an impractical and somewhat doomed idea, but it fills the sky magnificently. And so gracefully!"

He watched it sway back and forth. It didn't look graceful. It looked like a disaster in waiting.

"I *could* lower the winds to help Set land

that thing," he said to himself. "Or I *could* make it worse."

He could imagine Amaterasu's amused smile, chiding him that he's awful, neither encouraging or dissuading his mischief.

He shook his head as he started back towards the house.

No, even with all the powers of the sky and the bottle-lightning in his heart, he couldn't make it worse.

LUCIFER STOOD IN THE MAIN HALL of the mansion, back turned towards the prepared table. Simple fruits to begin with, apples most distinctly unforbidden. He studied himself in the window's reflection. Good looking in a bad way, suit as pristine as his soul was not, dual flicks of his hair giving him the faintest hint of horns, he was dapper. No—more than dapper. Wonderful! An impressive man in his impressive house.

He adjusted his focus and gazed north over the sea and pondered. Was the mansion not magnificent? It was not just magnificent. It was *wonderfully* magnificent. It should surely impress. It had to impress.

The projector mounted in the roof shuddered into life. Its gears whirred and a cone of light fell on the floor. Behind Lucifer, the flickering Butler emerged.

"I'm sorry to di-di-disturb you, sir," he said, "but Mistress S-S-Set and company are just arriving. It appears our company is-s-s complete. I have shown everyone else to their rooms. They await your summons, sir."

The Butler was the queerest thing, voice patched from a library recording of a fine English stage actor of Lucifer's acquaintance, guided by the building's new-fangled electrical brain. A celluloid ghost, a man of light. A miracle in an age of miracles. Lucifer thought it the very definition of "impressive".

Lucifer turned and walked through the unflustered Butler and took his seat at the head of the table. "Let the festivities begin," he said. "If we have but weeks to live, let them be weeks worth remembering, eh? Give me half an hour to assemble, then usher them in."

The Butler nodded and disappeared. Lucifer relaxed, breathing deeply, calmly. It all came to this. All this work. Why 'Lucifer?' The splinter had festered in him for two years. This was a mansion fit for Apollo. Surely his quality would be obvious *now*? He would prove that one can rise beyond their origins. The falling star can rise again.

The door opened. Lucifer's first guest entered.

"That was quick," Lucifer beamed, nonchalant as only the determinedly duplicitous can achieve. "I did want people to wait... but as it's you, come in. Please, take a seat. Take wines. Take..."

He sighed. He couldn't face the performance any more.

"So... put me out of my misery," he said. "Are you impressed?"

"I am," said his first guest. "I couldn't be more impressed."

Lucifer relaxed into his chair, smiled and closed his eyes.

Impressed! Impressed! It was all worth it.

A pair of fingers clicked.

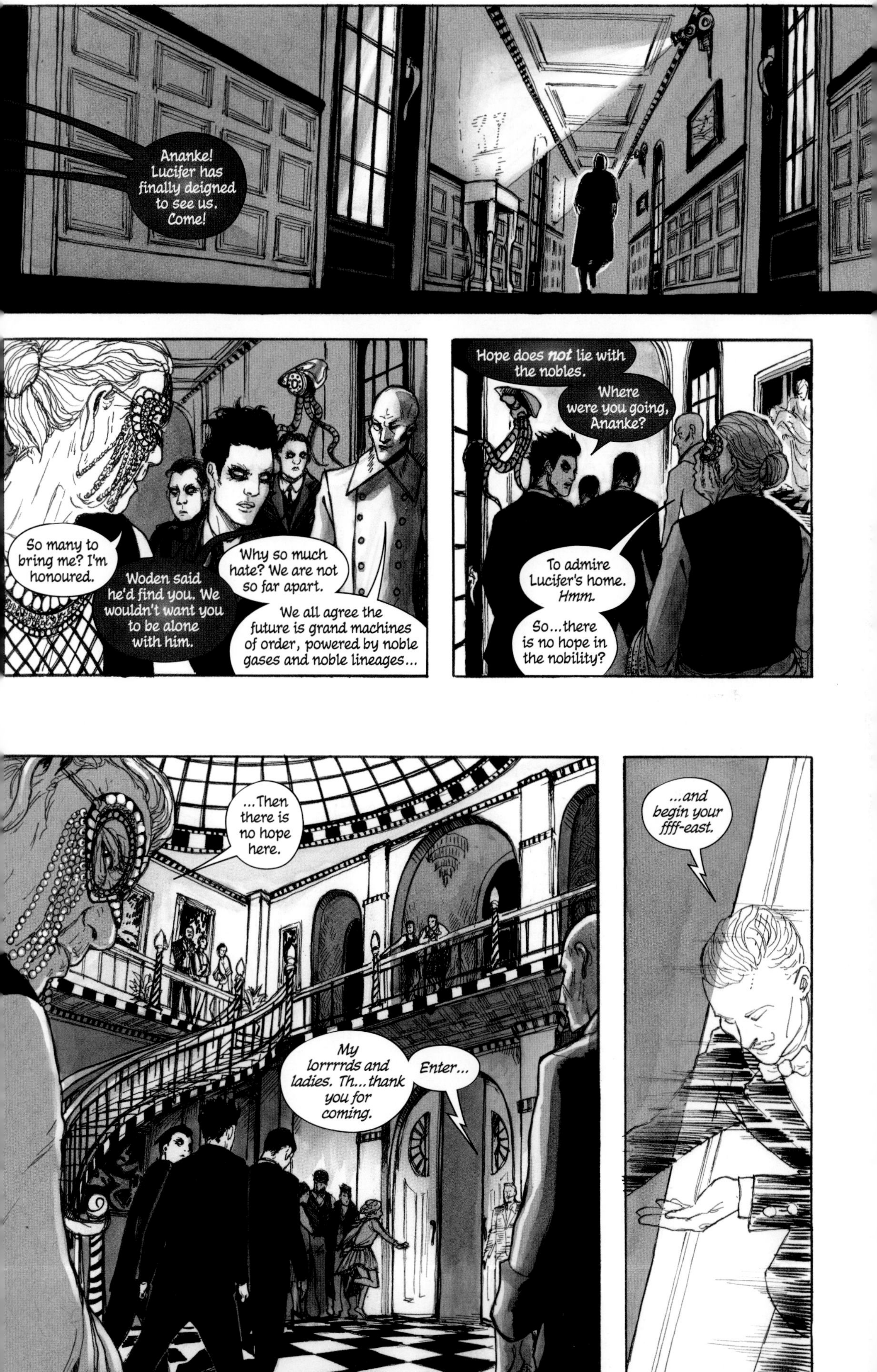

Ananke! Lucifer has finally deigned to see us. Come!
So many to bring me? I'm honoured.
Woden said he'd find you. We wouldn't want you to be alone with him.
Why so much hate? We are not so far apart.
We all agree the future is grand machines of order, powered by noble gases and noble lineages...
Hope does *not* lie with the nobles.
Where were you going, Ananke?
To admire Lucifer's home. *Hmm.*
So...there is no hope in the nobility?
...Then there is no hope here.
My lorrrrds and ladies. Th...thank you for coming.
Enter...
...and begin your ffff-east.

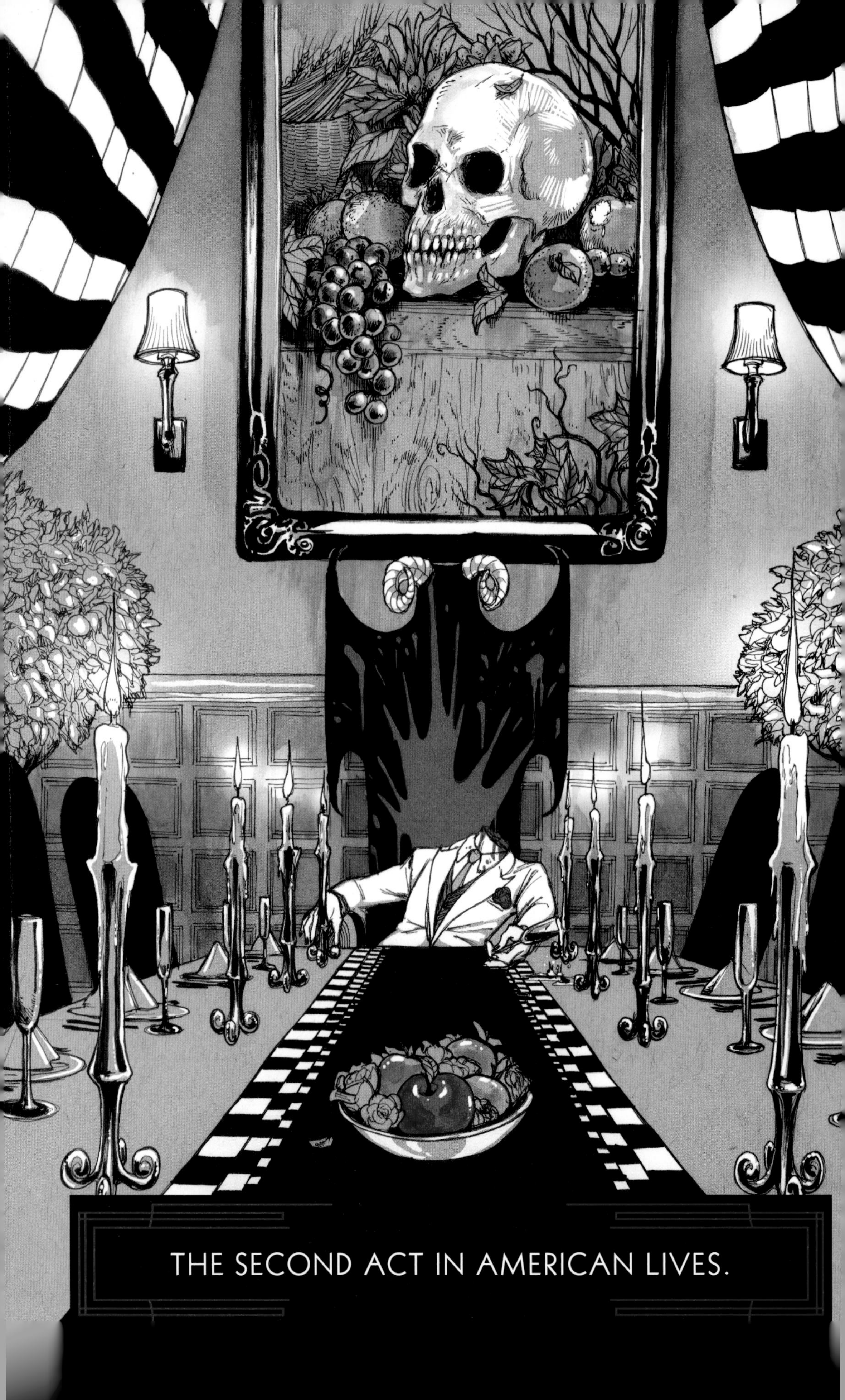
THE SECOND ACT IN AMERICAN LIVES.

2

MINERVA RUSHED FORWARD, then froze in the doorway, whimpering. It took a second for those closest to realise what she'd seen. Morrigan acted first, pulling her back. Neptune gathered her head against him, hiding the scene from her. Androgynously beautiful with Cleopatra's eyes, Set moved forwards.

She took in the scene and announced her expert opinion.

"Well, as Jesus Christ once told me in a tavern five days after his crucifixion," she said, "Lucifer's dead."

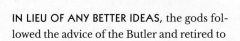

IN LIEU OF ANY BETTER IDEAS, the gods followed the advice of the Butler and retired to one of the building's many studies.

Matching the style of the majority of the house, it was the latest New York fashion with a splash of the scientific romances. The expected works of art and portraiture were joined by statues of light, filling empty alcoves. If that wasn't sufficient science, there was the matter of the staff. A mechanical servant made her way between the gods, a cable running from the small of her back to a disguised socket in the wall, with wide light-bulb eyes and gothic detailing. Hauntingly elegant, she delivered delicate canapés and champagne. The gods' appetites proved as small as the dishes.

"We c-c-ould eat in the pagoda, but then there would be no staff. There's insufficient power out there for the Metropolitans," said the Butler apologetically to everyone and no one in particular.

"No one cares about eating," said Neptune at the window. "Lucifer's been murdered."

"Can we be sure?" said Susanoo, throwing back his second brandy. "He's awful flighty at the best of times. I know sawing your own

head off would be a pretty extreme trick for a suicide, but Lucifer always did have a determined streak..."

"It wasn't a saw," said the Norns. "It was some manner of intense burst of energy. Perhaps heat. Perhaps electricity. Perhaps something we don't understand." They had sent their Little Brother floating into the room to examine the corpse, careful not to disturb whatever might be considered as evidence.

"What's happening?" said Minerva, sitting in a corner, legs crossed, rocking back and forth.

The gods had no answers in their eyes, and turned to their oracle, the old woman in the tall armchair. She considered the matter for a few minutes. All was silent except the click-clack of the gears and shuffle of the Metropolitan's feet.

"It is possible it is simply that Lucifer's two years were up," Ananke said. "Your times are ending. This manner of death is not unknown to me. It could be tragic, yet the natural tragedy that awaits you all."

"Is there some manner of recording of the room?" said Verðandi, gesturing at the cameras.

"I'm af-f-f-f-fraid not," said the Butler. "Those are projectorrrrrs. The building's systems recognise sound-sound as it's spoken and can act in response, but it does not record. All I can say is that Lucifer was ALIVE! when he called you all to supper, some ha-ha-half an hour ago."

"Convenient," said Amon-Ra from the far corner.

"It doesn't seem likely," said Set, "but are we seriously talking about some manner of assassination? This isn't a Byzantine court. I would have noticed. Who actually hates Lucifer?"

She paused.

"Very well," she corrected. "Who hates Lucifer enough to kill him? What's the motivation?"

"You are all aware of the Prometheus Gambit," said Ananke. "I have explained at length that it is nonsense. Humans cannot gain powers by murdering you, as much as they'd like to believe they can... but there is something that is true, that I haven't told you. For gods to ritually kill the kindred? It can add their time to yours."

She glanced around the room, carefully, measuring the responses. Some eyes were furtive. Some eyes were surprised.

"In my experience, this is more likely in the early days. To slay for an additional year or even two may seem logical. To slay for months or even weeks is hardly a motivation for such risk," she said, "though you gods were always intelligent. There are certainly rituals one of you could have discovered. You children make discoveries. Novelty is by definition novel, even if it builds upon an established theme. They are mysteries to me, if not to you."

"Oh, a mystery," sighed Susanoo. "You are always the great mystery writer."

Amaterasu touched his arm, and he grew quiet.

"We should consider contacting the authorities," Ananke said, carefully.

"Considered. Let's not," said Set.

No one disagreed. They were gods. What could the mortals do?

"So what now?" said Minerva, "Can we eat? I'm famished."

ANANKE LED THE GODS through the purgatorially austere garden, with more sculpture than greenery, and into the pagoda. A round table was waiting for them, surrounded by twelve seats. It was decorated in a simpler style: beautiful, and opulent, true, but still simple.

"Lucifer asked if I had any requests," said Ananke, "and I asked for this. I find a serious place to talk about serious matters most necessary."

As the gods looked around, Ananke opened a cupboard and retrieved a skull. She carried it with both hands and reverently placed it on the table, before the nearest seat.

"This seat is Lucifer's," she said. "You each have one. I shall stand."

"Firstly, I dare say a lady who brings skulls to a party is a trifle macabre for my tastes," said Susanoo. "Secondly—twelve chairs? Are the Norns meant to share one between them? That doesn't seem fair."

"What about this ever seemed fair, Storm God?" said Ananke. "This room... you must understand. I am old and sentimental. A circle reminds you you're all equal. The skulls remind you that you're all doomed. Normally, you'd have seen that earlier... but you have all been remarkably lucky. As I suspect some of you still consider your flesh to be immortal, the memento mori is perhaps most important now."

"Still seems creepy," said Susanoo. "Also... Memento Moriwhat?"

"'Remember that you have to die,'" said Baal, quotation marks like raised daggers around his words. "Any well-read person would know that. As would any who has studied the pantheon. This is all quite normal. The only thing that isn't normal is that we're all alive, although I have my theories on that."

"I'm sure you do," said Amon-Ra, taking a seat. "Can we pick up the beat?"

"I'm not sure what's required," said Set. "I'm unaware of the conventions in this form. Norse sagas I'd be able to help with, although it's been a long time since I helped darling Snorri with his little Edda. Not really my thing, this modern genre work."

"Oh, I know! Alibis!" said Minerva, "The rotter won't have one."

"How quaint," said Set. "Well, I do believe I'm in the clear. Baal and I were on our approach to the island. Which, I dare say, means we were off the island."

"How convenient. Well, Butler?" said Woden. "Is this correct?"

"Y-y-yes," said the Butler, flickering into existence. "All the arriving gods bar Baal, Set and Amon-Ra had been shown to their rooms at this point, where from I retrieved them for supper."

The collective attention shifted towards to the towering Amon-Ra expectantly.

"I talked with Baal on his ship. I went to the island and talked to Susanoo and Amaterasu," he said. "She asked me to fetch jam."

Amaterasu nodded her confirmation.

"Three rock-solid alibis and the rest abstractly in their rooms," said the Norns, turning towards the flickering man. "Any exceptions?"

"Yes, sir," said the Butler. "Amaterasu and Susanoo have been on the island since yesterday, and were wandering freely. Ms Ananke arrived th-th-this morning."

"Hmm," said Susanoo, swirling his drink around the glass. "I was making my way back to my room. I stayed there until I was called. Ammy?"

"I..." she paused. "I went to my room. I wanted to freshen up."

"Well, that seems perfectly reasonable," said Susanoo, turning to Ananke. "What about you, ma'am? Having a nice constitutional around the grounds and found that

you'd worked up a little appetite for murder?"

"The joke hides a good question," said the Norns. "You weren't in your room. Woden and I found you wandering the corridors. What were you doing?"

"Walking," said Ananke. "Lucifer had showed me the blueprints, and I wanted to see it all in the flesh."

"So you were following your wandering soul too. Did you find anything interesting?" asked Woden.

"Yes," said Ananke. "I find it all most impressive. Lucifers rarely show such determination. They—"

Ananke never finished, as she was interrupted when Neptune stood up and threw his glass against the wall.

"D—— it," he said. "This is no good. We'd have to be quick, but any of us on the island could have done it, if we wanted to."

"Morrigan considered the room. Friends? No. Peers? Too grand a word for this collection of lucky unlucky dice," said Morrigan, *"but if the company was comprised of tawdry gods, the place itself was grand, like a skyscraper made of the sky, and the boy from Dublin thought of the man who gathered them here, and what his plans could have been, and the only ones who he might have confided in on his final night..."*

"Wait for it. Wait for it..." said Susanoo, drumming the table.

"MORRIGAN (cautiously): Ananke. Amaterasu. Susanoo. You were here earliest. Did you speak to Lucifer? What was on his mind?" said Morrigan.

"Unfortunately not," said Ananke. "The Butler said he was too busy."

"Well, too busy for you," said Susanoo. "We had the pleasure of the last meal with the man—assuming that he skipped breakfast. Supper last night. We talked a lot and said little of any weight. But it's Lucifer! That was quite normal. He was quite normal."

"He wasn't," said Amaterasu, as if she was testing the ground to see if it would fall beneath her. "He made jokes and you saw the jokes... but I saw the drama. He was different. He was anxious. He seemed like a little boy, more than usual. When you were getting more brandy, Su-su, he leaned to me and said... *Oh, Amykins, darling, haven't you read the papers? I think it's better to die while it's a little more exclusive, as it's going to become painfully popular again soon enough. At least death is fashionable now.*"

She relaxed. The performance had been uncanny. It it was as if Lucifer had been reborn before them.

Dionysus stood up sharply, grasping the table, then exploded into light. His eye curled in his head, becoming a shape akin to a pentagon, before collapsing back together. He leaned on the table, palms flat, gasping.

"Brandy?" asked Susanoo, tilting the decanter.

"I... it's war. Again. I've seen it. Harpies sending bombs crashing to earth. Cities burned from fortresses in the sky. Ovens...

full of people. It's there, it's coming. There... there's nothing we can do. It... it..." he said in a rush, and showed no signs of ceasing.

Neptune stood up, walked around the table, and with a single back-handed blow hit Dionysus across the face.

"You're unmanned," said Neptune, taking his shoulder and leading him out.

"Where do you think you're going?" asked Set.

"I'm taking him to bed. He needs to sleep. He's a great artist but not a strong man," said Neptune, "and most of all, he is wrong. The war was *the* war. If I thought that there was anything worse than that, I'd kill the whole d—— species. We don't deserve to live."

The silence stretched on.

"Well, I believe that's it for the evening. Shall we retire, or shall we have a nightcap?" said Susanoo.

THE GODS MADE their way into the house, separating. Amaterasu retired to the main hall, wanting to show some light sculptures she'd been working on. Amon-Ra, Baal and Morrigan expressed relative degrees of interest, and joined her. Susanoo winced, thinking of the things she previously had shown Amon-Ra, and considered it was time for a distraction. That nightcap called. The studies and their decanters summoned half the gods.

Woden gestured at one of the rooms, a sliver of ebony technology showing at the cuff of his trench coat. "Perhaps there is a matter we could debate with a drink? I have some fascinating ideas I'd love to share," he said. "Germany is febrile. The clubs! The art! The ideas! Have you heard Mr Hitler's speeches yet? You simply must? National socialism. It's—"

"We know what Nazis are," said the Norns,

opening the door to the adjoining room, "And we have no interest in them."

"Will I like them?" said Susanoo, about to follow Woden.

"No," said the Norns.

"Oh," said Susanoo, turning on his heel and following the Norns. "Sorry, Woden, old chap."

"Well, as I once told Temuchin, I won't turn from a fight, though hopefully I won't have to show off my Parthian shot," said Set, stepping in after Woden. "Let's hear what an Austrian peasant has to tell his betters, eh?"

The Norns took three seats while Susanoo explored their room. Woden's and Set's voices were already raised next door. Susanoo shuddered, and found the brandy. Rémy Martin. A tiny note, in Lucifer's hand. *"I know it's your favourite, Susanoo. Have one on me."* Susanoo hid his tears. The poor doomed fool, he thought, just like the rest of us.

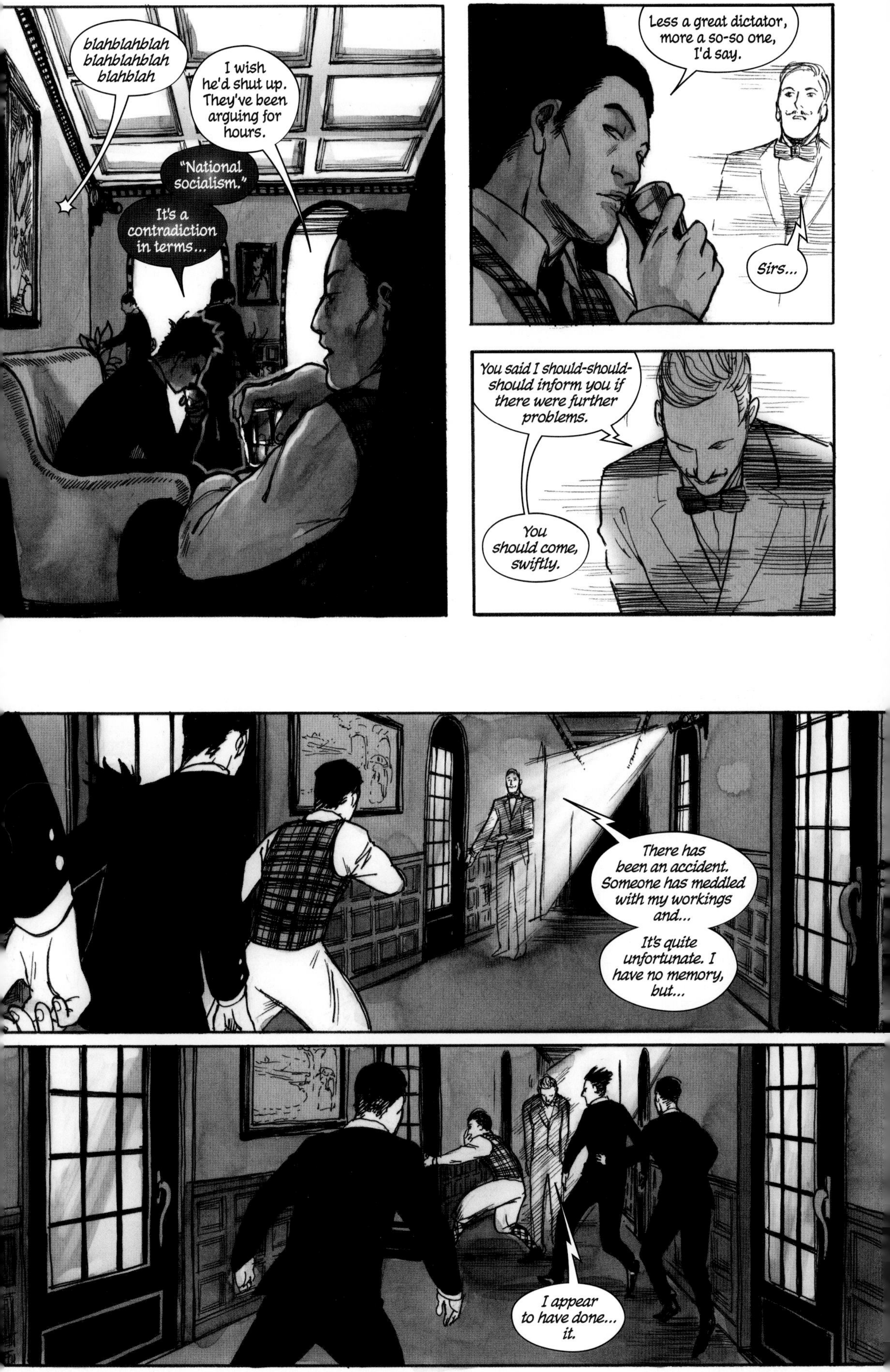
blahblahblah blahblahblah blahblah
I wish he'd shut up. They've been arguing for hours.
"National socialism."
It's a contradiction in terms...
Less a great dictator, more a so-so one, I'd say.
Sirs...
You said I should-should-should inform you if there were further problems.
You should come, swiftly.
There has been an accident. Someone has meddled with my workings and...
It's quite unfortunate. I have no memory, but...
I appear to have done... it.

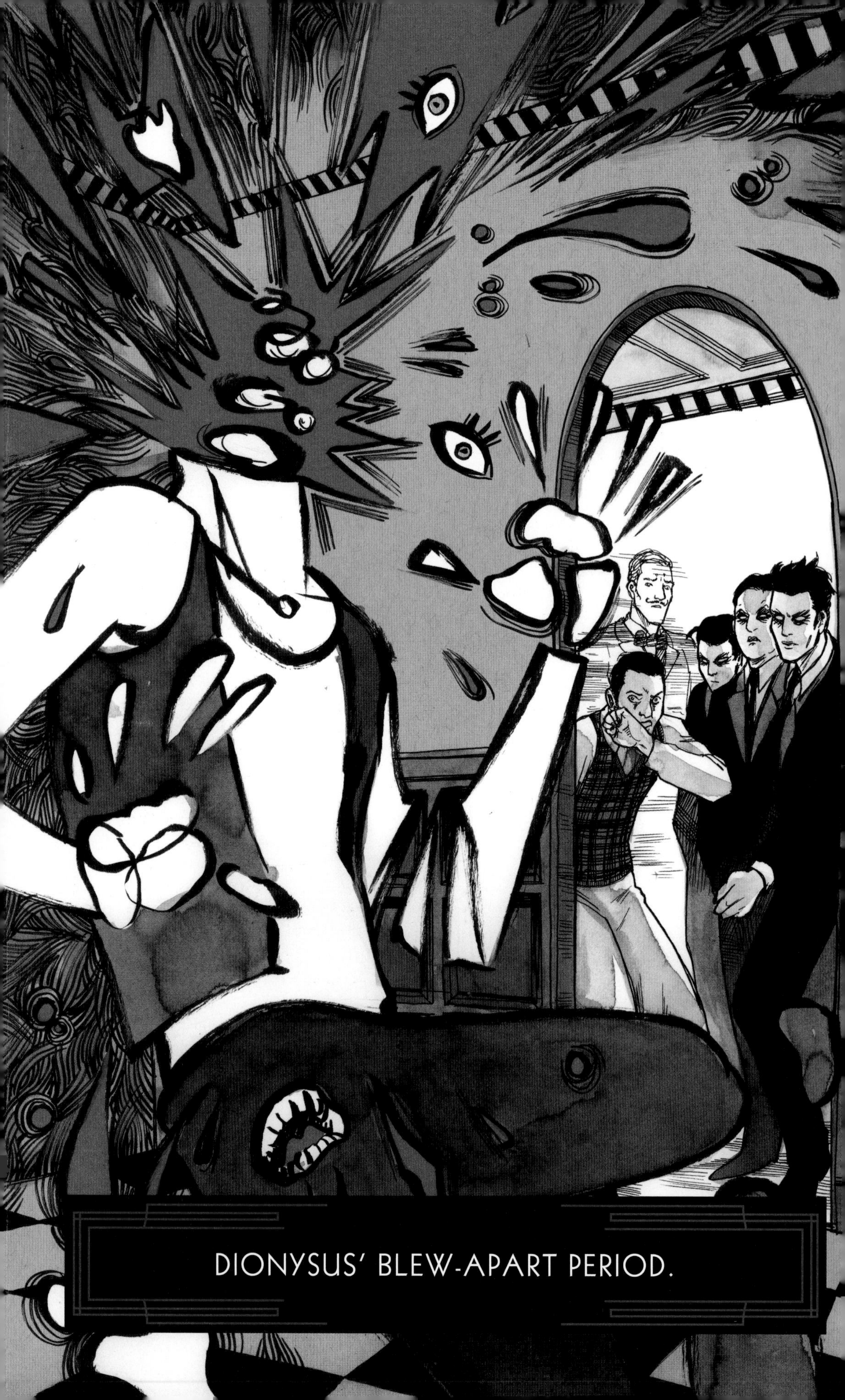

DIONYSUS' BLEW-APART PERIOD.

3

ANANKE PLACED A SKULL in front of Dionysus' empty chair and retreated to the pagoda's shadows.

The gods watched the ceremony in silence, several degrees more respectful. The atmosphere had changed. They'd lived under a hanging sword for two years, but it had never dropped. The curse had been distant, yet to become real. The first death could have been considered a singular event. Lucifer was not loved, as charming as he could be. But Dionysus? Feelings varied, but his passing changed things from a death to a pattern. It spoke to everyone in the room.

"And then there were..." said Susanoo, "ten gods, thirteen people or twelve godly beings and a mysteriously immortal one. How are we counting this?"

"Enough," said Neptune. "A man is dead. No time for jest, little time for anything else."

"The man *you* last saw alive, old chap," said Susanoo, eyes sharp over the rim of his glass. "If we've no time for jests, perhaps you've got time to explain why you shouldn't be suspect *numero uno*."

"Because I was the only one who cared about him enough to get him to bed?" Neptune said, stormy-faced. "I took him to his room. I lay him down. I left. I went to walk the grounds. I collected my thoughts. I wish I'd stayed with him, but it's too late now. The bell tolls."

Neptune picked up the skull from before Dionysus' empty seat, and raised it like a bludgeon.

"And if you repeat that insinuation, I will beat you," he said. "If I want a man dead, I'll come at him straight."

"How did he die?" said Minerva, hands twisting and curling her petticoats.

"It actually *was* the Butler," said the Norns. "Somehow his systems have been interfered with. Instead of a simple projection, there was some manner of focused *light*. The records have been purged, but it appears that the beam decapitated him. Dionysus was frozen in the moment of his death. When the projector was turned off, he dispersed."

"This all sounds overwhelmingly technical, so if you'd pardon a question," said Set, "how can you tell this *exactly*?"

"There was a tiny mark where the light focused, directly opposite the projector. A tiny burn. It speaks of light turned to weapons," said Amaterasu. "It's obvious to any creature of light. Amon-Ra agreed with me."

"So either of you pair could have done it?" said Set. "How interesting."

"Oh please!" said Amaterasu. "I... am drama and light. I wouldn't have done it, and I wouldn't have used a machine. I'm more akin to you than—"

"No," interrupted Baal, "you're not. Set's work is about history. Yours is of the moment. Your dramas of light may appeal now, but they are transitory as the substance of which they consist."

"You're wrong," said Woden, firmly. "There is power in light, and it would be foolish for us to ignore it. There is a power in distraction too. Light is needed to cast the shadows. Mine will be long indeed."

"Yes," said the Norns, "and you have firm futurist leanings. If any one of us was going to subvert the system, it would be you."

"Says one futurist to the other," said Woden, gesturing to the mechanical Little Brother floating around the room. "If I could have done it, so could you. We're not too different. Perhaps... two-thirds different."

"Can we just stop this?" snapped Neptune. "We are all smart. We can spout theories. What's the d—— evidence? Where was everyone when Dionysus was murdered?"

"Hey! Let's not leap to conclusions here," said Susanoo. "A weapon implies a killer, but not that the killer was a murderer. Why not suicide? He did seem jolly maudlin." He didn't seem convinced by the argument, but knew someone had to play the part.

Susanoo spoke and everyone ignored him, said Morrigan. *"His words were like branches banging against a window too late at night. Annoying, but not sufficient to make one care enough to crawl from the bed and silence them. Still, come morning or the morning after that, one would take a saw and solve the problem..."*

"Did you hear that? Morrigan's threatening me too now!" said Susanoo. "Or at least I'm pretty sure it was a threat..."

"He's speaking what we all are thinking, Susanoo. It's part of what makes him great," said Neptune, tired. "So, alibis. I've given mine. I have none. What about everyone else?"

The truths were gathered. Minerva and Ananke were in Minerva's room. The smallest god was upset and Ananke was calming her. The Norns and Susanoo were in one of the studies, having a little light conversation on the nature of light. Woden and Set were next door, arguing loudly about the nature of national socialism. Amaterasu was performing in the main hall. She had summoned skeletons of light to create the illusion of a ball. Baal, Morrigan and Amon-Ra watched, though Amon-Ra left five minutes before the Butler reported the murder.

"I did wonder why you left," said Baal. "What was so urgent?"

"I'm in love with Amaterasu," said Amon-Ra. "I love to see her perform. I cannot bear to see her perform. I can only take so much."

Candour, it seemed, was the one thing that disarmed the Pantheon. Neptune clapped his hands together, pleased. "A more convincing alibi than mine, old friend, but it does mean that only you and I are possible suspects..."

"Perhaps," said the Norns. "We live in an age of impossibilities. Still... I think logic dictates how we proceed. The projection system must be deactivated, in case any would try to repeat the method."

Amaterasu thought of all the statues of light filling the building and how sullen the mansion would be without them, and sighed, then felt embarrassed she was so audibly distressed over the loss of such small beauty. Susanoo smiled at her, encouragingly.

"More importantly, we must all stay in couples, at the absolute least," said Urðr. "Murders have only happened when someone has been left alone. If a murder happens while we are paired, there will be only one suspect. If it scares them off? Good. No one dies, and if we can prevent them from striking, we have more time to ascertain the nature of the killer."

"Assuming it is one of us. There are other enemies," said Ananke. "There is always the Great Darkness."

"Yes, yes, yes," said Susanoo. "But I'm less worried about elusive nefarious shadows and more worried by the sea god who promised to bash in my skull with another skull, and Morrigan's threat to do... something with a saw?"

Neptune bristled, but it was Morrigan who stood up. *"Susanoo doesn't understand the work, surprising no one. Morrigan flushed, as half-cut with fury as Susanoo was with drink, hating that he was angry with him. Morrigan alone values men like Susanoo, the average clown, the wonderful average. Normality in all* its majesty is all that matters, and it is a shame that Susanoo's fears make him an enemy, when Morrigan would rather stand with him than those who think themselves better and—"

"Say it!" shouted Susanoo.

"MORRIGAN (embarrassed)," said Morrigan. *"Perhaps Minerva should get to bed. I'll read her a bedtime tale."*

"Goodie!" yelped Minerva.

"I'll join you," said Neptune. "You're annoyed by Susanoo's clowning, which is a fine mark of a man. Plus, I have stories too."

"Baal," said Woden, "this is possibly badly timed, but if we're all sitting around waiting to die, there is a small matter I'd like to take up. You mocked the possibility of film, but I think I can convince you otherwise with some selected—"

"Banalities," said Baal. "It is not possibly badly timed. It is definitely badly timed. However, I'm intrigued. Would anyone like to join us for some of Woden's creaky machines and creakier plotting?"

"Woden told me all about them earlier. I dare say I'd rather die. When you've seen historical epics first-hand, film really does

pale," said Set, "but I would love to see a little of Amaterasu's performance she's so proud of. Would anyone care to join us?"

Susanoo and Amon-Ra both did, surprising no one, least of all themselves.

"It is late, and the commencement of your passing has left me maudlin. I would rather retire," said Ananke. "But there's no one to stay with me..."

"I will," said Urðr. "The other two Norns will ensure everyone is where they claimed."

"Er... aren't you all basically one person? Surely two of you together is basically you being by yourself!" said Susanoo.

"Wrong. We disagree all the time," said Urðr. "Skuld thinks the primary threat to civilisation is pacification via some manner of soporific culture or drugs. Verðandi thinks it's the impulse towards totalitarianism. We are men who chart the future. If we could agree what the future might be, there would be no need for us."

It was decided. The gods returned to the house. The Norns and Woden disconnected the projection system and the electronic brain. The house darkened.

MINERVA SAT ON HER BED, legs dangling, determined to drag out getting ready for bed for as long as possible. She'd managed an hour so far, and the performance seemed to have no end in sight.

"I would really like some ginger beer!" said Minerva. "Or a posset! I do love a posset. Can you make me a posset?"

"To fill you with sugar?" said Neptune, staring out of the window. "You'll never sleep."

"I don't want to sleep! I hate sleeping," said Minerva. "It's like being dead. We'll be *that* soon enough so it feels terribly unfair to have to do it earlier."

Verðandi and Skuld looked in from the doorway. The adults exchanged nods. Minerva waved. The two Norns left.

"They are so creepy," said Minerva, in a

stage whisper.

"They are, but..." Neptune paused, "they are serious men. If you speak to them about the future, you'll get something. Maybe not true, but something to fear, something to be aware of. I'm glad to be dead. I saw one war. To live to see another that's even worse? It would be cruel."

"MORRIGAN (fearfully): Have you changed your mind?" asked Morrigan.

"No," said Neptune, "but I'm considering it, and considering what a man should do to prevent it."

"And what's that?" said Minerva.

"Whatever is required," said Neptune.

He frowned, paused and peered through the window. He squinted a little, confused, and came to a decision.

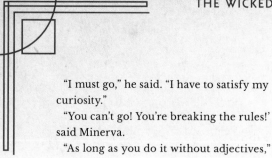

"I must go," he said. "I have to satisfy my curiosity."

"You can't go! You're breaking the rules!' said Minerva.

"As long as you do it without adjectives," said Neptune, stomping out, "there are no rules for a man."

Morrigan and Minerva exchanged glances. "*Now* can I have a posset?" she asked.

THE HALL-AS-BALLROOM WAS A STAGE. Amaterasu filled it with dreams. It was half performance, half new life. It was wonderful. She was wonderful, and ever more wonderful, a sun turning supernova. She bowed, brow wet, a stage-smile on her face, and stepped down for a break. Amon-Ra seized the moment, and took her aside.

Amon-Ra had been her lover. He knew her. He knew when she was happy, that radiance that seemed to burn through her skin. He knew when she was sad, the cloud covering its brilliance. He knew when she lied, as she did when she said there was no one else, as she did when she said she'd love him forever, as she did today, when she said she was in her room when Lucifer was murdered.

The god of the sun asked the god of the sun where she had been.

She swallowed, looked him in the eye and told him.

Amon-Ra took his seat when she started the next act of her performance. To his credit, he managed almost three minutes before leaving.

Outside the mansion, a storm broke.

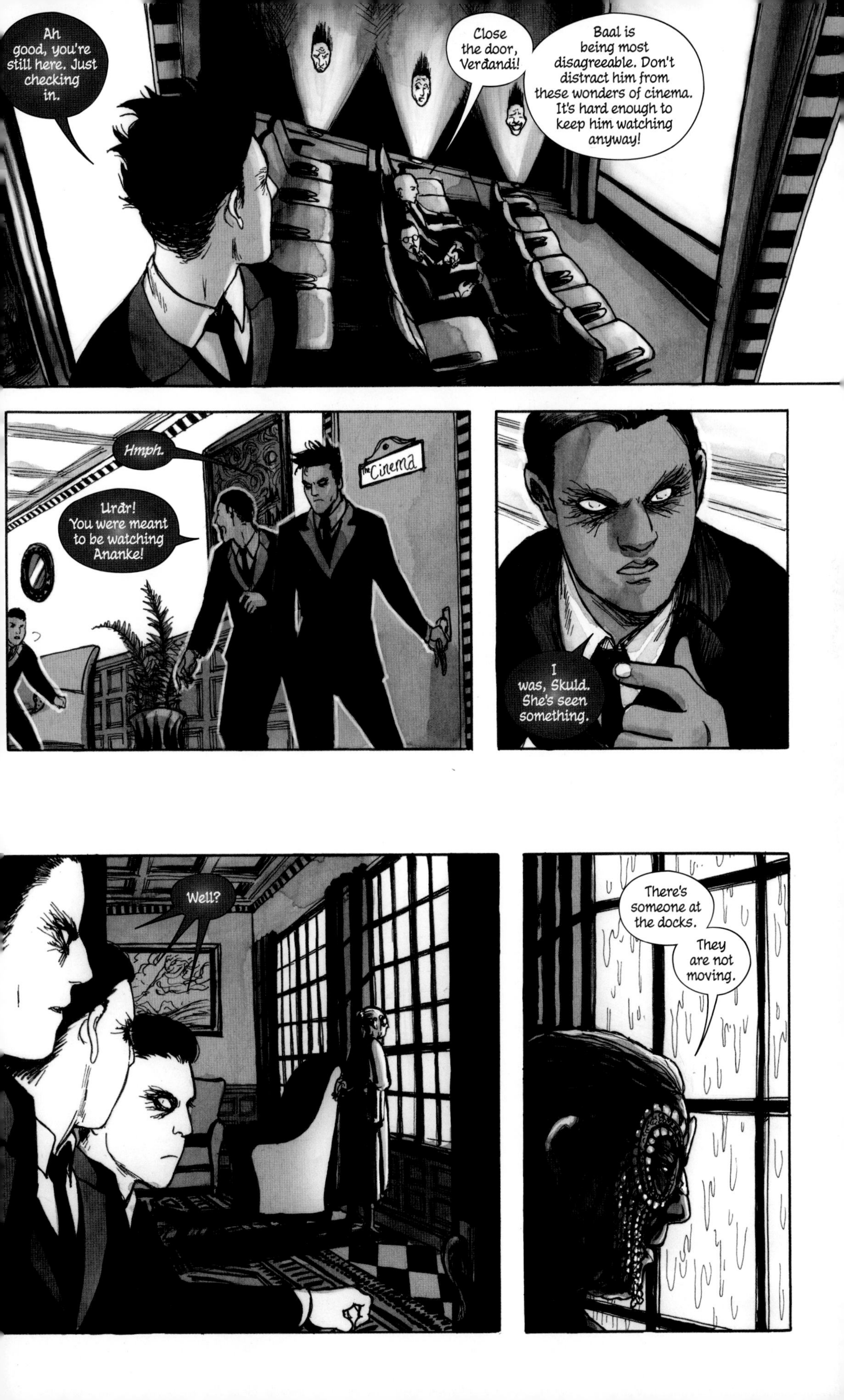
Ah good, you're still here. Just checking in.
Close the door, Verdandi!
Baal is being most disagreeable. Don't distract him from these wonders of cinema. It's hard enough to keep him watching anyway!
Hmph.
The Cinema
Urdr! You were meant to be watching Ananke!
I was, Skuld. She's seen something.
Well?
There's someone at the docks.
They are not moving.

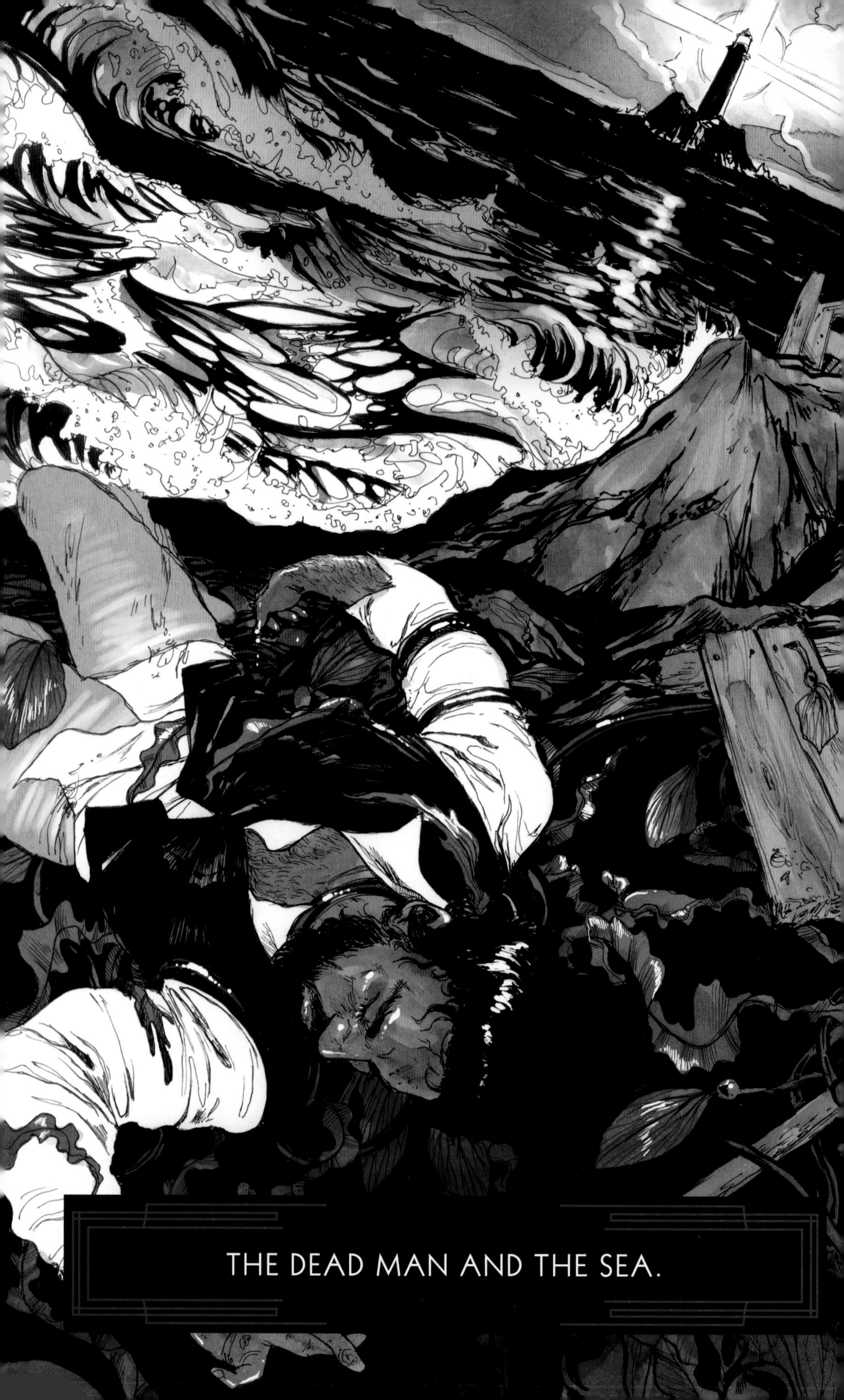
THE DEAD MAN AND THE SEA.

4

NEPTUNE'S CORPSE LAY SPRAWLED and broken on the rocks. It was a terrible vision, framed by the debris of the dock and his ship, lashed by rain from the still furious heavens. The Norns and Ananke had made their way down from the mansion, silently, urgently. The three men and their mechanism studied the body as if they were witches around a cauldron, or Neptune was a sacrificial lamb in whose entrails they could divine the future, or at least the near past.

"He drowned," said the Norns, flatly. "I always said he should have learnt to swim."

That the god of the sea couldn't swim would be a surprise to any who had not sat with him in a bar in Venice, throwing back drinks, and sharing stories. "To learn to swim would be to imply the sea might rebel," Neptune said. "A man's mastery is what matters. My tools. My will. The spray in my face. It is joy."

Beneath his corpse eyes, brine dripped from his open mouth.

"We should gather the others," said Ananke, still on the steps up to the mansion, seemingly happy to be the audience.

The Norns looked up, out to sea, to the north. Bleak. The lighthouse kept its silent vigil. The Norns murmured a three-voiced, "Hmm."

"No," said the Norns. "This is an opportunity for clear thought and action. With us, Ananke. We need to talk."

They headed back up the path. After one final look back towards the corpse, Ananke followed.

THE MANSION WAS LIFELESS, seemingly more haunted now that the ghosts of light had been banished. The Norns led Ananke to a study, lit its open fire. Ananke settled in her tall chair, hands curling around the arm-rests. The Norns paced in a circle, like if they were a cog in some manner of mechanical brain, trying to calculate an answer.

"Speak of what troubles you, my Norns?" said Ananke.

"The mystery and the solving of it," they said. "We think we are close to the murderer."

"Oh," said Ananke, "that's interesting. I admit, I find myself somewhat lost. Perhaps you could enlighten me?"

"We can, as we have removed you from the list of suspects," said the Norns. "You were with Urðr when Neptune died, so we can talk together... and we may divine the murderer from the facts."

"I hope so," said Ananke. "This has gone on so long."

The Norns stopped their circling and sat in three seats in three motions. They leaned forward, a three-formed study of the great detective. They seemed confident. Ananke was not.

"I cannot see how we are closer," said Ananke. "Neptune's ship was destroyed when he was sailing. Surely any of the gods could do that?"

"Yes, obviously," said the Norns, "but there was a storm. A somewhat suspiciously sudden storm. That would speak of the mastery of the skies."

"Susanoo and Baal are our party of storm gods. Perhaps Set, though she is difficult. All could have done it, but they were being watched," said Ananke. "This becomes most difficult. I believe you checked everyone's alibis, yes?"

"Baal was with Woden in the projection theatre. Susanoo and Set were with the larger party watching Amaterasu's displays of living people," said Skuld.

"We can't be sure they were in the hall. It's possible that Amaterasu made a living statue of them," said Urðr.

"Susanoo made a few jokes. Set referenced a party in Babylon. They were there," said Skuld.

"But I didn't speak to Baal," said Verðandi. "Baal was silent throughout our visit to the picture theatre. He even watched Woden's film without comment. To go so long without critique is unusual in him…"

"That was the one room where the building's light statue system was still operating. The cinematic projection system wouldn't work otherwise. One who knew the system well could create a facsimile…" said Skuld.

"Are you sure Woden could manage such a feat?" said Ananke.

"Yes," said the Norns, at once. "*We* could have done it, and we *don't* know the system well."

"So… am I in the room with the killer?" said Ananke, guardedly.

"Yes, you should be more careful," said Urðr. "We are a prime suspect. Our abilities are sufficient for many of the murderer's tasks. The only reason why we removed ourselves from the list of possible culprits is that we know we are not the murderer."

"Oh, I am so relieved," said Ananke. "Then who do you suspect?"

"Woden," said the Norns, "who clearly built this mansion."

"I thought it was Lucifer?" said Ananke.

"The art and design is Lucifer's," said Urðr, "but the technology that underpins it? No. Never. Look at the Metropolitan servant's casings, the projectors, the tubing on the docks. I was immediately struck by how closely it all matched the gilded curves of his grotesque submarine. Woden may as well have signed this mansion, it's so obvious to a trained eye."

"It is suspicious that he didn't admit to having a hand in it, especially given his grandiosity of character, but Woden and Baal can't possibly be responsible." said Ananke. "Both had alibis for the murder of Lucifer. Woden was with you and Baal wasn't even on the island. He was with Set, landing her ship. Amon-Ra saw him."

"Think! Think it through!" said the Norns, frustrated. "Amon-Ra saw Baal aboard Set's ship… but he didn't see Set. We heard Set and Woden arguing, but only have their word they were both actually there…"

"What are you suggesting?" said Ananke.

"It's quite simple," said the Norns. "We have Set, who claimed to be arguing with Woden, when Woden could be using his mastery of the building's projectors to kill Dionysus. We have Woden, who claimed to be watching a projected narrative with Baal, when Baal could have been bringing the rage of the storm against Neptune. And Baal, who claimed that Set was dressing herself, when she was secretly already on the island, killing Lucifer…"

The study door opened.

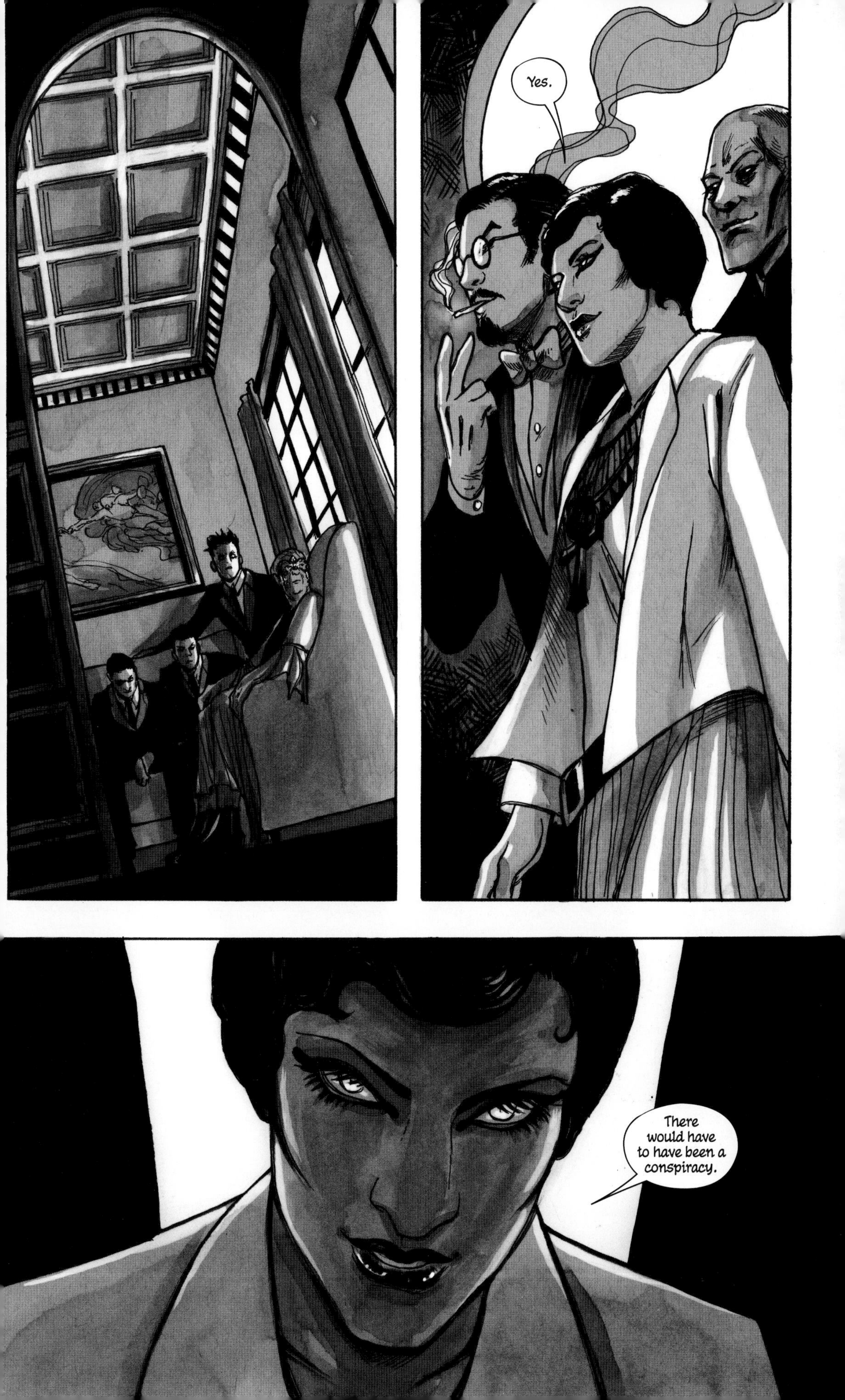
Yes.
There would have to have been a conspiracy.

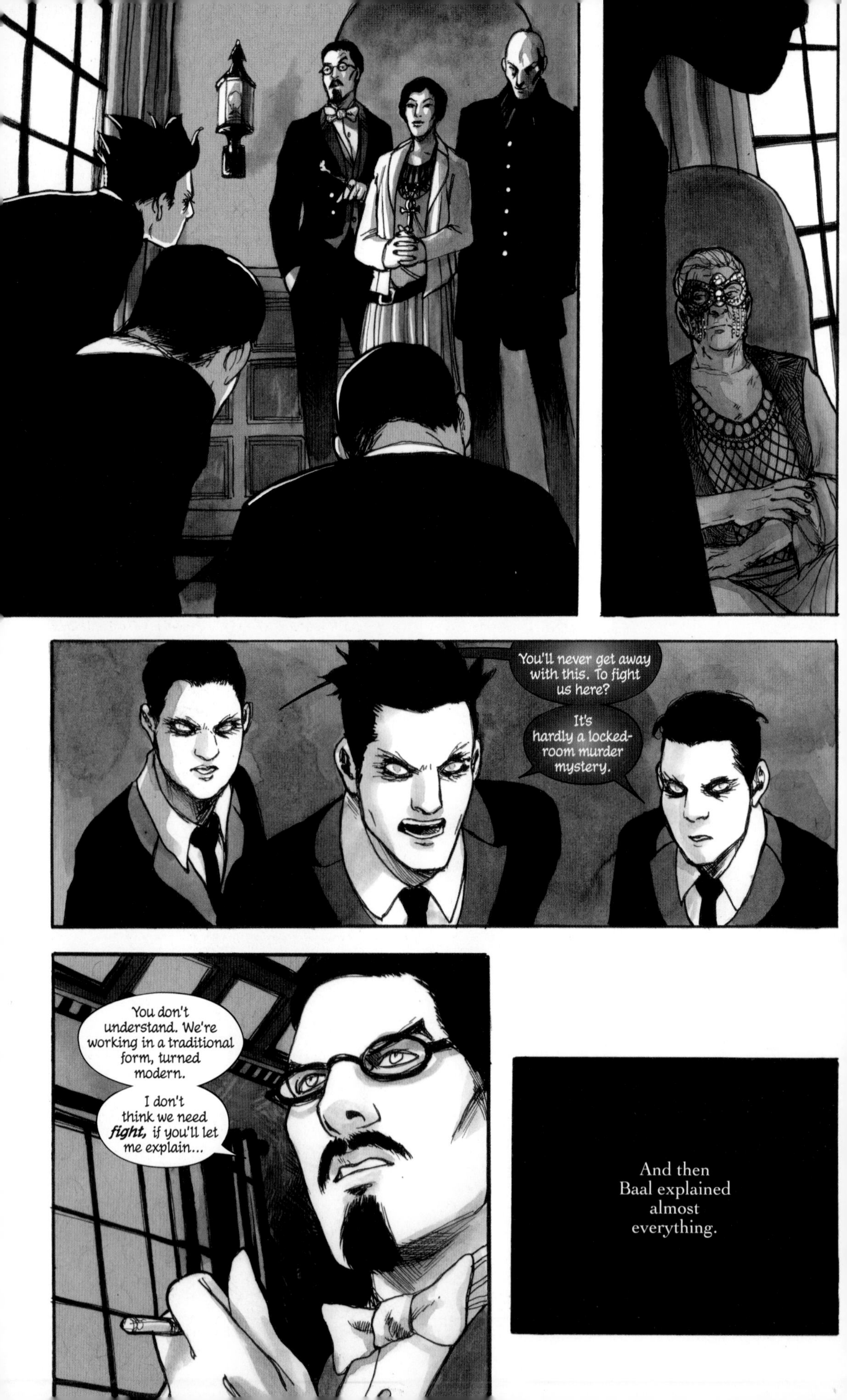
You'll never get away with this. To fight us here?
It's hardly a locked-room murder mystery.
You don't understand. We're working in a traditional form, turned modern.
I don't think we need *fight,* if you'll let me explain...
And then Baal explained almost everything.

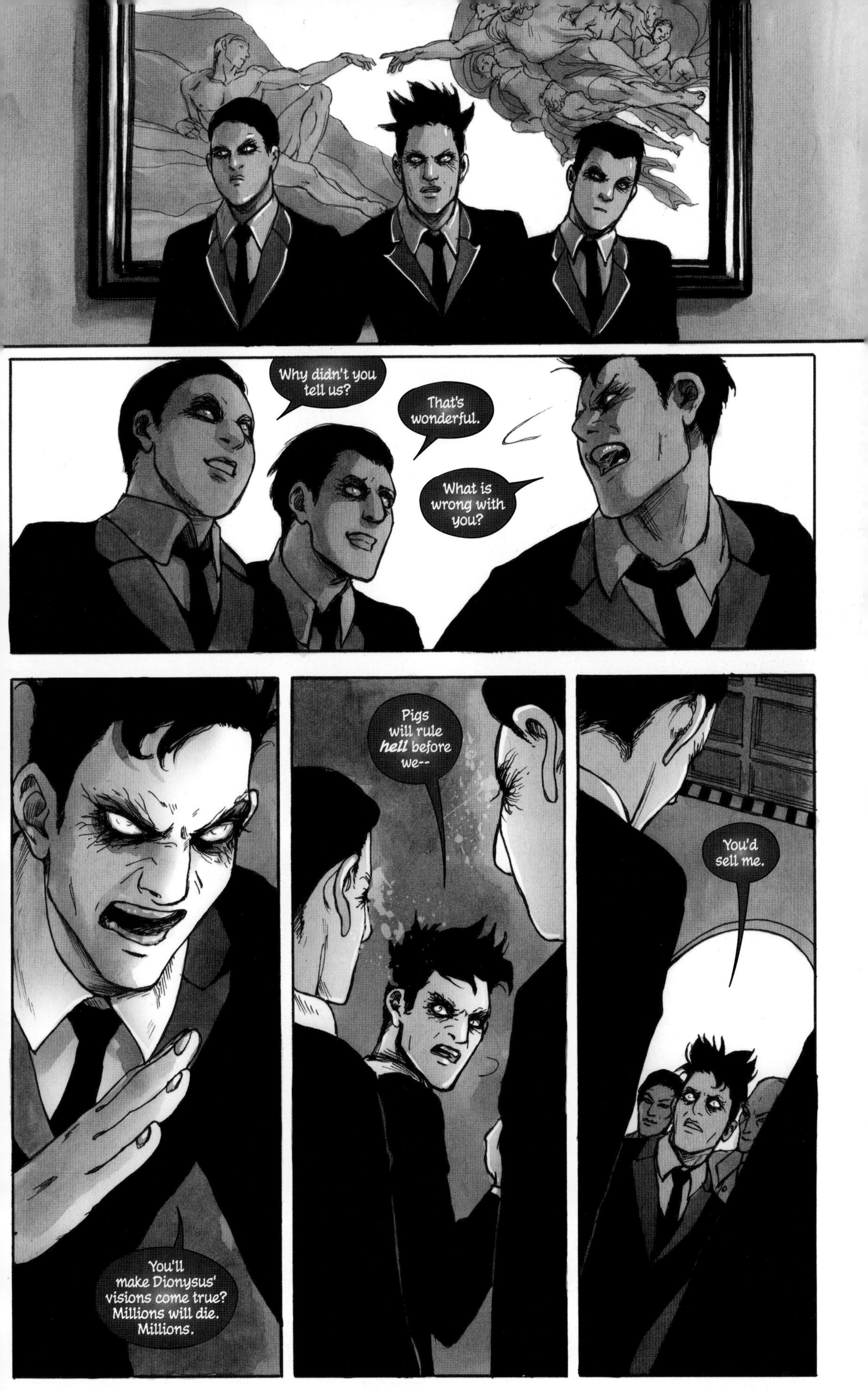
Why didn't you tell us?
That's wonderful.
What is wrong with you?
You'll make Dionysus' visions come true? Millions will die. Millions.
Pigs will rule **hell** before we--
You'd sell me.

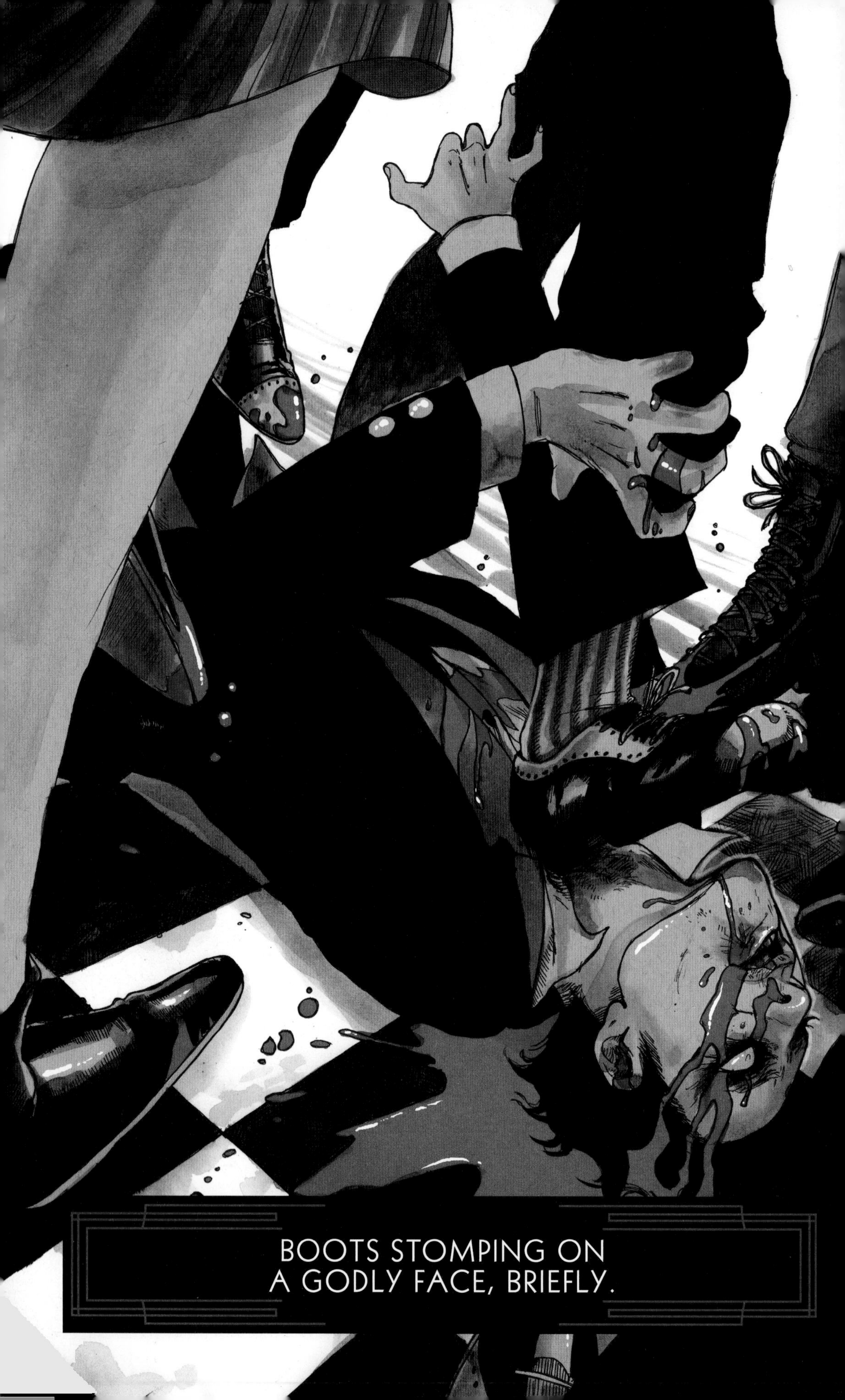
BOOTS STOMPING ON A GODLY FACE, BRIEFLY.

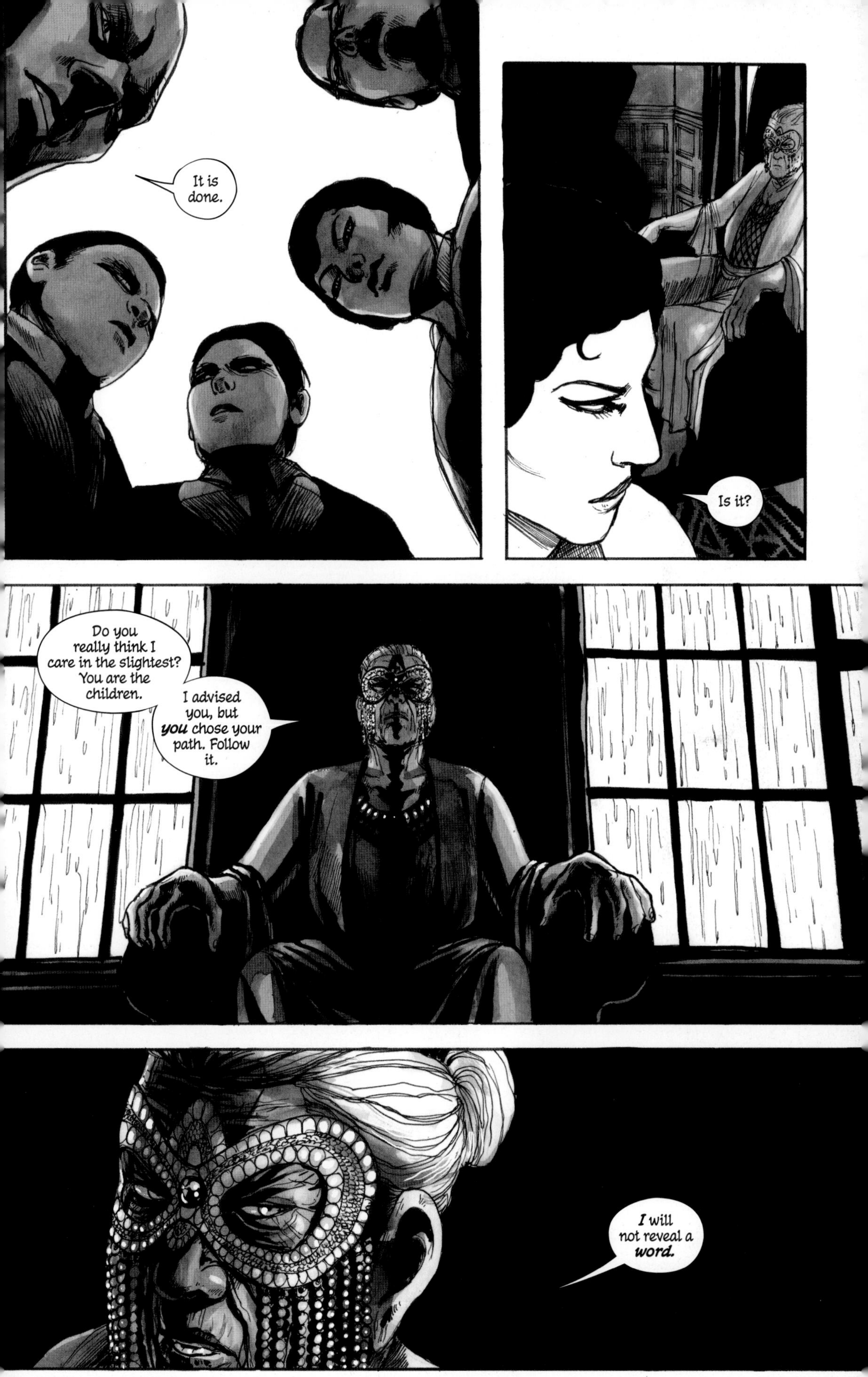
It is done.
Is it?
Do you really think I care in the slightest? You are the children.
I advised you, but **you** chose your path. Follow it.
I will not reveal a ***word.***

5

MINERVA RAN.

She had to get to the main hall. The gods had to know. They had to act. Cold stone busts of gods long dead watched accusingly.

The clock tick-tocked its warning as she ran past, petticoats raised, feet in a frenzy. Quick! Quick! Quick!

Never enough time.

THE HALL WAS FULL OF LIGHT. Amaterasu had done this twice before. By her third performance, she knew this space and filled it. Her light-summoned dancers moved in silence, conducted by gentle twists of her fingers. In their arms, they miraculously carried empty chairs, a romance of luminescence and carpentry. Susanoo watched, enrapt. Amon-Ra likewise. Amaterasu was lost in her art, the little theatre just for the delight of her friends. When she performed, she thought everyone her friend. They came to the darkened space to see the light and be transported. She smiled to herself, and wished it was always as simple as it was in these moments. She allowed herself the sentimentality of the urge: she wished it could go on forever.

Minerva ran into the room and screamed.

A room full of people vanished, two dozen chairs falling to the floor. A couple shattered, scattering splinters across the marble.

Minerva had stopped in the doorway, alone, tears on her face, news in her mouth.

"They killed Verðandi!"

Susanoo rushed over, so quickly it almost appeared to be a pratfall.

"They?"

"I was walking over here and passed the study," she said. "I saw Set and Baal and nasty old Woden go in and I think they've killed Neptune too! Poor Neptune! I didn't hear what they said. But the two Norns joined the baddies, and they stomped Mr Verðandi to death. And then I ran here and..."

She erupted into tears, throwing her arms around Susanoo, hiding her face in his waistcoat.

"Oh, this is all so awful," she bawled. "What are we going to do?"

The three older gods glanced between each other. Baal and Woden had arrived some minutes earlier, entering into conversation with Set before the trio left quietly. Baal hadn't even made a comment about the silliness of Amaterasu's performance. That should have been a clue.

"Stay here. If I don't come back, you can assume it's true," said Amon-Ra, heading towards the door.

"I'm almost glad," said Susanoo, looking towards Amaterasu. "When I covered for you not being in your room, I did wonder if I was an accessory to murder. When a feller says he'll do anything for a girl, he hopes it doesn't stretch to something like that. What *were* you doing?"

"She was—," said Amon-Ra at the doorway, and stopped, looking at Amaterasu for permission. She nodded.

"She was speaking to Ananke on the matter of marriage between brother and sister gods," he said, "and whether the godly part matters more than being unrelated as mortals."

Amon-Ra left. He had nothing else to say.

"What did she say?" said Susanoo, quiet, perhaps for the first time.

"She said that gods make our own rules, and no one can judge us," said Amaterasu, burning.

Susanoo took Amaterasu's hand, then blushed.

"I don't have a ring," said Susanoo, weakly, "or a future."

"At least Till Death Do Us Part is easier," said Amaterasu. She turned, her eyes bright as lanterns. She projected beams of light onto the marble, showing two monochrome rings. Susanoo reached into the image, and withdrew the flickering circles of silvered gold. He slid a ring on her finger. She slid a ring on his. They hung on their skin for a second, then twinkled away.

"You know, I'm not sure if this is weird or romantic or both. Both, I think," ventured Minerva, seemingly soothed by the melodrama, "but, er, shouldn't we be doing something about the baddies? I feel awful about not guessing. Mr Baal's sneaky beard should have been a clue. Baddies do like their sneaky beards."

"It's Judgement Day," said Amon-Ra, returning. "Verðandi is dead. They're gone."

"I told you!" said Minerva.

"There is the question of why were you wandering the corridors by yourself," said Amon-Ra. "We were meant to stick together."

"M... Morrigan," Minerva said. "He said he wanted to be alone. At least, I think he did. He is jolly hard to understand at times."

The gods exchanged glances.

Minerva looked somewhat shamefaced.

"Was that a mistake?" she said.

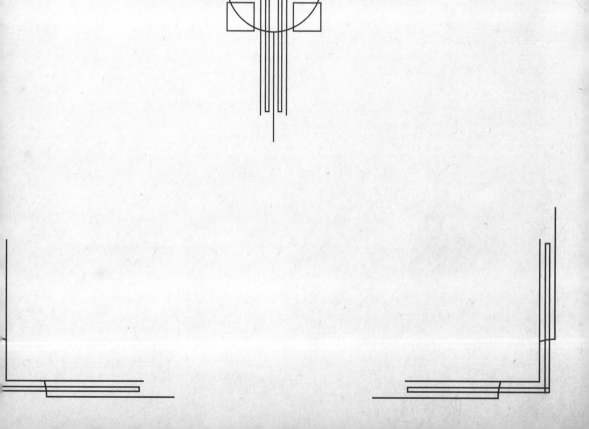

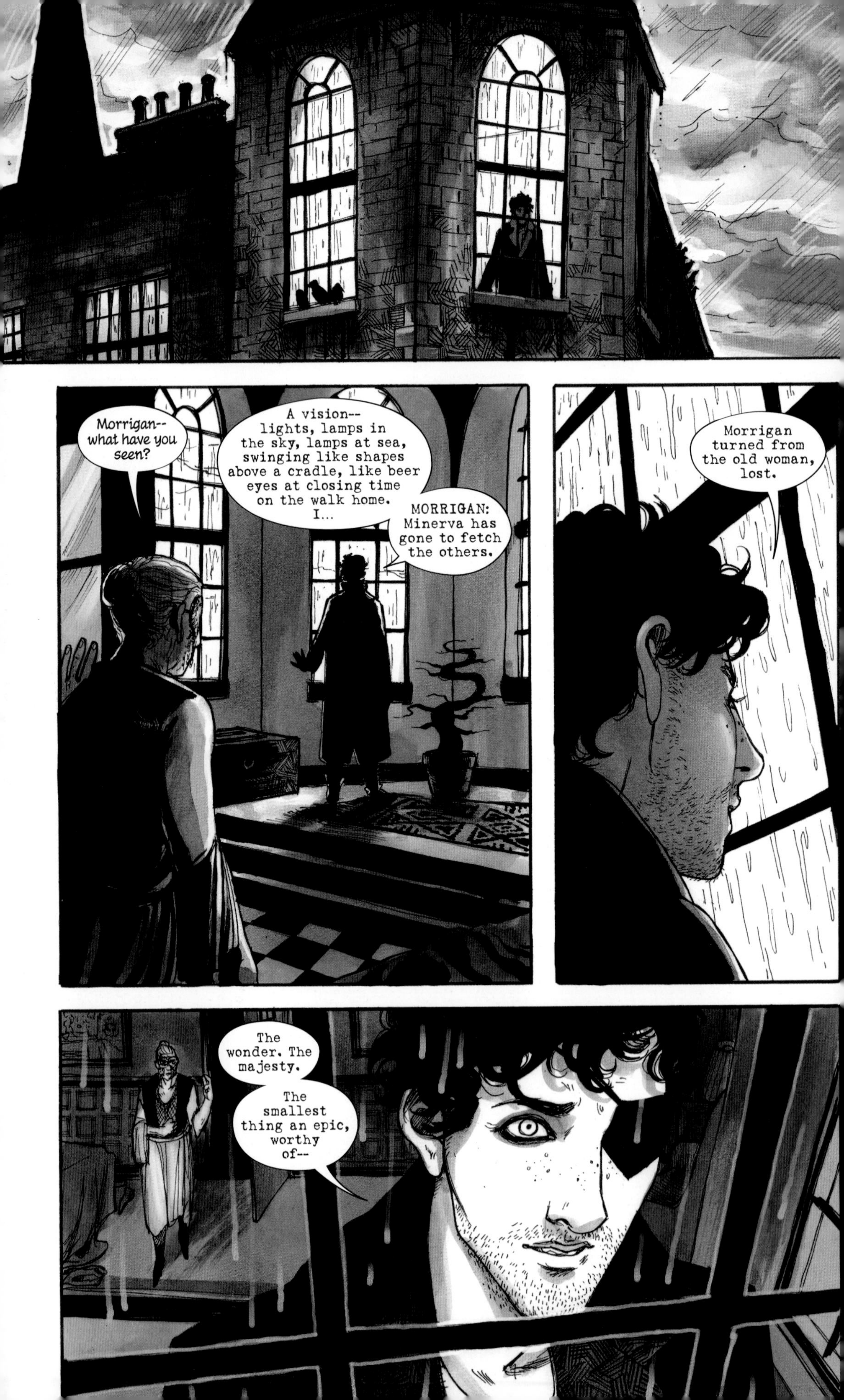
Morrigan--what have you seen?
A vision--lights, lamps in the sky, lamps at sea, swinging like shapes above a cradle, like beer eyes at closing time on the walk home. I...
MORRIGAN: Minerva has gone to fetch the others.
Morrigan turned from the old woman, lost.
The wonder. The majesty.
The smallest thing an epic, worthy of--

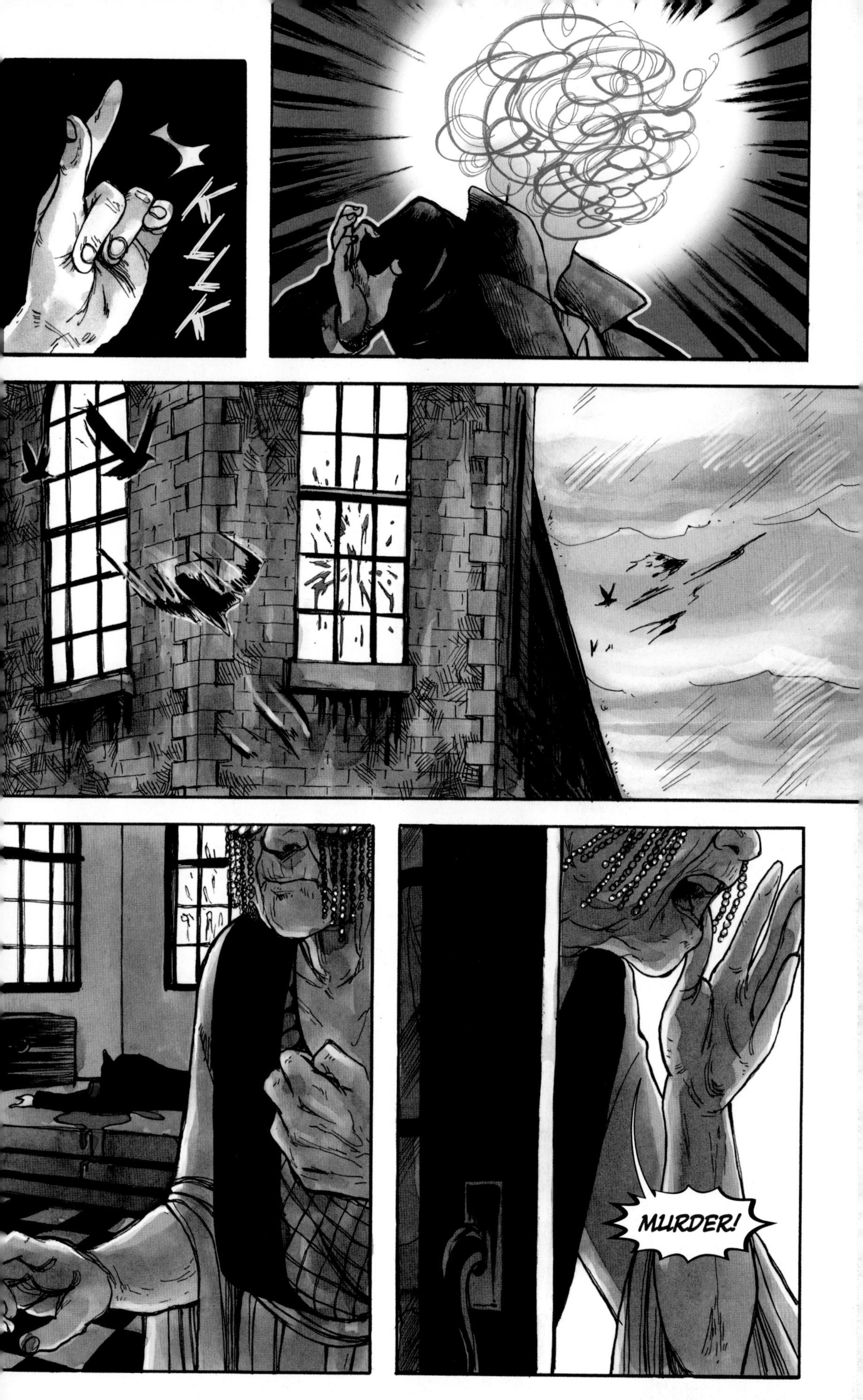
KLLK
MURDER!

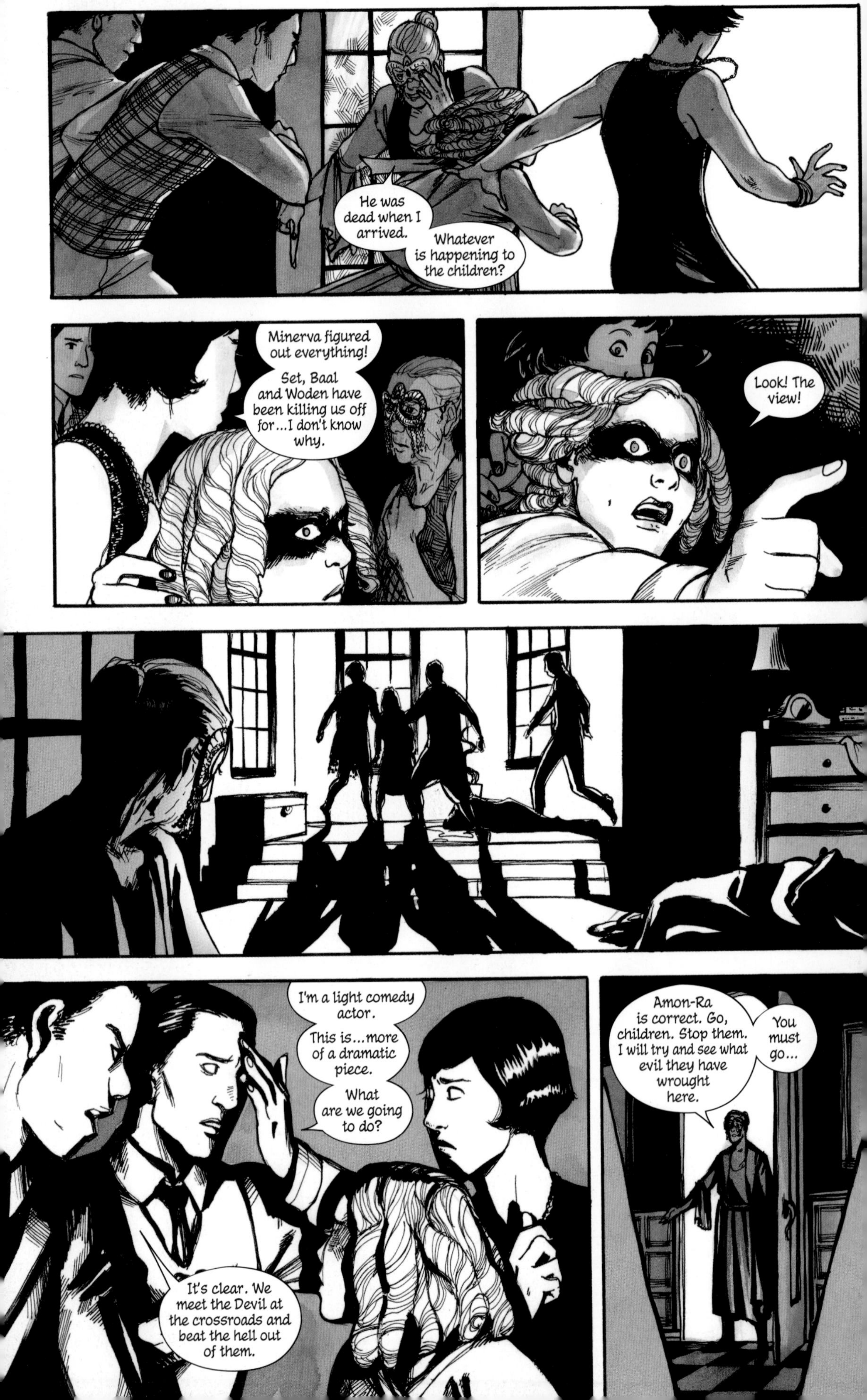
He was dead when I arrived.
Whatever is happening to the children?
Minerva figured out everything!
Set, Baal and Woden have been killing us off for...I don't know why.
Look! The view!
I'm a light comedy actor.
This is...more of a dramatic piece.
What are we going to do?
It's clear. We meet the Devil at the crossroads and beat the hell out of them.
Amon-Ra is correct. Go, children. Stop them. I will try and see what evil they have wrought here.
You must go...

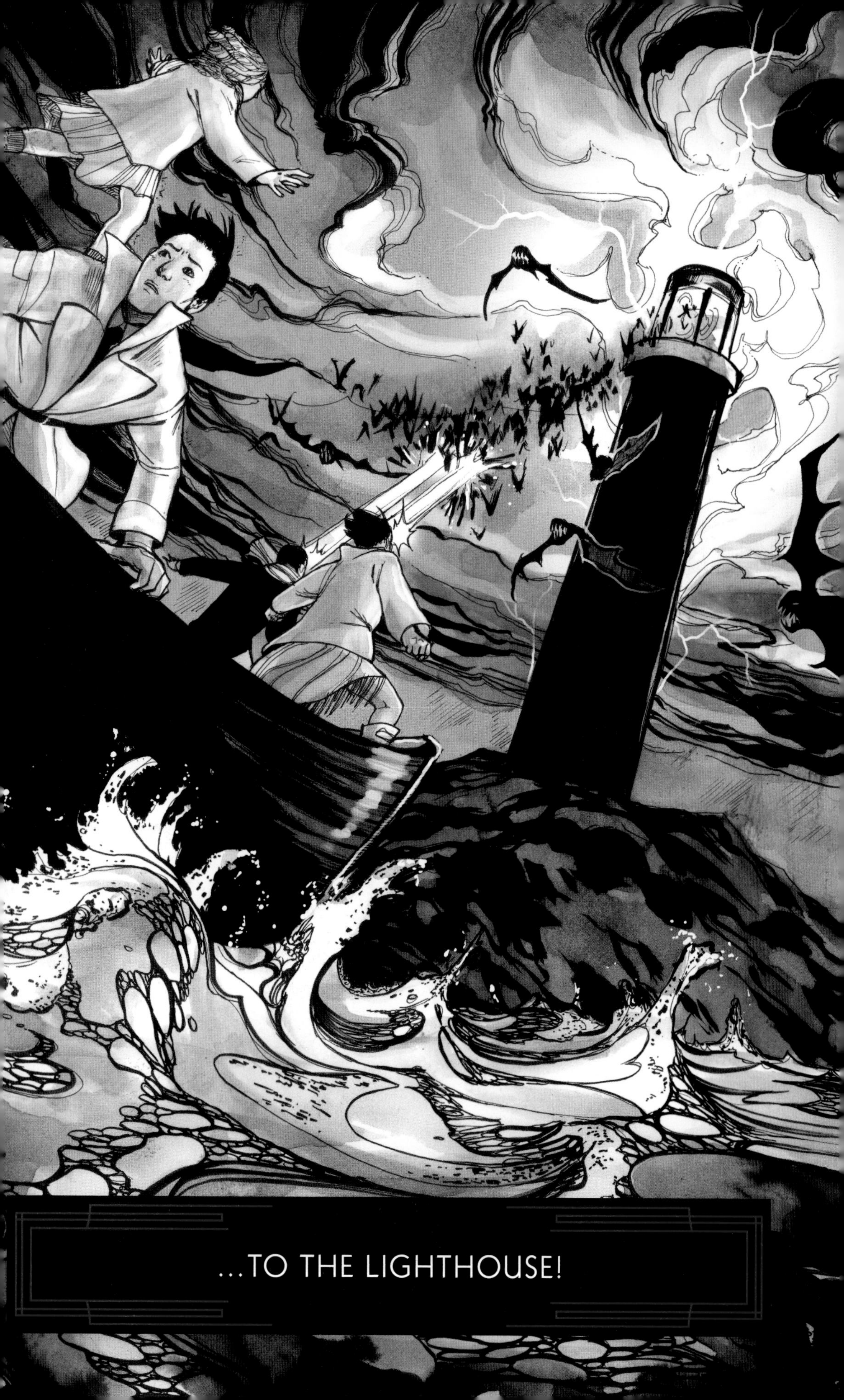
...TO THE LIGHTHOUSE!

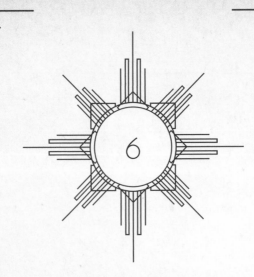

6

THE LIGHTHOUSE SHOOK, Baal's storm a frenzied lash at its walls. Eldritch energies snaked through the stonework, like mortar dredged up from hell. The lighthouse was little more than its shell, its original floors having been torn away to make room for Woden's machinery. At the base, a squat terminal sat with a crystal finger pointing aggressively upwards. Far above it, a sister crystal mounted where the lamp should have been. Above the lighthouse, danced... what? Words failed to truly describe what the eyes failed to truly see.

Instead of a light, the impossible opposite: an ebony luminescence with streaks of blue beyond blue. As much as Set and Baal would have loathed to admit it, it was beyond their gifts to describe. The machine was leeching this force from the heavens. In the midst of the uncanny storm there almost seemed to be a figure forming...

The gods gathered around the machine, studying how it almost *distilled* the sky. Woden was outside, harrying the approach of the gods of light. The remaining two Norns worked the controls, a frenzy of hands, as if two could do with sufficient effort what three had achieved without. Baal watched, measured, judged. Set amused herself by what Lucifer would have surely described as "swatting" the head of Lucifer. It was a poor choice of words. "Swatting" was too much. It was barely a tap, sufficient to send it bobbing back and forth on the string that suspended it from the machine.

With a tug she tore it down, and rolled it into a corner. The head was an unnecessary trophy she should put firmly behind her. She had played with the boy enough.

Woden rejoined them, slamming the door to the lighthouse. He had released the last of his bats, their awful jagged wings almost like a grotesque parody of an old Hindu symbol of good fortune.

"They're coming. We need to finish, quickly," said Woden.

"To quote Leonardo: art is never finished, only abandoned," said Baal, "and we are almost done. The moment is ours."

"And the future!" said the Norns, caught up in the excitement.

Baal and Set exchanged scowls. They heard the exclamation mark and shuddered. Verðandi was their enemy, but at least he had taste... still, the Norns served their purpose for now.

In their position, Set would have loathed that the idea wasn't solely her own, but inspired by another. She knew Ananke had no idea what she was setting in motion. Baal and Set had despaired for the future. What they loved was being debased. Art was holy, the poet a king. They had seen the performances of gods such as Amaterasu and Susanoo, and thought them little better than vaudevillians. But the crowds lapped them up, these swarms of semi-literate clerks filling the libraries... Art was higher culture, and it was impossible to soar with so many people dragging them down. The hordes were quicksand of the soul.

They saw the direction in which the masses were shambling. They were heading whichever way the crowd's momentary desires would take them, and away from the rightful elite. That the age of mass literacy should lead to the end of literature was a sharp irony, but a far from pleasing one.

Their dissatisfaction was enough that Ananke had warned them. "Gods are inspiration," she said. "Your desires will shape the future anyway. You should not try to go further. The spirit of the age belongs to all of you. None of you should try to possess her." She had seen those who would sacrifice their peers to siphon their power and reshape the ghost of the times, but it never ended well. "Murdering your fraternity is an abomination," she warned.

"Perhaps", said Baal, later, when they were alone. "But a necessary one."

They would die for art in any case. Killing for art was far easier. Baal and Set were agreed. They would murder their peers and use the energies to shape the spirit of the age more to their liking.

Woden was recruited later, a simple tool. His silly little Teutonic beliefs were a useful structure. A totalitarianism was required, as democracy would clearly fail. There was even some irony in the way he would conquer the masses. This living light which Amaterasu and Susanoo were so fond of would rule the coming century, but it could so easily be used simply to control. The elite would craft a lesser art to bewitch the masses. It'd keep them in their correct place, and not give them any ideas above their station which, at least as far as Set and Baal saw it, meant any ideas at all.

They came to an arrangement. Woden would provide the means to warp this zeitgeist. Baal and Set would provide the ideas. All would perform the deed.

Lucifer had been the easiest to manipulate. He was smitten with Set. Before it was stripped bare, Set had lived in her private retreat in this lighthouse, her personal ivory tower. He came calling, and she challenged him. Show us what manner of man you are. The climbing little wretch tried so hard with his bauble of a mansion. As if she would care about such silly things,

but it provided the perfect way to conceal Woden's workings.

If any gods died on the island, the conspirators could use that power to lure the spirit of the age to the lighthouse and reforge it in their image.

But which gods to kill?

Lucifer knew most, and it was possible he may see past his vanity and desire. He had to be the first. In death, at least, he was useful to Set. He died with a fool's smile. There are worse fates.

They thought they would have to kill Ananke but, when the gods shared their alibis and she blithered about mysteries being for them, they understood her subtext. Ananke was washing her hands of them. They had, if not permission, at least a blind eye.

After that it was a case of grasping opportunities. They would have preferred one of the new world gods of light—after all, murder is the most sincere form of criticism. Alas, their little clique stuck together and would not be separated.

Conversely Dionysus, confused and alone, seemed almost too easy. Besides... his prophesying had disturbed the three. Totalitarianism would mean war with the democracies, and anyone who read the papers would realise that war would be terrible, if necessary. Perhaps if left alone he would have realised their involvement? Better he die, with Woden's beams of light shredding his flesh.

The next choice was made for them. Neptune's bellicosity took him to the lighthouse. The machine was active. The lighthouse was alive, venting arcs of crackling light, and draping itself with a queer miasma. Nothing compared to its present magnificence, but noticeable to the attentive eye. Perhaps Neptune saw it. Perhaps. It was as likely his drive would take him to the lighthouse simply to see what was there. He had no idea of the old world sophistication he was dealing with. Perhaps he thought himself great, his trip to the new world a chance to find a grand story? There is nothing novel or great in the Americas, thought Baal as he smashed Neptune's boat, drowned him and dragged him to the dock to breathe his last. Baal had a moment of doubt afterwards, standing over the broken body. Consider Neptune. Once handsome and tall. Now dead. It only reminded him how little time there was remaining and how swiftly he had to act.

Two-thirds of the Norns were sold into the conspiracy. They liked conspiracies. They felt the future needed organisation, and by warping the spirit of the future, they'd achieve it. Baal, Set and Woden hadn't said what death and war there would be along the way, perhaps including civilisation burned back to a reasonable size in atomic fire... but they didn't need to know that. Verðandi alone saw the dangers, but Verðandi saw dangers in all things. Of course they didn't believe him when they should have. The Norns' war was far from civil.

Four deaths. That would be sufficient. They'd tame the spirit and the future would be a future worth leaving behind...

Set and Baal shared a fey smile, and toasted one another's brilliance.

"It's working," shouted Woden over the machines' scream. Lightning darted from the swirling skies, cloaking the lighthouse's tip with a feral energy. Now would be the sensible time to be afraid, considered Set, too delighted by the vision to dream of ever doing so. This wild child of the times was theirs. The machine would twist her to their purposes...

The lighthouse burst into darkness one last time, the machine's crystal shuddering, and then it was done. A figure fell from far above, colliding with the machine and then was drawn into it. The energy above faded, like a light bulb's afterglow. It was done.

"And so it begins," said Woden, proudly. "We—"

Woden was the only one touching the machine at that moment. A crackle ran through his body, his skeleton visible through thick leather. With a scream, he started to unravel. This was not according to plan. Woden was not meant to die.

Baal didn't care. Neither did Set. While the Norns were horrified, they shrugged. It was done. The spirit was their spirit, and the world would be formed of their ideas, not those of the gods of the failing light. What's another death when they were prepared to plunge the world into war to ensure a world worth living in emerged? Destroy a world. Make a world.

"This is the way the world ends," said Baal, "because we say so."

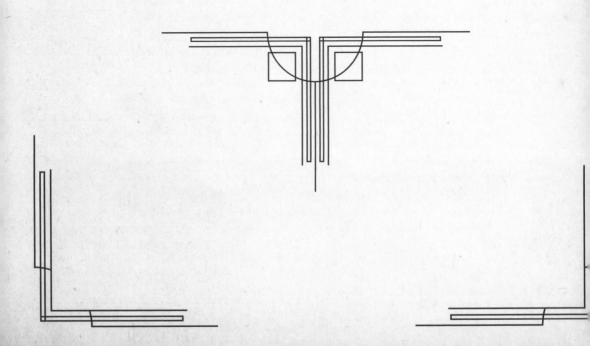

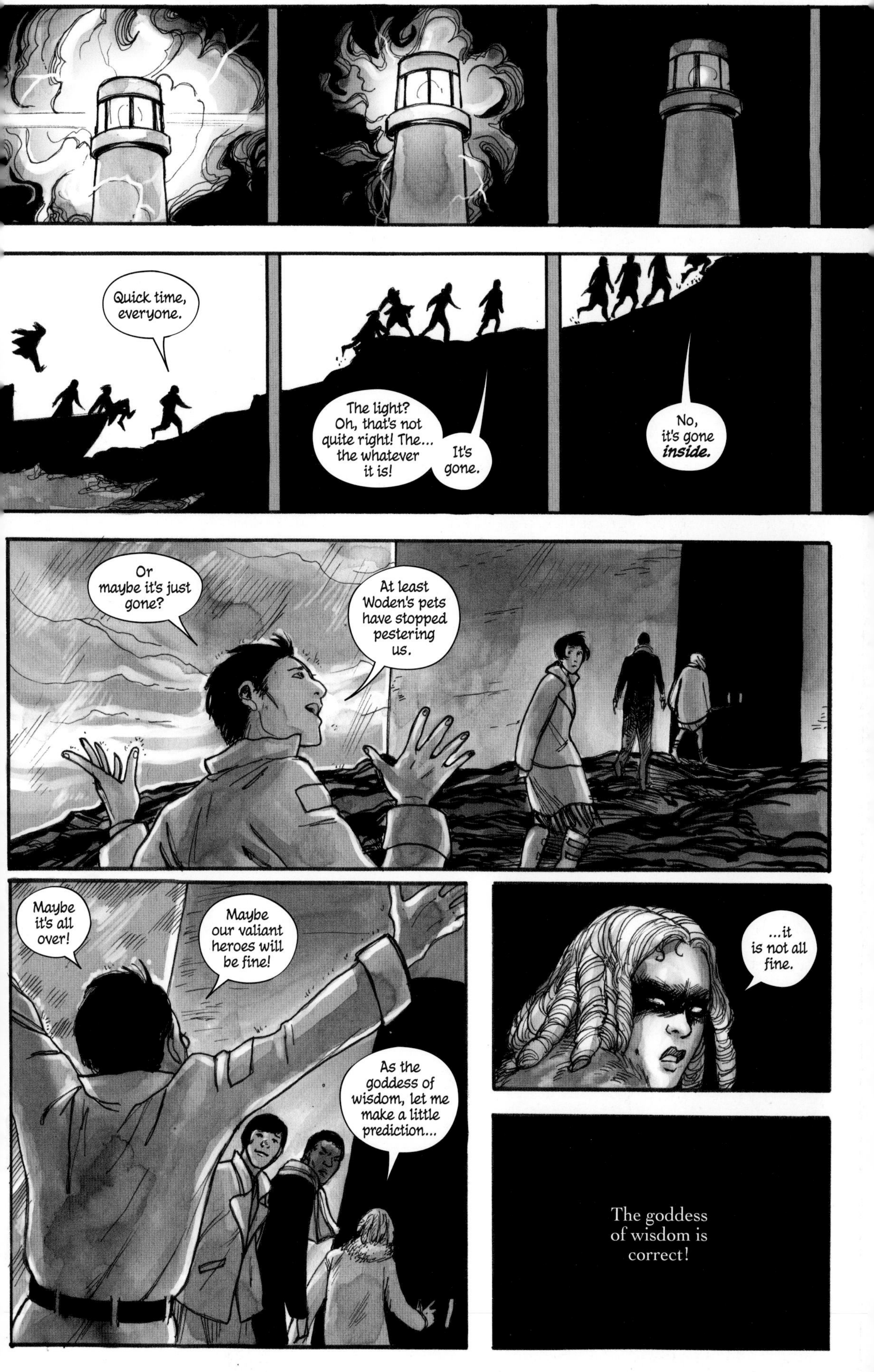
Quick time, everyone.
The light? Oh, that's not quite right! The... the whatever it is!
It's gone.
No, it's gone *inside.*
Or maybe it's just gone?
At least Woden's pets have stopped pestering us.
Maybe it's all over!
Maybe our valiant heroes will be fine!
As the goddess of wisdom, let me make a little prediction...
...it is not all fine.
The goddess of wisdom is correct!

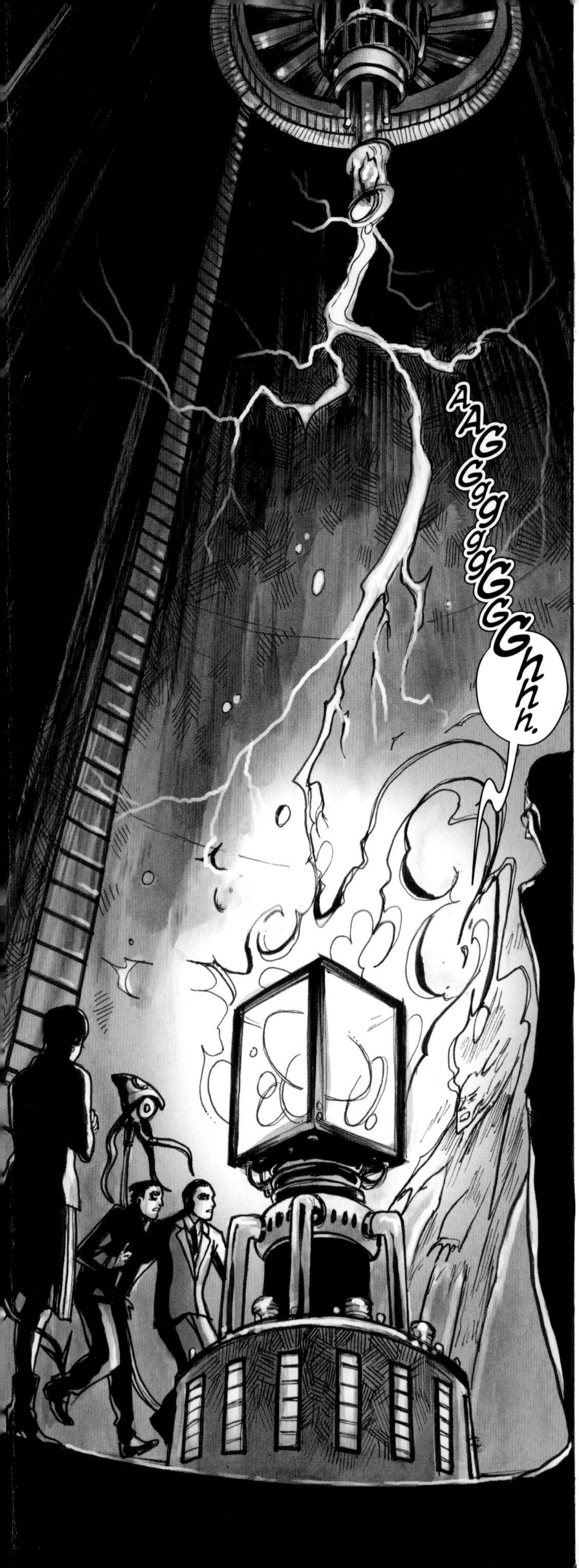
AAGGgggGGGhhh.

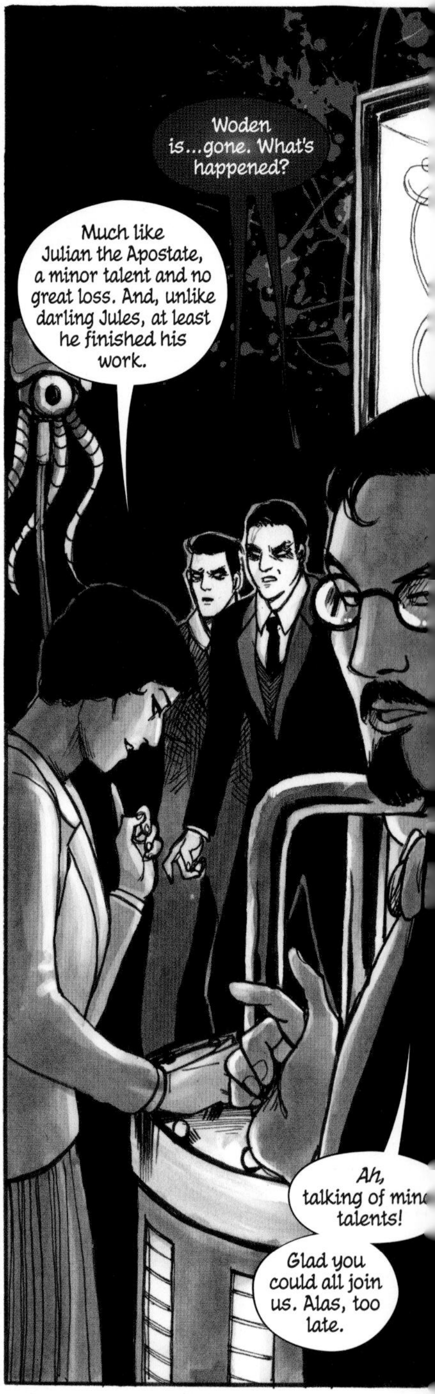
Woden is...gone. What's happened?
Much like Julian the Apostate, a minor talent and no great loss. And, unlike darling Jules, at least he finished his work.
Ah, talking of mino
talents!
Glad you could all join us. Alas, too late.

But too late for what?

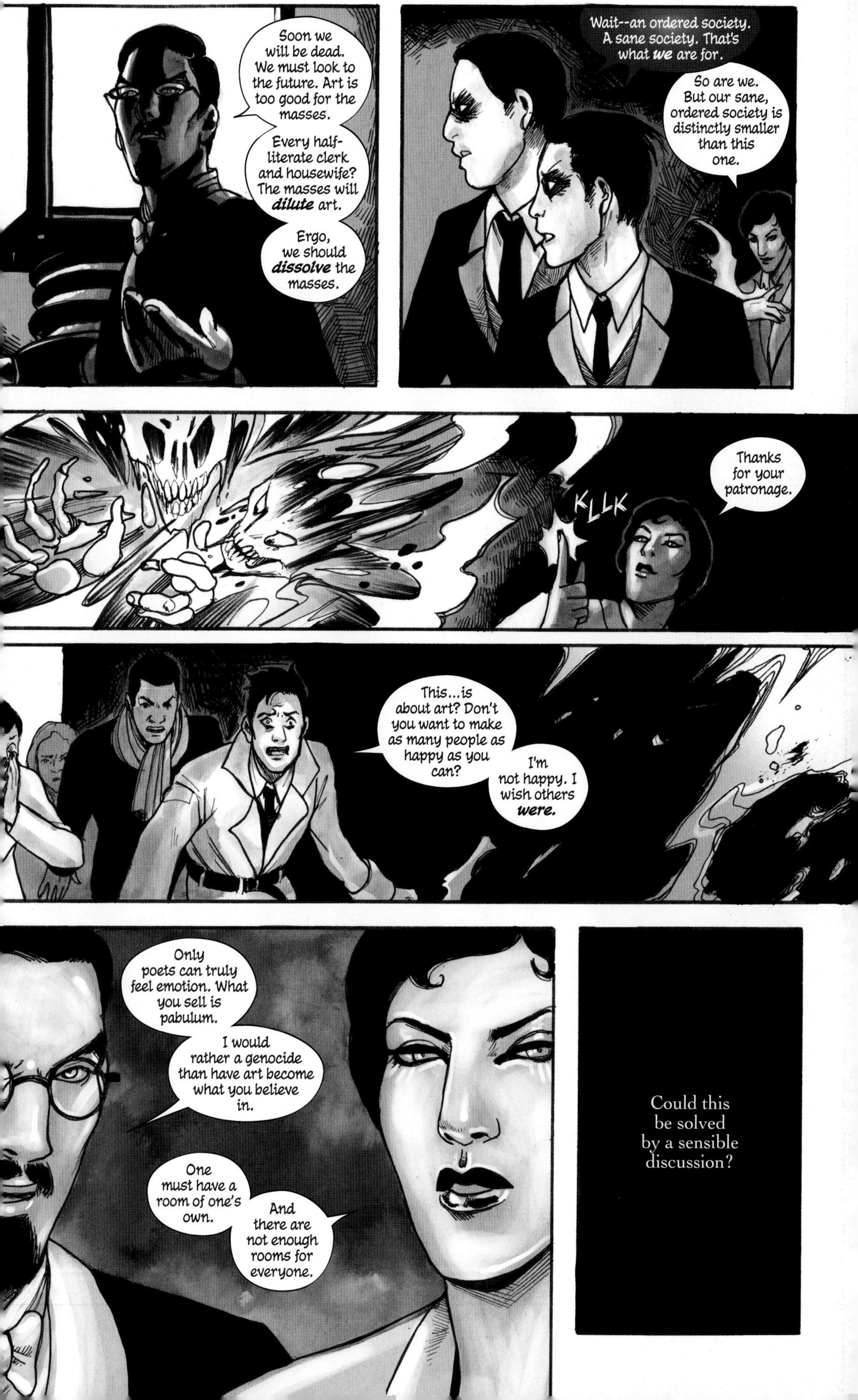

Soon we will be dead. We must look to the future. Art is too good for the masses.
Every half-literate clerk and housewife? The masses will *dilute* art.
Ergo, we should *dissolve* the masses.
Wait--an ordered society. A sane society. That's what *we* are for.
So are we. But our sane, ordered society is distinctly smaller than this one.
KLLK
Thanks for your patronage.
This...is about art? Don't you want to make as many people as happy as you can?
I'm not happy. I wish others *were.*
Only poets can truly feel emotion. What you sell is pabulum.
I would rather a genocide than have art become what you believe in.
One must have a room of one's own.
And there are not enough rooms for everyone.
Could this be solved by a sensible discussion?

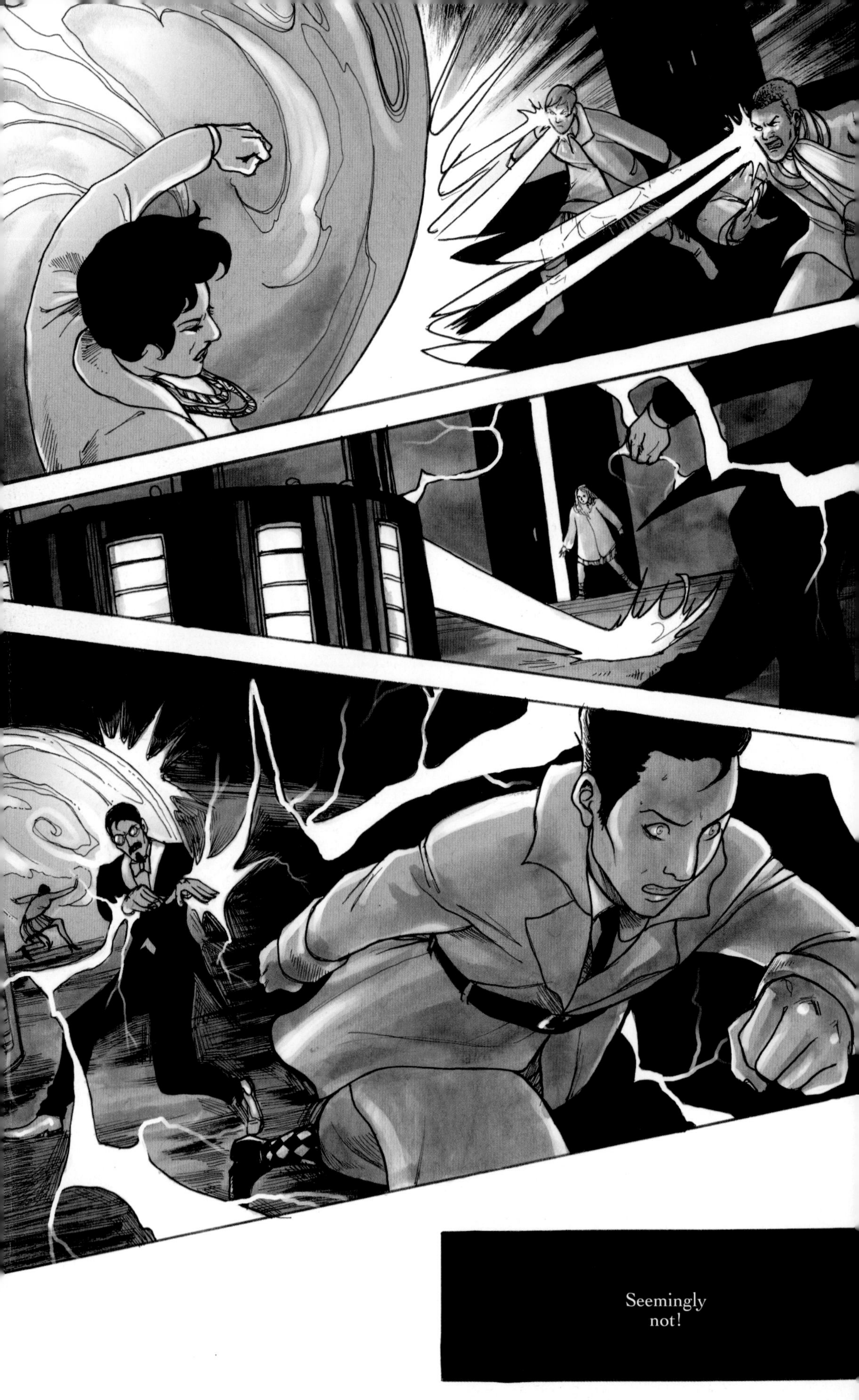
Seemingly
not!

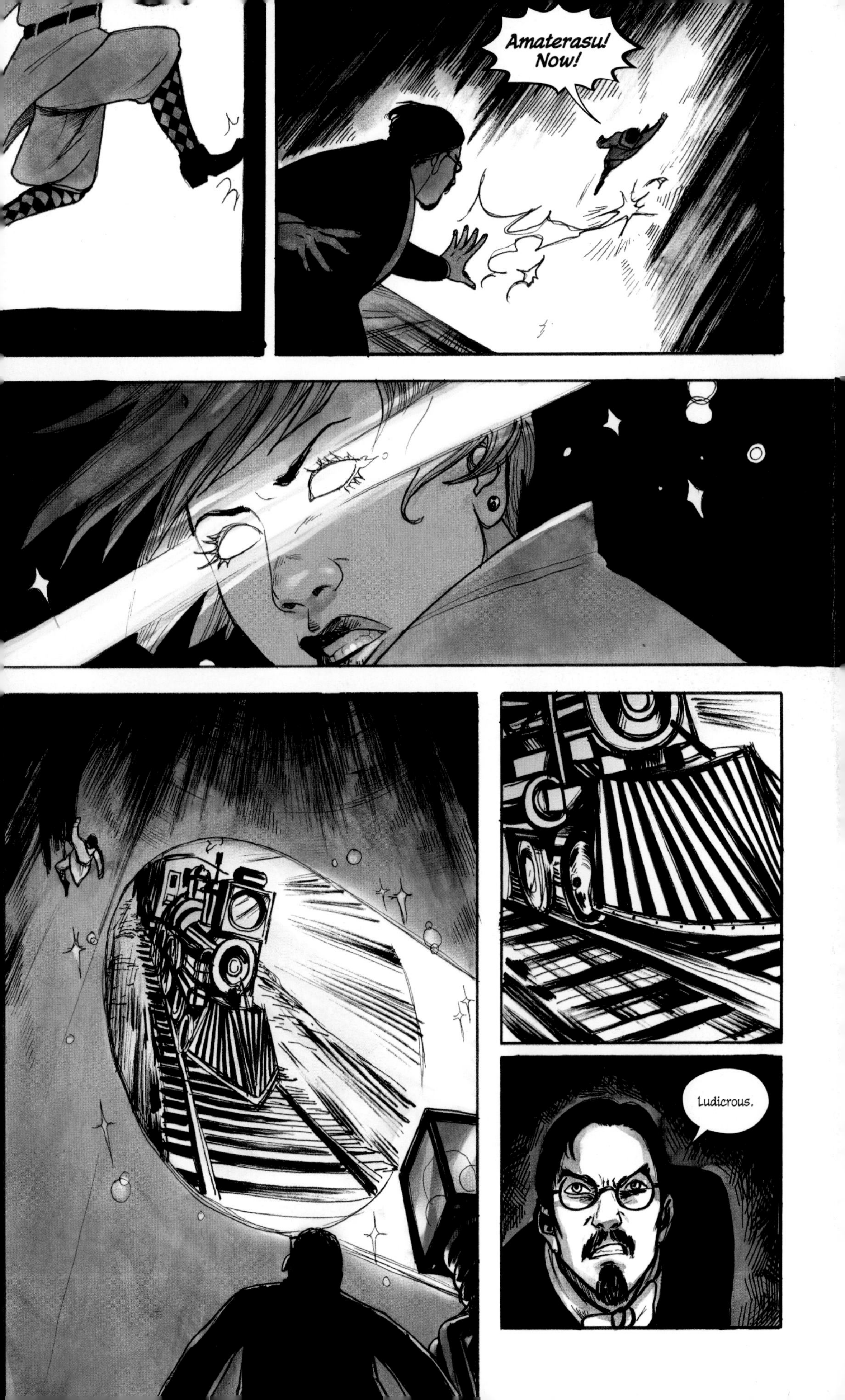
Amaterasu! Now!
Ludicrous.

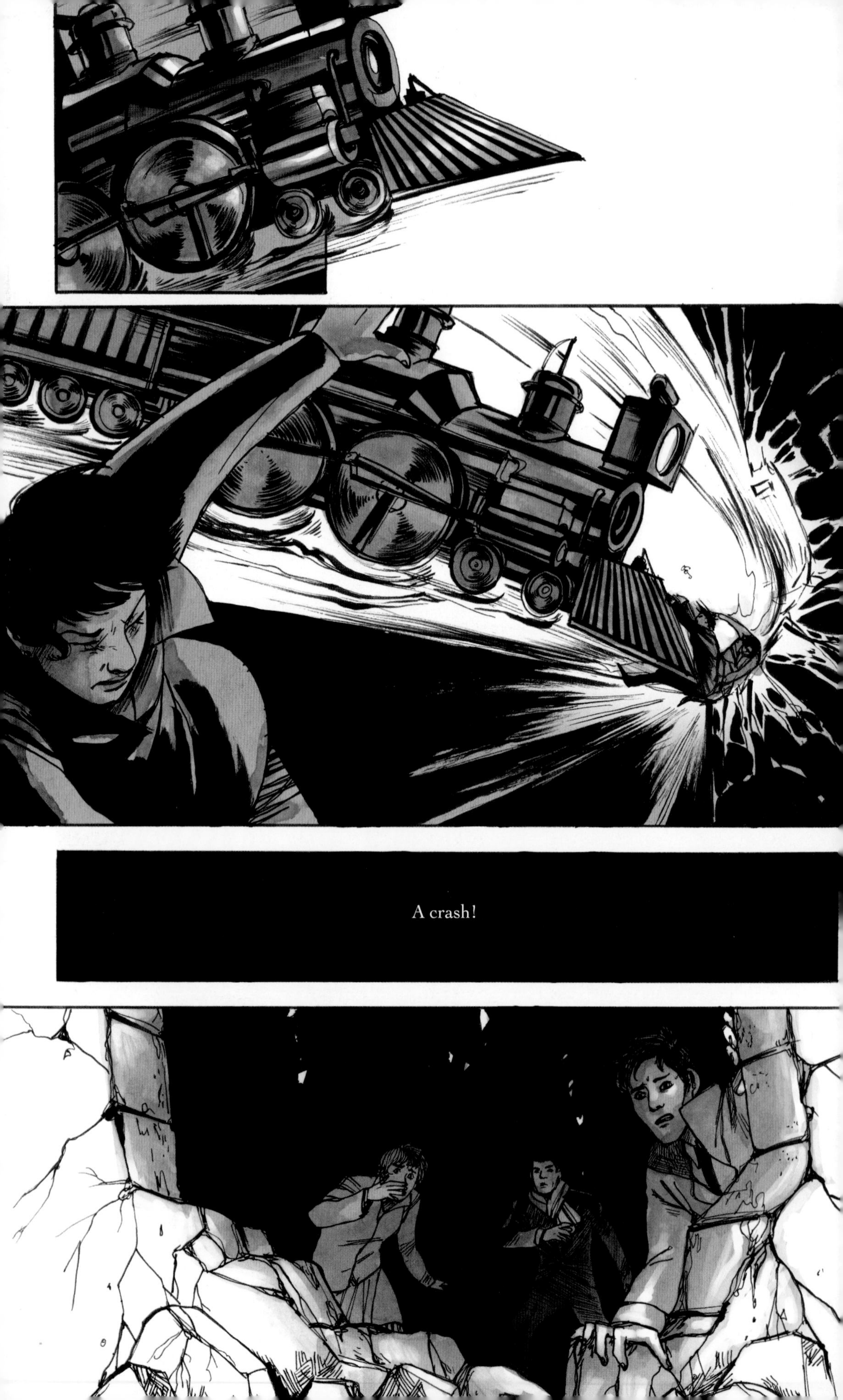
A crash!

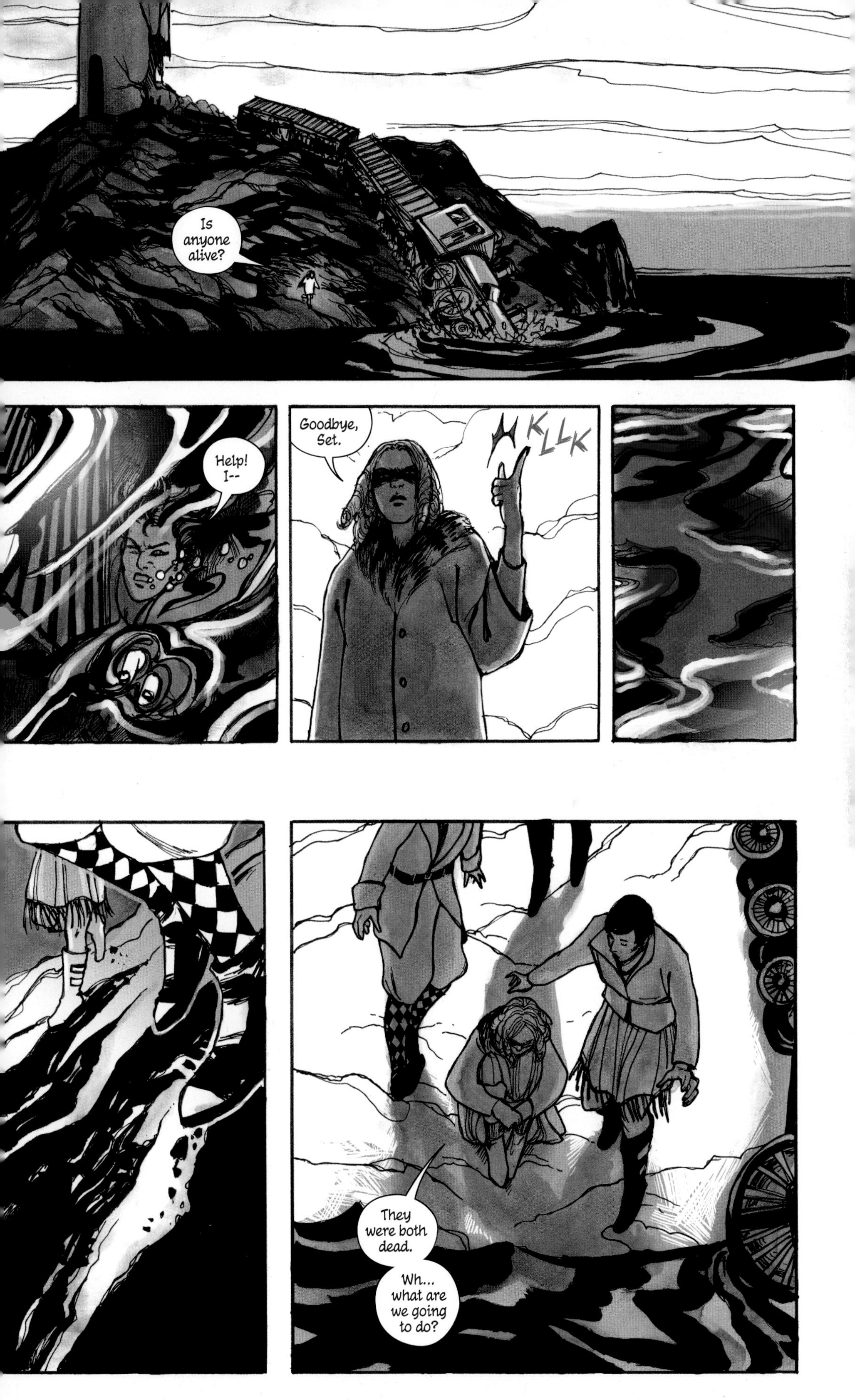
Is anyone alive?
Help! I--
Goodbye, Set.
KLLK
They were both dead.
Wh... what are we going to do?

THE GODS HEADED BACK to Lucifer's island in silence. The angry seas had calmed with Baal's violent passing. Susanoo had summoned breeze enough to pull the sails taut, and carry them home to the black rock and its darkened mansion. For most of the journey they could see nothing ahead but blackness.

They were ten metres from the docks when they realised Ananke was waiting, amongst the debris.

The gods explained. Ananke listened. When they were done, she began to weep.

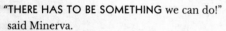

"THERE HAS TO BE SOMETHING we can do!" said Minerva.

They had gathered in the study where, mere hours earlier, the Norns and Susanoo had discussed the finer things in life. The topic had since turned, moving to life, simple life on Earth, and its continuance. What Set, Baal and their Woden stooge had wrought was a monstrosity, too large to comprehend. Susanoo finished pouring the drinks for everyone, Minerva included.

"Well, Ananke," said Susanoo, "Is there anything?"

"Possibly," said Ananke, carefully, "but it is only a chance. The mathematics are distinctly not in our favour…"

"If there's chance at all, it's enough," said Amaterasu. "I'm not afraid of hope. Please! A chance is better than the lights going out over the whole world."

"What they have done is perform a ritual sacrifice," she said. "Five gods were slaughtered… and perhaps six. We cannot truly understand what happened to Woden on the island."

"I hope it hurt," said Susanoo. For once, no one could tell if it was a joke. For once, no one disagreed.

"We also cannot truly understand what function they thought the machine served. We know only that their sacrifice must be countered to the best of our abilities," said Ananke, "opposed by one of our own."

For the world to live, it seemed they all must die.

"But there's only four of us," said Minerva. "Even if we all die we can't match them!"

"Yes," said Ananke, "but it would perhaps curtail the full effect. Five or six wishes for Armageddon are very different from one or two. Perhaps it could be survived? I cannot know for certain, in truth."

"All Woden's mechanisms," said Amaterasu. "We really don't understand them. We don't have time to understand them."

"Neither did they, I dare say," said Ananke. "Such rituals are actually simple. It is about will and art. The machines… in my experience, they are little more than props. All that matters is your action and intent. They killed so the world would die. You die so the world can live."

She stood up and moved as if the weight of the years had finally crushed her.

"I will leave you to consider the matter," she said. "I will go to the lighthouse to see if there is anything I can discern which may be useful. Think carefully. Whatever decision you make, I am proud of you." At the threshold of the room she stopped, glancing back, eyes wet beneath the mask.

"I'm sorry," she said. "I would never have thought they could be so cruel. But I would never have thought you to be so selfless. After all these years, you still have the capacity to surprise."

She left them alone with the silence.

Susanoo refilled his brandy, making his way to the arm of Amaterasu's chair.

"Even saving half the world from darkness would be better than saving none," he said with a sigh. "That's simple math."

"And honestly?" said Amaterasu, holding Susanoo's hand. "If we only have weeks to live anyway, that's hardly something to be precious about."

Amaterasu and Susanoo kissed, and cried. Minerva hugged Amon-Ra. Amon-Ra grew tense then relaxed. A decision was made.

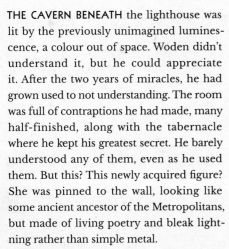

THE CAVERN BENEATH the lighthouse was lit by the previously unimagined luminescence, a colour out of space. Woden didn't understand it, but he could appreciate it. After the two years of miracles, he had grown used to not understanding. The room was full of contraptions he had made, many half-finished, along with the tabernacle where he kept his greatest secret. He barely understood any of them, even as he used them. But this? This newly acquired figure? She was pinned to the wall, looking like some ancient ancestor of the Metropolitans, but made of living poetry and bleak lightning rather than simple metal.

What was it?

Baal and Set and the futurists would never know. They thought they were only warping the zeitgeist. Woden had tricked them. They were capturing it, permanently. Now the Zeitgeist was his!

This creature of science and fiction would give Germany the future she deserved.

He stared in wonder, and thought of what awaited them. He'd barely moved since teleporting to the secret cavern. A necessary illusion if he was to survive this mess of egos. Still, perhaps history will understand he was the true artist, who should have always been gifted godhood, not the lesser degenerate bohemian whose abilities he had repurposed.

"Beautiful," he said, with a shiver, taking in the wonder of this zeitgeist on the wall.

"Quite numinous," said Ananke, entering through the hidden staircase from the lighthouse above.

Ananke made her way across the cavern, watching the figure intensely, a collector admiring a rare prize.

"Of course, she isn't the zeitgeist. I doubt there's any such thing," said Ananke, "but numinous she is all the same."

"What... what do you mean?" said Woden. Ananke smiled, and declined to answer.

"Where do you keep what I gave you?" said Ananke.

"You can't have it!" said Woden, stepping instinctively towards the grand tabernacle. "You can't have it back!"

"You just gave away where you were keeping it, Woden," said Ananke. "But worry not. It is useless to me. I don't want it back."

Woden relaxed for a half-second, before Ananke clicked her fingers and the box was destroyed in a ball of fire. He fell to his knees. He felt his suit's abilities falter. His link to the godhead was gone. It was over.

"You're going to kill me," said once-Woden, Woden no more.

"Correct," said Ananke, walking towards him, ignoring the white greasepaint running down his face in streams of tears.

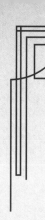

"What now?" said Woden.

"Will the Reich you desire come? Perhaps. It is likely, even. I think Versailles alone implies another war," said Ananke. "But is it more likely *because* of this ritual? It is difficult to say. Metaphor is difficult. Inspiration is difficult. I don't really care. I just needed this creature..."

She glanced at the captured ghost, proudly, before resuming her steady progress.

"But why?" said Woden. "Why do all this to get it? I watched all the gods—none of them would have done this if you didn't encourage it. You've done this and things like this before. I'll bet you have! I can see in your face I'm right. Please, if I'm to die, tell me. If it's not the zeitgeist, what is it? Why do you want it? What is going on?"

"Perhaps eventually someone will work it out," said Ananke. "Alas for you, Joseph, it will remain a mystery."

She clicked her fingers, turning the not-Woden into an abstract smear of red on the far wall. It was nearly done. All she required was an ending.

Messier than she had hoped. Not a masterpiece, she had to admit, but the deadlines were crushing. Next time she'd do better.

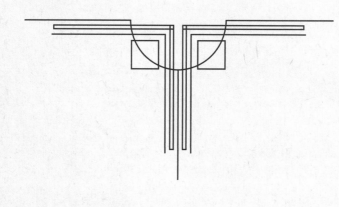

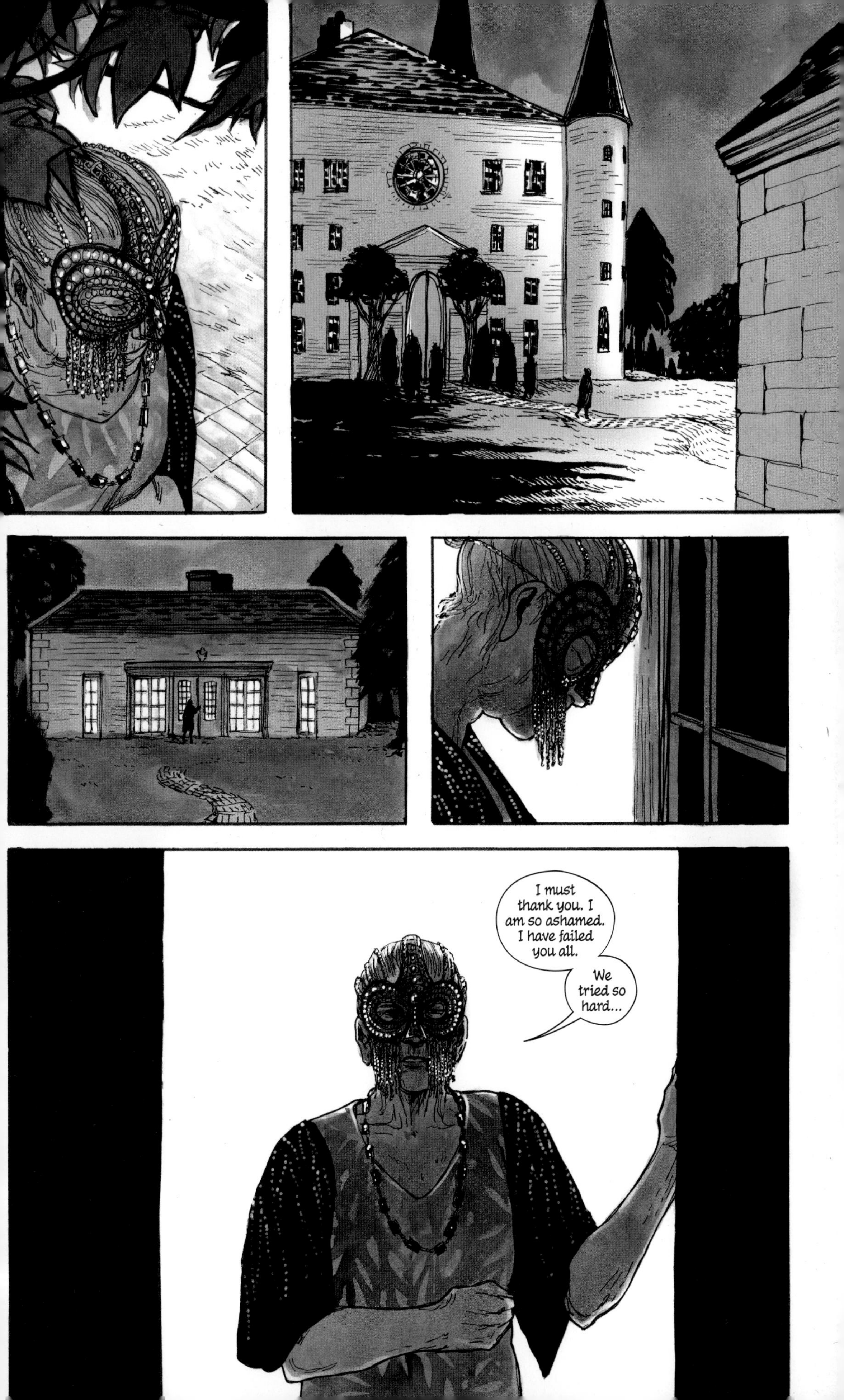
I must thank you. I am so ashamed. I have failed you all.
We tried so hard...

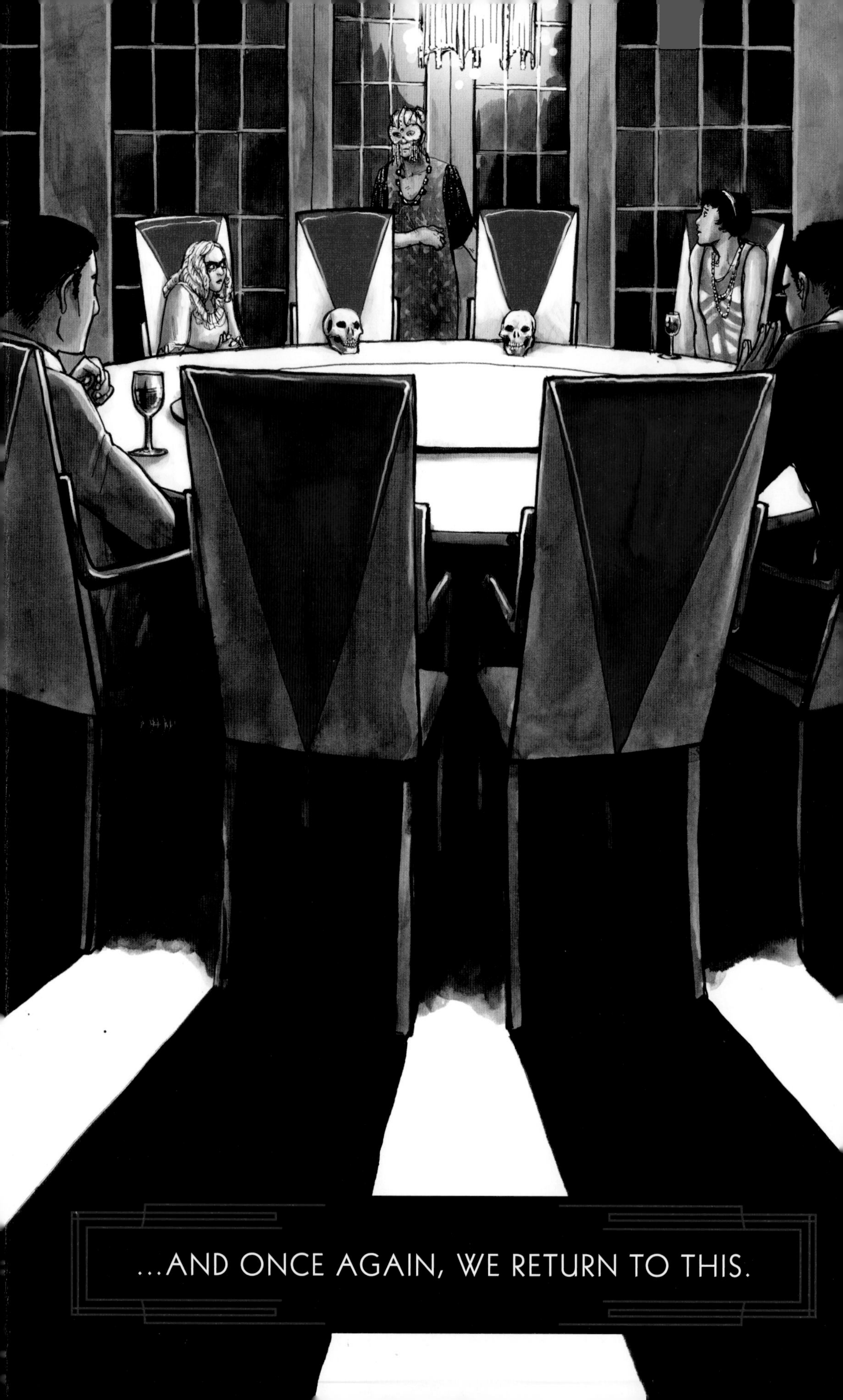
...AND ONCE AGAIN, WE RETURN TO THIS.

THE
WICKED
+
THE DIVINE

CHRISTMAS ANNUAL

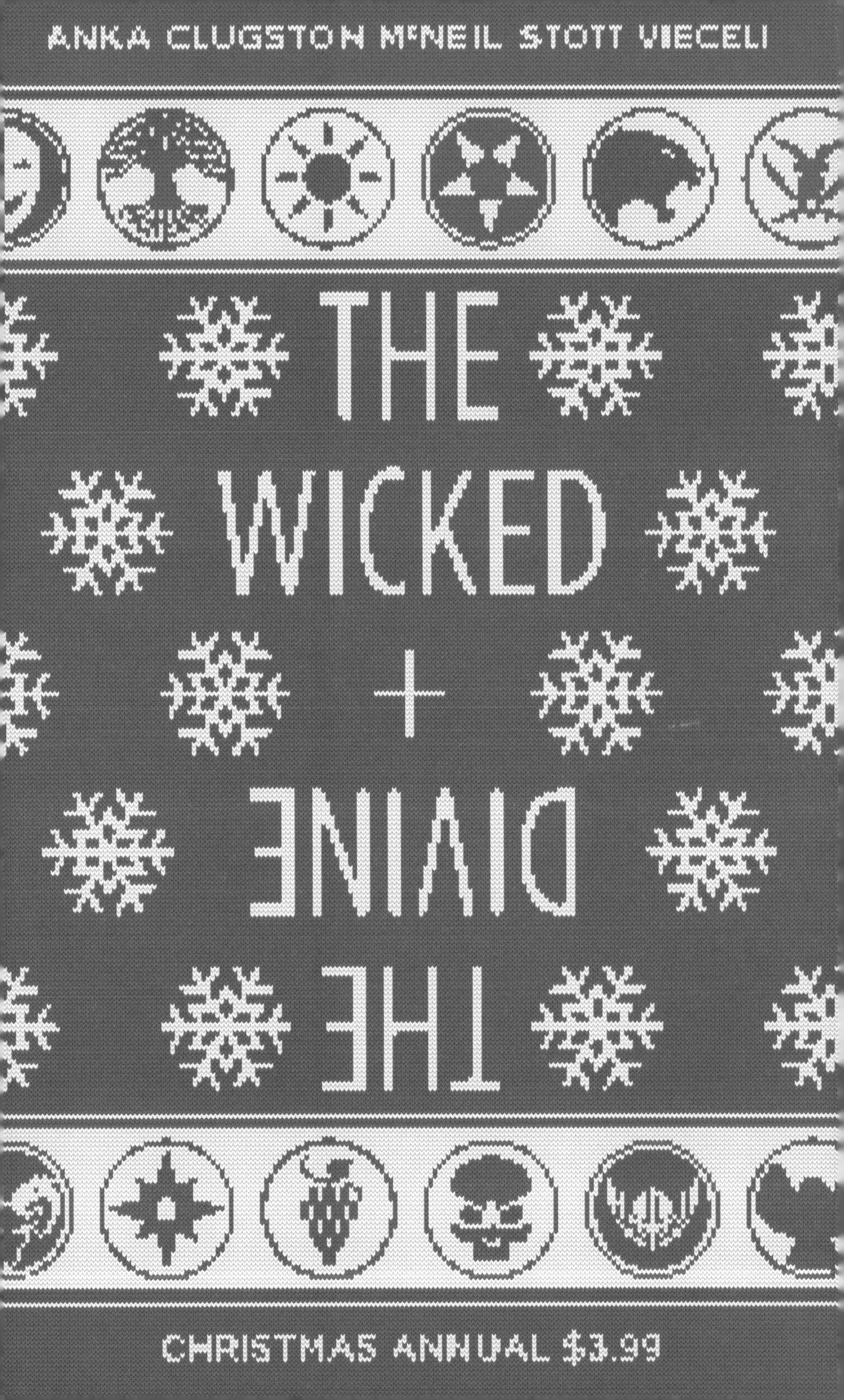
ANKA CLUGSTON McNEIL STOTT VIECELI
THE
WICKED
+
DIVINE
THE
CHRISTMAS ANNUAL $3.99

Seasonal Hellos!

When structuring *The Wicked + The Divine*, we just sort of... dived in. Fancy thinky folks would call it "in medias res". We wanted readers to join the story at the point where there's a huge plot engine driving the thing — namely, the Murder Mystery with Lucifer. As such, we skipped a lot of things that happened in the first six months of the Recurrence.

While we've skipped back and shown various key moments, there's still a lot we haven't shown. Amaterasu and Lucifer's pre-godhood friendship. How Dionysus and Baphomet became friends. Inanna and Baal, getting it on. Lucifer and Sakhmet, getting it on. Later in the story, we skipped Laura and Baal, getting it on. Basically, we've skipped a lot of Getting It On.

It's Christmas. Let's make amends.

We're joined by our artistic friends Kris Anka (with Jen Bartel helping on inks), Emma Vieceli, Chynna Clugston Flores, Carla Speed McNeil and Rachael Stott to provide art. Tamra Bonvillain and our very own Matt Wilson split the colours. Kieron dived through a bunch of scenes he always wanted to write, to show odd sparkling moments that made the characters happy. Well... for a *WicDiv* value of happy. Bittersweet is our thing. Jamie did an excellent sweater cover, which is clearly the piece of merch we should work out how to make real. We had a fun time. Hopefully you will too.

Anyway! See you soon — in spring, or late winter, depending on how Global Warming is feeling.

Thanks for riding through the past year with us. It's been a hard one, but you've always made it better. You're the best readers in the whole wide world!

Yes, we've been drinking, why do you ask?

Hugs!

Kieron and Jamie!

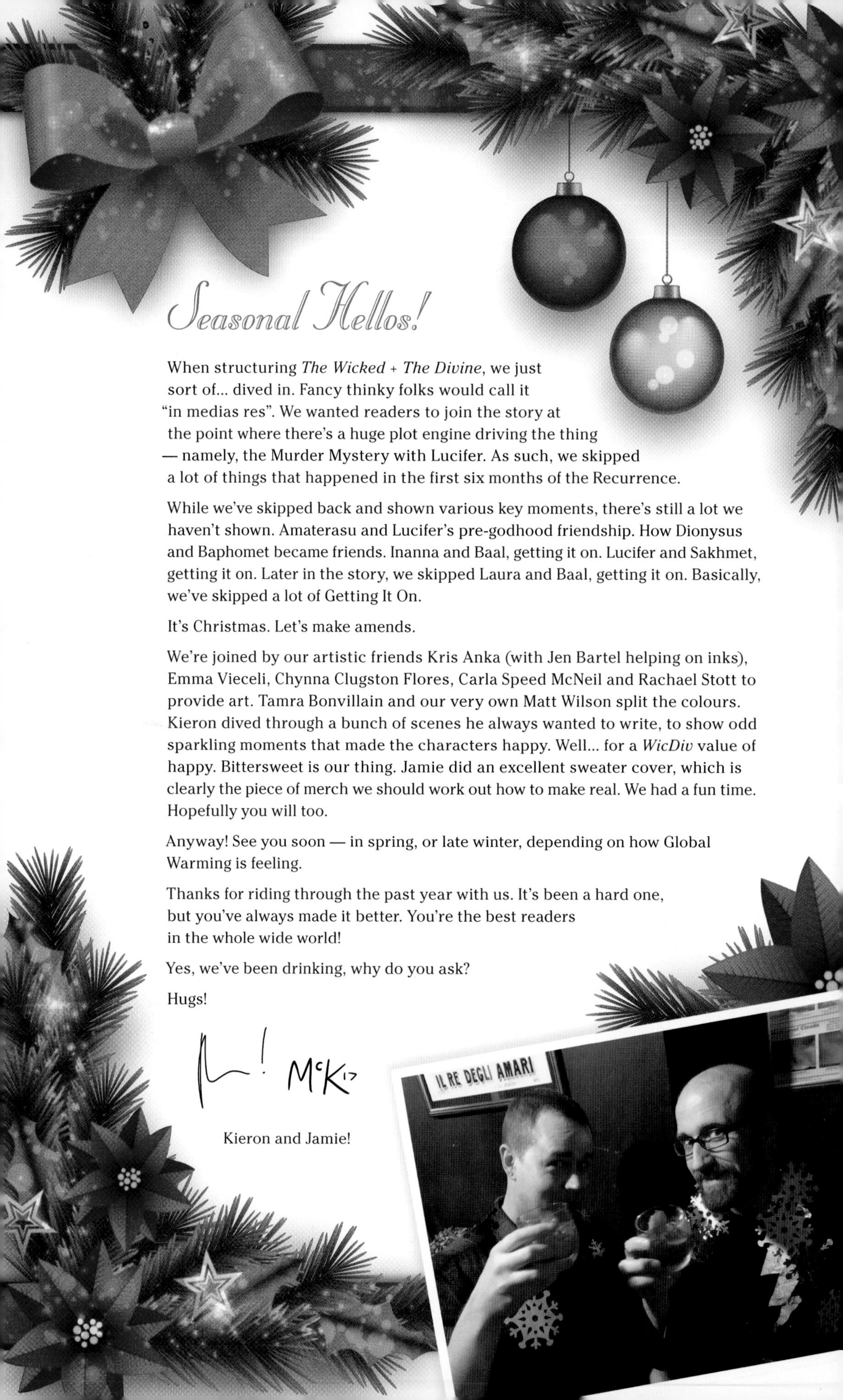
IL RE DEGLI AMARI

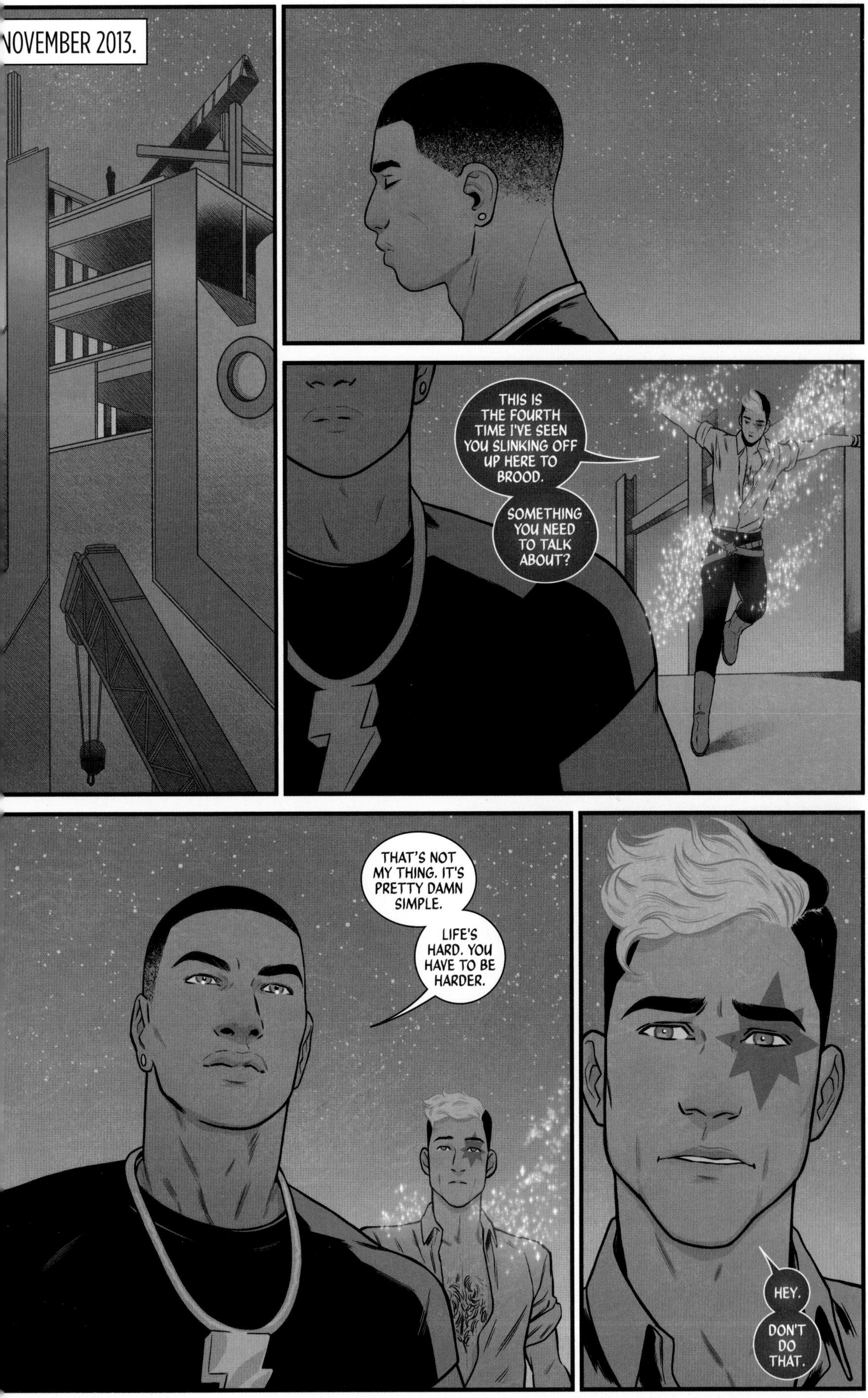
NOVEMBER 2013.
THIS IS THE FOURTH TIME I'VE SEEN YOU SLINKING OFF UP HERE TO BROOD.
SOMETHING YOU NEED TO TALK ABOUT?
THAT'S NOT MY THING. IT'S PRETTY DAMN SIMPLE.
LIFE'S HARD. YOU HAVE TO BE HARDER.
HEY.
DON'T DO THAT.

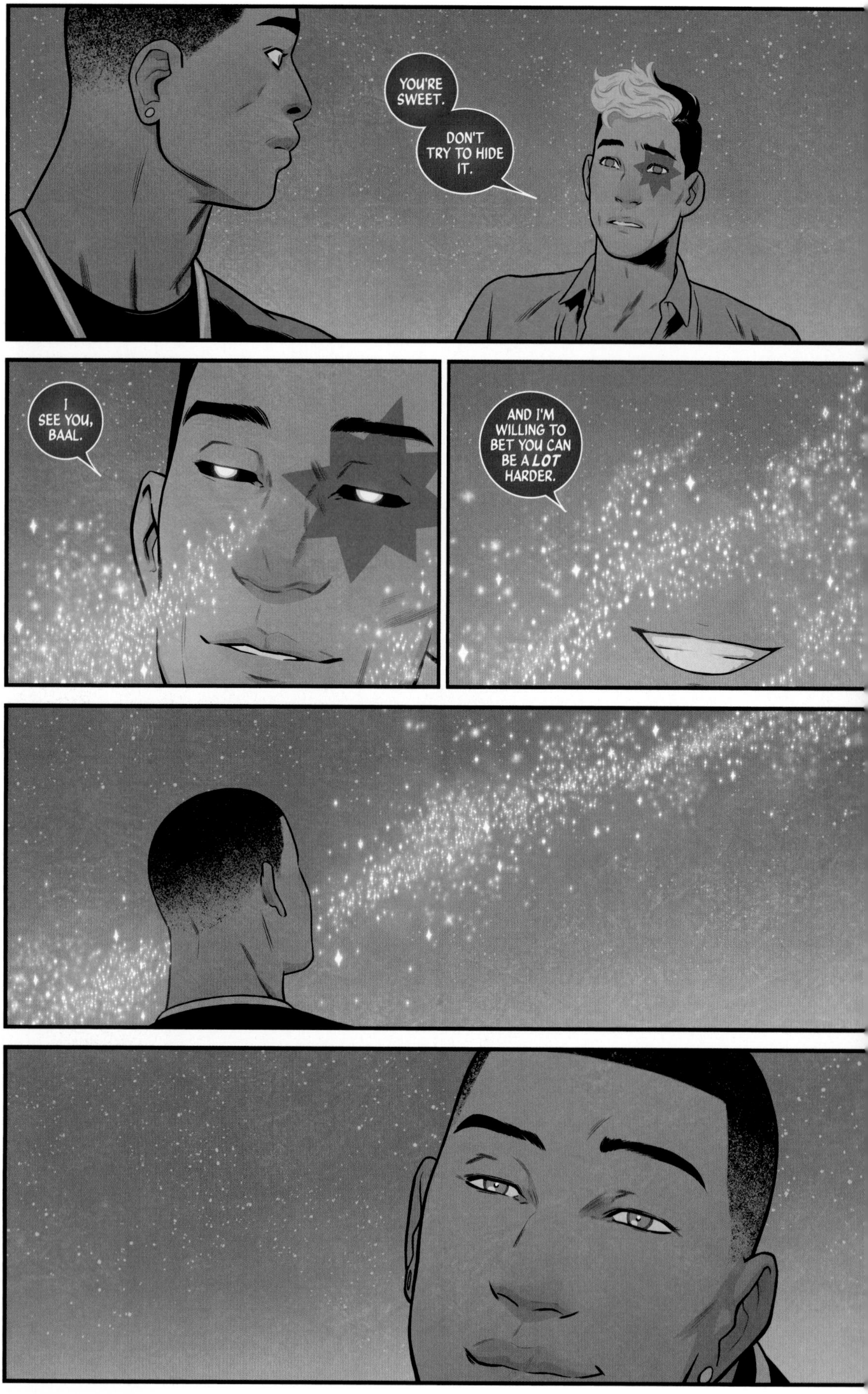
YOU'RE SWEET.
DON'T TRY TO HIDE IT.
I SEE YOU, BAAL.
AND I'M WILLING TO BET YOU CAN BE A *LOT* HARDER.

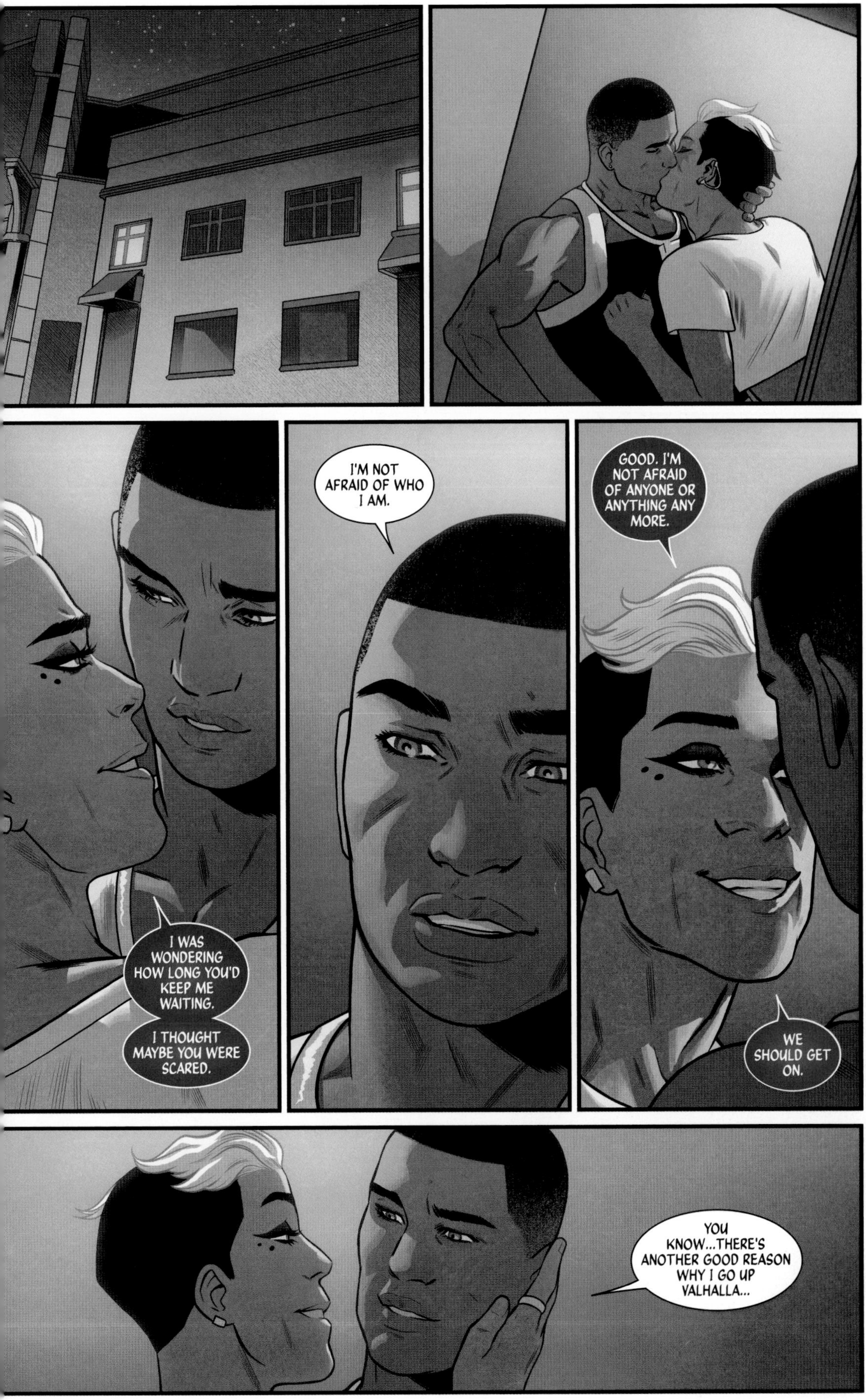

I WAS WONDERING HOW LONG YOU'D KEEP ME WAITING.
I THOUGHT MAYBE YOU WERE SCARED.
I'M NOT AFRAID OF WHO I AM.
GOOD. I'M NOT AFRAID OF ANYONE OR ANYTHING ANY MORE.
WE SHOULD GET ON.
YOU KNOW...THERE'S ANOTHER GOOD REASON WHY I GO UP VALHALLA...

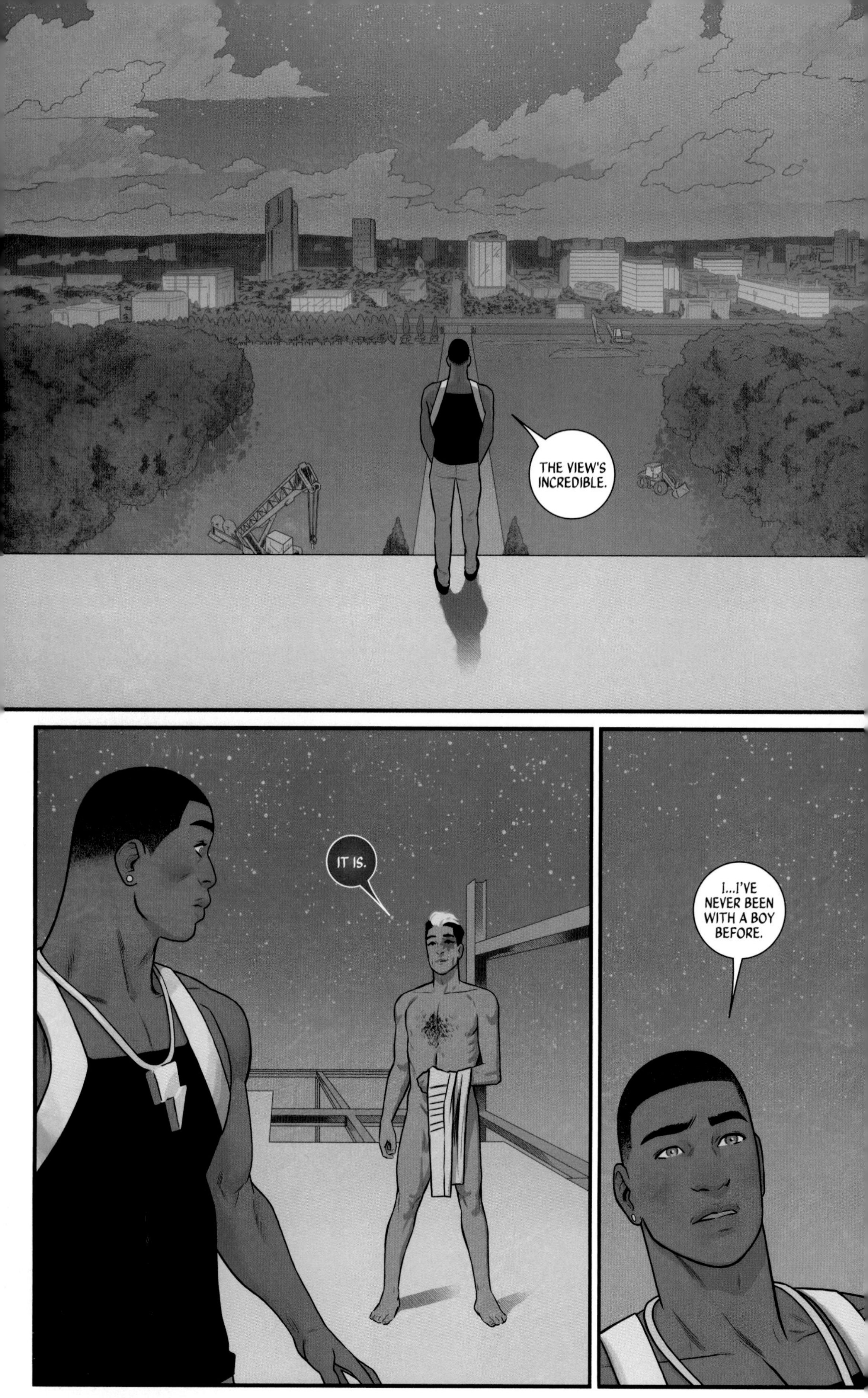
THE VIEW'S INCREDIBLE.
IT IS.
I...I'VE NEVER BEEN WITH A BOY BEFORE.

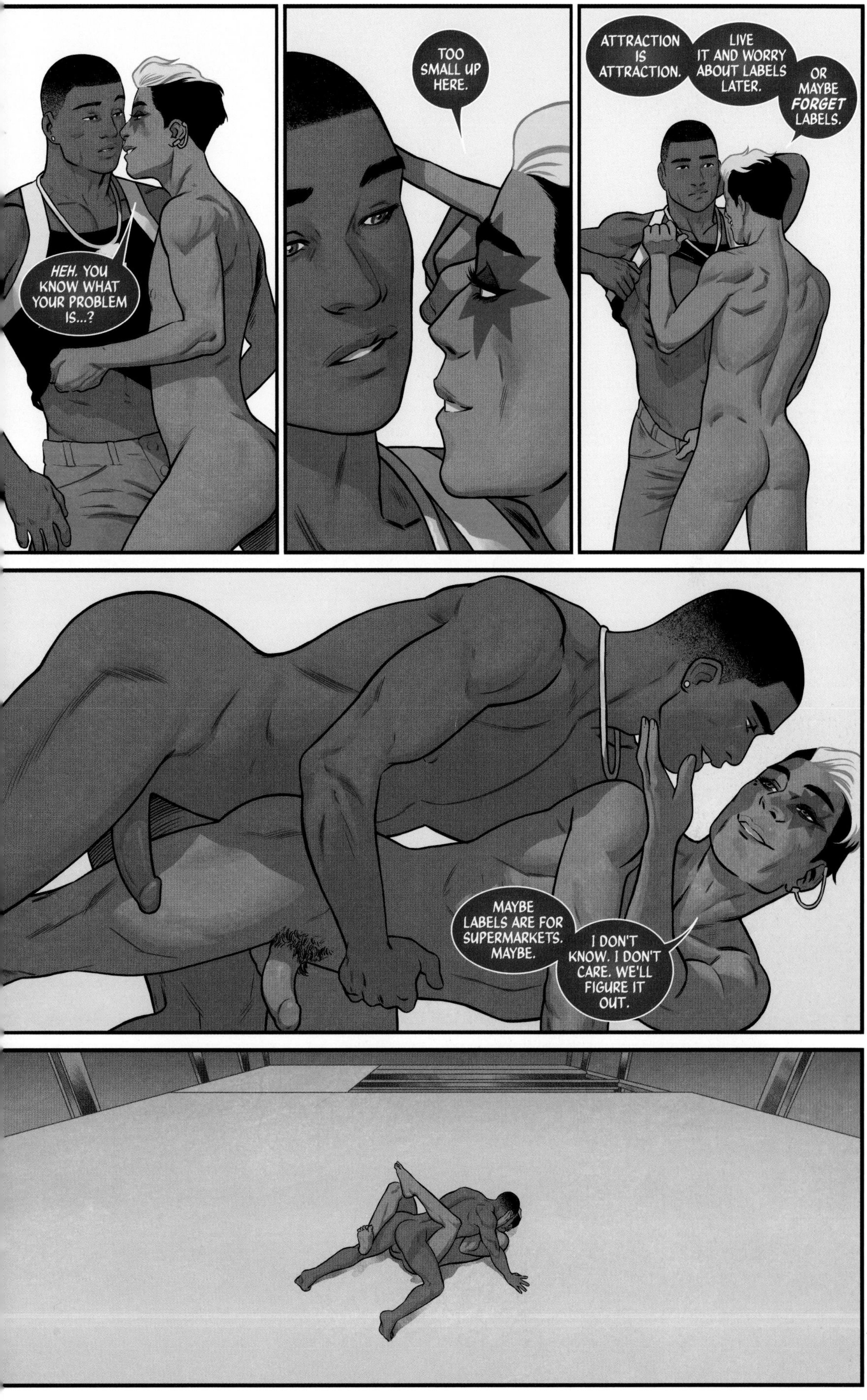
HEH. YOU KNOW WHAT YOUR PROBLEM IS...?
TOO SMALL UP HERE.
ATTRACTION IS ATTRACTION.
LIVE IT AND WORRY ABOUT LABELS LATER.
OR MAYBE FORGET LABELS.
MAYBE LABELS ARE FOR SUPERMARKETS. MAYBE.
I DON'T KNOW. I DON'T CARE. WE'LL FIGURE IT OUT.

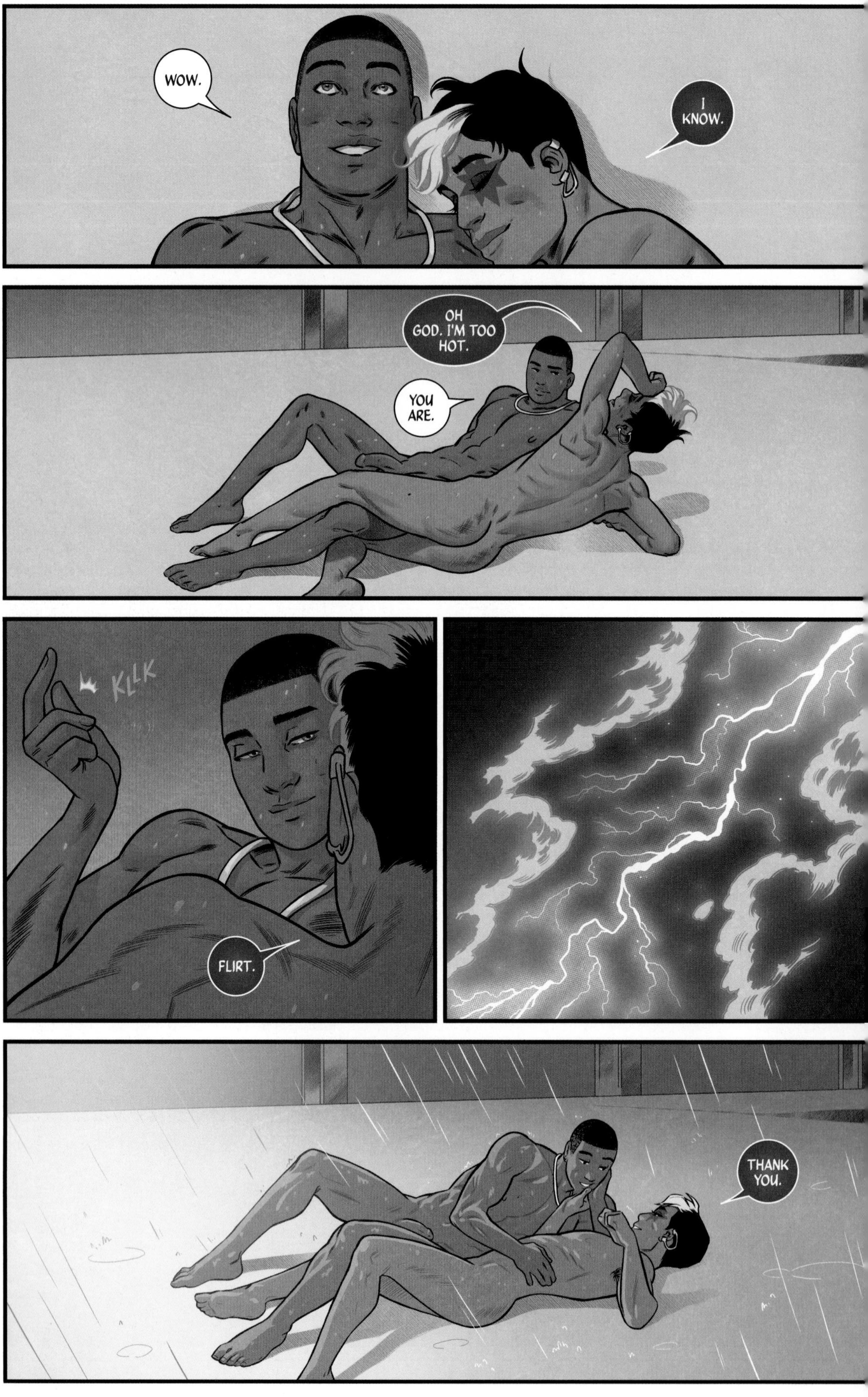
WOW.
I KNOW.
OH GOD. I'M TOO HOT.
YOU ARE.
KLLK
FLIRT.
THANK YOU.

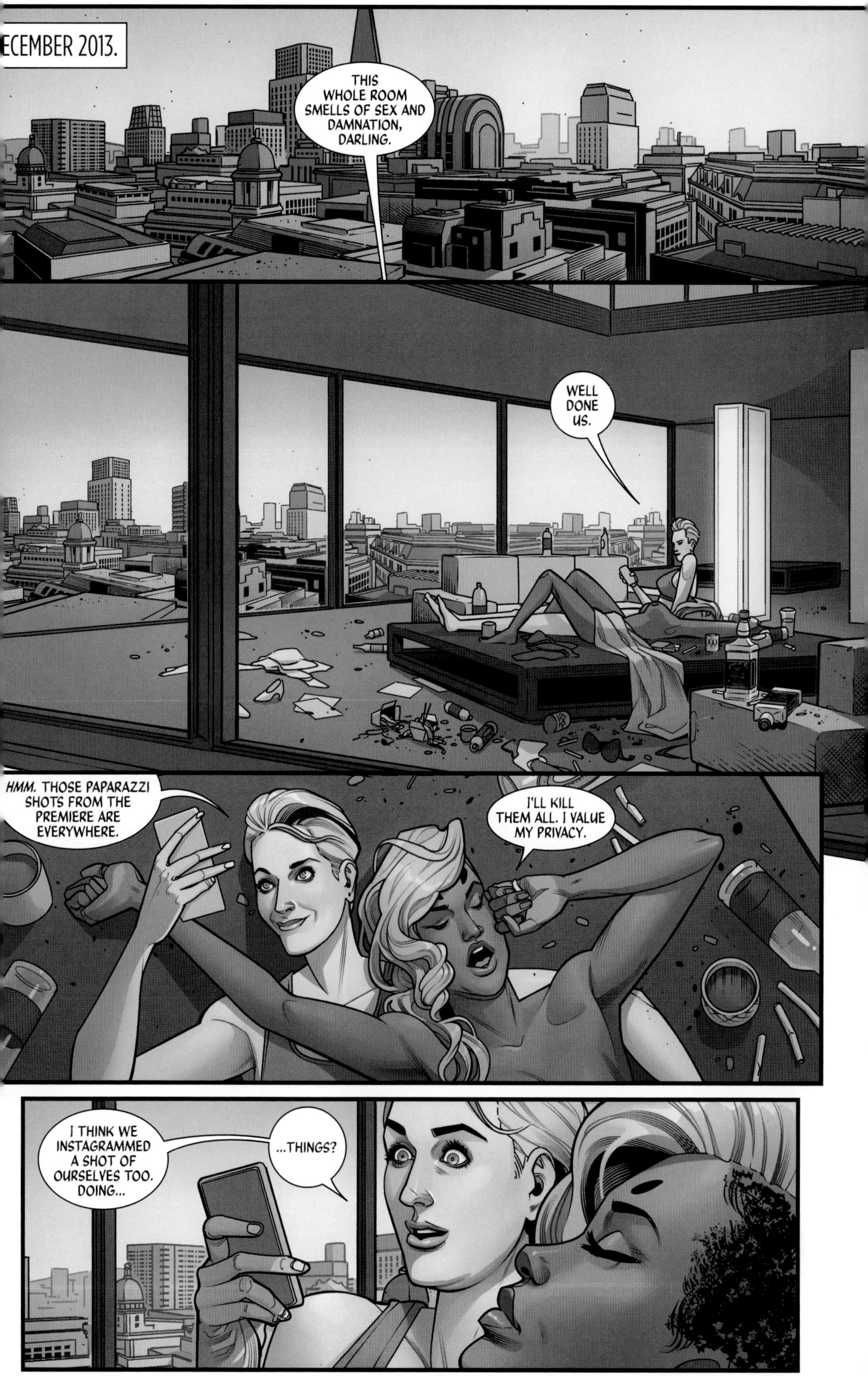
ECEMBER 2013.
THIS WHOLE ROOM SMELLS OF SEX AND DAMNATION, DARLING.
WELL DONE US.
HMM. THOSE PAPARAZZI SHOTS FROM THE PREMIERE ARE EVERYWHERE.
I'LL KILL THEM ALL. I VALUE MY PRIVACY.
I THINK WE INSTAGRAMMED A SHOT OF OURSELVES TOO. DOING...
...THINGS?

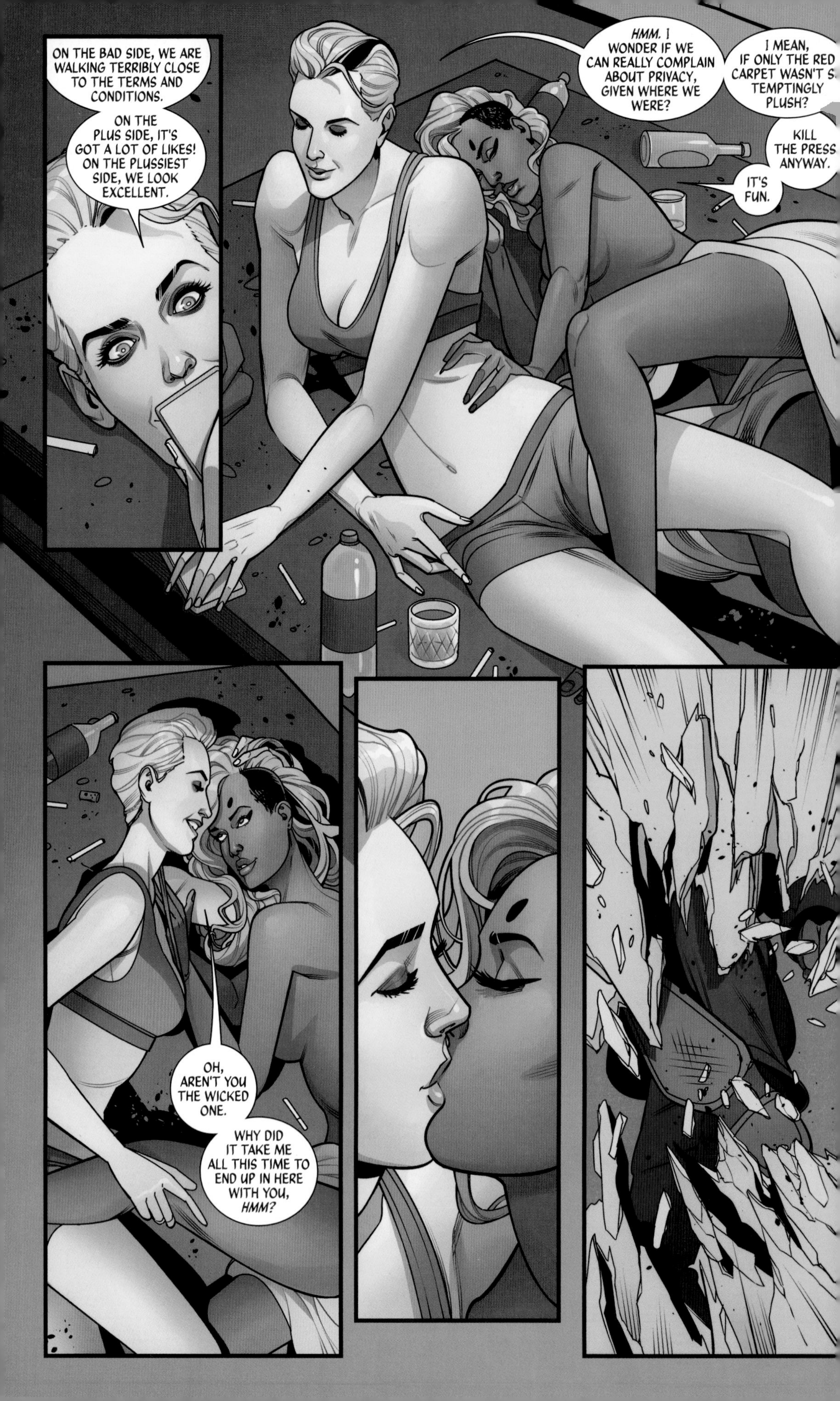
ON THE BAD SIDE, WE ARE WALKING TERRIBLY CLOSE TO THE TERMS AND CONDITIONS.
ON THE PLUS SIDE, IT'S GOT A LOT OF LIKES! ON THE PLUSSIEST SIDE, WE LOOK EXCELLENT.
HMM. I WONDER IF WE CAN REALLY COMPLAIN ABOUT PRIVACY, GIVEN WHERE WE WERE?
I MEAN, IF ONLY THE RED CARPET WASN'T S TEMPTINGLY PLUSH?
KILL THE PRESS ANYWAY.
IT'S FUN.
OH, AREN'T YOU THE WICKED ONE.
WHY DID IT TAKE ME ALL THIS TIME TO END UP IN HERE WITH YOU, HMM?

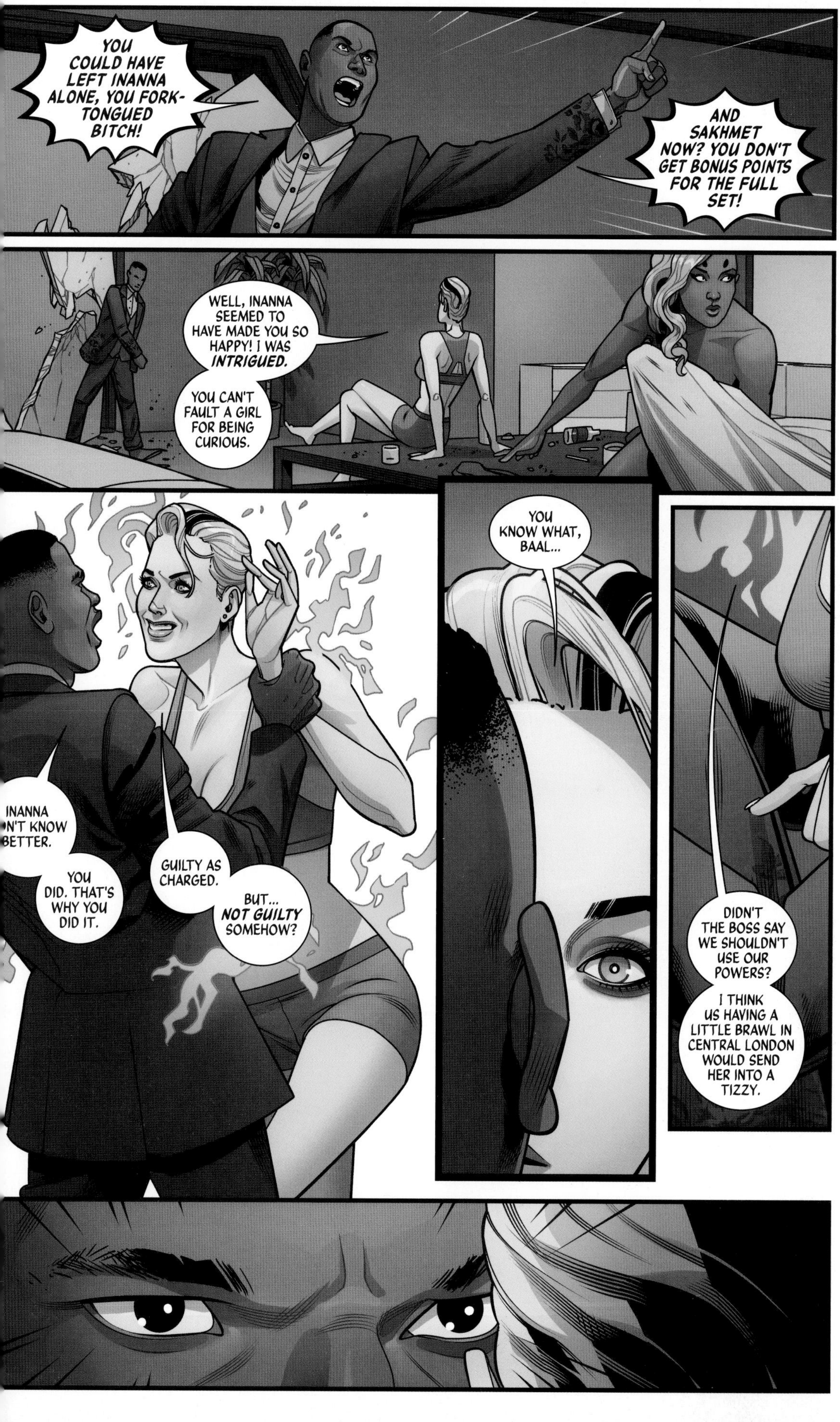
YOU COULD HAVE LEFT INANNA ALONE, YOU FORK-TONGUED BITCH!
AND SAKHMET NOW? YOU DON'T GET BONUS POINTS FOR THE FULL SET!
WELL, INANNA SEEMED TO HAVE MADE YOU SO HAPPY! I WAS *INTRIGUED.*
YOU CAN'T FAULT A GIRL FOR BEING CURIOUS.
INANNA N'T KNOW BETTER.
YOU DID. THAT'S WHY YOU DID IT.
GUILTY AS CHARGED.
BUT... *NOT GUILTY* SOMEHOW?
YOU KNOW WHAT, BAAL...
DIDN'T THE BOSS SAY WE SHOULDN'T USE OUR POWERS?
I THINK US HAVING A LITTLE BRAWL IN CENTRAL LONDON WOULD SEND HER INTO A TIZZY.

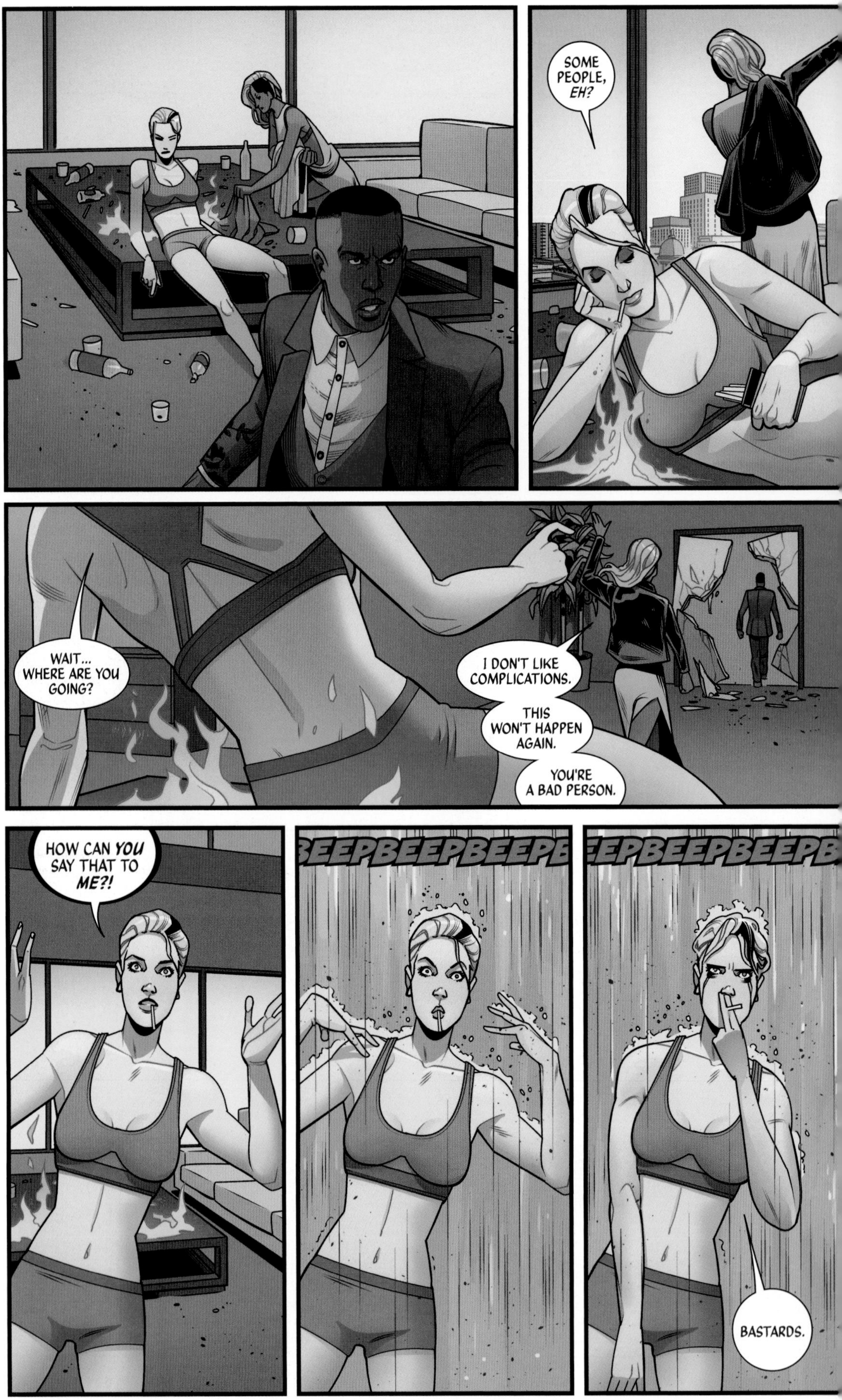
SOME PEOPLE, *EH?*
WAIT... WHERE ARE YOU GOING?
I DON'T LIKE COMPLICATIONS.
THIS WON'T HAPPEN AGAIN.
YOU'RE A BAD PERSON.
HOW CAN ***YOU*** SAY THAT TO ***ME?!***
EEPBEEPBEEPB
EEPBEEPBEEPB
BASTARDS.

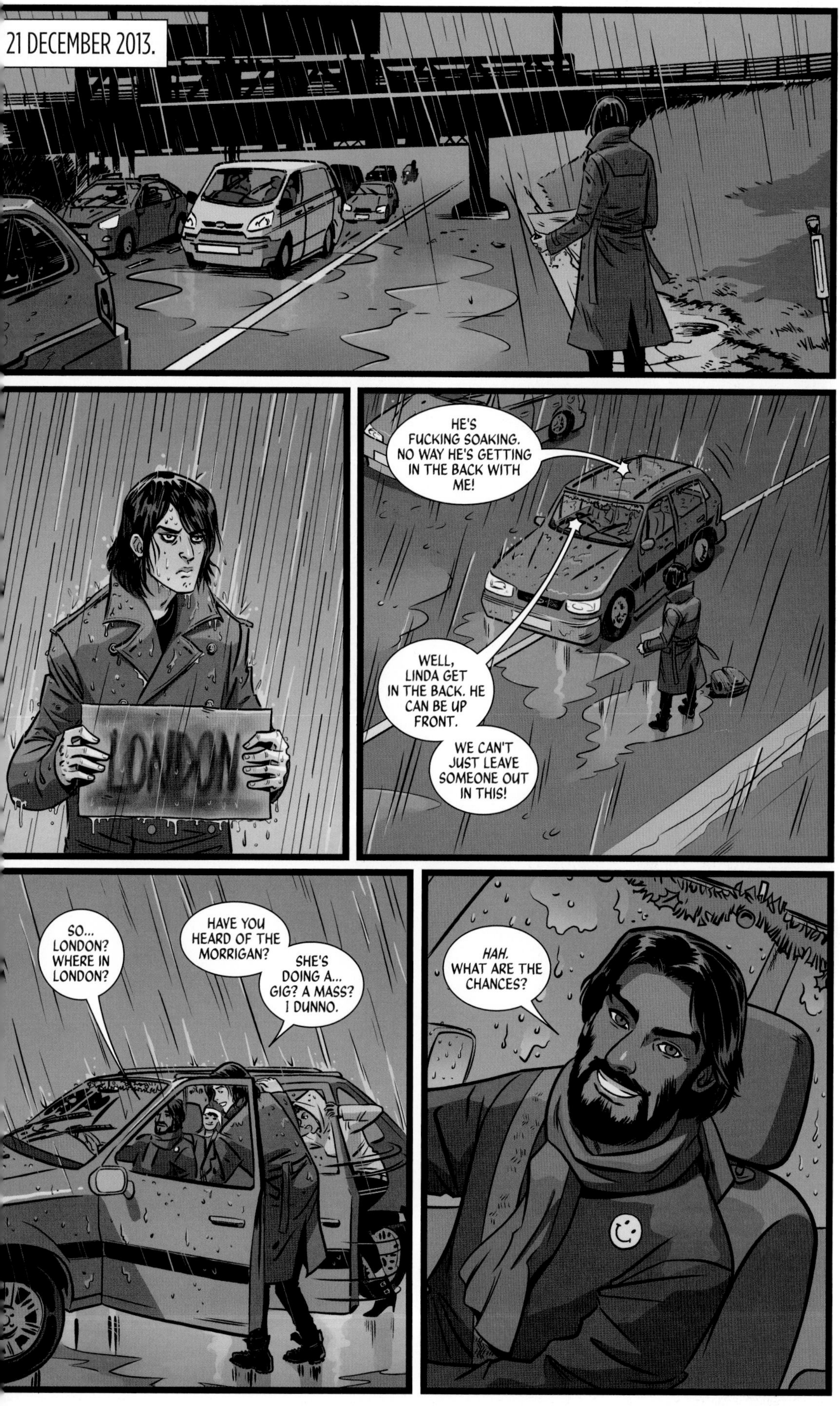
21 DECEMBER 2013.
LONDON
HE'S FUCKING SOAKING. NO WAY HE'S GETTING IN THE BACK WITH ME!
WELL, LINDA GET IN THE BACK. HE CAN BE UP FRONT.
WE CAN'T JUST LEAVE SOMEONE OUT IN THIS!
SO... LONDON? WHERE IN LONDON?
HAVE YOU HEARD OF THE MORRIGAN?
SHE'S DOING A... GIG? A MASS? I DUNNO.
HAH. WHAT ARE THE CHANCES?

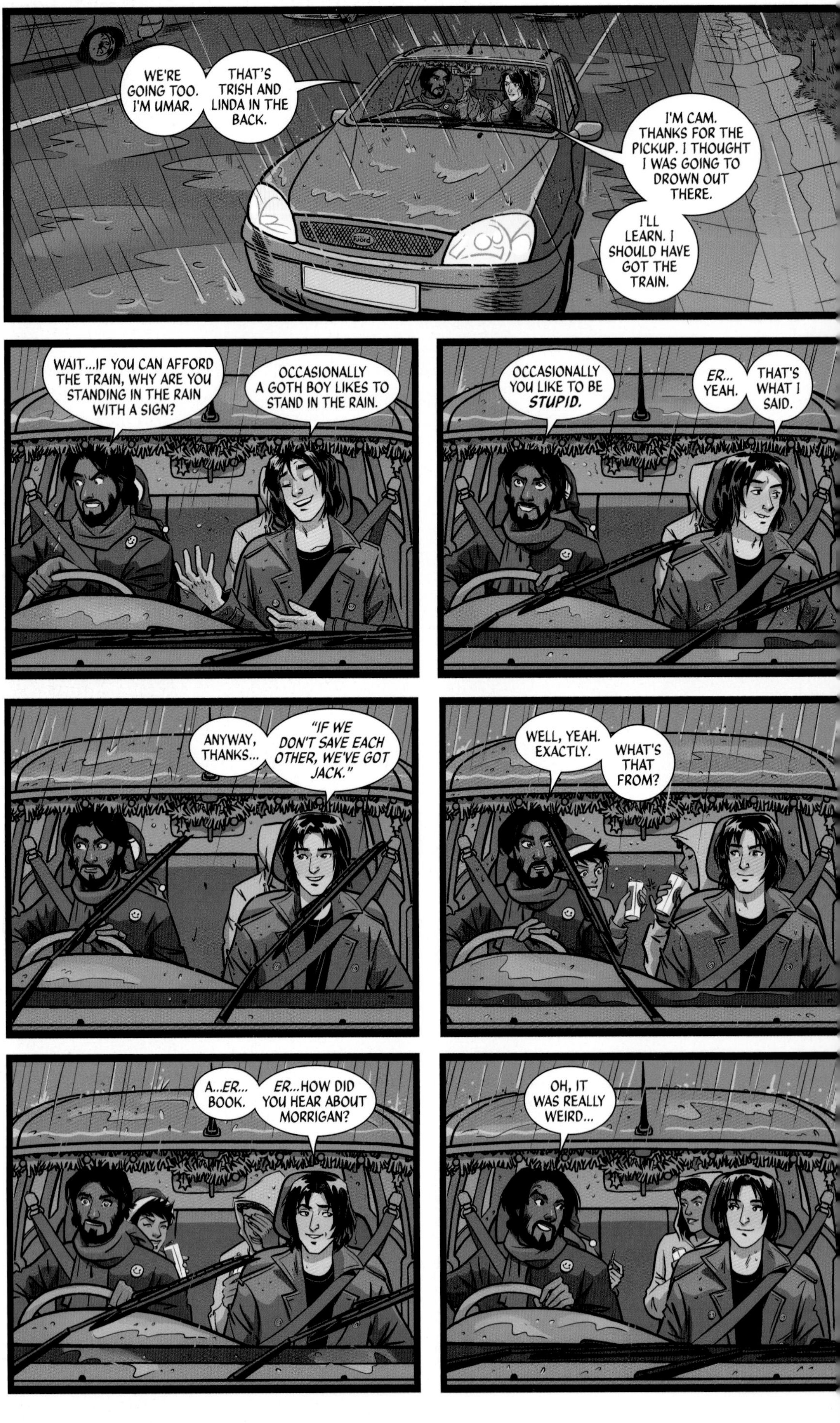
WE'RE GOING TOO. I'M UMAR.
THAT'S TRISH AND LINDA IN THE BACK.
I'M CAM. THANKS FOR THE PICKUP. I THOUGHT I WAS GOING TO DROWN OUT THERE.
I'LL LEARN. I SHOULD HAVE GOT THE TRAIN.
WAIT...IF YOU CAN AFFORD THE TRAIN, WHY ARE YOU STANDING IN THE RAIN WITH A SIGN?
OCCASIONALLY A GOTH BOY LIKES TO STAND IN THE RAIN.
OCCASIONALLY YOU LIKE TO BE *STUPID.*
ER... YEAH.
THAT'S WHAT I SAID.
ANYWAY, THANKS...
"IF WE DON'T SAVE EACH OTHER, WE'VE GOT JACK."
WELL, YEAH. EXACTLY.
WHAT'S THAT FROM?
A...*ER...* BOOK.
*ER...*HOW DID YOU HEAR ABOUT MORRIGAN?
OH, IT WAS REALLY WEIRD...

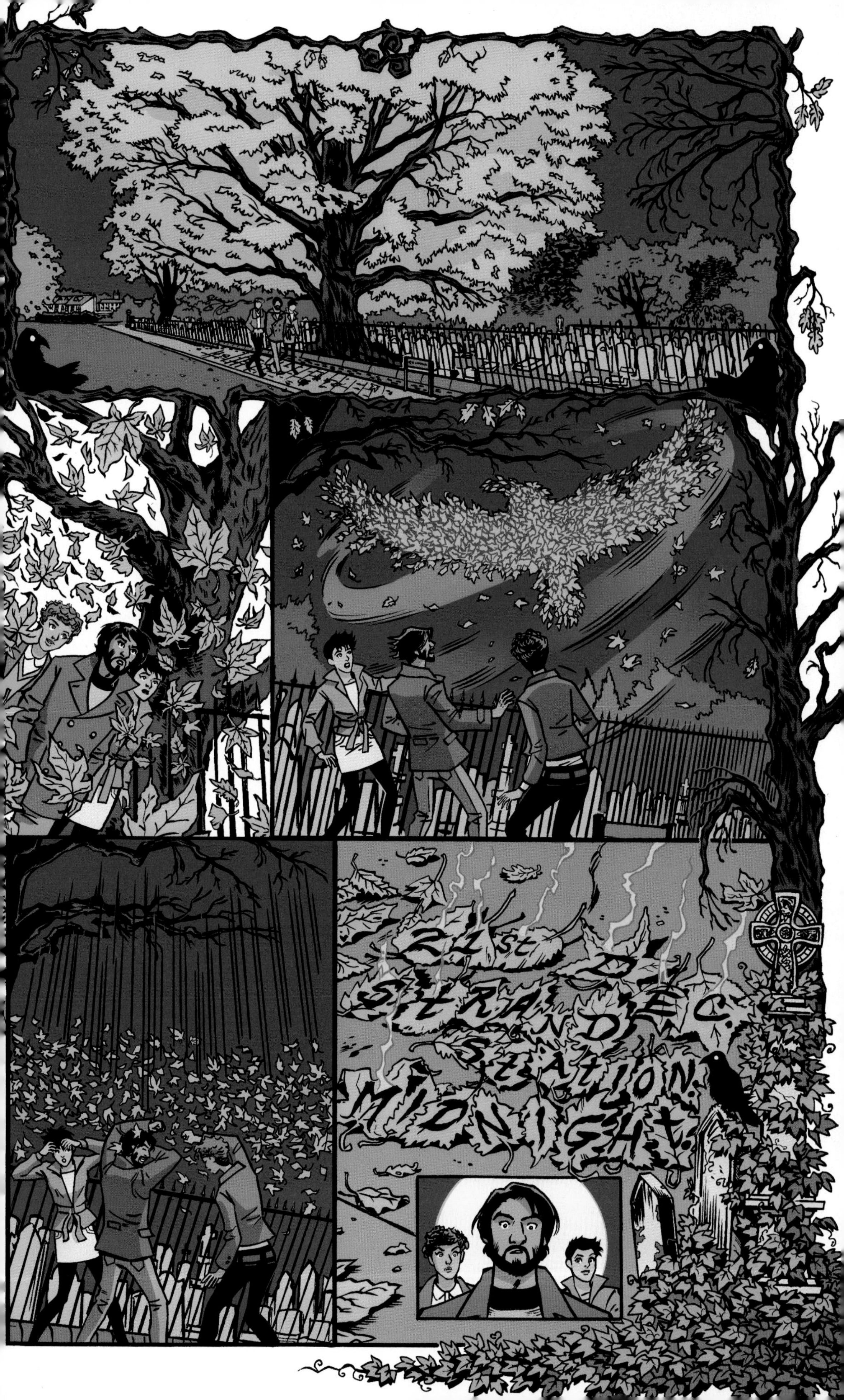
21st DEC.
STRAND STATION.
MIDNIGHT.

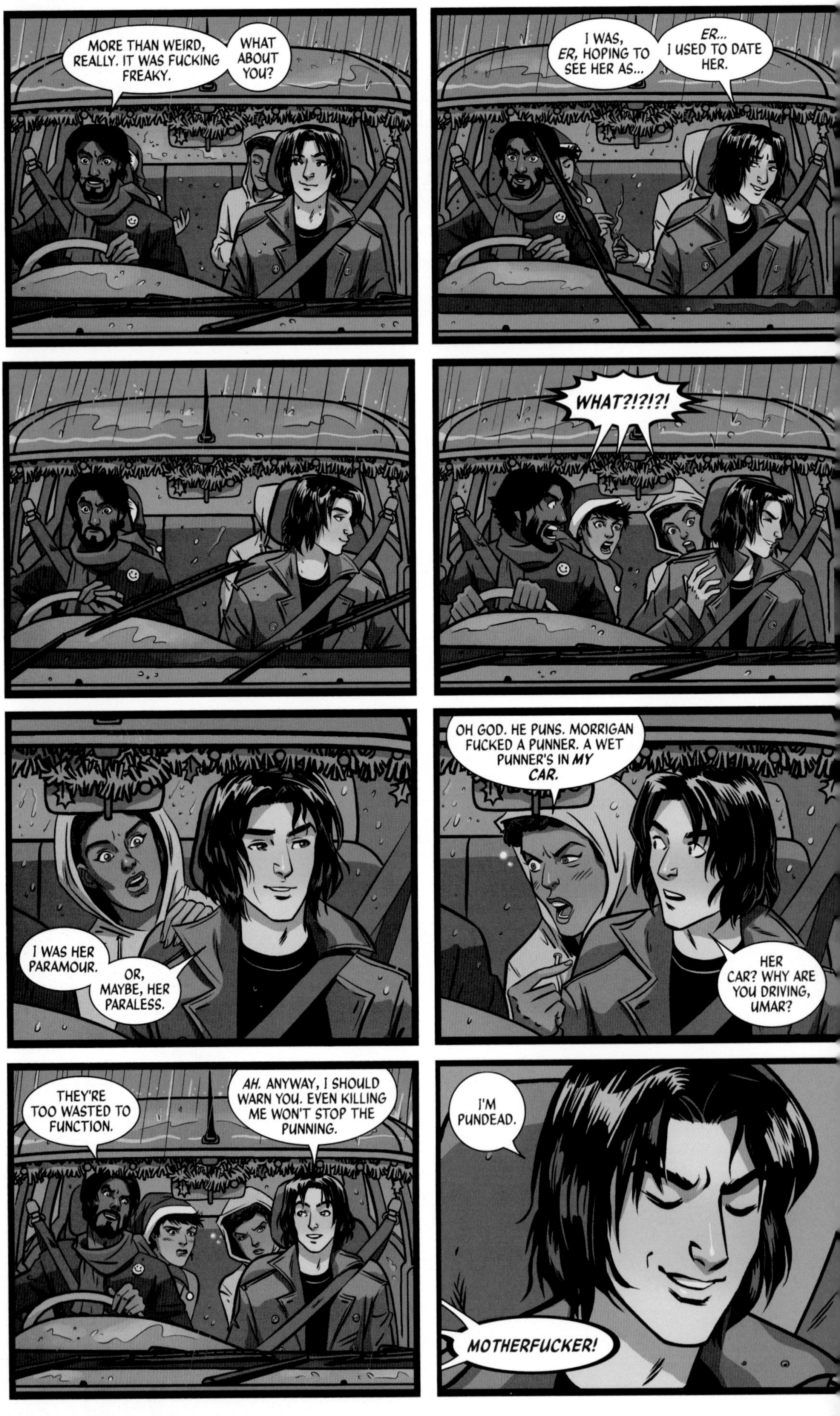
MORE THAN WEIRD, REALLY. IT WAS FUCKING FREAKY.
WHAT ABOUT YOU?
I WAS, *ER,* HOPING TO SEE HER AS...
ER... I USED TO DATE HER.
WHAT?!?!?!
I WAS HER PARAMOUR.
OR, MAYBE, HER PARALESS.
OH GOD. HE PUNS. MORRIGAN FUCKED A PUNNER. A WET PUNNER'S IN *MY CAR.*
HER CAR? WHY ARE YOU DRIVING, UMAR?
THEY'RE TOO WASTED TO FUNCTION.
AH. ANYWAY, I SHOULD WARN YOU. EVEN KILLING ME WON'T STOP THE PUNNING.
I'M PUNDEAD.
MOTHERFUCKER!

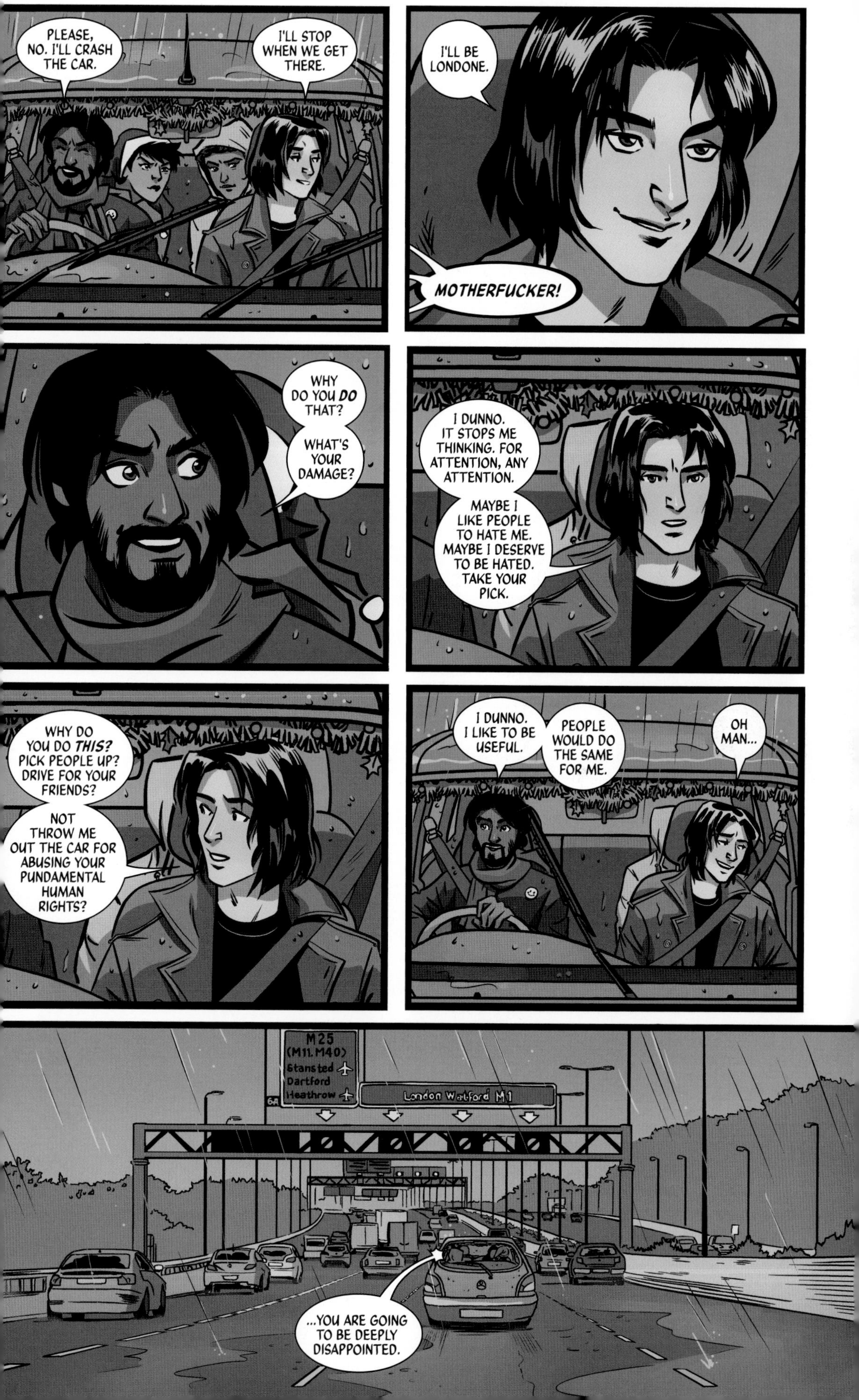
PLEASE, NO. I'LL CRASH THE CAR.
I'LL STOP WHEN WE GET THERE.
I'LL BE LONDONE.
MOTHERFUCKER!
WHY DO YOU DO THAT?
WHAT'S YOUR DAMAGE?
I DUNNO. IT STOPS ME THINKING. FOR ATTENTION, ANY ATTENTION.
MAYBE I LIKE PEOPLE TO HATE ME. MAYBE I DESERVE TO BE HATED. TAKE YOUR PICK.
WHY DO YOU DO THIS? PICK PEOPLE UP? DRIVE FOR YOUR FRIENDS?
NOT THROW ME OUT THE CAR FOR ABUSING YOUR PUNDAMENTAL HUMAN RIGHTS?
I DUNNO. I LIKE TO BE USEFUL.
PEOPLE WOULD DO THE SAME FOR ME.
OH MAN...
M25
(M11, M40)
Stansted
Dartford
Heathrow
6A
London Watford M1
...YOU ARE GOING TO BE DEEPLY DISAPPOINTED.

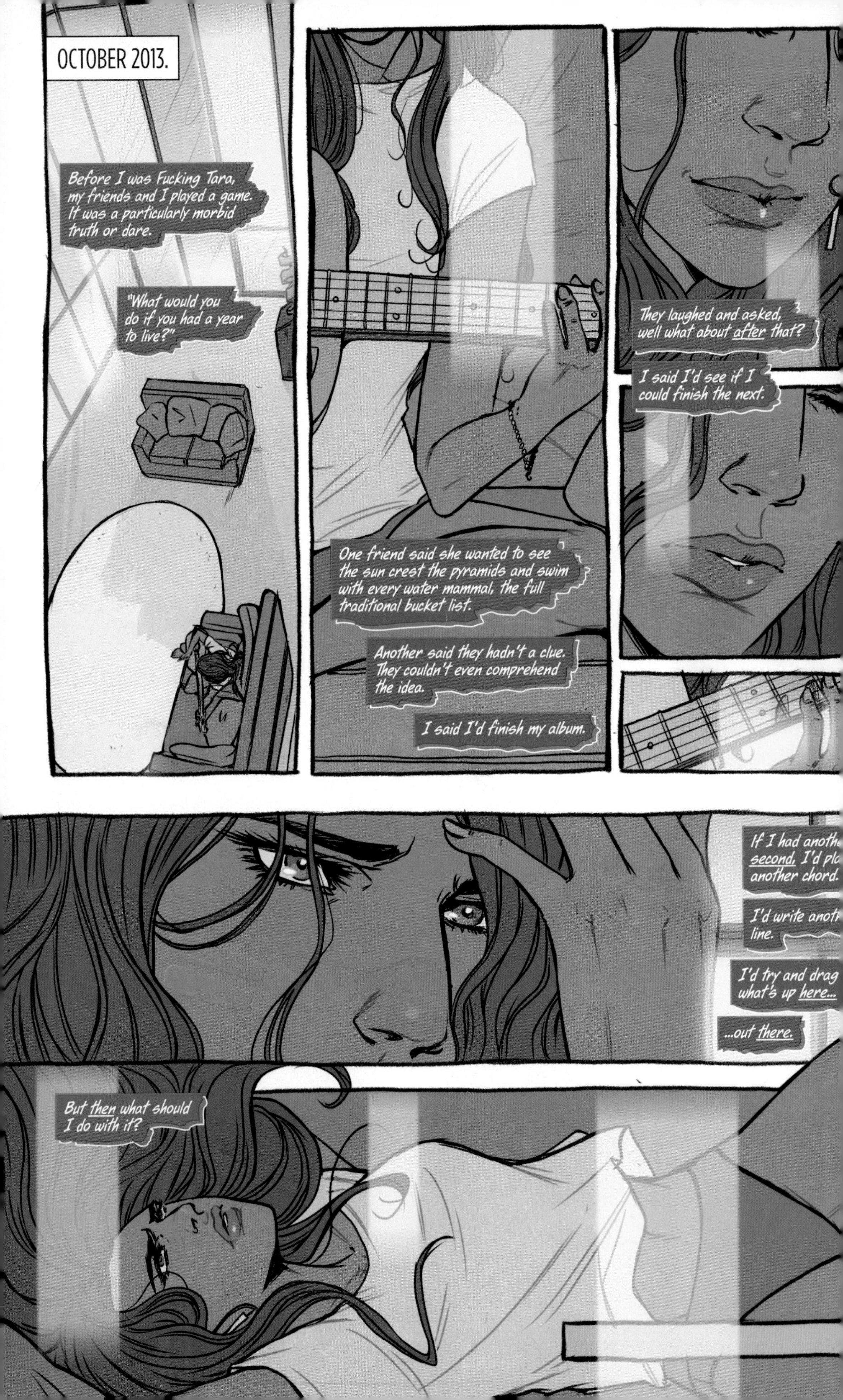
OCTOBER 2013.
Before I was Fucking Tara, my friends and I played a game. It was a particularly morbid truth or dare.
"What would you do if you had a year to live?"
One friend said she wanted to see the sun crest the pyramids and swim with every water mammal, the full traditional bucket list.
Another said they hadn't a clue. They couldn't even comprehend the idea.
I said I'd finish my album.
They laughed and asked, well what about after that?
I said I'd see if I could finish the next.
If I had anoth second, I'd pla another chord.
I'd write anot line.
I'd try and drag what's up here...
...out there.
But then what should I do with it?

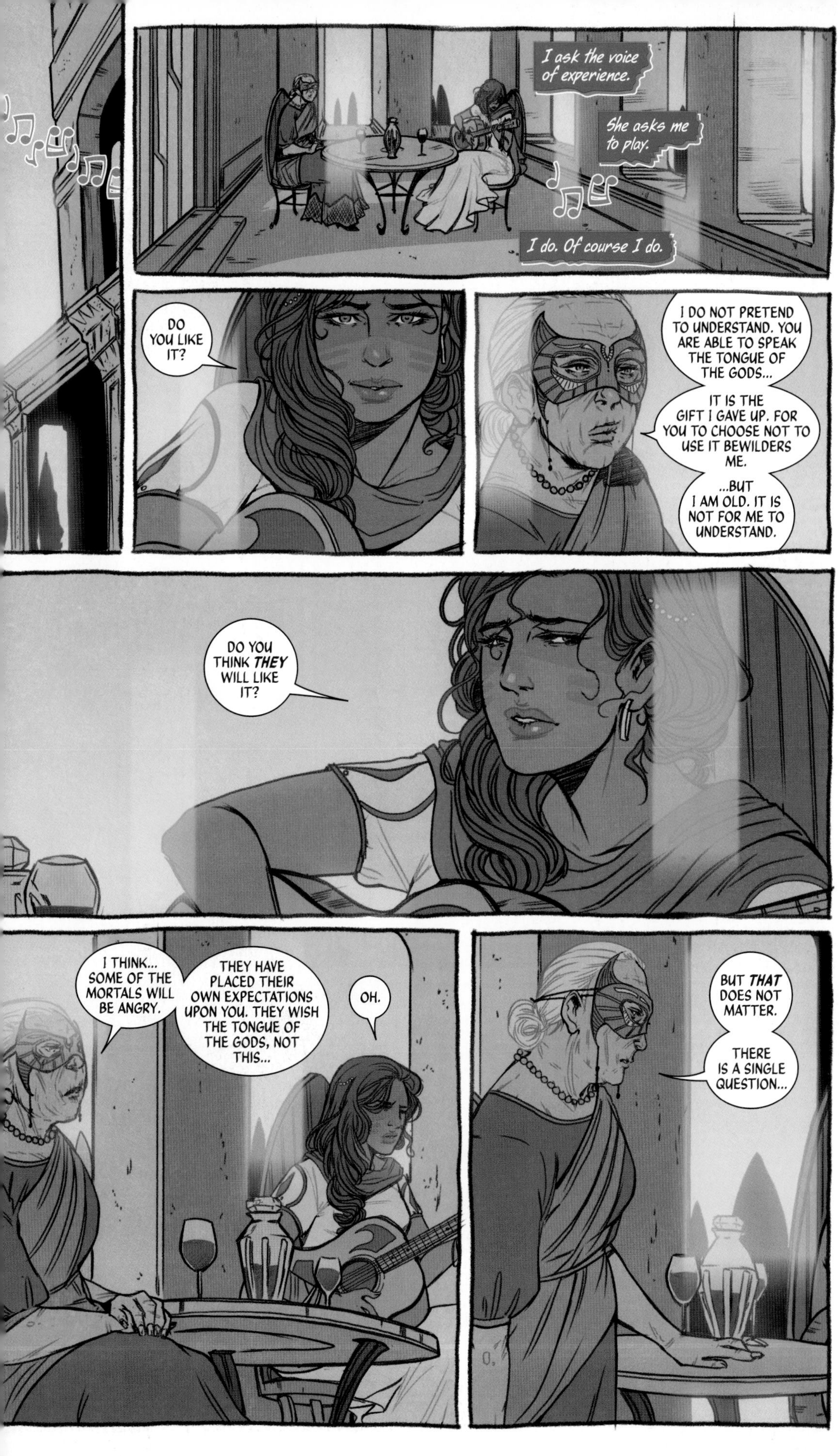
I ask the voice of experience.
She asks me to play.
I do. Of course I do.
DO YOU LIKE IT?
I DO NOT PRETEND TO UNDERSTAND. YOU ARE ABLE TO SPEAK THE TONGUE OF THE GODS...
IT IS THE GIFT I GAVE UP. FOR YOU TO CHOOSE NOT TO USE IT BEWILDERS ME.
...BUT I AM OLD. IT IS NOT FOR ME TO UNDERSTAND.
DO YOU THINK *THEY* WILL LIKE IT?
I THINK... SOME OF THE MORTALS WILL BE ANGRY.
THEY HAVE PLACED THEIR OWN EXPECTATIONS UPON YOU. THEY WISH THE TONGUE OF THE GODS, NOT THIS...
OH.
BUT *THAT* DOES NOT MATTER.
THERE IS A SINGLE QUESTION...

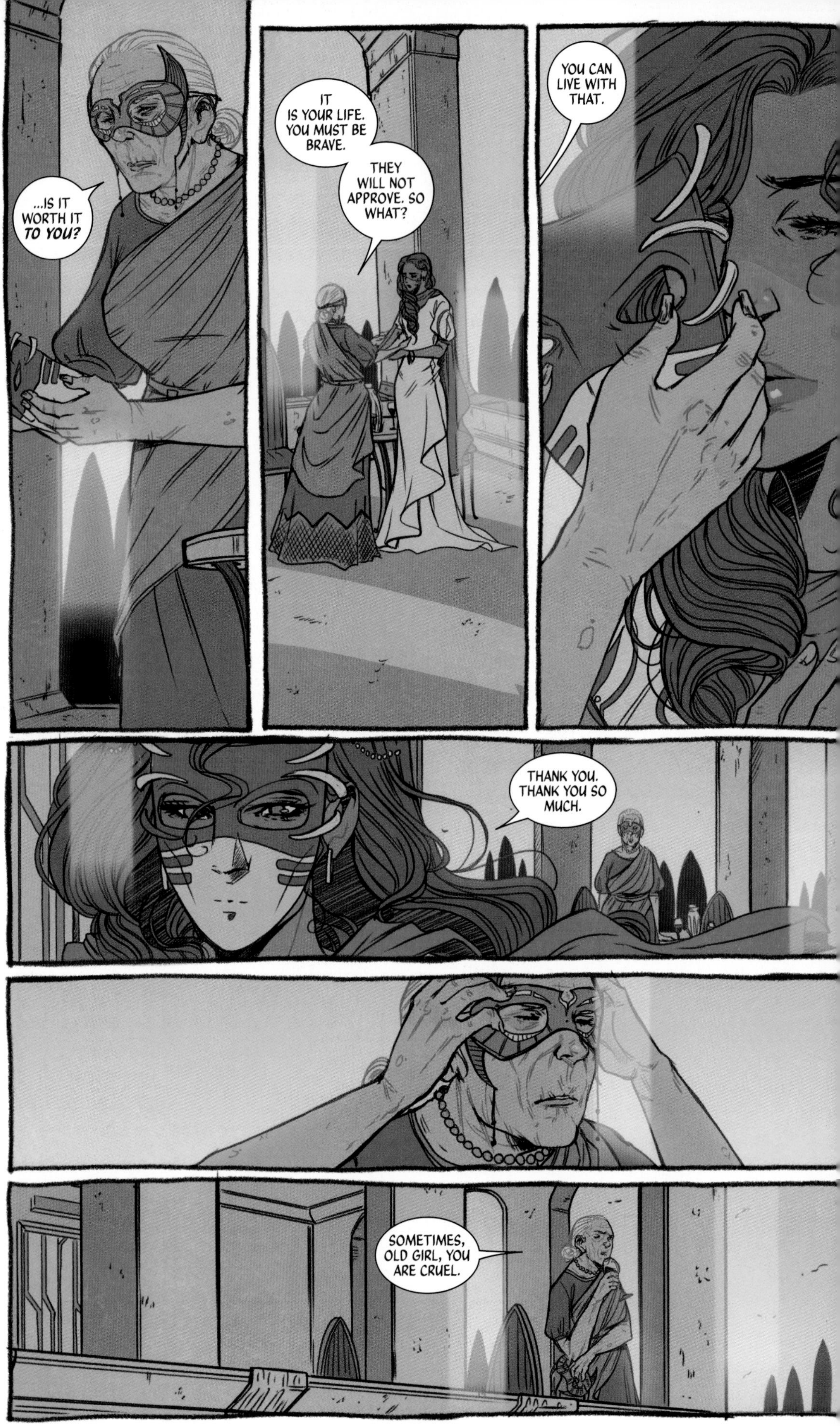
...IS IT WORTH IT *TO YOU?*
IT IS YOUR LIFE. YOU MUST BE BRAVE.
THEY WILL NOT APPROVE. SO WHAT?
YOU CAN LIVE WITH THAT.
THANK YOU. THANK YOU SO MUCH.
SOMETIMES, OLD GIRL, YOU ARE CRUEL.

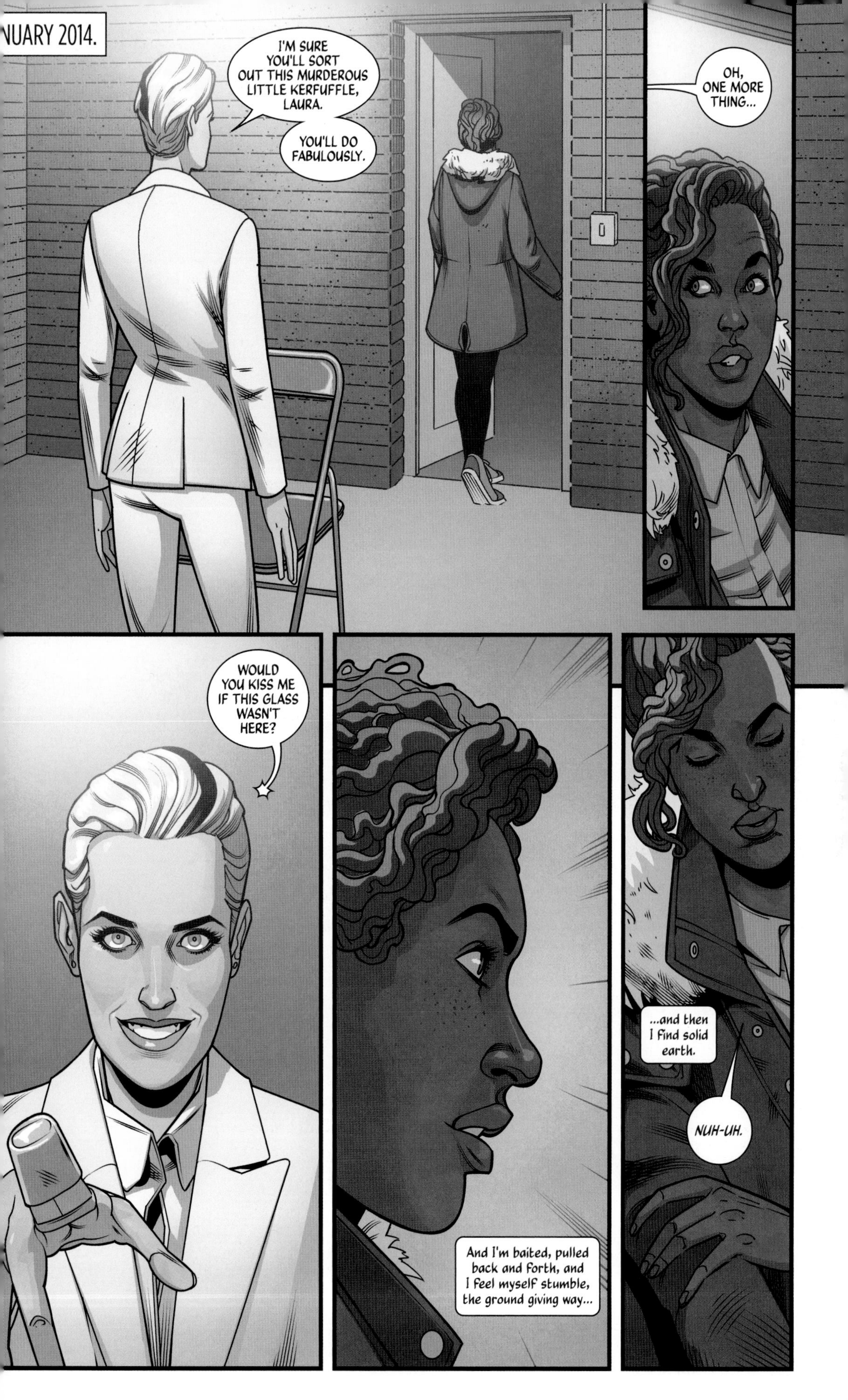

NUARY 2014.
I'M SURE YOU'LL SORT OUT THIS MURDEROUS LITTLE KERFUFFLE, LAURA.
YOU'LL DO FABULOUSLY.
OH, ONE MORE THING...
WOULD YOU KISS ME IF THIS GLASS WASN'T HERE?
And I'm baited, pulled back and forth, and I feel myself stumble, the ground giving way...
...and then I find solid earth.
NUH-UH.

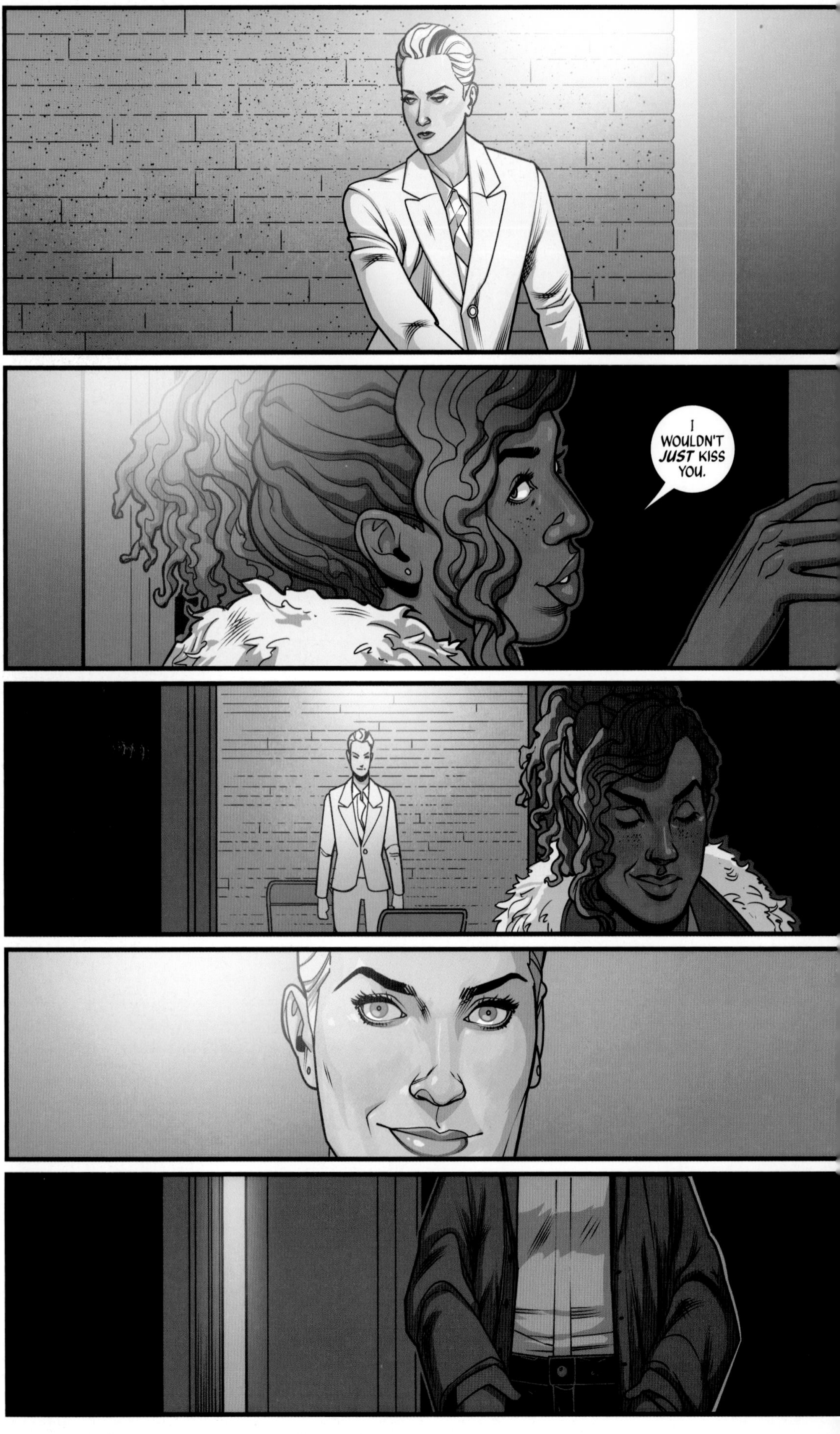
I WOULDN'T JUST KISS YOU.

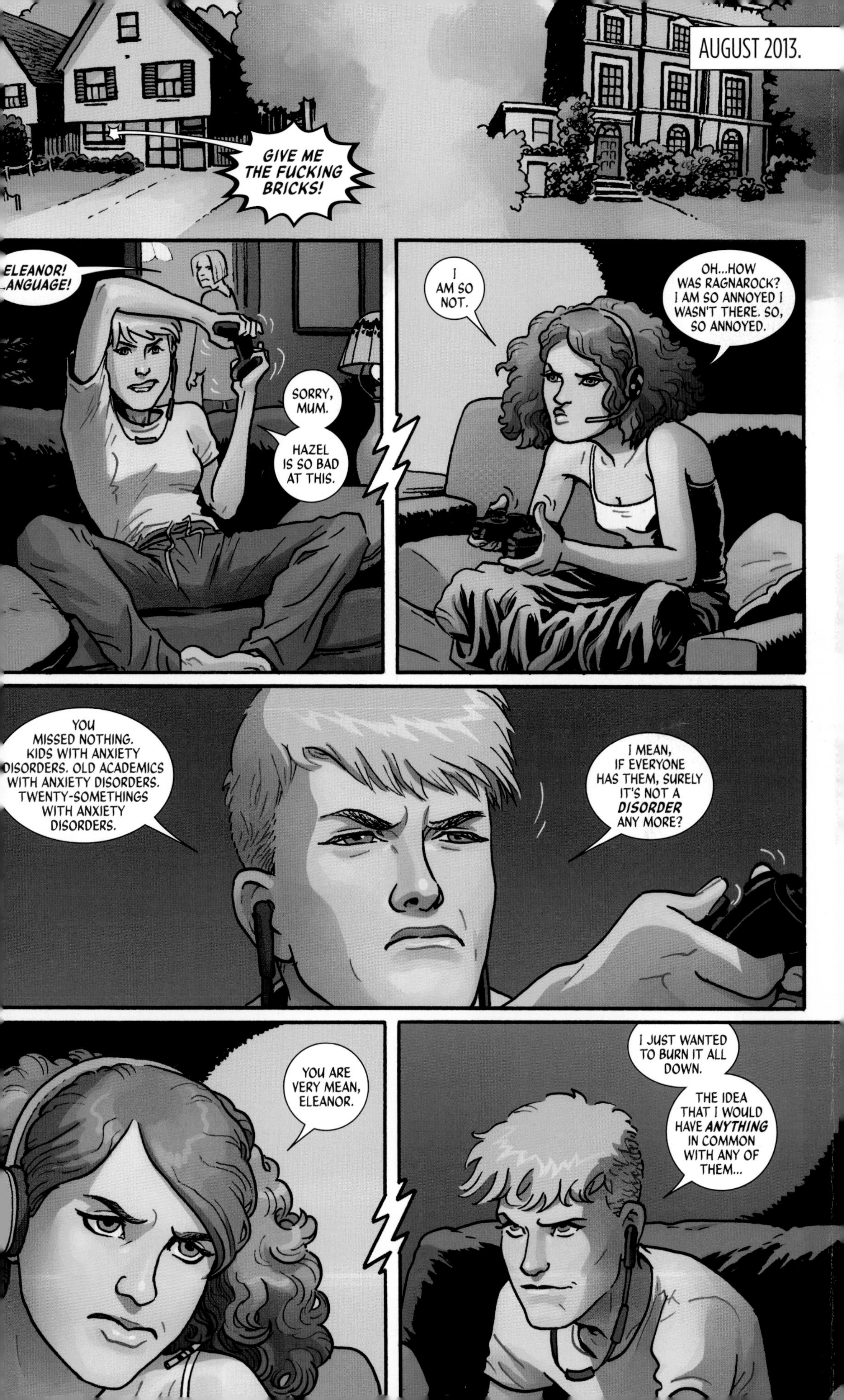
AUGUST 2013.
GIVE ME THE FUCKING BRICKS!
ELEANOR! LANGUAGE!
SORRY, MUM.
HAZEL IS SO BAD AT THIS.
I AM SO NOT.
OH...HOW WAS RAGNAROCK? I AM SO ANNOYED I WASN'T THERE. SO, SO ANNOYED.
YOU MISSED NOTHING. KIDS WITH ANXIETY DISORDERS. OLD ACADEMICS WITH ANXIETY DISORDERS. TWENTY-SOMETHINGS WITH ANXIETY DISORDERS.
I MEAN, IF EVERYONE HAS THEM, SURELY IT'S NOT A *DISORDER* ANY MORE?
YOU ARE VERY MEAN, ELEANOR.
I JUST WANTED TO BURN IT ALL DOWN.
THE IDEA THAT I WOULD HAVE *ANYTHING* IN COMMON WITH ANY OF THEM...

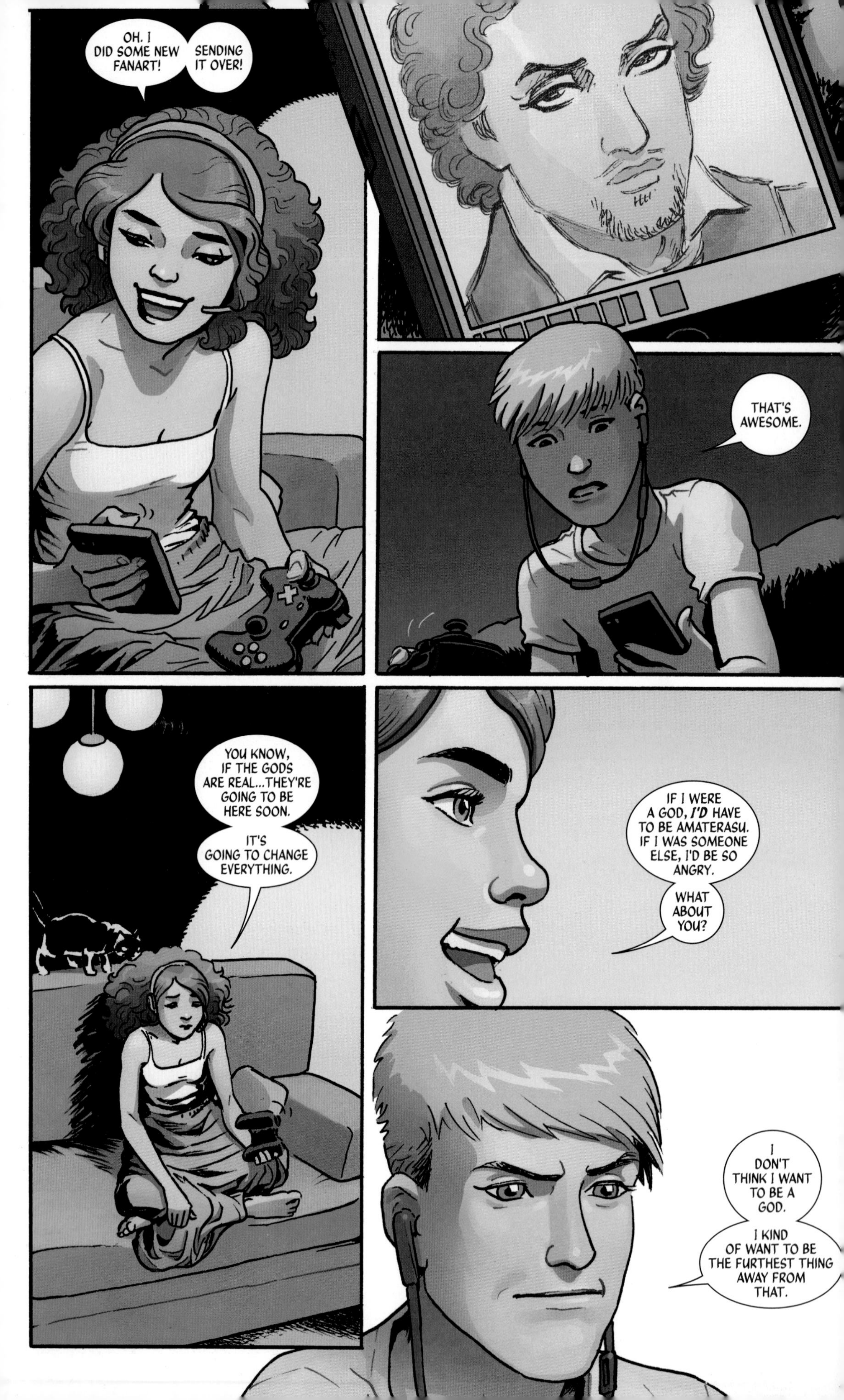
OH. I DID SOME NEW FANART!
SENDING IT OVER!
THAT'S AWESOME.
YOU KNOW, IF THE GODS ARE REAL...THEY'RE GOING TO BE HERE SOON.
IT'S GOING TO CHANGE EVERYTHING.
IF I WERE A GOD, *I'D* HAVE TO BE AMATERASU. IF I WAS SOMEONE ELSE, I'D BE SO ANGRY.
WHAT ABOUT YOU?
I DON'T THINK I WANT TO BE A GOD.
I KIND OF WANT TO BE THE FURTHEST THING AWAY FROM THAT.

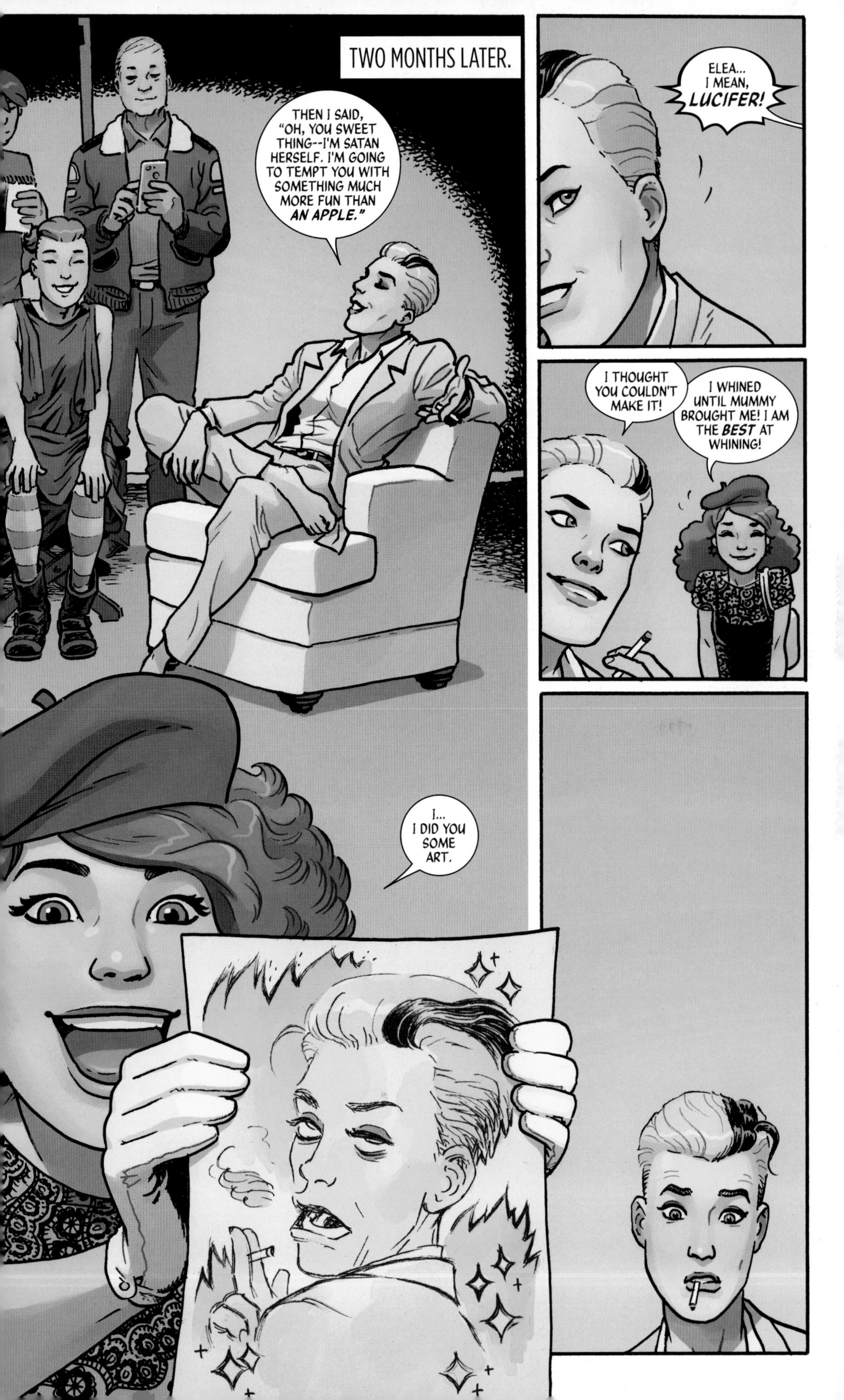
TWO MONTHS LATER.
THEN I SAID, "OH, YOU SWEET THING--I'M SATAN HERSELF. I'M GOING TO TEMPT YOU WITH SOMETHING MUCH MORE FUN THAN *AN APPLE.*"
ELEA... I MEAN, *LUCIFER!*
I THOUGHT YOU COULDN'T MAKE IT!
I WHINED UNTIL MUMMY BROUGHT ME! I AM THE *BEST* AT WHINING!
I... I DID YOU SOME ART.

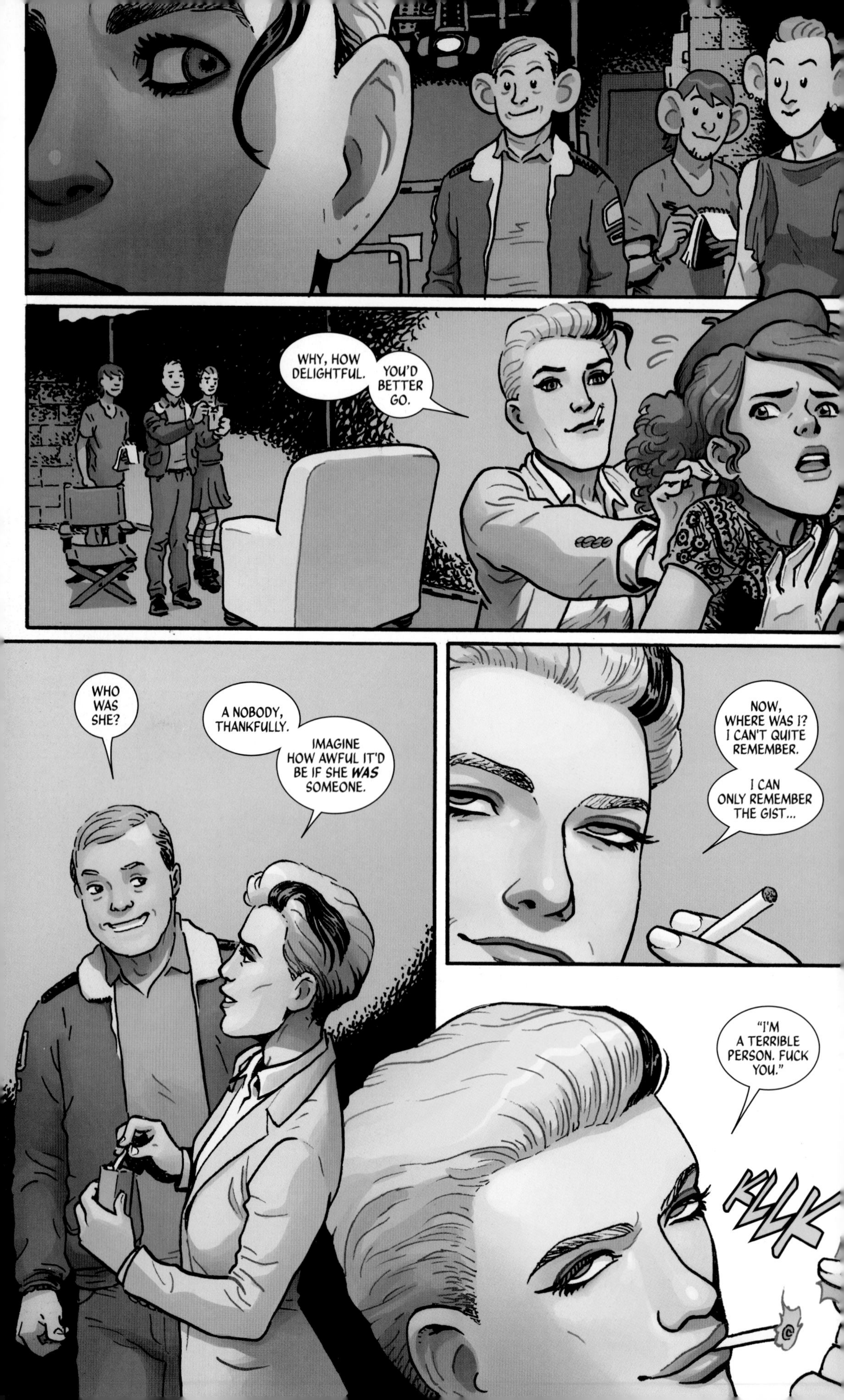
WHY, HOW DELIGHTFUL.
YOU'D BETTER GO.
WHO WAS SHE?
A NOBODY, THANKFULLY.
IMAGINE HOW AWFUL IT'D BE IF SHE WAS SOMEONE.
NOW, WHERE WAS I? I CAN'T QUITE REMEMBER.
I CAN ONLY REMEMBER THE GIST...
"I'M A TERRIBLE PERSON. FUCK YOU."
KLIK

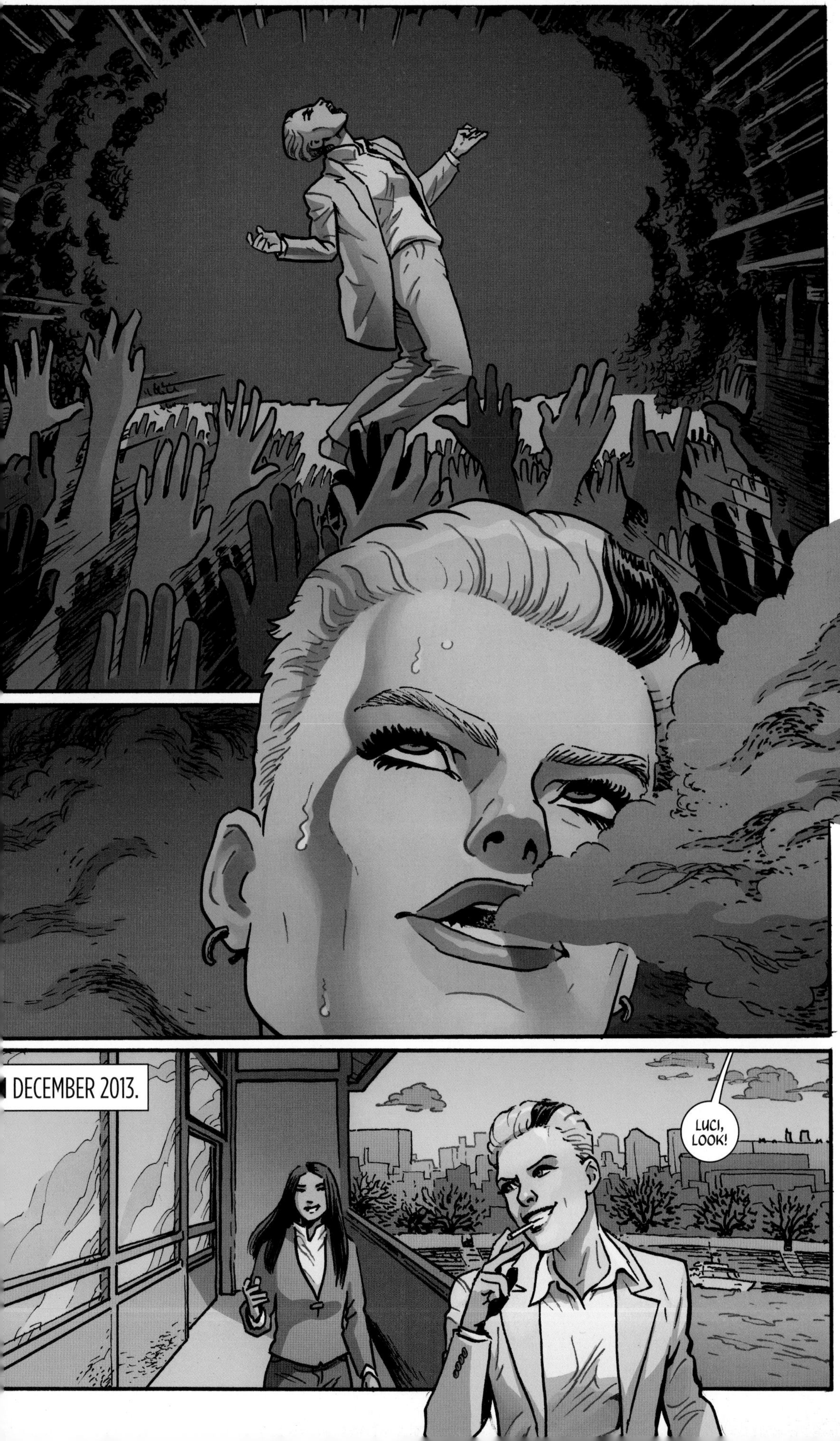
DECEMBER 2013.
LUCI, LOOK!

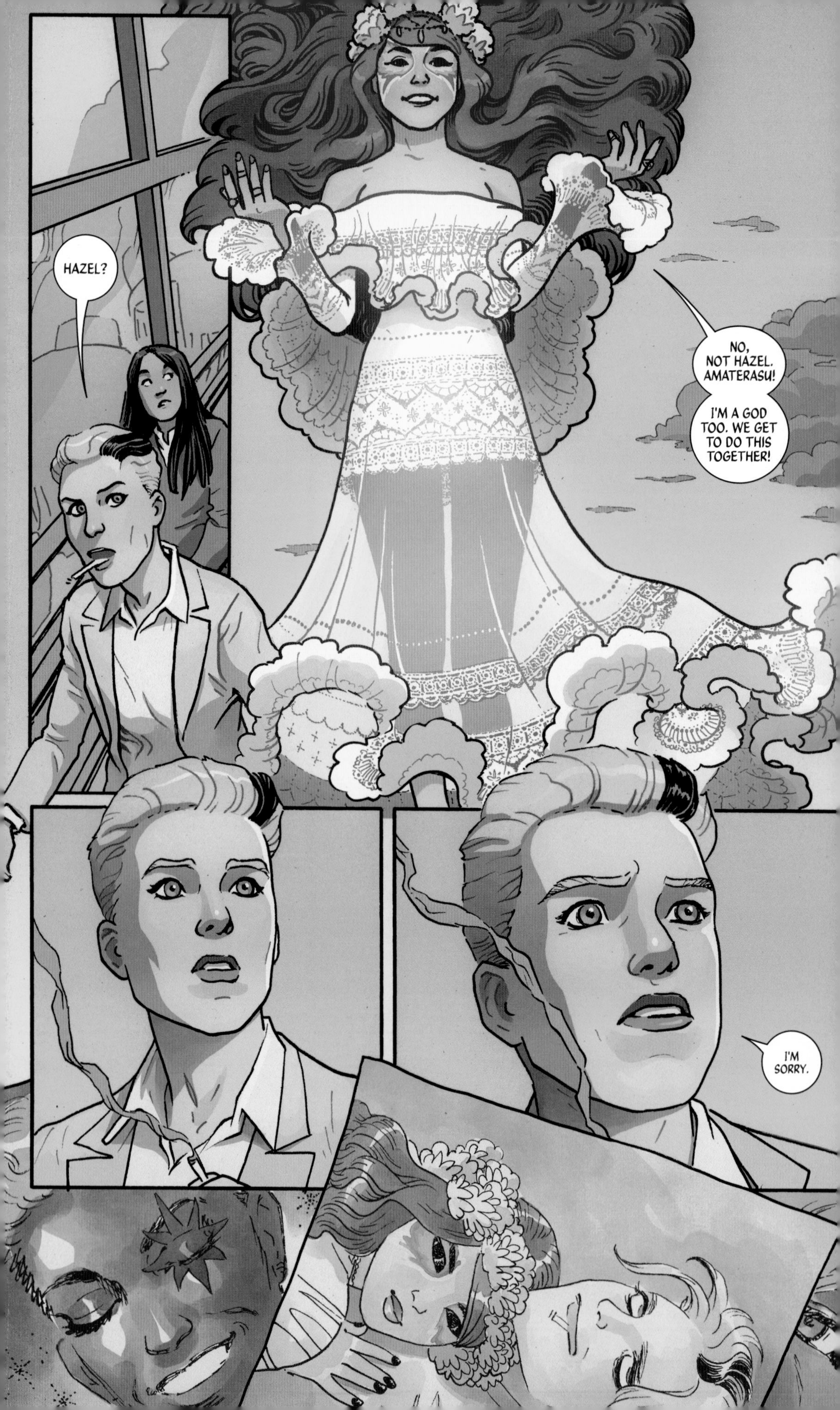
HAZEL?
NO, NOT HAZEL. AMATERASU!
I'M A GOD TOO. WE GET TO DO THIS TOGETHER!
I'M SORRY.

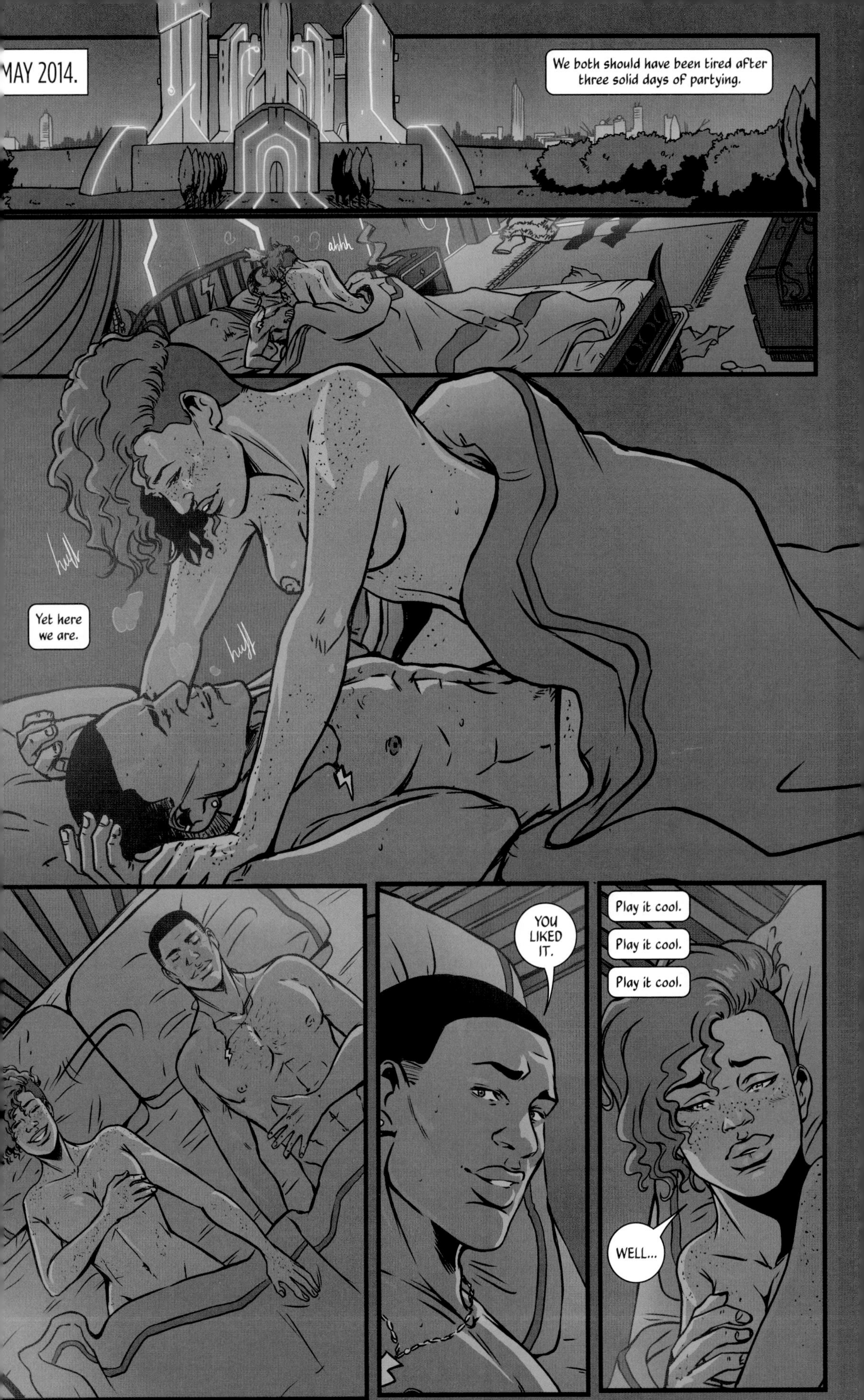
MAY 2014.
We both should have been tired after three solid days of partying.
ahhh
huff
Yet here we are.
huff
YOU LIKED IT.
Play it cool.
Play it cool.
Play it cool.
WELL...

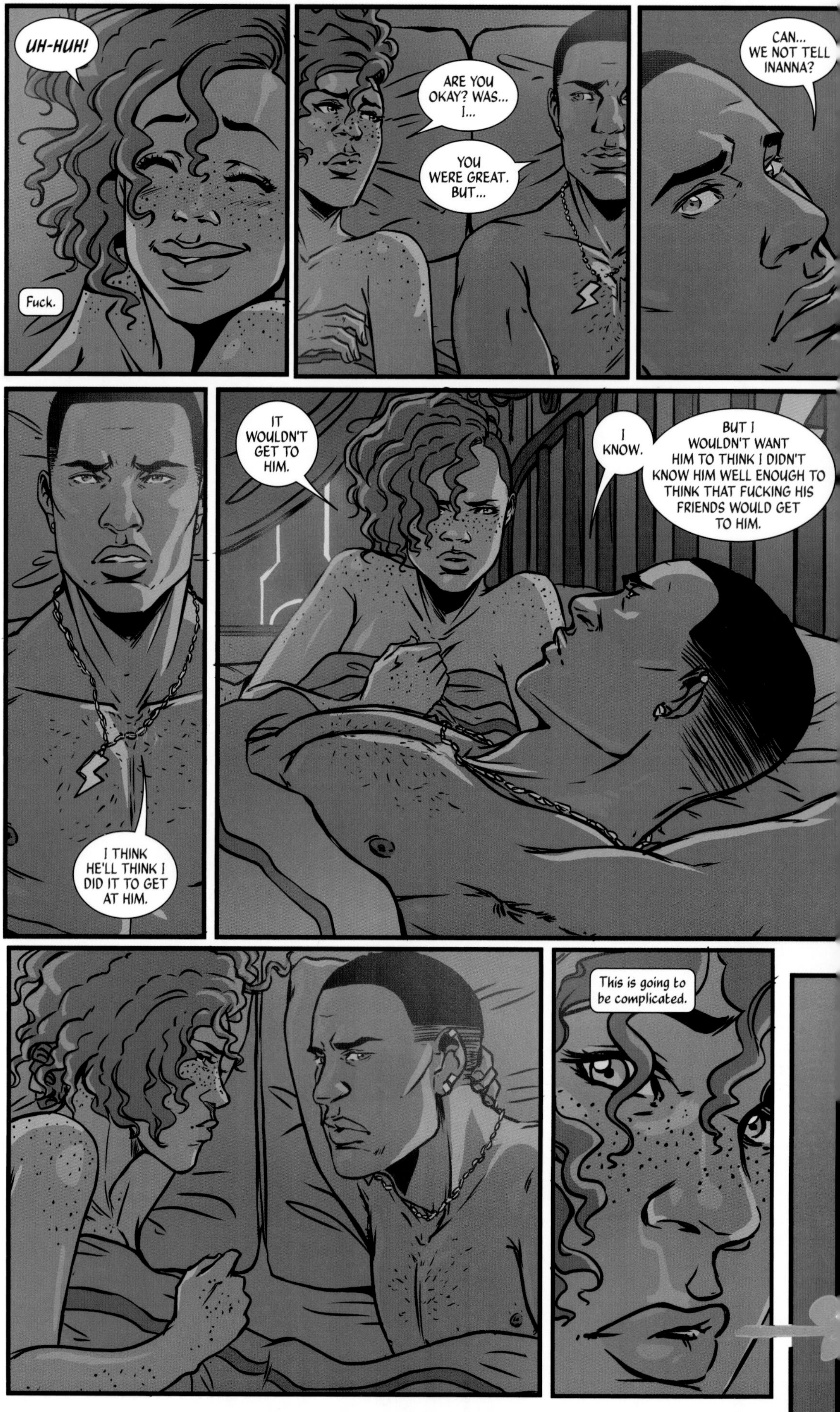
UH-HUH!
Fuck.
ARE YOU OKAY? WAS... I...
YOU WERE GREAT. BUT...
CAN... WE NOT TELL INANNA?
I THINK HE'LL THINK I DID IT TO GET AT HIM.
IT WOULDN'T GET TO HIM.
I KNOW.
BUT I WOULDN'T WANT HIM TO THINK I DIDN'T KNOW HIM WELL ENOUGH TO THINK THAT FUCKING HIS FRIENDS WOULD GET TO HIM.
This is going to be complicated.

THE
WICKED
+
THE DIVINE

THE
FUNNIES

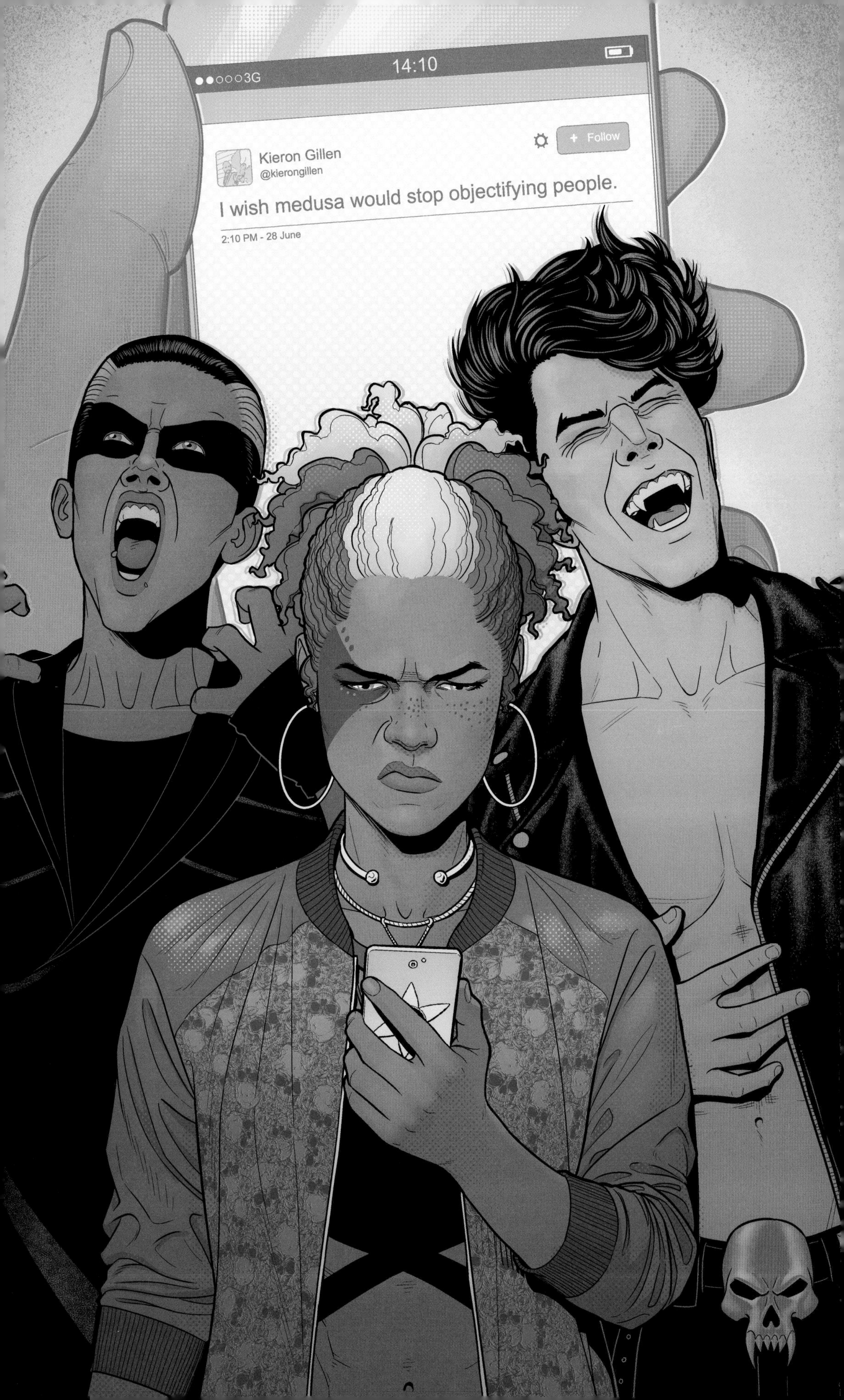
14:10
3G
Follow
Kieron Gillen
@kierongillen
I wish medusa would stop objectifying people.
2:10 PM - 28 June

THE FUNNIES #1

THE WICKED + THE DIVINE

DOGS!

CATS!

RAPS!

LABOURED PUNS!

OUR COMIC SERIES IS NEARLY OVER. One more arc to go. As such, when we realised we had space for a final Special, we had to decide what to do. We'd hit all the necessary historical ones. We'd touched on some minor scenes with the annual. What's left?

In short: having some fun.

This Special is the equivalent of the last day of school where instead of doing the work, you're allowed to bunk off and mess around. We invited some of our good friends to write comedy stories about our characters. Or to mock our characters. Or to mock us. Or to just take our money and run because we love them that much.

When setting up something like this, the urge is to try and take from the widest part of comics, from indie to hyper-mainstream, from the ultra-credible to Chip Zdarsky. Kate Leth has been mocking us in person for as long as we've known her, so she had to be hit up to do it in the eternal form of paper, with art from Sisters of Mercy Supremo Margaux Saltel (whose *Superfreaks* over on Amazon is an astounding showcase for her). Lizz Lunney has been delighting us with her minimalist comics ever since we've come up in the zine scene, and scaring us with her intense glare, so we had to invite her. Hamish Steele's *Pantheon* is the best mythology comic in the last thousand years, so we were overjoyed that he could jump along. Kitty Curran and Larissa Zageris' illustrated prose micronovel *Taylor Swift: Girl Detective* ("The Secrets of the Starbucks Lovers") was such a delight we had to charm them aboard.

We kidnapped Romesh Ranganathan outside a recording studio for *Judge Romesh* and refused to let him leave until he wrote a comic. He did, and we grabbed Julia Madrigal (best known for her issues of *Giant Days*) to draw it, entirely making her complicit in our crime. I'm sorry you had to find out like this, Julia. Editor Chrissy wanted to prove that this writing comics thing was actually easy, so I gave her enough rope to hang herself, and instead she has made a magical rope sculpture and now has all the moral authority to tell us we suck she will ever need. She teamed up with usual letterer Clayton and usual flatter Dee, and generally tore things up. I wrote a couple too. Jamie did one for — er — "closure" as he put it. For the opener, we have Erica Henderson who we lured into joining us with a once-in-a-lifetime chance to draw all the dogs in the world. Always Give Artists What They Want.

We also asked Chip.

See you when the final arc kicks off. It's called *"OKAY"* as we really like making it easy for sarcastic reviewers. Until then, relax with a glass of fizzy pop and enjoy yourselves.

Love,

MᶜK

Kieron and Jamie

THE END

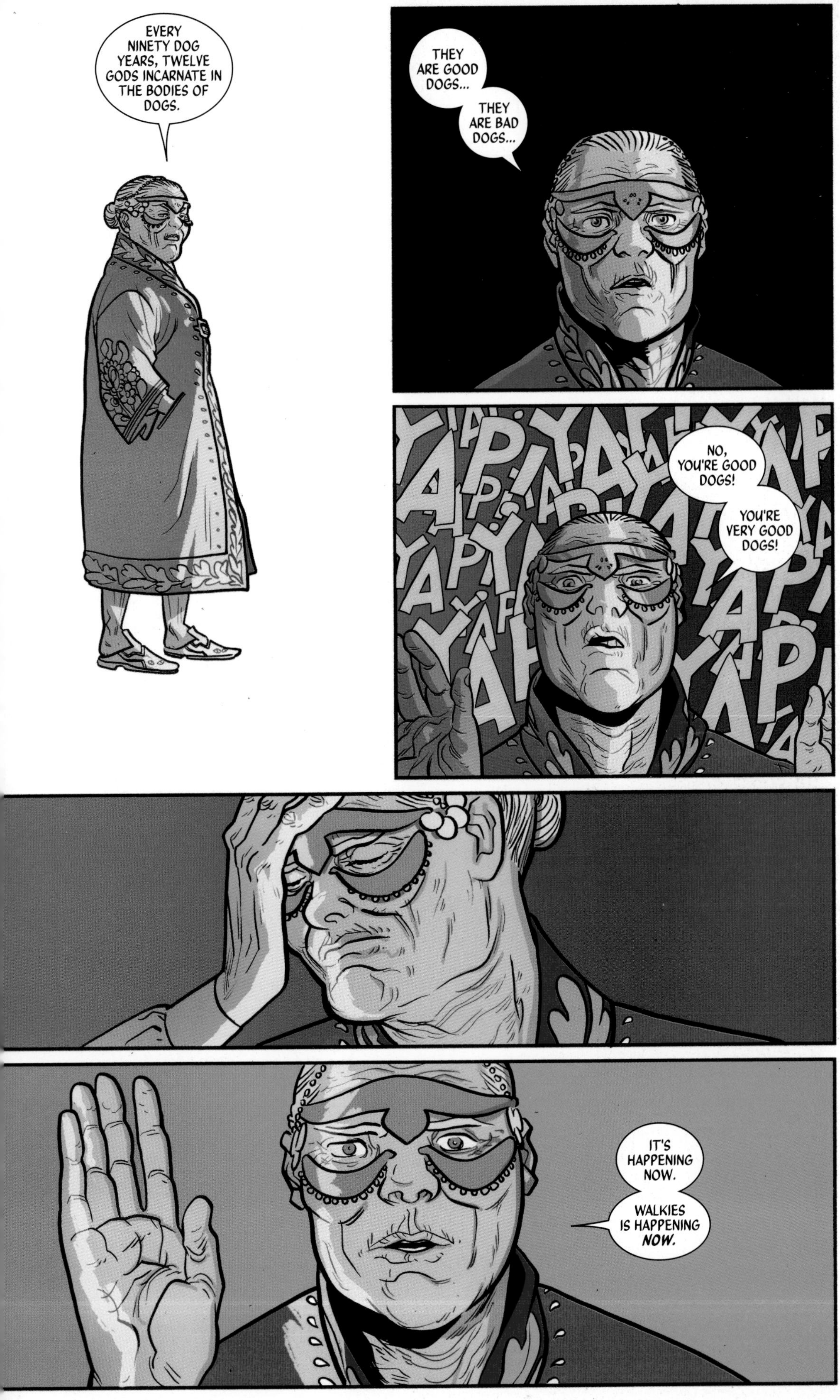
EVERY NINETY DOG YEARS, TWELVE GODS INCARNATE IN THE BODIES OF DOGS.
THEY ARE GOOD DOGS...
THEY ARE BAD DOGS...
NO, YOU'RE GOOD DOGS!
YOU'RE VERY GOOD DOGS!
IT'S HAPPENING NOW.
WALKIES IS HAPPENING *NOW.*

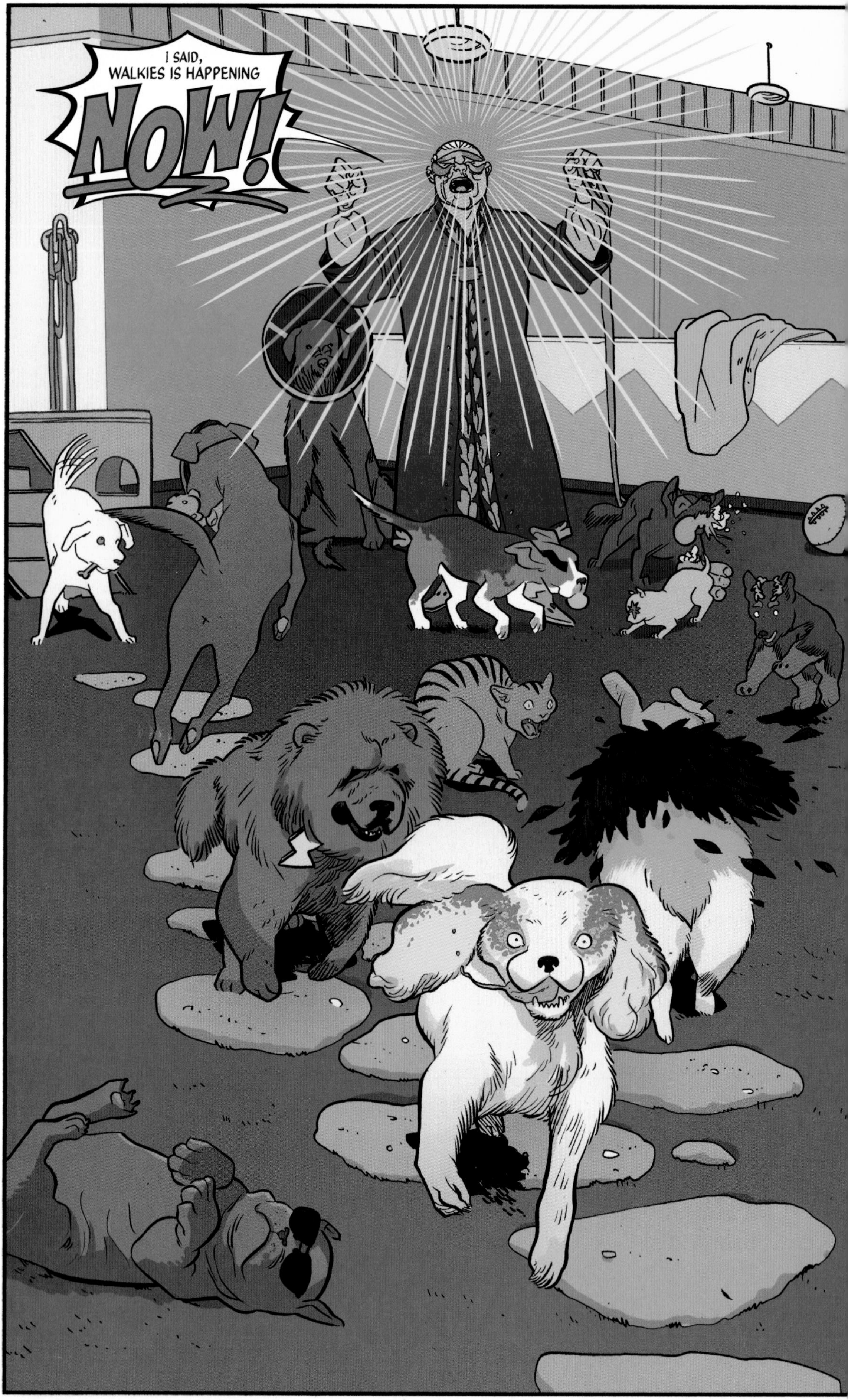
I SAID, WALKIES IS HAPPENING
NOW!

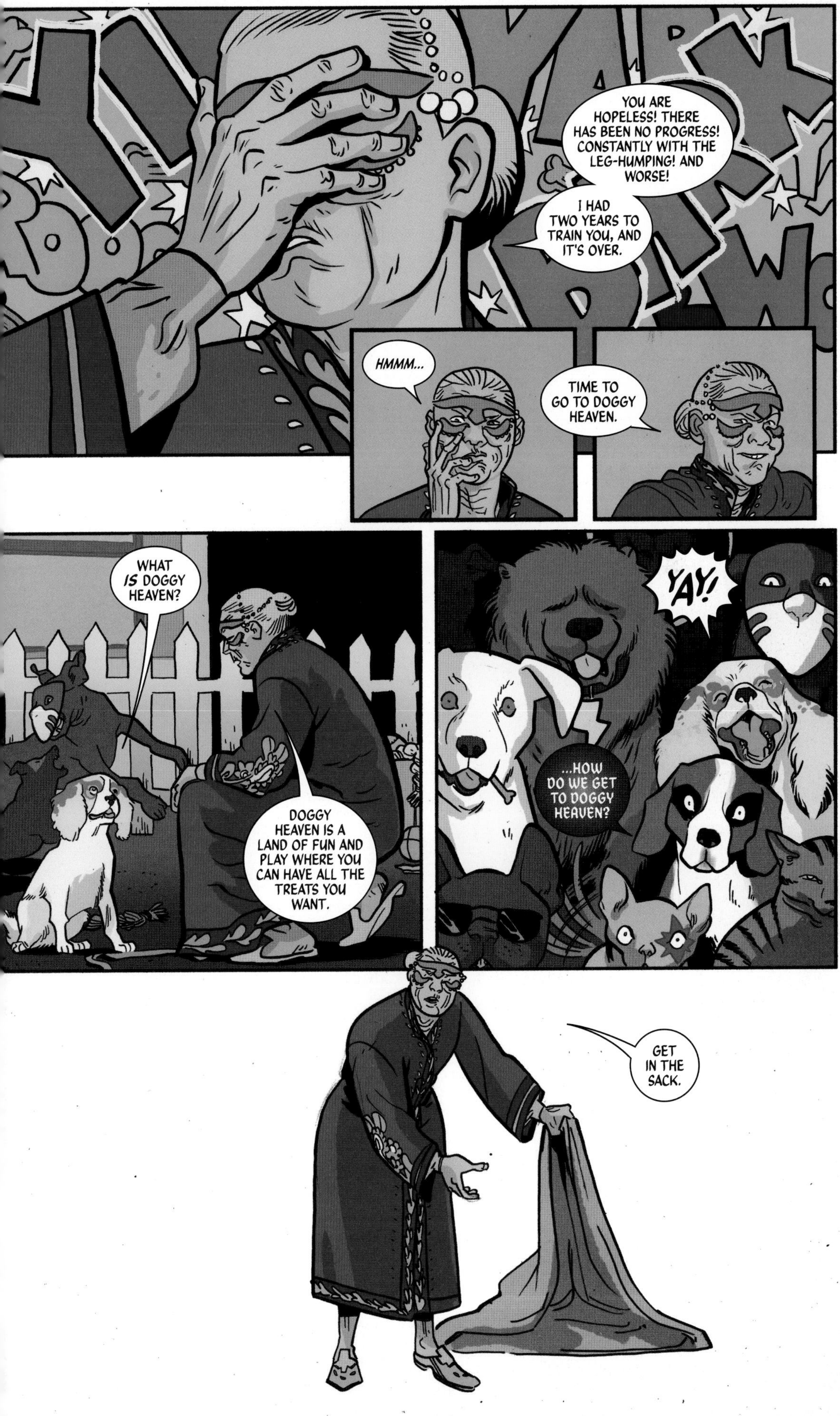

YOU ARE HOPELESS! THERE HAS BEEN NO PROGRESS! CONSTANTLY WITH THE LEG-HUMPING! AND WORSE!
I HAD TWO YEARS TO TRAIN YOU, AND IT'S OVER.
HMMM...
TIME TO GO TO DOGGY HEAVEN.
WHAT *IS* DOGGY HEAVEN?
DOGGY HEAVEN IS A LAND OF FUN AND PLAY WHERE YOU CAN HAVE ALL THE TREATS YOU WANT.
YAY!
...HOW DO WE GET TO DOGGY HEAVEN?
GET IN THE SACK.

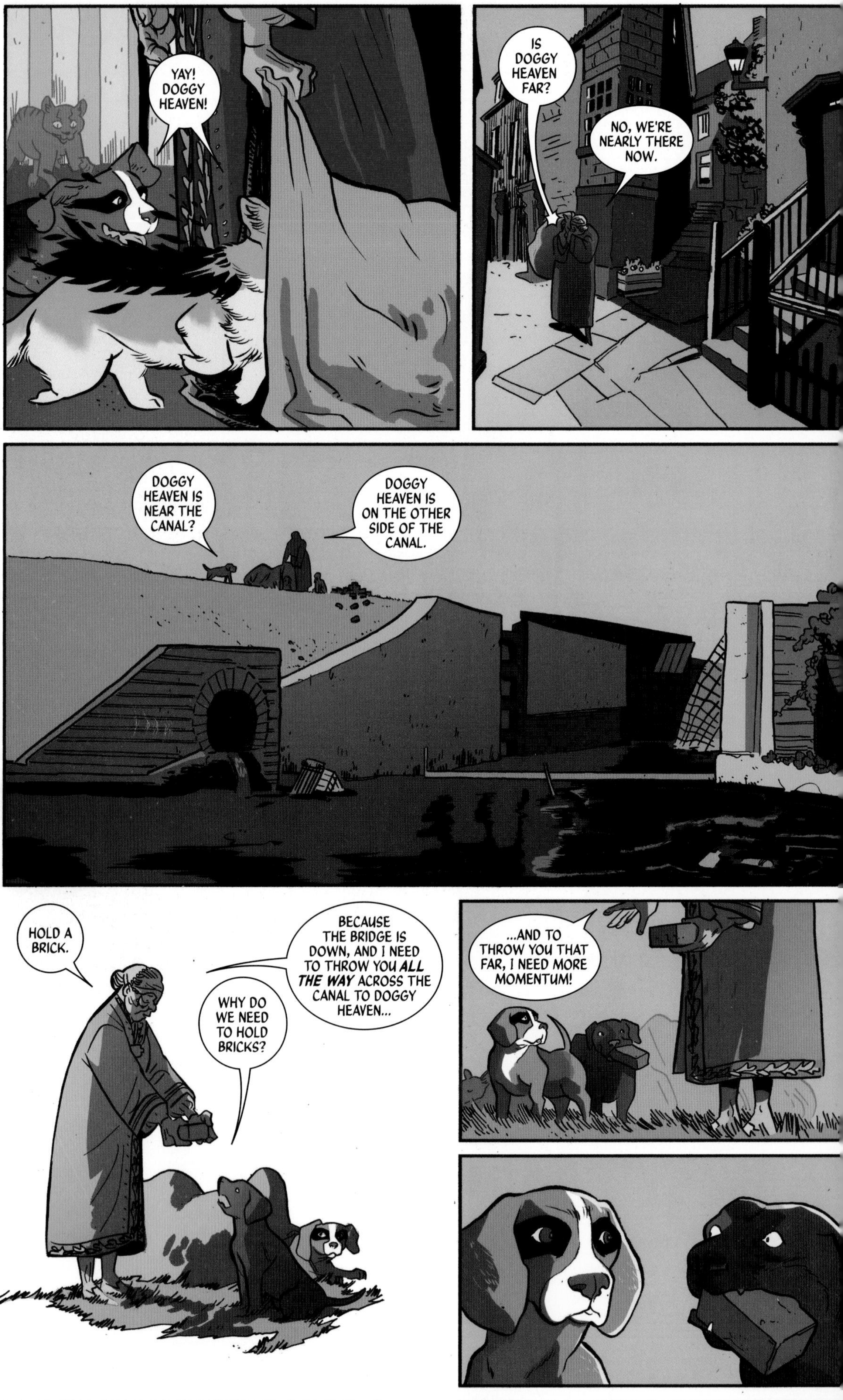
YAY! DOGGY HEAVEN!
IS DOGGY HEAVEN FAR?
NO, WE'RE NEARLY THERE NOW.
DOGGY HEAVEN IS NEAR THE CANAL?
DOGGY HEAVEN IS ON THE OTHER SIDE OF THE CANAL.
HOLD A BRICK.
WHY DO WE NEED TO HOLD BRICKS?
BECAUSE THE BRIDGE IS DOWN, AND I NEED TO THROW YOU ALL THE WAY ACROSS THE CANAL TO DOGGY HEAVEN...
...AND TO THROW YOU THAT FAR, I NEED MORE MOMENTUM!

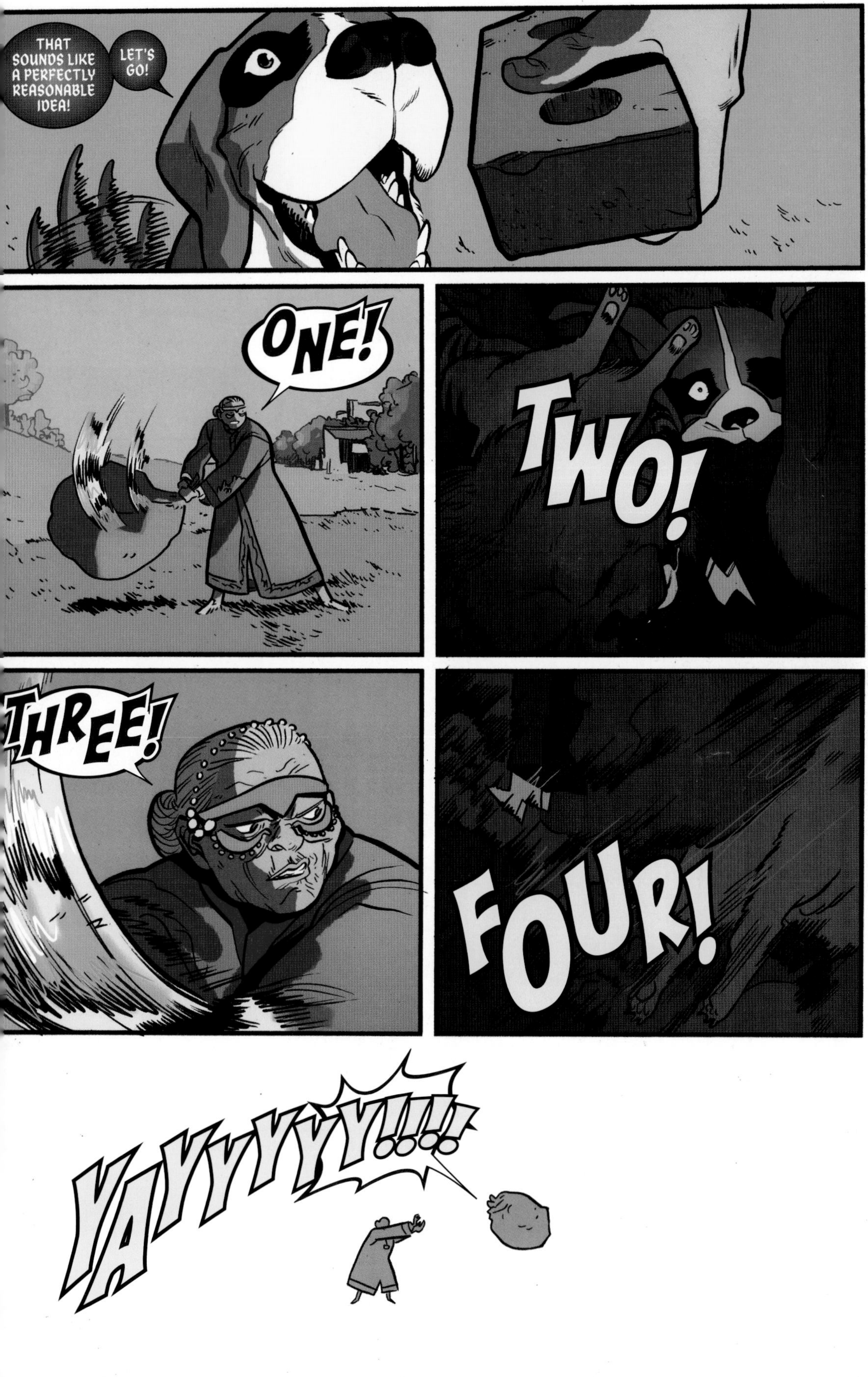
THAT SOUNDS LIKE A PERFECTLY REASONABLE IDEA!
LET'S GO!
ONE!
TWO!
THREE!
FOUR!
YAYYYYYY!!!!

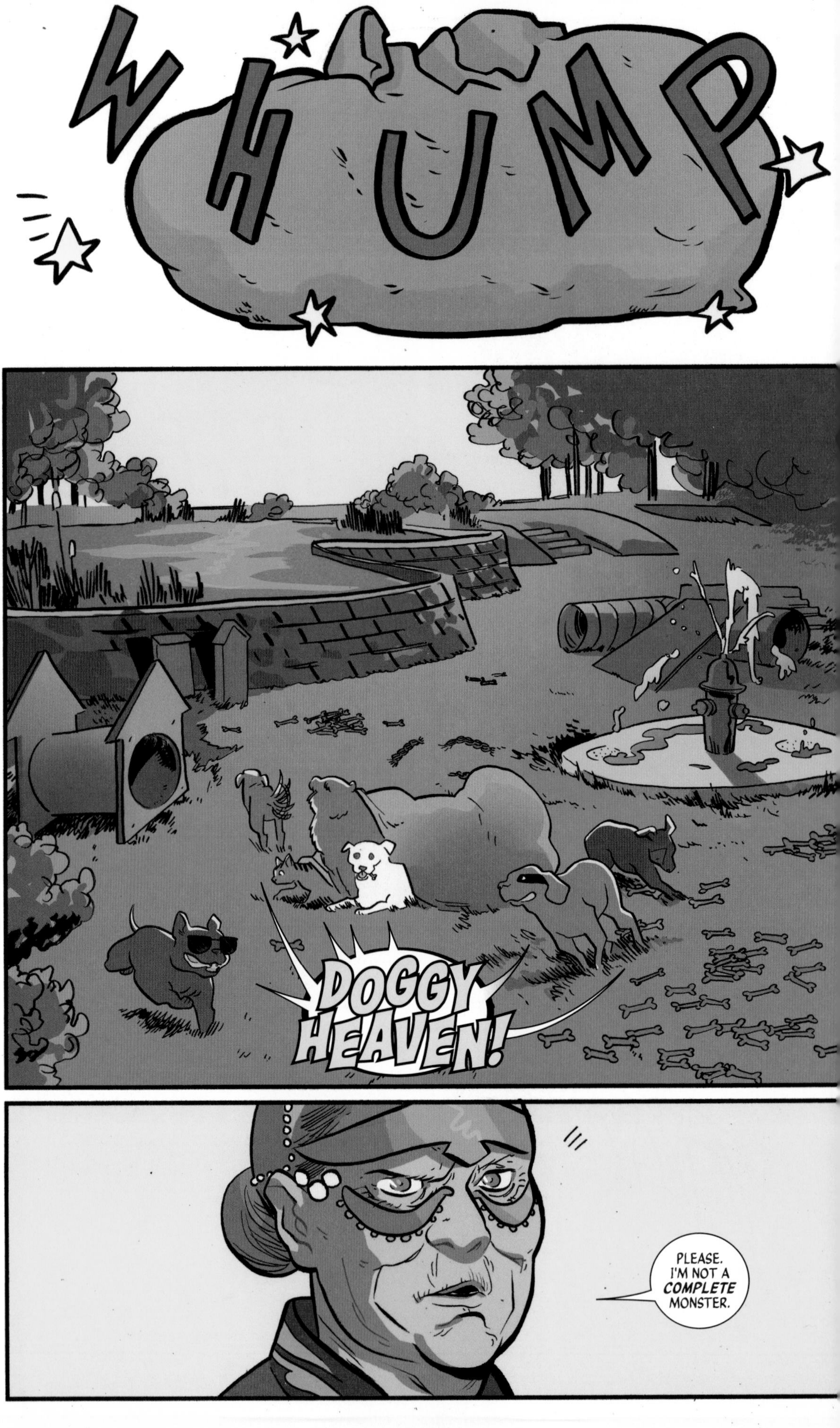
WHUMP
DOGGY HEAVEN!
PLEASE. I'M NOT A *COMPLETE* MONSTER.

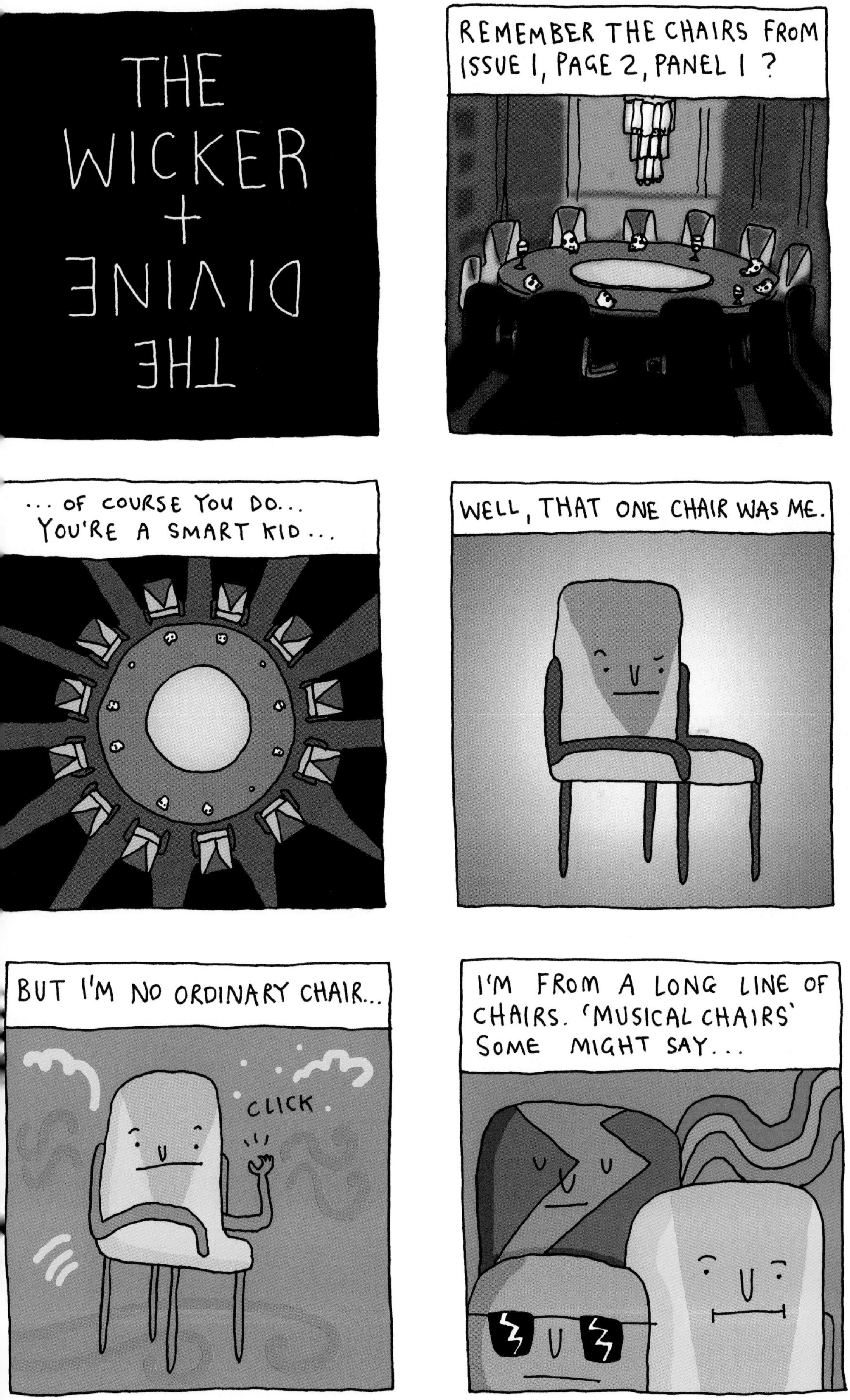
THE
WICKER
+
DIVINE
THE
REMEMBER THE CHAIRS FROM ISSUE 1, PAGE 2, PANEL 1 ?
... OF COURSE YOU DO... YOU'RE A SMART KID...
WELL, THAT ONE CHAIR WAS ME.
BUT I'M NO ORDINARY CHAIR...
CLICK
I'M FROM A LONG LINE OF CHAIRS. 'MUSICAL CHAIRS' SOME MIGHT SAY...

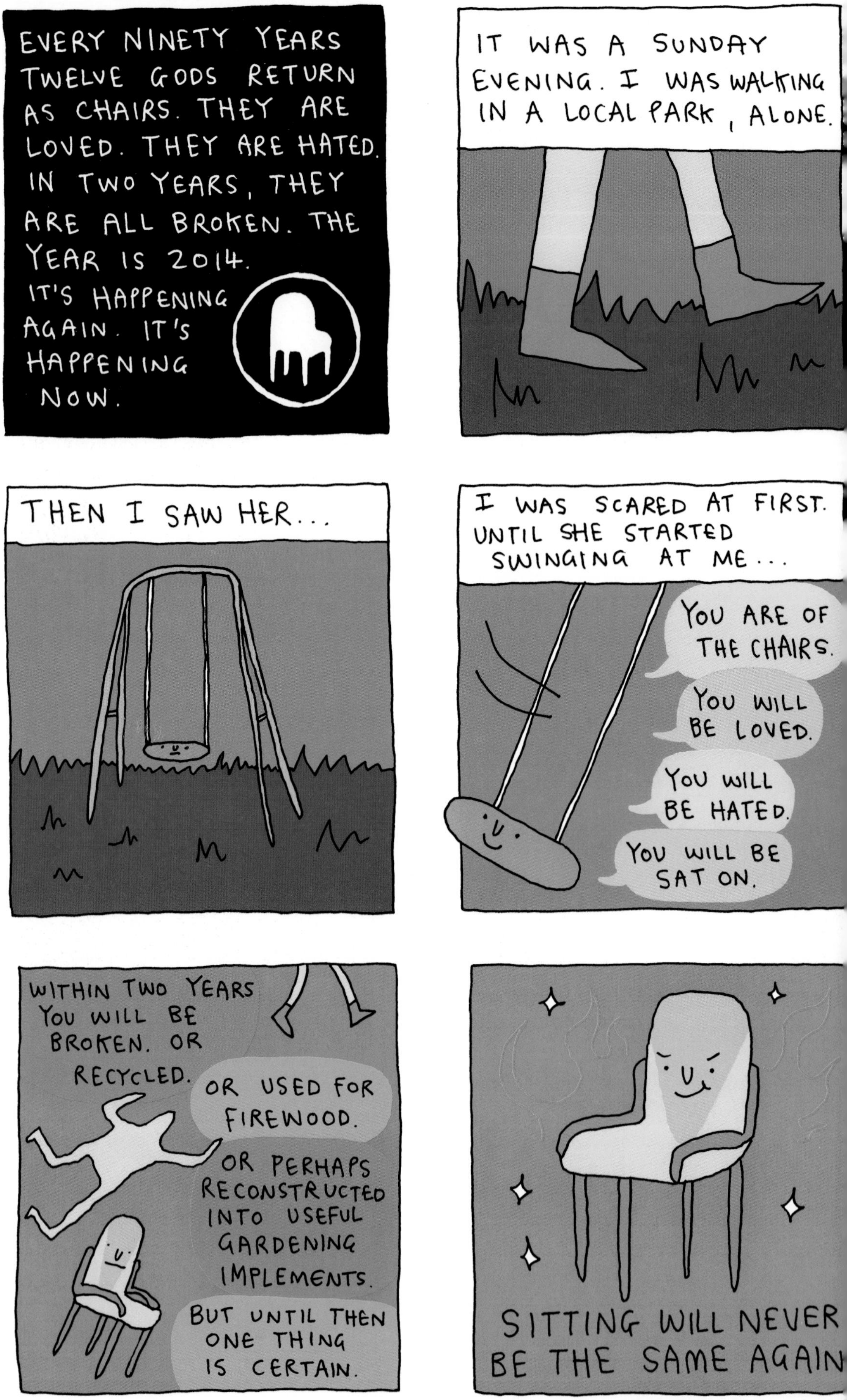
EVERY NINETY YEARS TWELVE GODS RETURN AS CHAIRS. THEY ARE LOVED. THEY ARE HATED. IN TWO YEARS, THEY ARE ALL BROKEN. THE YEAR IS 2014.
IT'S HAPPENING AGAIN. IT'S HAPPENING NOW.
IT WAS A SUNDAY EVENING. I WAS WALKING IN A LOCAL PARK, ALONE.
THEN I SAW HER...
I WAS SCARED AT FIRST. UNTIL SHE STARTED SWINGING AT ME...
YOU ARE OF THE CHAIRS.
YOU WILL BE LOVED.
YOU WILL BE HATED.
YOU WILL BE SAT ON.
WITHIN TWO YEARS YOU WILL BE BROKEN. OR RECYCLED.
OR USED FOR FIREWOOD.
OR PERHAPS RECONSTRUCTED INTO USEFUL GARDENING IMPLEMENTS.
BUT UNTIL THEN ONE THING IS CERTAIN.
SITTING WILL NEVER BE THE SAME AGAIN

BY LIZZ LUNNEY

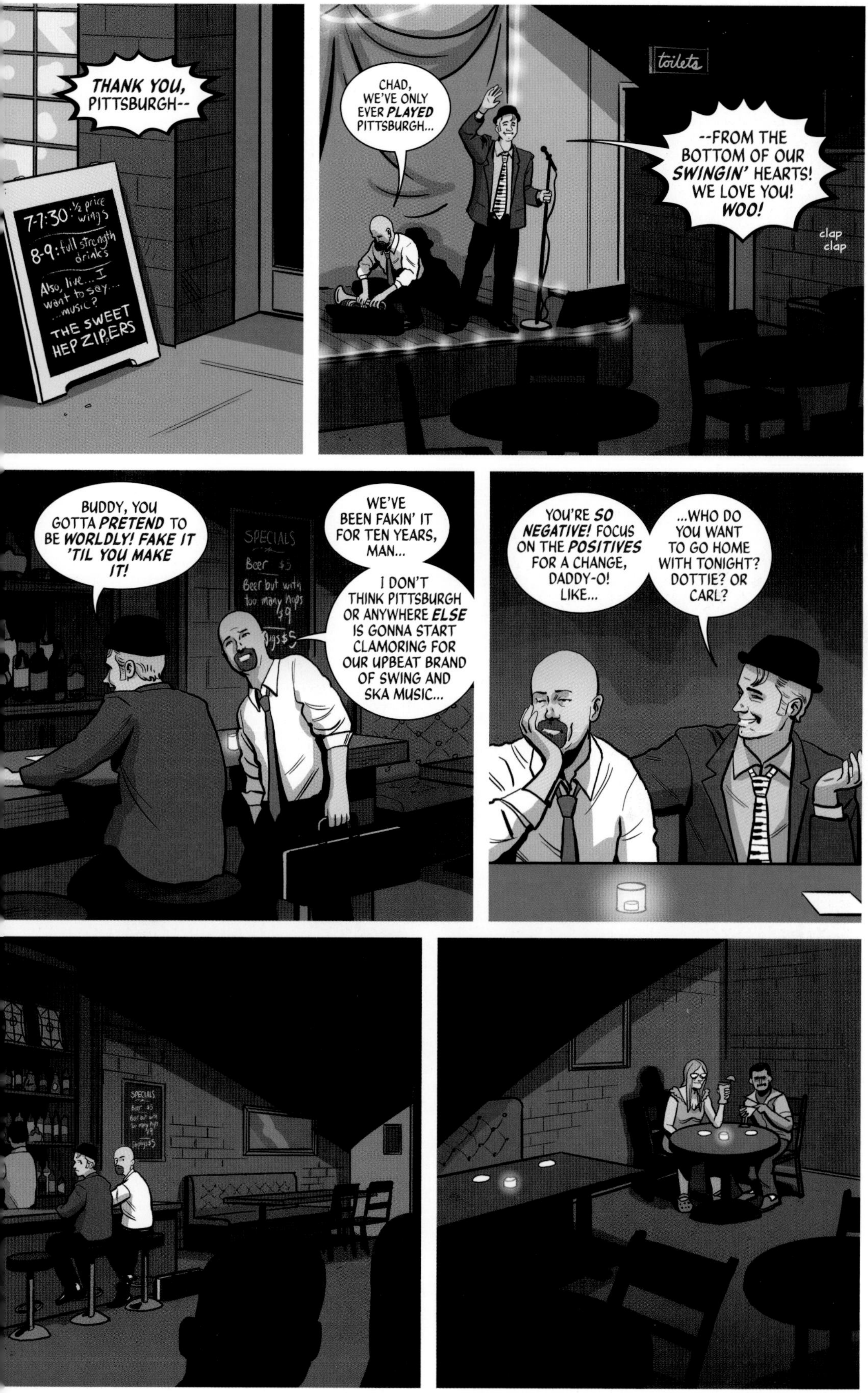
THANK YOU, PITTSBURGH--
7-7:30: ½ price wings
8-9: full strength drinks
Also, live... I want to say... ...music?
THE SWEET HEP ZIPPERS
CHAD, WE'VE ONLY EVER PLAYED PITTSBURGH...
toilets
--FROM THE BOTTOM OF OUR SWINGIN' HEARTS! WE LOVE YOU! WOO!
clap clap
BUDDY, YOU GOTTA PRETEND TO BE WORLDLY! FAKE IT 'TIL YOU MAKE IT!
SPECIALS
Beer $5
Beer but with too many hops $9
WE'VE BEEN FAKIN' IT FOR TEN YEARS, MAN...
I DON'T THINK PITTSBURGH OR ANYWHERE ELSE IS GONNA START CLAMORING FOR OUR UPBEAT BRAND OF SWING AND SKA MUSIC...
YOU'RE SO NEGATIVE! FOCUS ON THE POSITIVES FOR A CHANGE, DADDY-O! LIKE...
...WHO DO YOU WANT TO GO HOME WITH TONIGHT? DOTTIE? OR CARL?

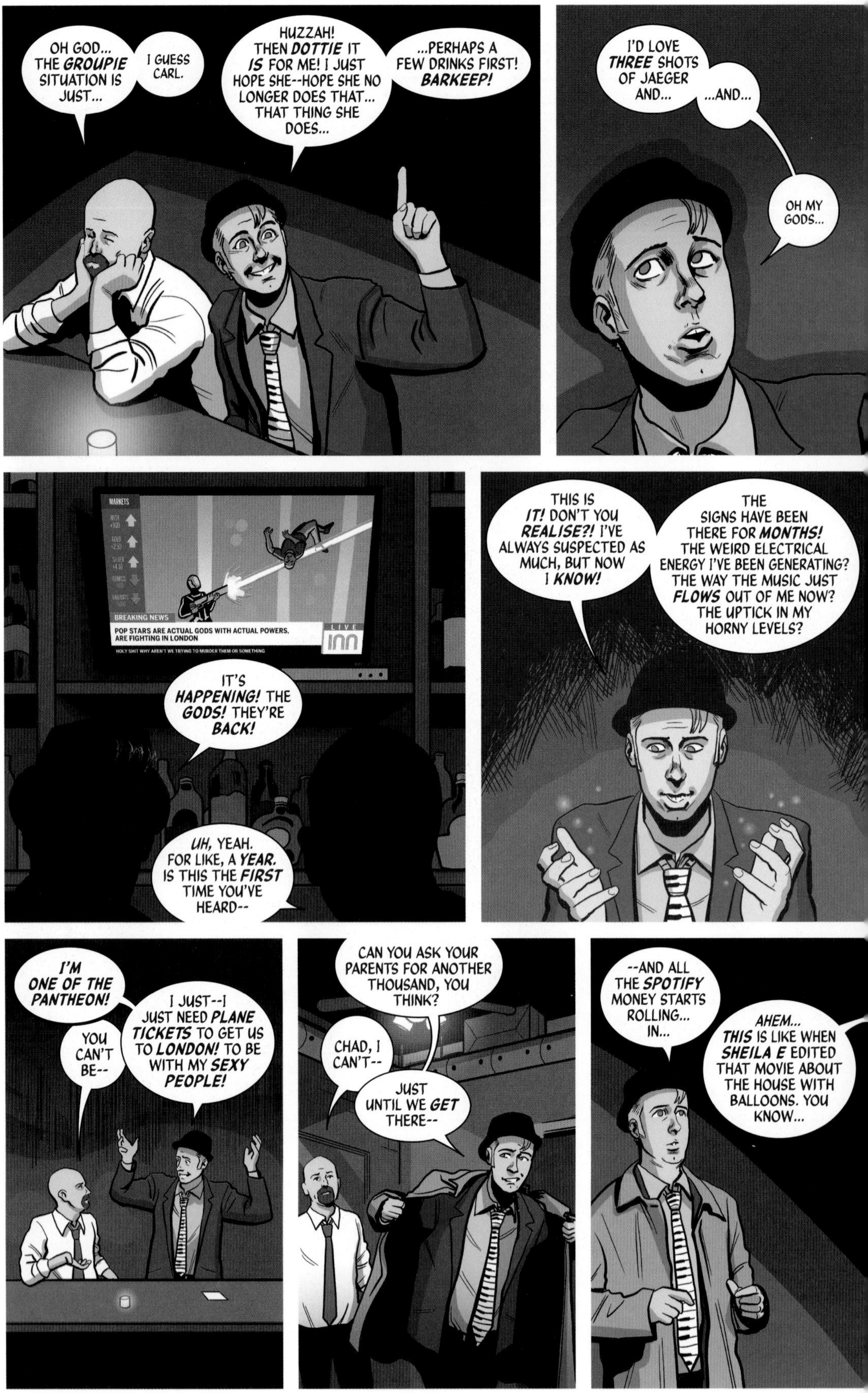
OH GOD... THE GROUPIE SITUATION IS JUST...
I GUESS CARL.
HUZZAH! THEN DOTTIE IT IS FOR ME! I JUST HOPE SHE--HOPE SHE NO LONGER DOES THAT... THAT THING SHE DOES...
...PERHAPS A FEW DRINKS FIRST! BARKEEP!
I'D LOVE THREE SHOTS OF JAEGER AND...
...AND...
OH MY GODS...
MARKETS
BREAKING NEWS
POP STARS ARE ACTUAL GODS WITH ACTUAL POWERS, ARE FIGHTING IN LONDON
HOLY SHIT WHY AREN'T WE TRYING TO MURDER THEM OR SOMETHING
LIVE
INN
IT'S HAPPENING! THE GODS! THEY'RE BACK!
UH, YEAH. FOR LIKE, A YEAR. IS THIS THE FIRST TIME YOU'VE HEARD--
THIS IS IT! DON'T YOU REALISE?! I'VE ALWAYS SUSPECTED AS MUCH, BUT NOW I KNOW!
THE SIGNS HAVE BEEN THERE FOR MONTHS! THE WEIRD ELECTRICAL ENERGY I'VE BEEN GENERATING? THE WAY THE MUSIC JUST FLOWS OUT OF ME NOW? THE UPTICK IN MY HORNY LEVELS?
I'M ONE OF THE PANTHEON!
YOU CAN'T BE--
I JUST--I JUST NEED PLANE TICKETS TO GET US TO LONDON! TO BE WITH MY SEXY PEOPLE!
CAN YOU ASK YOUR PARENTS FOR ANOTHER THOUSAND, YOU THINK?
CHAD, I CAN'T--
JUST UNTIL WE GET THERE--
--AND ALL THE SPOTIFY MONEY STARTS ROLLING... IN...
AHEM... THIS IS LIKE WHEN SHEILA E EDITED THAT MOVIE ABOUT THE HOUSE WITH BALLOONS. YOU KNOW...

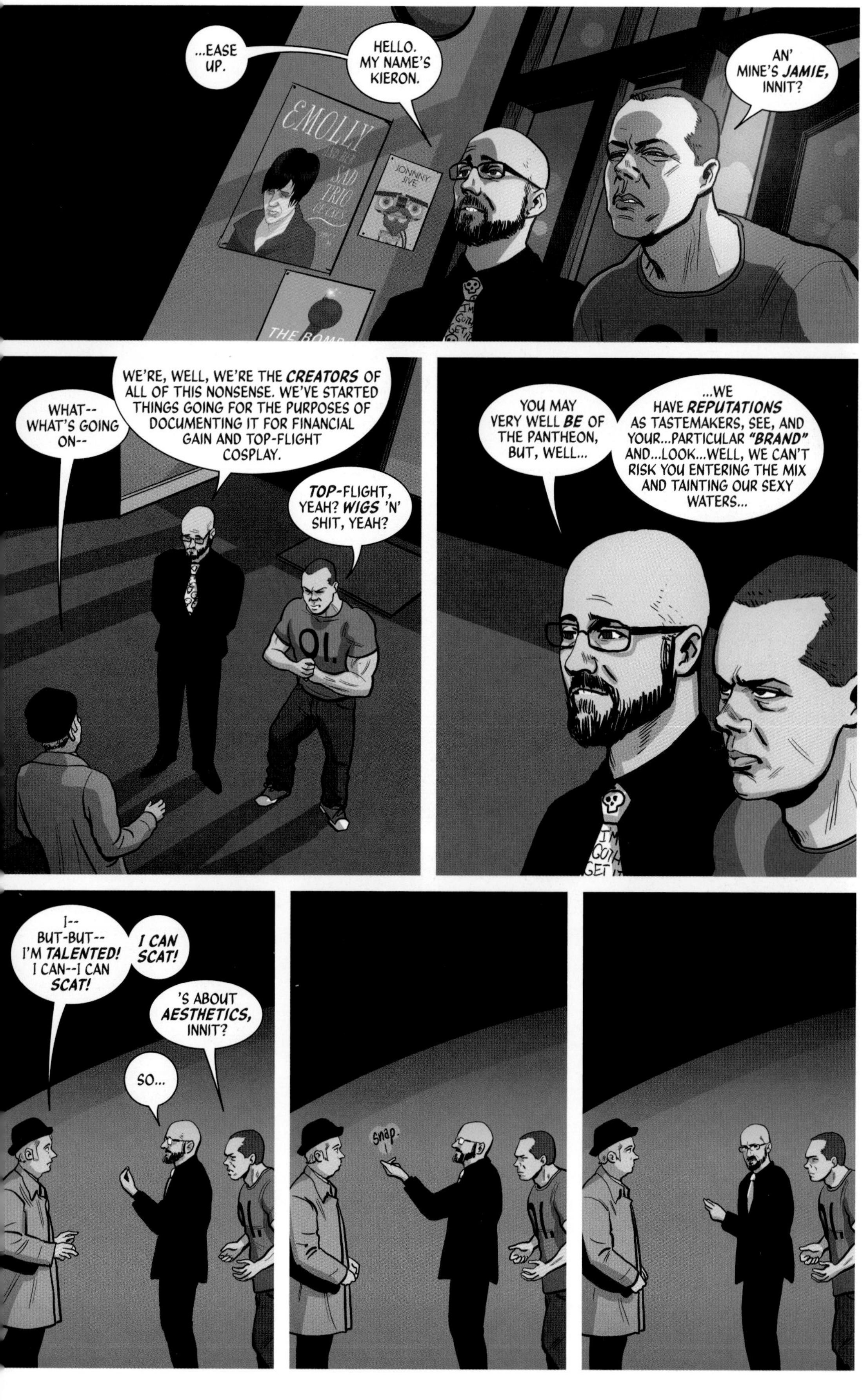
HELLO. MY NAME'S KIERON.
...EASE UP.
AN' MINE'S *JAMIE*, INNIT?
EMOLLY AND HER SAD TRIO
JONNY JIVE
THE BOMB
WHAT-- WHAT'S GOING ON--
WE'RE, WELL, WE'RE THE *CREATORS* OF ALL OF THIS NONSENSE. WE'VE STARTED THINGS GOING FOR THE PURPOSES OF DOCUMENTING IT FOR FINANCIAL GAIN AND TOP-FLIGHT COSPLAY.
TOP-FLIGHT, YEAH? *WIGS* 'N' SHIT, YEAH?
YOU MAY VERY WELL *BE* OF THE PANTHEON, BUT, WELL...
...WE HAVE *REPUTATIONS* AS TASTEMAKERS, SEE, AND YOUR...PARTICULAR *"BRAND"* AND...LOOK...WELL, WE CAN'T RISK YOU ENTERING THE MIX AND TAINTING OUR SEXY WATERS...
I-- BUT-BUT-- I'M *TALENTED!* I CAN--I CAN *SCAT!*
I CAN SCAT!
'S ABOUT *AESTHETICS,* INNIT?
SO...
snap.

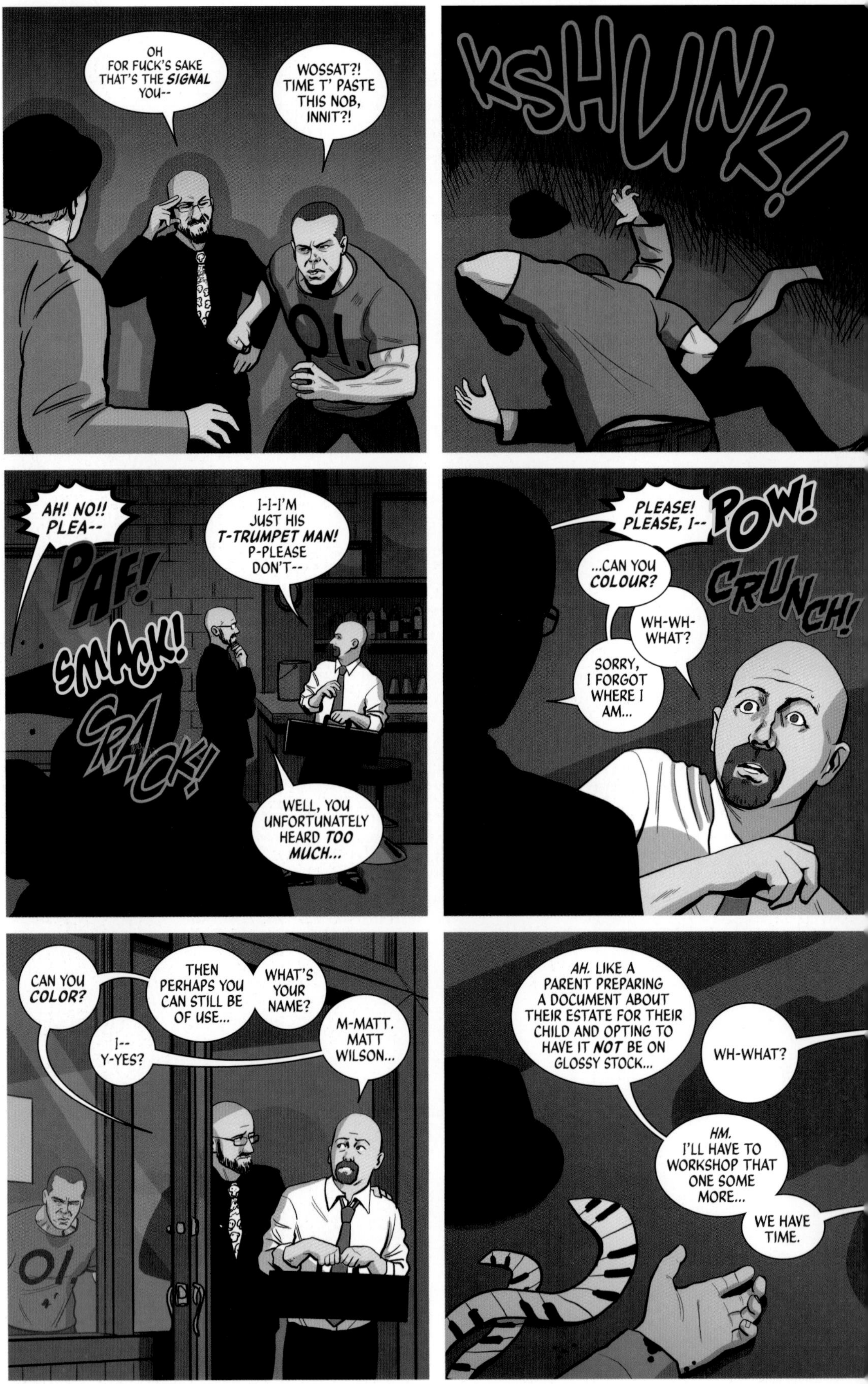
OH FOR FUCK'S SAKE THAT'S THE SIGNAL YOU--
WOSSAT?! TIME T' PASTE THIS NOB, INNIT?!
KSHUNK!
AH! NO!! PLEA--
PAF!
SMACK!
CRACK!
I-I-I'M JUST HIS T-TRUMPET MAN! P-PLEASE DON'T--
WELL, YOU UNFORTUNATELY HEARD TOO MUCH...
PLEASE! PLEASE, I--
POW!
CRUNCH!
...CAN YOU COLOUR?
WH-WH-WHAT?
SORRY, I FORGOT WHERE I AM...
CAN YOU COLOR?
I-- Y-YES?
THEN PERHAPS YOU CAN STILL BE OF USE...
WHAT'S YOUR NAME?
M-MATT. MATT WILSON...
AH. LIKE A PARENT PREPARING A DOCUMENT ABOUT THEIR ESTATE FOR THEIR CHILD AND OPTING TO HAVE IT NOT BE ON GLOSSY STOCK...
WH-WHAT?
HM. I'LL HAVE TO WORKSHOP THAT ONE SOME MORE...
WE HAVE TIME.

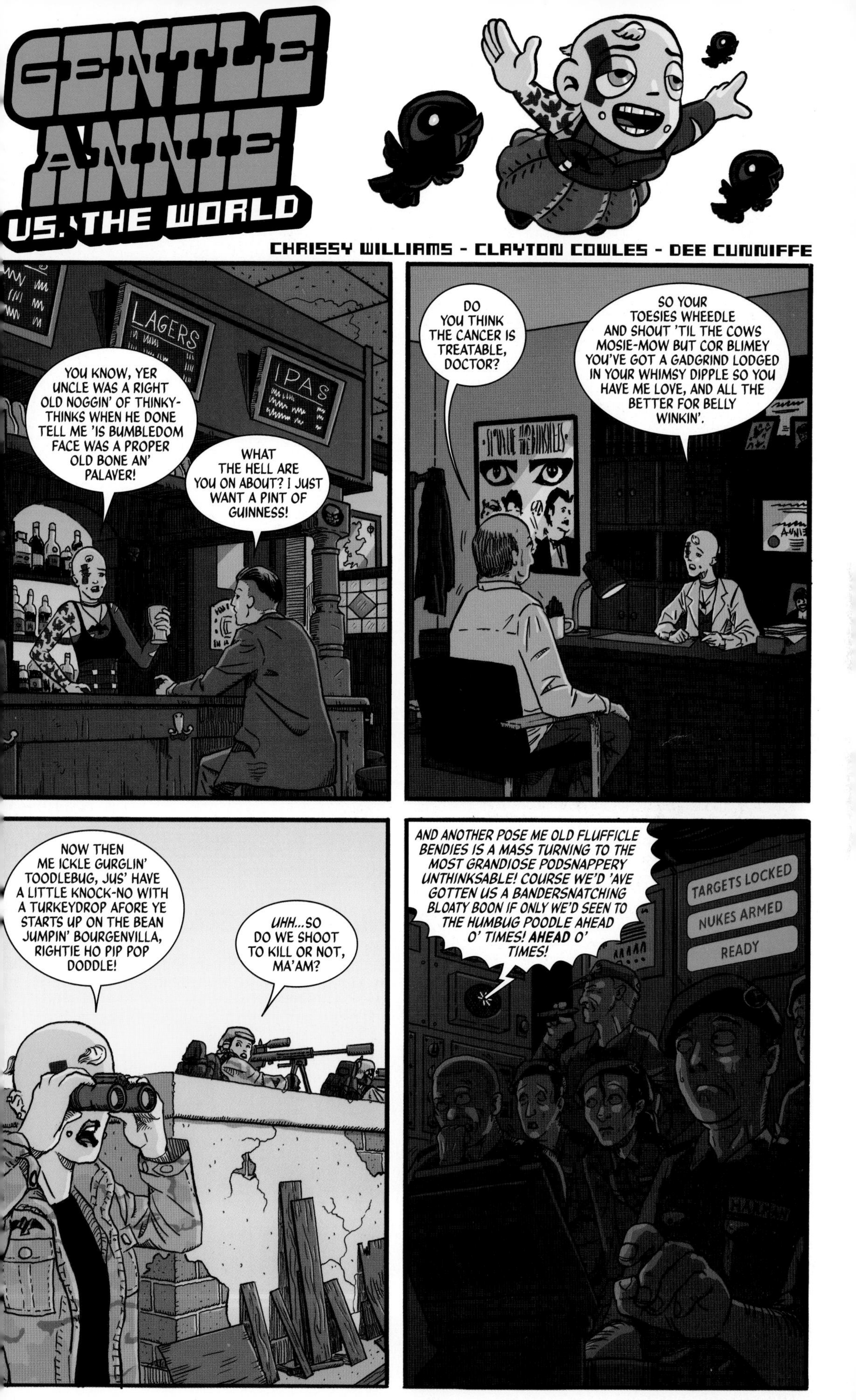
GENTLE ANNIE VS. THE WORLD
CHRISSY WILLIAMS - CLAYTON COWLES - DEE CUNNIFFE
LAGERS
IPAS
YOU KNOW, YER UNCLE WAS A RIGHT OLD NOGGIN' OF THINKY-THINKS WHEN HE DONE TELL ME 'IS BUMBLEDOM FACE WAS A PROPER OLD BONE AN' PALAVER!
WHAT THE HELL ARE YOU ON ABOUT? I JUST WANT A PINT OF GUINNESS!
DO YOU THINK THE CANCER IS TREATABLE, DOCTOR?
SO YOUR TOESIES WHEEDLE AND SHOUT 'TIL THE COWS MOSIE-MOW BUT COR BLIMEY YOU'VE GOT A GADGRIND LODGED IN YOUR WHIMSY DIPPLE SO YOU HAVE ME LOVE, AND ALL THE BETTER FOR BELLY WINKIN'.
NOW THEN ME ICKLE GURGLIN' TOODLEBUG, JUS' HAVE A LITTLE KNOCK-NO WITH A TURKEYDROP AFORE YE STARTS UP ON THE BEAN JUMPIN' BOURGENVILLA, RIGHTIE HO PIP POP DODDLE!
UHH...SO DO WE SHOOT TO KILL OR NOT, MA'AM?
AND ANOTHER POSE ME OLD FLUFFICLE BENDIES IS A MASS TURNING TO THE MOST GRANDIOSE PODSNAPPERY UNTHINKSABLE! COURSE WE'D 'AVE GOTTEN US A BANDERSNATCHING BLOATY BOON IF ONLY WE'D SEEN TO THE HUMBUG POODLE AHEAD O' TIMES! AHEAD O' TIMES!
TARGETS LOCKED
NUKES ARMED
READY

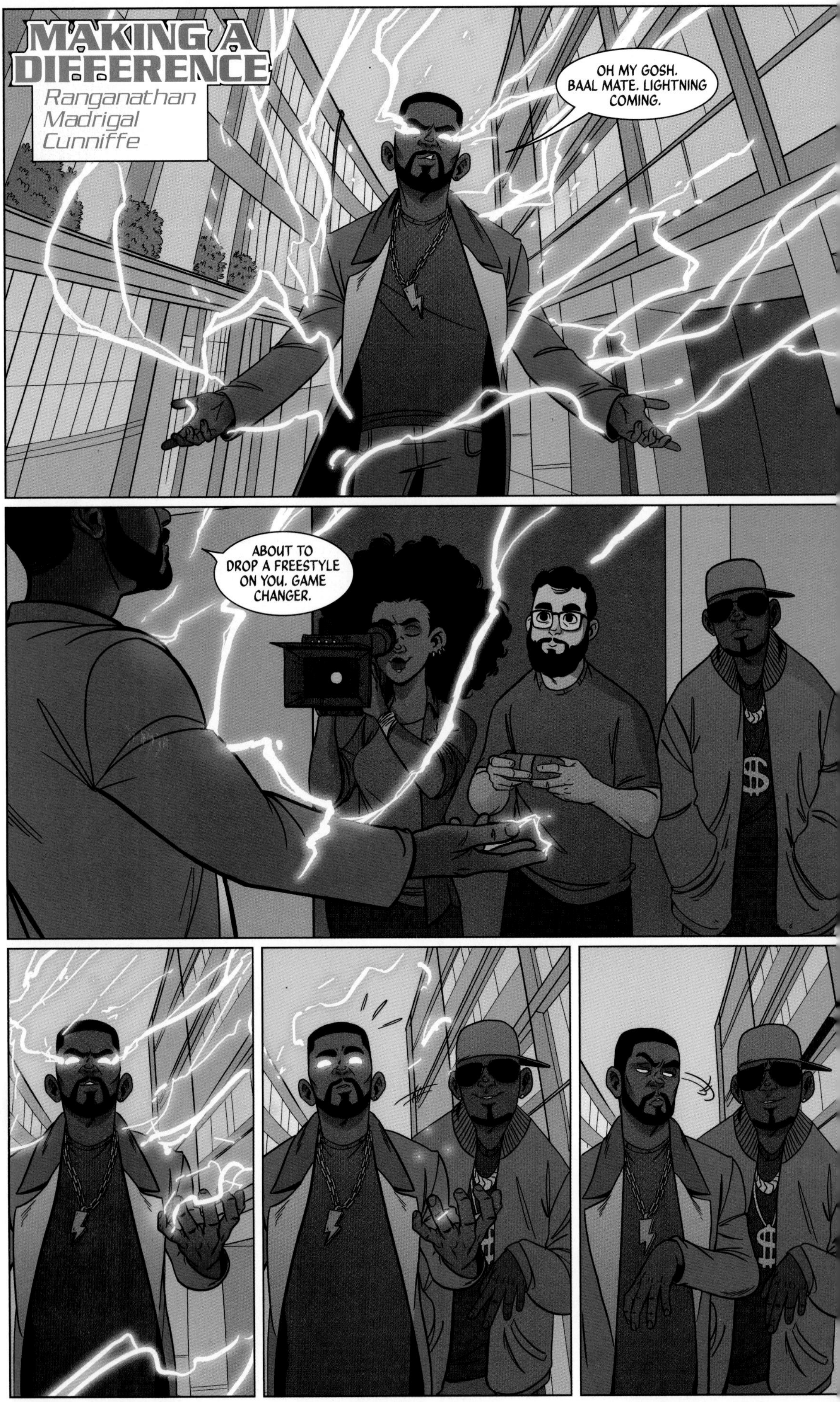
MAKING A DIFFERENCE
Ranganathan
Madrigal
Cunniffe
OH MY GOSH. BAAL MATE. LIGHTNING COMING.
ABOUT TO DROP A FREESTYLE ON YOU. GAME CHANGER.

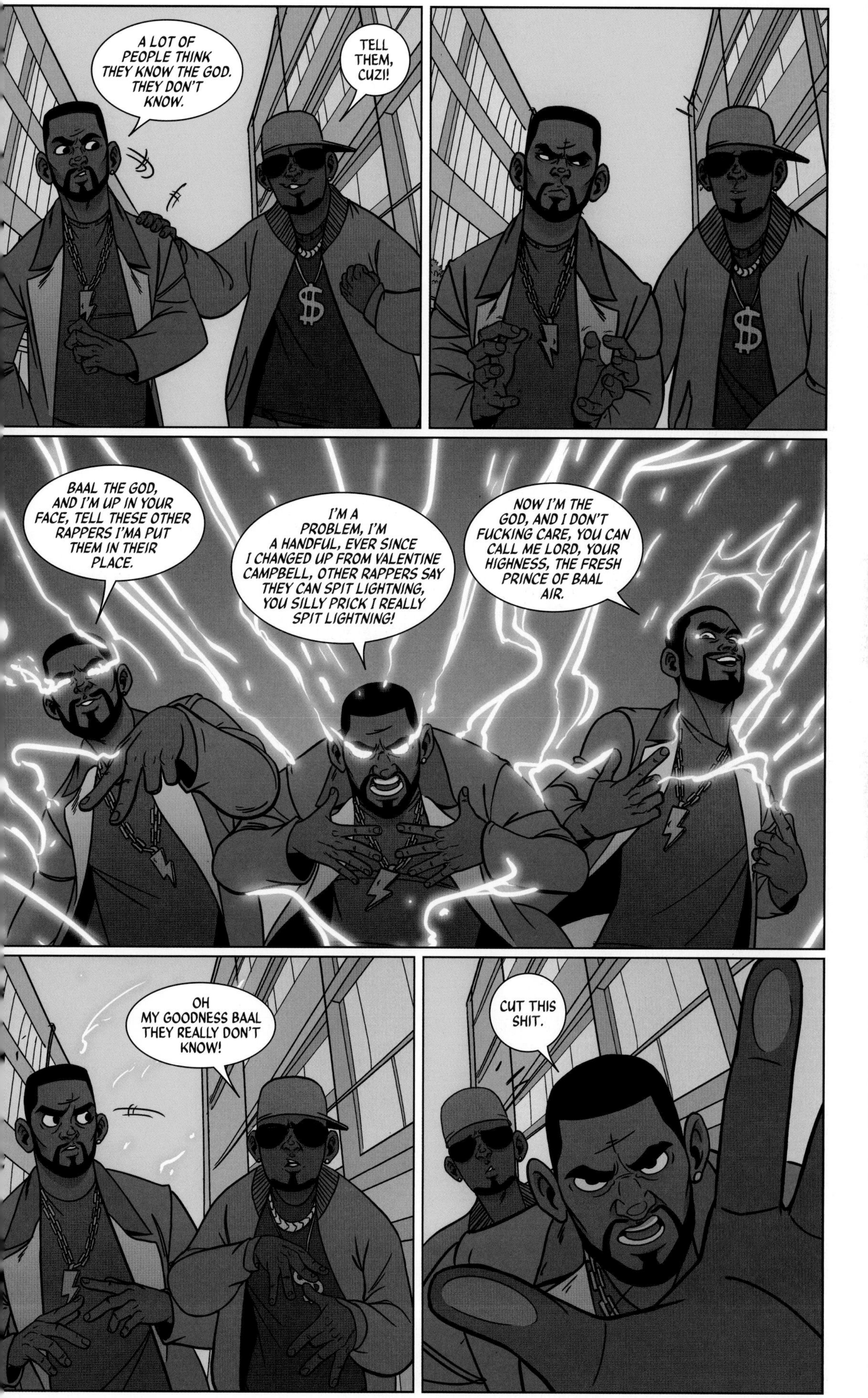
A LOT OF PEOPLE THINK THEY KNOW THE GOD. THEY DON'T KNOW.
TELL THEM, CUZI!
BAAL THE GOD, AND I'M UP IN YOUR FACE, TELL THESE OTHER RAPPERS I'MA PUT THEM IN THEIR PLACE.
I'M A PROBLEM, I'M A HANDFUL, EVER SINCE I CHANGED UP FROM VALENTINE CAMPBELL, OTHER RAPPERS SAY THEY CAN SPIT LIGHTNING, YOU SILLY PRICK I REALLY SPIT LIGHTNING!
NOW I'M THE GOD, AND I DON'T FUCKING CARE, YOU CAN CALL ME LORD, YOUR HIGHNESS, THE FRESH PRINCE OF BAAL AIR.
OH MY GOODNESS BAAL THEY REALLY DON'T KNOW!
CUT THIS SHIT.

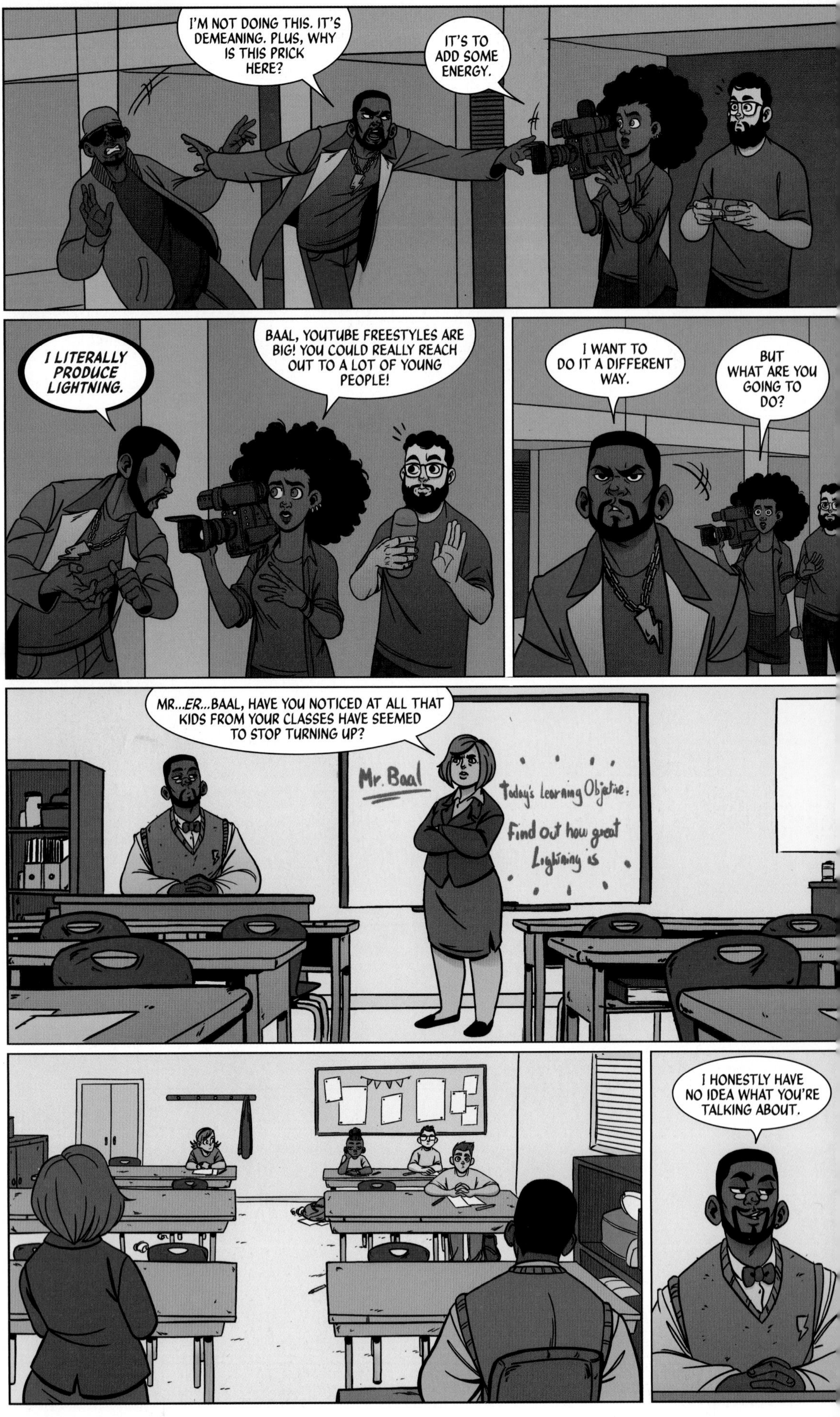
I'M NOT DOING THIS. IT'S DEMEANING. PLUS, WHY IS THIS PRICK HERE?
IT'S TO ADD SOME ENERGY.
I LITERALLY PRODUCE LIGHTNING.
BAAL, YOUTUBE FREESTYLES ARE BIG! YOU COULD REALLY REACH OUT TO A LOT OF YOUNG PEOPLE!
I WANT TO DO IT A DIFFERENT WAY.
BUT WHAT ARE YOU GOING TO DO?
MR...ER...BAAL, HAVE YOU NOTICED AT ALL THAT KIDS FROM YOUR CLASSES HAVE SEEMED TO STOP TURNING UP?
Mr. Baal
Today's Learning Objective:
Find out how great Lightning is
I HONESTLY HAVE NO IDEA WHAT YOU'RE TALKING ABOUT.

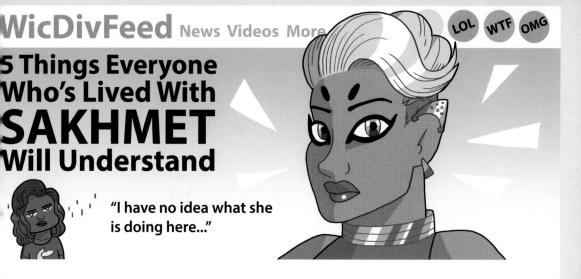

WicDivFeed News Videos More

LOL WTF OMG

5 Things Everyone Who's Lived With SAKHMET Will Understand

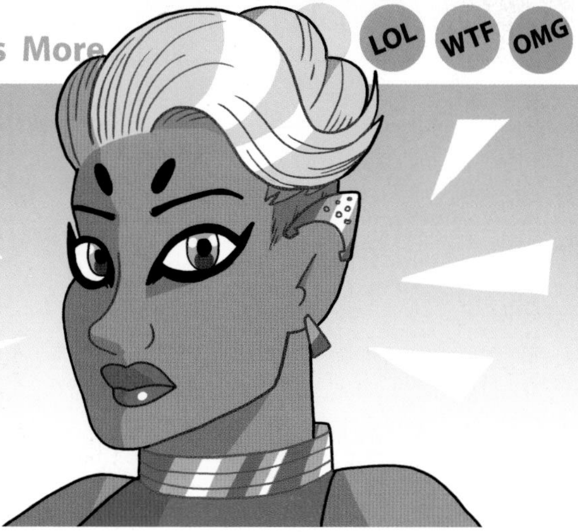

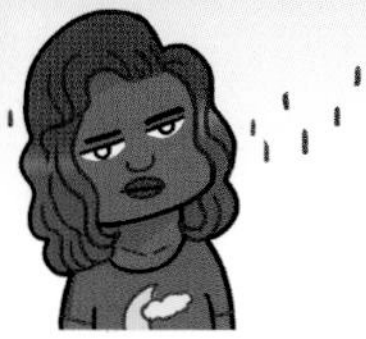

"I have no idea what she is doing here..."

1. She'll never appreciate the effort you put into your cohabitation.

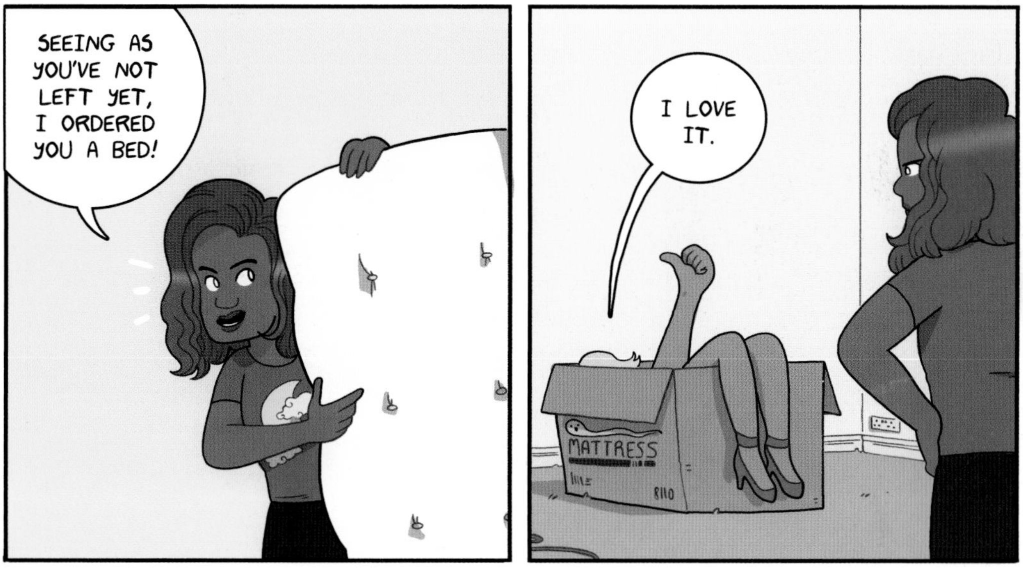

SEEING AS YOU'VE NOT LEFT YET, I ORDERED YOU A BED!
I LOVE IT.
MATTRESS

2. And she will never respect personal space...

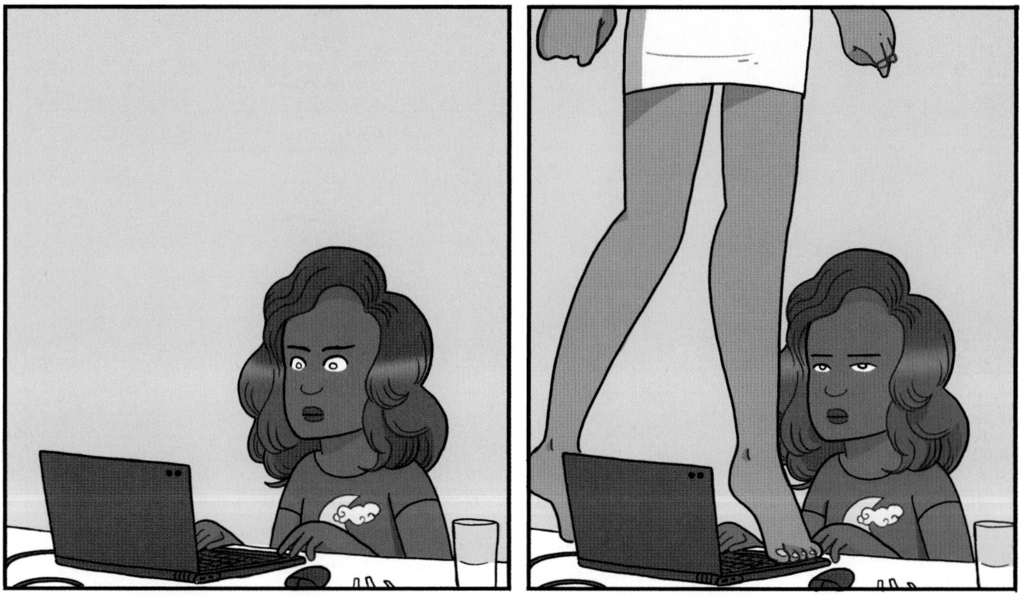

3. Or... personal belongings.

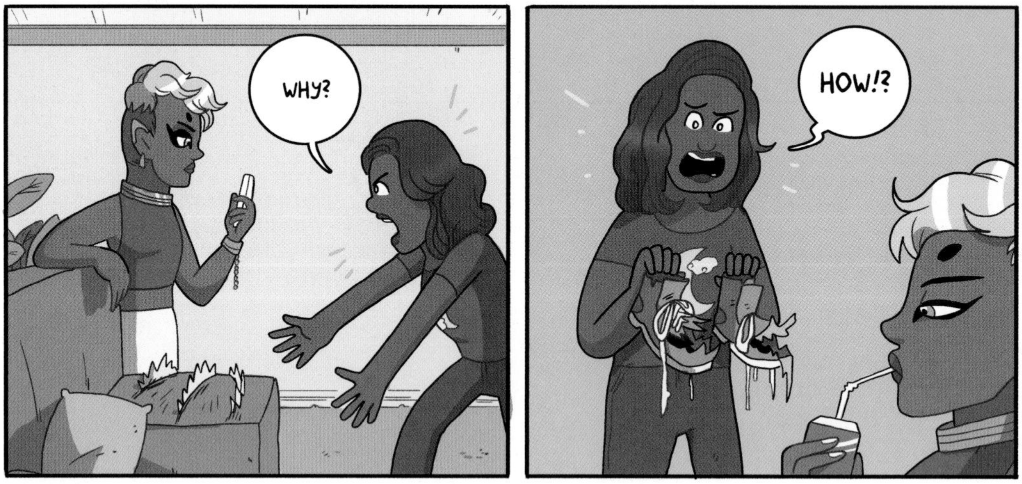
WHY?
HOW!?

4. In fact, you'll soon learn that anything in the house is hers for the taking.

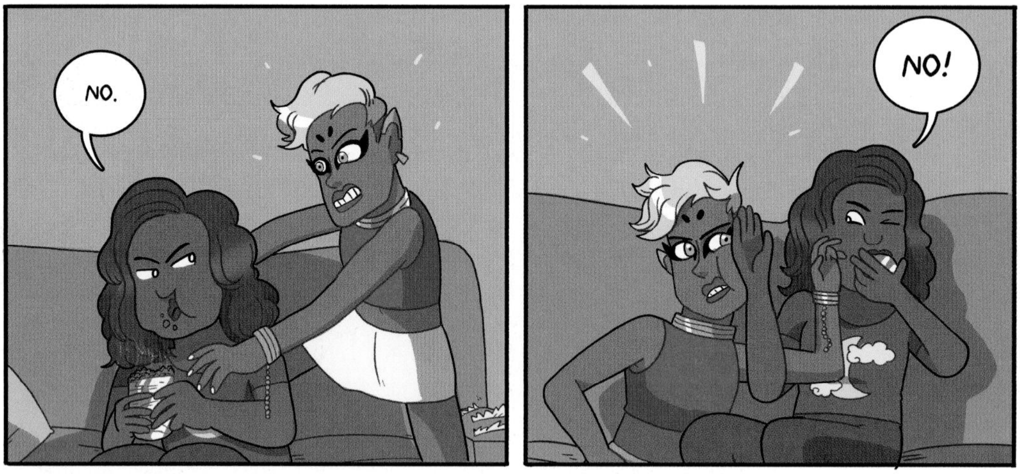
NO.
NO!

5. But at the end of the day, she still loves you.
... Just be ready to deal with the unique way she expresses this ...

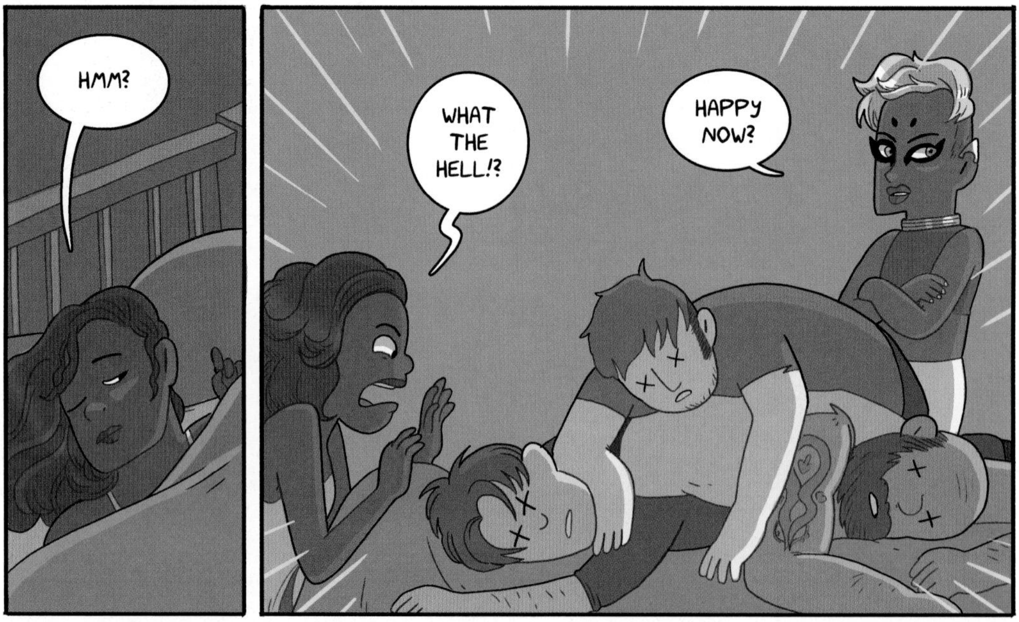
HMM?
WHAT THE HELL!?
HAPPY NOW?

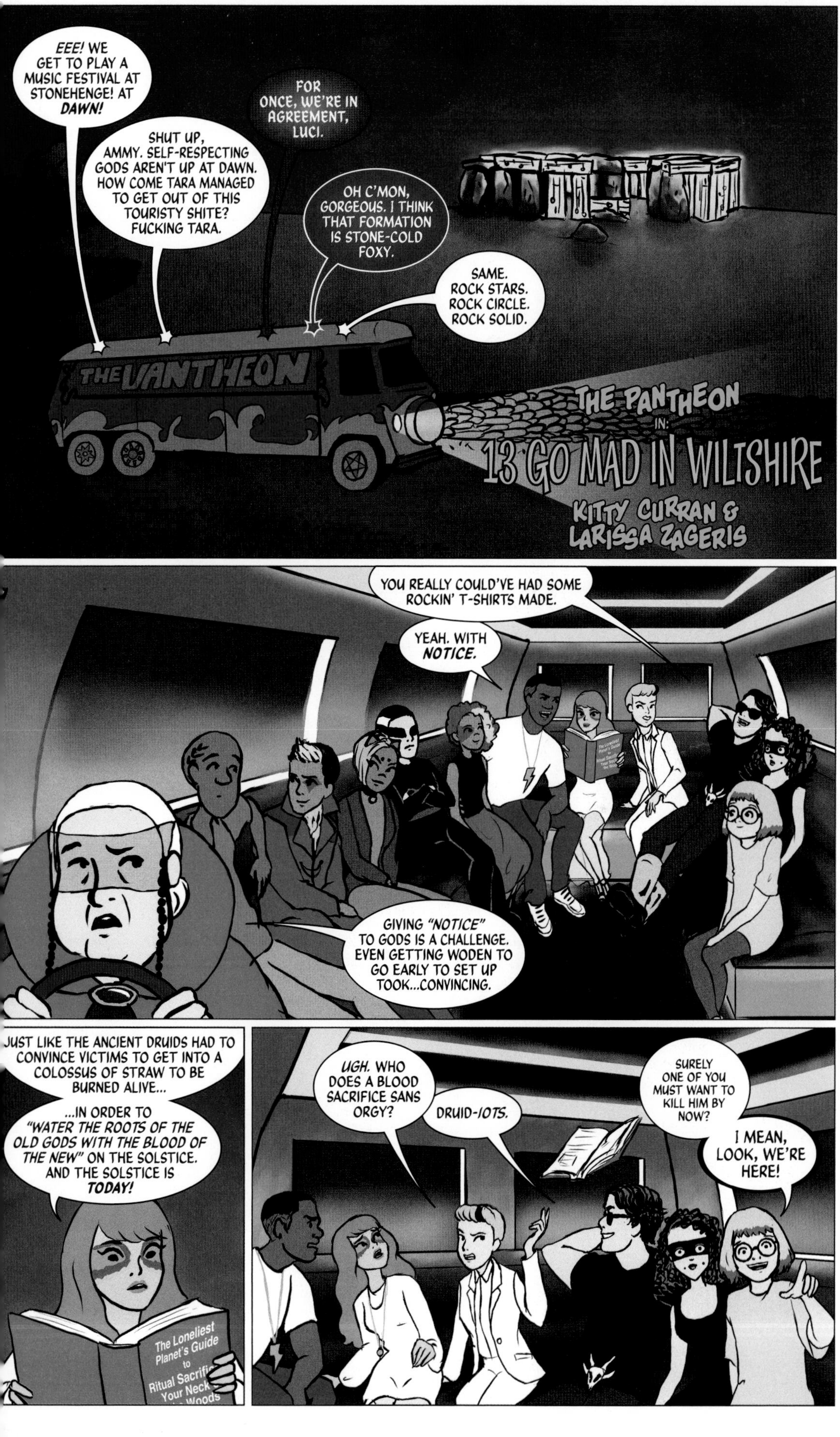
EEE! WE GET TO PLAY A MUSIC FESTIVAL AT STONEHENGE! AT DAWN!
SHUT UP, AMMY. SELF-RESPECTING GODS AREN'T UP AT DAWN. HOW COME TARA MANAGED TO GET OUT OF THIS TOURISTY SHITE? FUCKING TARA.
FOR ONCE, WE'RE IN AGREEMENT, LUCI.
OH C'MON, GORGEOUS. I THINK THAT FORMATION IS STONE-COLD FOXY.
SAME. ROCK STARS. ROCK CIRCLE. ROCK SOLID.
THE VANTHEON
THE PANTHEON IN:
13 GO MAD IN WILTSHIRE
KITTY CURRAN & LARISSA ZAGERIS
YOU REALLY COULD'VE HAD SOME ROCKIN' T-SHIRTS MADE.
YEAH. WITH NOTICE.
GIVING "NOTICE" TO GODS IS A CHALLENGE. EVEN GETTING WODEN TO GO EARLY TO SET UP TOOK...CONVINCING.
JUST LIKE THE ANCIENT DRUIDS HAD TO CONVINCE VICTIMS TO GET INTO A COLOSSUS OF STRAW TO BE BURNED ALIVE...
...IN ORDER TO "WATER THE ROOTS OF THE OLD GODS WITH THE BLOOD OF THE NEW" ON THE SOLSTICE. AND THE SOLSTICE IS TODAY!
The Loneliest Planet's Guide to
UGH. WHO DOES A BLOOD SACRIFICE SANS ORGY?
DRUID-IOTS.
SURELY ONE OF YOU MUST WANT TO KILL HIM BY NOW?
I MEAN, LOOK, WE'RE HERE!

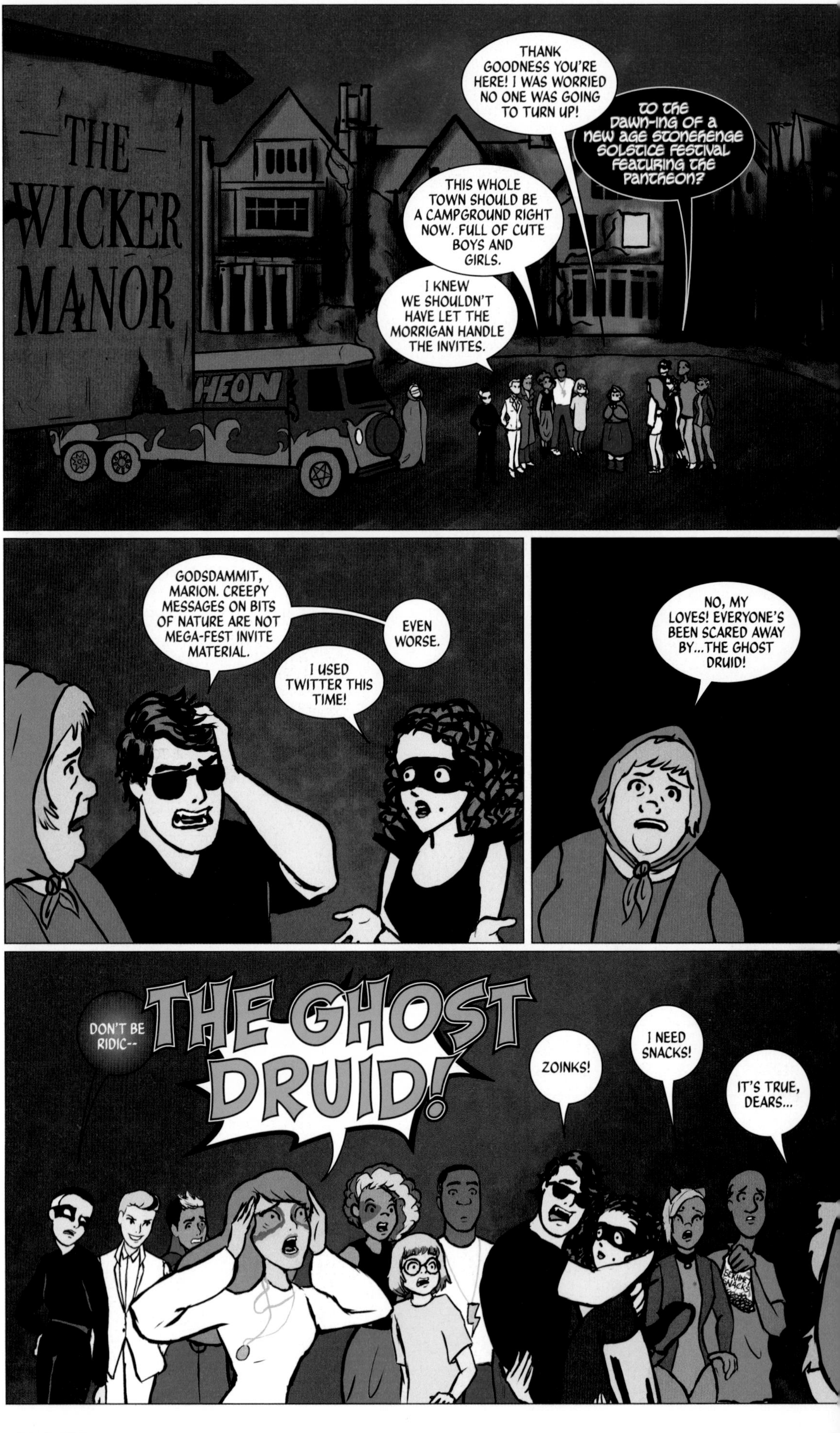
THE WICKER MANOR
HEON
THANK GOODNESS YOU'RE HERE! I WAS WORRIED NO ONE WAS GOING TO TURN UP!
TO THE DAWN-ING OF A NEW AGE STONEHENGE SOLSTICE FESTIVAL FEATURING THE PANTHEON?
THIS WHOLE TOWN SHOULD BE A CAMPGROUND RIGHT NOW. FULL OF CUTE BOYS AND GIRLS.
I KNEW WE SHOULDN'T HAVE LET THE MORRIGAN HANDLE THE INVITES.
GODSDAMMIT, MARION. CREEPY MESSAGES ON BITS OF NATURE ARE NOT MEGA-FEST INVITE MATERIAL.
EVEN WORSE.
I USED TWITTER THIS TIME!
NO, MY LOVES! EVERYONE'S BEEN SCARED AWAY BY...THE GHOST DRUID!
DON'T BE RIDIC--
THE GHOST DRUID!
ZOINKS!
I NEED SNACKS!
IT'S TRUE, DEARS...

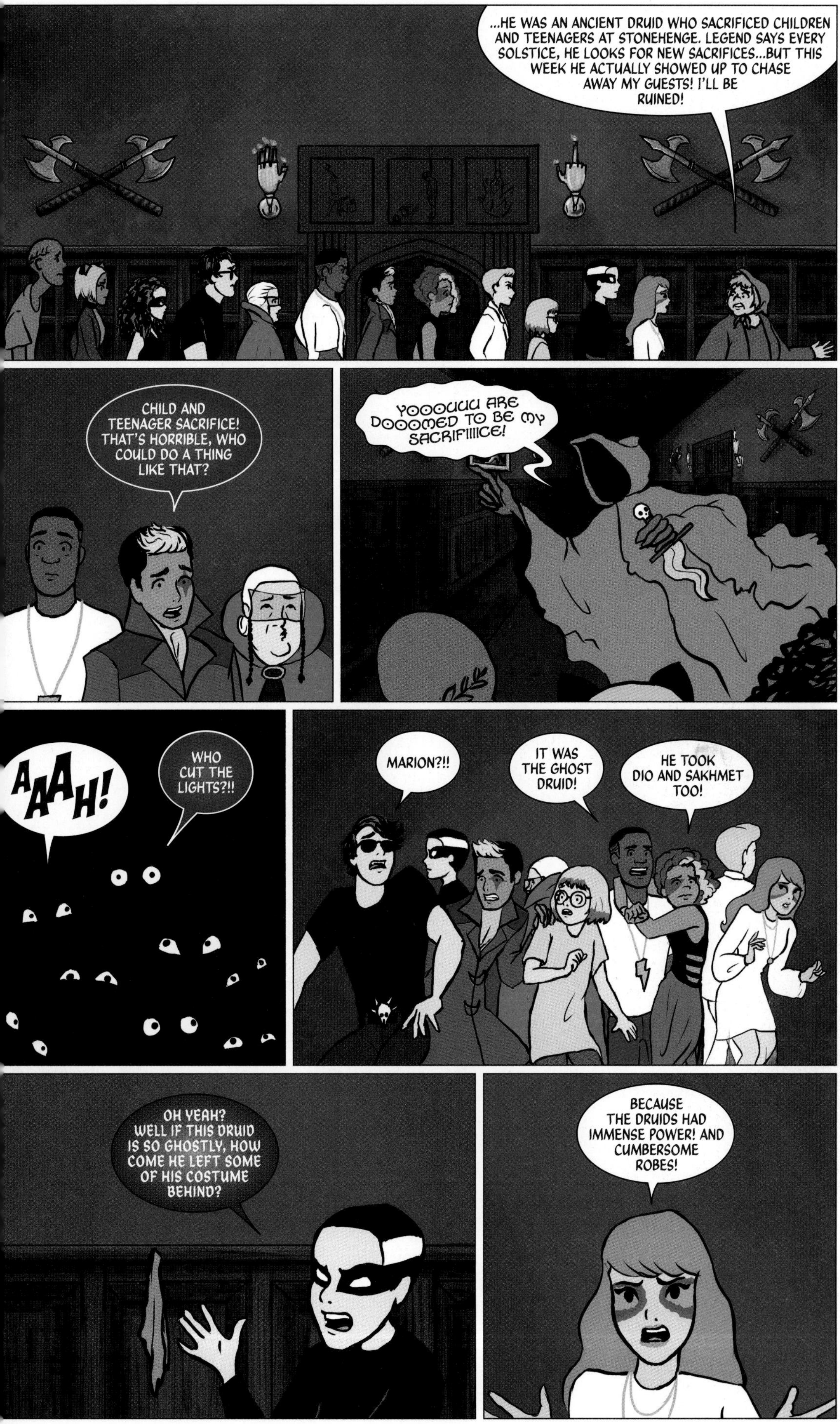
...HE WAS AN ANCIENT DRUID WHO SACRIFICED CHILDREN AND TEENAGERS AT STONEHENGE. LEGEND SAYS EVERY SOLSTICE, HE LOOKS FOR NEW SACRIFICES...BUT THIS WEEK HE ACTUALLY SHOWED UP TO CHASE AWAY MY GUESTS! I'LL BE RUINED!
CHILD AND TEENAGER SACRIFICE! THAT'S HORRIBLE, WHO COULD DO A THING LIKE THAT?
YOOOUUU ARE DOOOMED TO BE MY SACRIFIIIICE!
AAAH!
WHO CUT THE LIGHTS?!!
MARION?!!
IT WAS THE GHOST DRUID!
HE TOOK DIO AND SAKHMET TOO!
OH YEAH? WELL IF THIS DRUID IS SO GHOSTLY, HOW COME HE LEFT SOME OF HIS COSTUME BEHIND?
BECAUSE THE DRUIDS HAD IMMENSE POWER! AND CUMBERSOME ROBES!

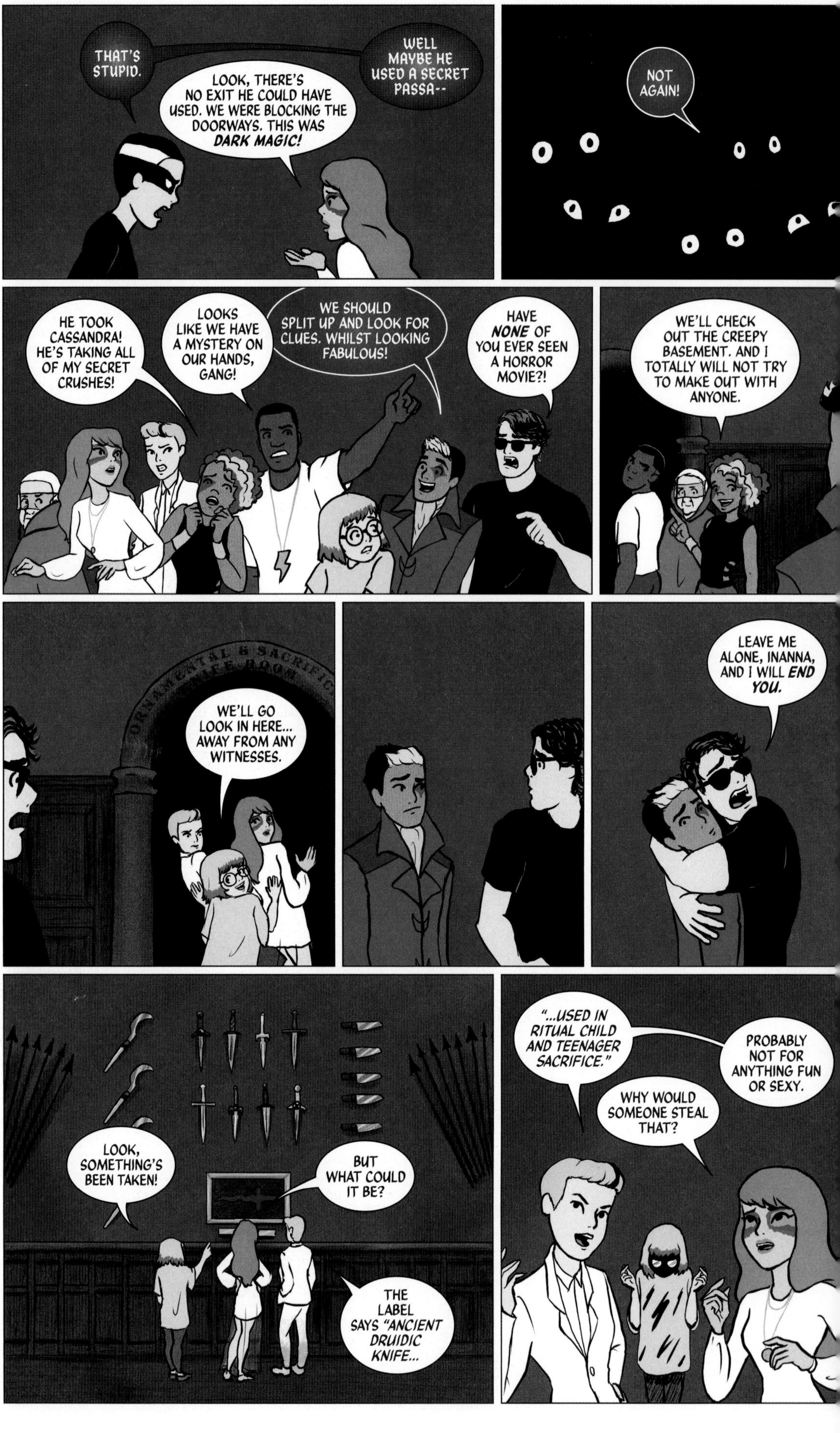
THAT'S STUPID.
LOOK, THERE'S NO EXIT HE COULD HAVE USED. WE WERE BLOCKING THE DOORWAYS. THIS WAS *DARK MAGIC!*
WELL MAYBE HE USED A SECRET PASSA--
NOT AGAIN!
HE TOOK CASSANDRA! HE'S TAKING ALL OF MY SECRET CRUSHES!
LOOKS LIKE WE HAVE A MYSTERY ON OUR HANDS, GANG!
WE SHOULD SPLIT UP AND LOOK FOR CLUES. WHILST LOOKING FABULOUS!
HAVE *NONE* OF YOU EVER SEEN A HORROR MOVIE?!
WE'LL CHECK OUT THE CREEPY BASEMENT. AND I TOTALLY WILL NOT TRY TO MAKE OUT WITH ANYONE.
ORNAMENTAL & SACRIFICIAL KNIFE ROOM
WE'LL GO LOOK IN HERE... AWAY FROM ANY WITNESSES.
LEAVE ME ALONE, INANNA, AND I WILL *END YOU.*
LOOK, SOMETHING'S BEEN TAKEN!
BUT WHAT COULD IT BE?
THE LABEL SAYS "*ANCIENT DRUIDIC KNIFE...*
"*...USED IN RITUAL CHILD AND TEENAGER SACRIFICE.*"
PROBABLY NOT FOR ANYTHING FUN OR SEXY.
WHY WOULD SOMEONE STEAL THAT?

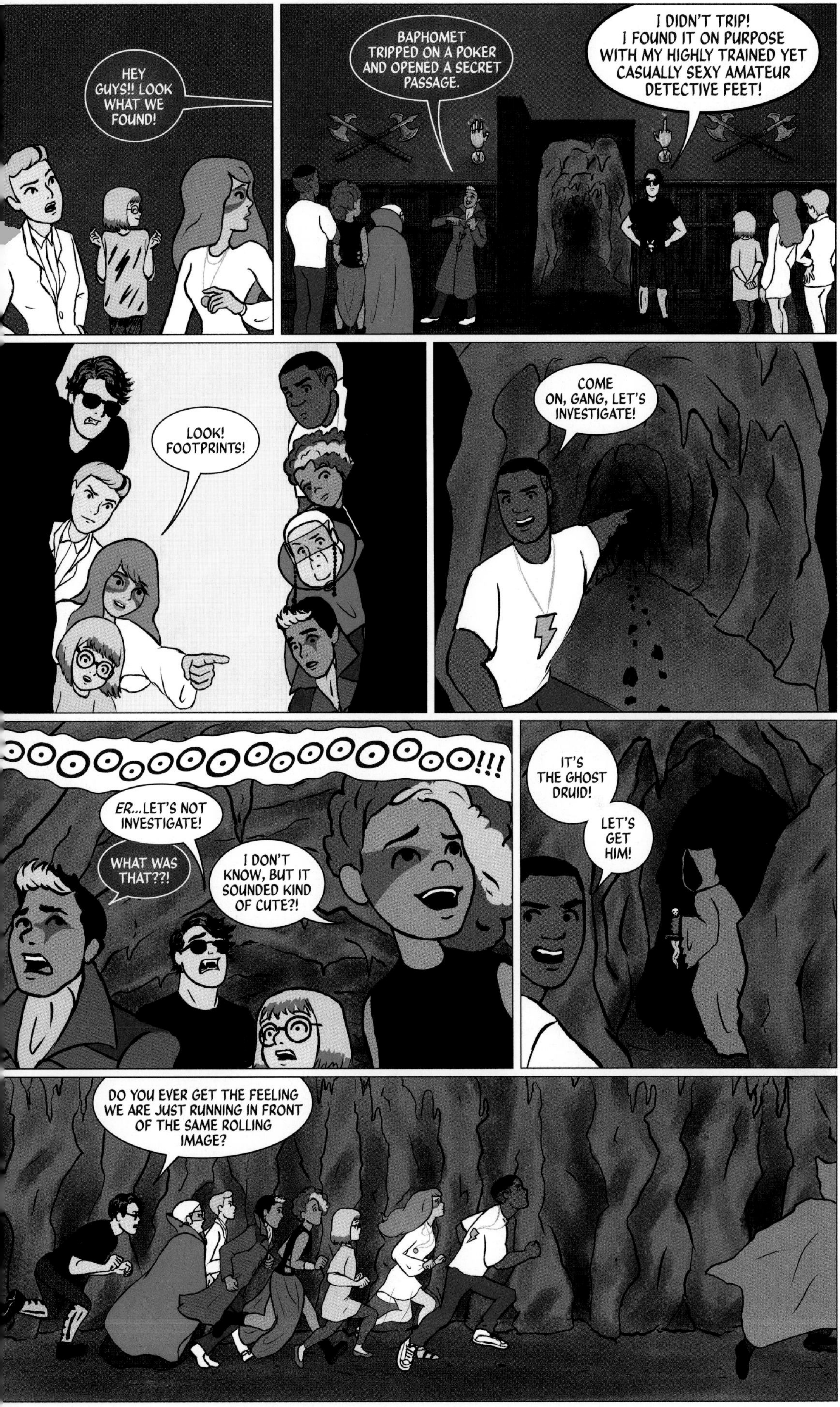
HEY GUYS!! LOOK WHAT WE FOUND!
BAPHOMET TRIPPED ON A POKER AND OPENED A SECRET PASSAGE.
I DIDN'T TRIP! I FOUND IT ON PURPOSE WITH MY HIGHLY TRAINED YET CASUALLY SEXY AMATEUR DETECTIVE FEET!
LOOK! FOOTPRINTS!
COME ON, GANG, LET'S INVESTIGATE!
OOOOOOOOOOOOOOOOOOOO!!!
ER...LET'S NOT INVESTIGATE!
WHAT WAS THAT??!
I DON'T KNOW, BUT IT SOUNDED KIND OF CUTE?!
IT'S THE GHOST DRUID!
LET'S GET HIM!
DO YOU EVER GET THE FEELING WE ARE JUST RUNNING IN FRONT OF THE SAME ROLLING IMAGE?

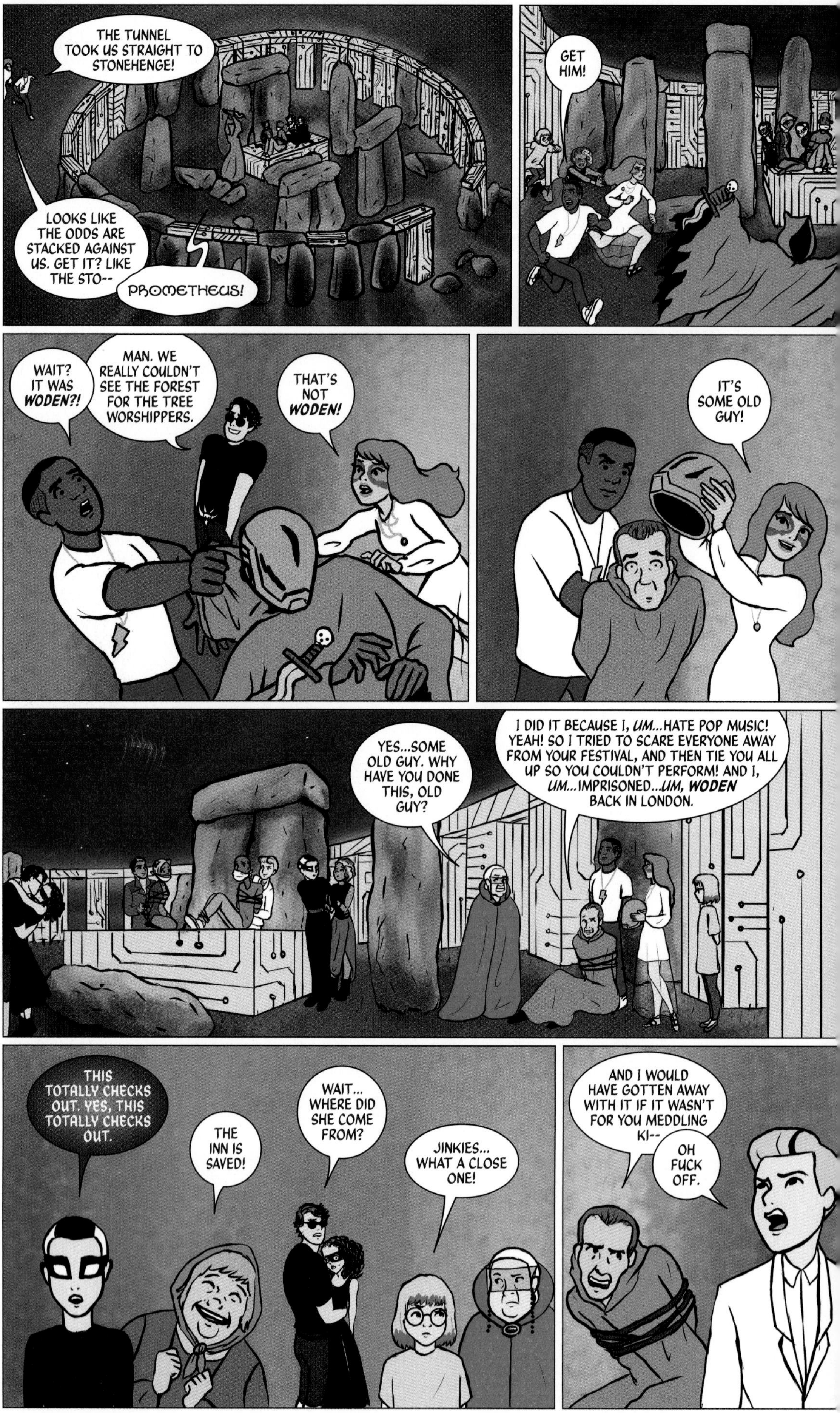
THE TUNNEL TOOK US STRAIGHT TO STONEHENGE!
LOOKS LIKE THE ODDS ARE STACKED AGAINST US. GET IT? LIKE THE STO--
PROMETHEUS!
GET HIM!
WAIT? IT WAS *WODEN?!*
MAN. WE REALLY COULDN'T SEE THE FOREST FOR THE TREE WORSHIPPERS.
THAT'S NOT *WODEN!*
IT'S SOME OLD GUY!
YES...SOME OLD GUY. WHY HAVE YOU DONE THIS, OLD GUY?
I DID IT BECAUSE I, *UM*...HATE POP MUSIC! YEAH! SO I TRIED TO SCARE EVERYONE AWAY FROM YOUR FESTIVAL, AND THEN TIE YOU ALL UP SO YOU COULDN'T PERFORM! AND I, *UM*...IMPRISONED...*UM, WODEN* BACK IN LONDON.
THIS TOTALLY CHECKS OUT. YES, THIS TOTALLY CHECKS OUT.
THE INN IS SAVED!
WAIT... WHERE DID SHE COME FROM?
JINKIES... WHAT A CLOSE ONE!
AND I WOULD HAVE GOTTEN AWAY WITH IT IF IT WASN'T FOR YOU MEDDLING KI--
OH FUCK OFF.

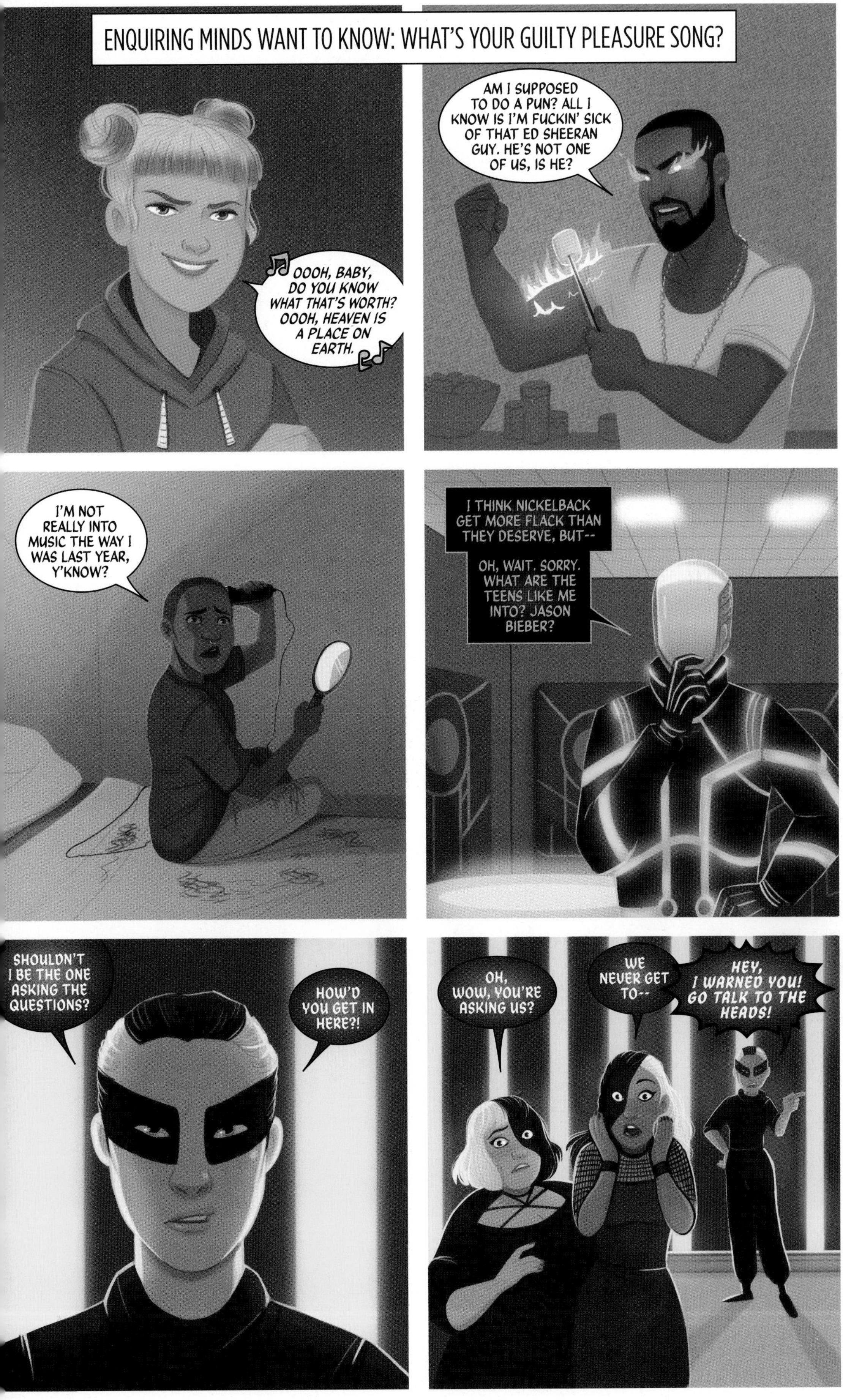

ENQUIRING MINDS WANT TO KNOW: WHAT'S YOUR GUILTY PLEASURE SONG?
OOOH, BABY, DO YOU KNOW WHAT THAT'S WORTH? OOOH, HEAVEN IS A PLACE ON EARTH.
AM I SUPPOSED TO DO A PUN? ALL I KNOW IS I'M FUCKIN' SICK OF THAT ED SHEERAN GUY. HE'S NOT ONE OF US, IS HE?
I'M NOT REALLY INTO MUSIC THE WAY I WAS LAST YEAR, Y'KNOW?
I THINK NICKELBACK GET MORE FLACK THAN THEY DESERVE, BUT--
OH, WAIT. SORRY. WHAT ARE THE TEENS LIKE ME INTO? JASON BIEBER?
SHOULDN'T I BE THE ONE ASKING THE QUESTIONS?
HOW'D YOU GET IN HERE?!
OH, WOW, YOU'RE ASKING US?
WE NEVER GET TO--
HEY, I WARNED YOU! GO TALK TO THE HEADS!

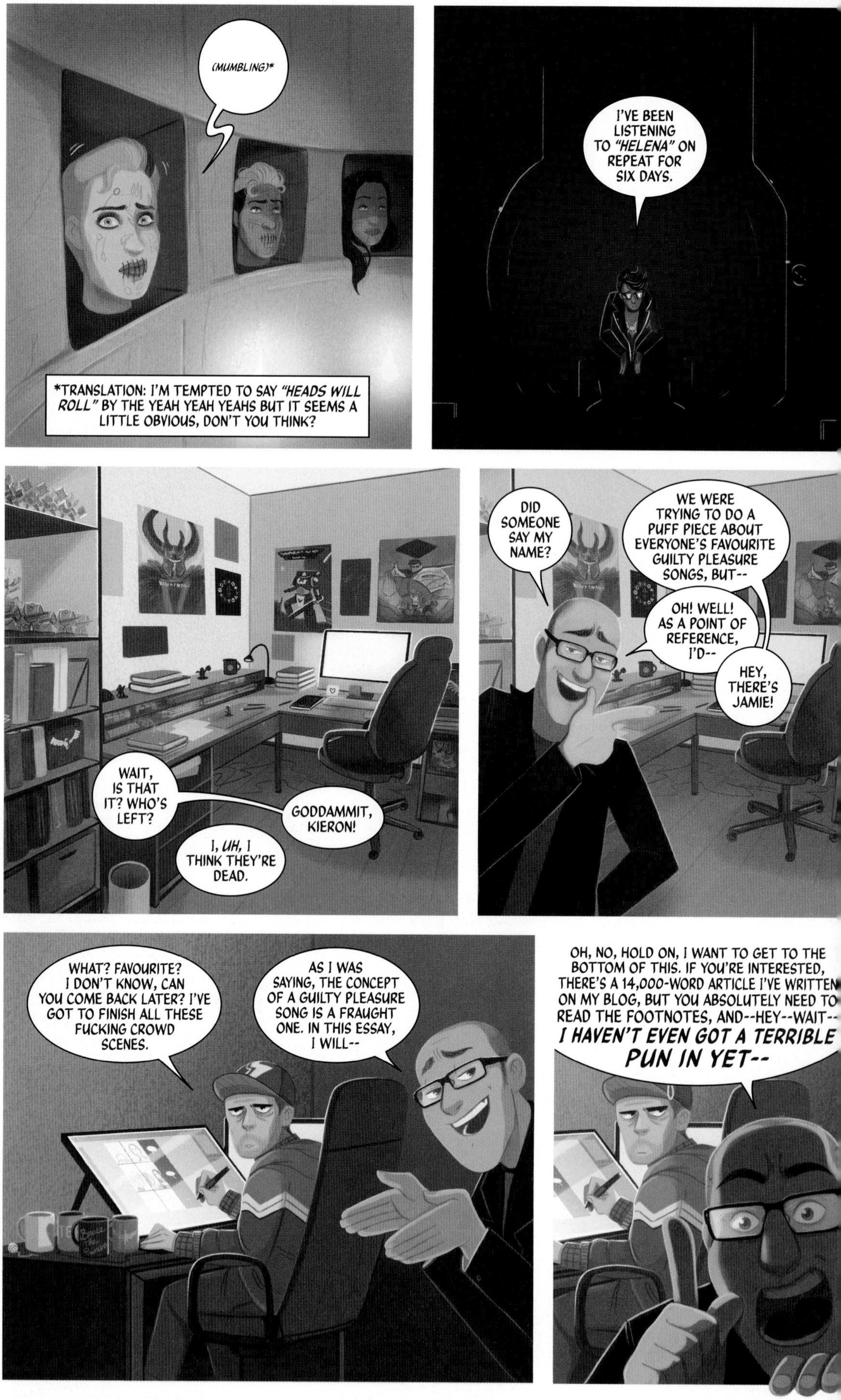
(MUMBLING)*
*TRANSLATION: I'M TEMPTED TO SAY "HEADS WILL ROLL" BY THE YEAH YEAH YEAHS BUT IT SEEMS A LITTLE OBVIOUS, DON'T YOU THINK?
I'VE BEEN LISTENING TO "HELENA" ON REPEAT FOR SIX DAYS.
WAIT, IS THAT IT? WHO'S LEFT?
GODDAMMIT, KIERON!
I, UH, I THINK THEY'RE DEAD.
DID SOMEONE SAY MY NAME?
WE WERE TRYING TO DO A PUFF PIECE ABOUT EVERYONE'S FAVOURITE GUILTY PLEASURE SONGS, BUT--
OH! WELL! AS A POINT OF REFERENCE, I'D--
HEY, THERE'S JAMIE!
WHAT? FAVOURITE? I DON'T KNOW, CAN YOU COME BACK LATER? I'VE GOT TO FINISH ALL THESE FUCKING CROWD SCENES.
AS I WAS SAYING, THE CONCEPT OF A GUILTY PLEASURE SONG IS A FRAUGHT ONE. IN THIS ESSAY, I WILL--
OH, NO, HOLD ON, I WANT TO GET TO THE BOTTOM OF THIS. IF YOU'RE INTERESTED, THERE'S A 14,000-WORD ARTICLE I'VE WRITTEN ON MY BLOG, BUT YOU ABSOLUTELY NEED TO READ THE FOOTNOTES, AND--HEY--WAIT-- I HAVEN'T EVEN GOT A TERRIBLE PUN IN YET--

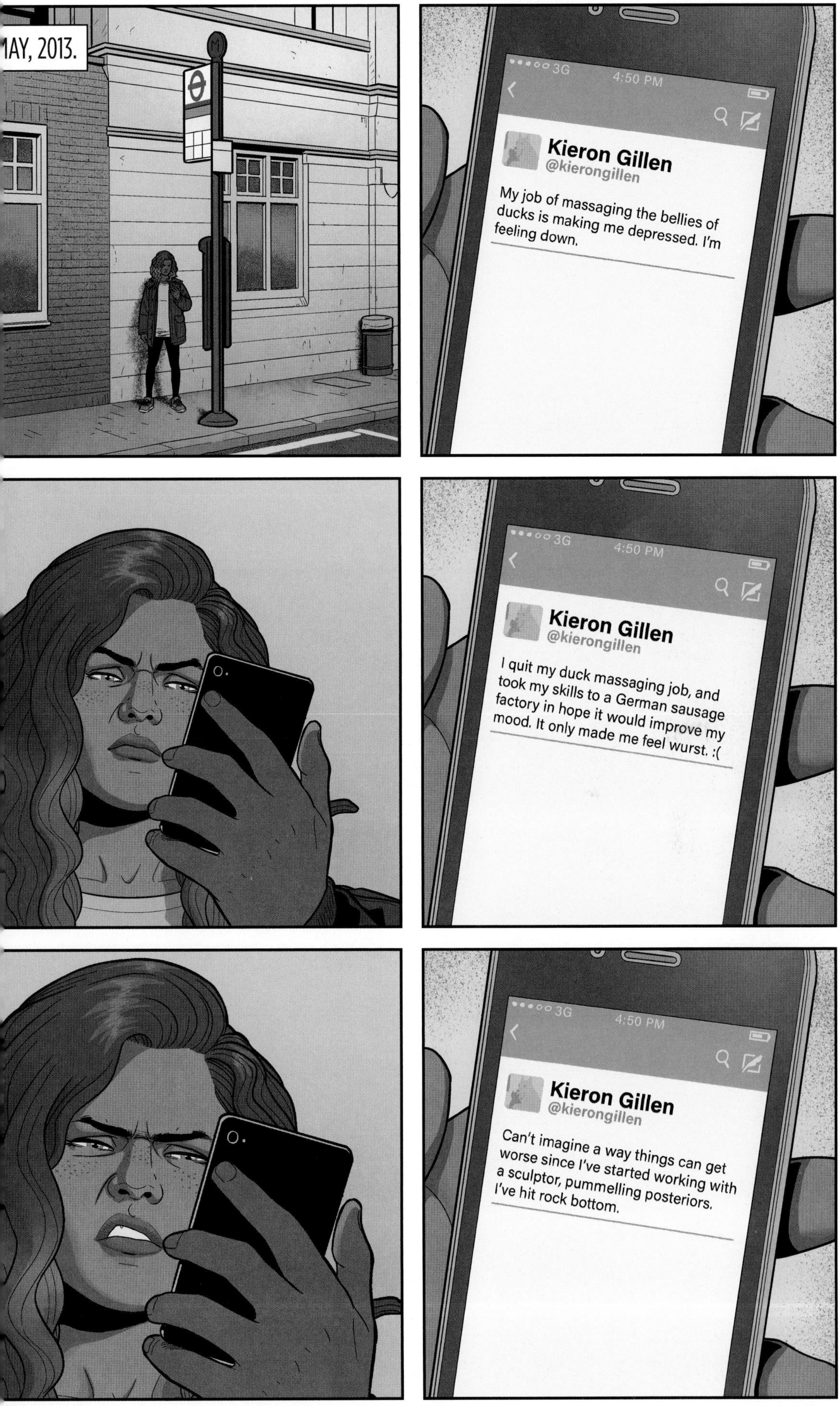
AY, 2013.
Kieron Gillen
@kierongillen
My job of massaging the bellies of ducks is making me depressed. I'm feeling down.
Kieron Gillen
@kierongillen
I quit my duck massaging job, and took my skills to a German sausage factory in hope it would improve my mood. It only made me feel wurst. :(
Kieron Gillen
@kierongillen
Can't imagine a way things can get worse since I've started working with a sculptor, pummelling posteriors. I've hit rock bottom.

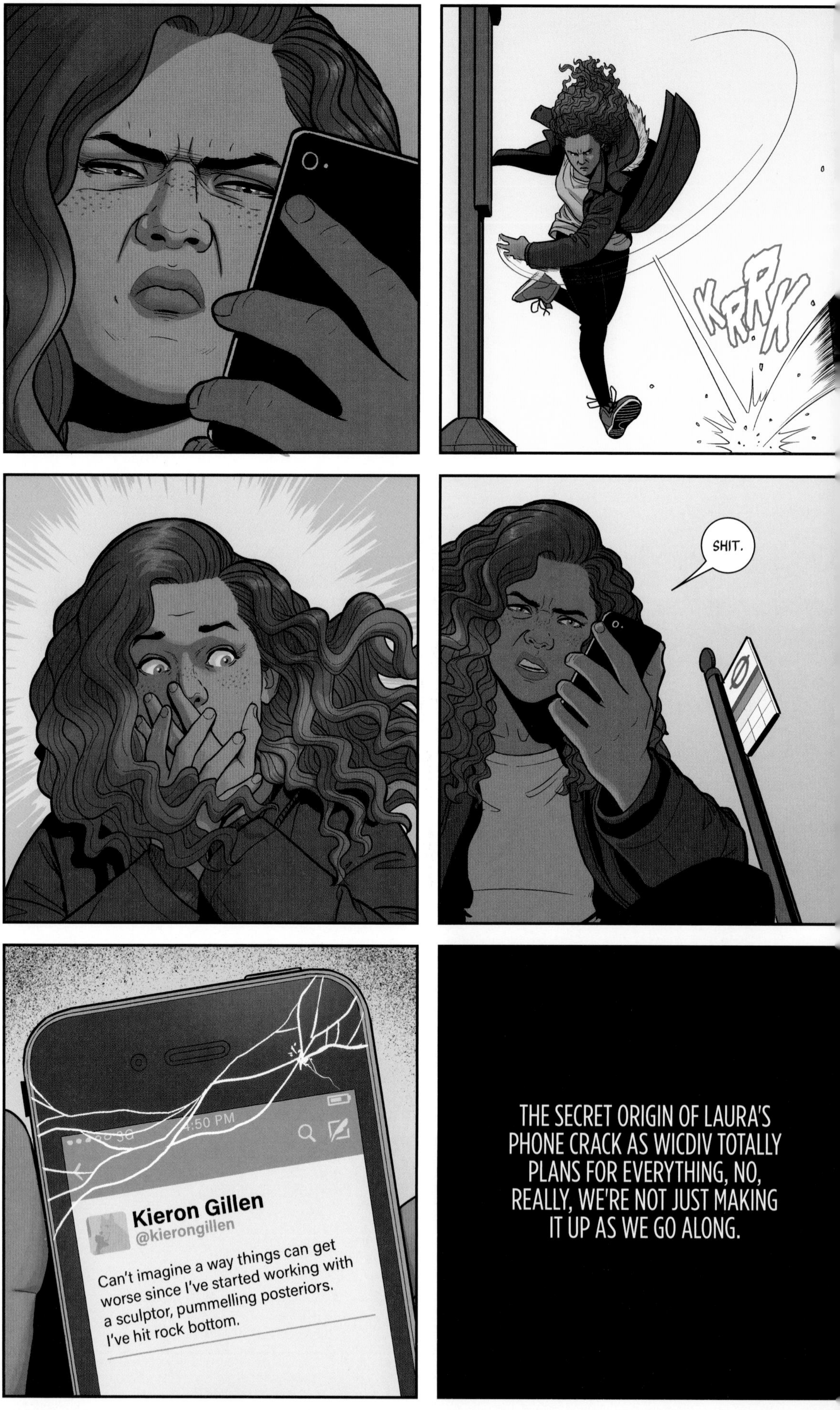
KRRK
SHIT.
4:50 PM
Kieron Gillen
@kierongillen
Can't imagine a way things can get worse since I've started working with a sculptor, pummelling posteriors. I've hit rock bottom.
THE SECRET ORIGIN OF LAURA'S PHONE CRACK AS WICDIV TOTALLY PLANS FOR EVERYTHING, NO, REALLY, WE'RE NOT JUST MAKING IT UP AS WE GO ALONG.

THE
WICKED
+
DIVINE
THE

VARIANT ART

In the main series issues, the alternate covers are a chance for our talented friends to get to play with (and expand) the iconography of the series. With the Specials, they take on a different purpose. As they're drawn by the interior artists, it's their chance to introduce their story, and capture a moment. That they're done months before release also means they're often the first thing the artists draw — it's their own introduction to the characters as much as ours. Also, very pretty.

André Araújo and Matthew Wilson
455AD cover

Ryan Kelly and Matthew Wilson
1373AD cover

Stephanie Hans
1831AD cover

Jamie McKelvie and Matthew Wilson
1831AD second printing

Aud Koch
1923AD cover

Jamie McKelvie
1923AD Image Expo cover

Jamie McKelvie
1923AD Image Expo cover

Kris Anka
Christmas Annual cover

Margaux Saltel
The Funnies cover

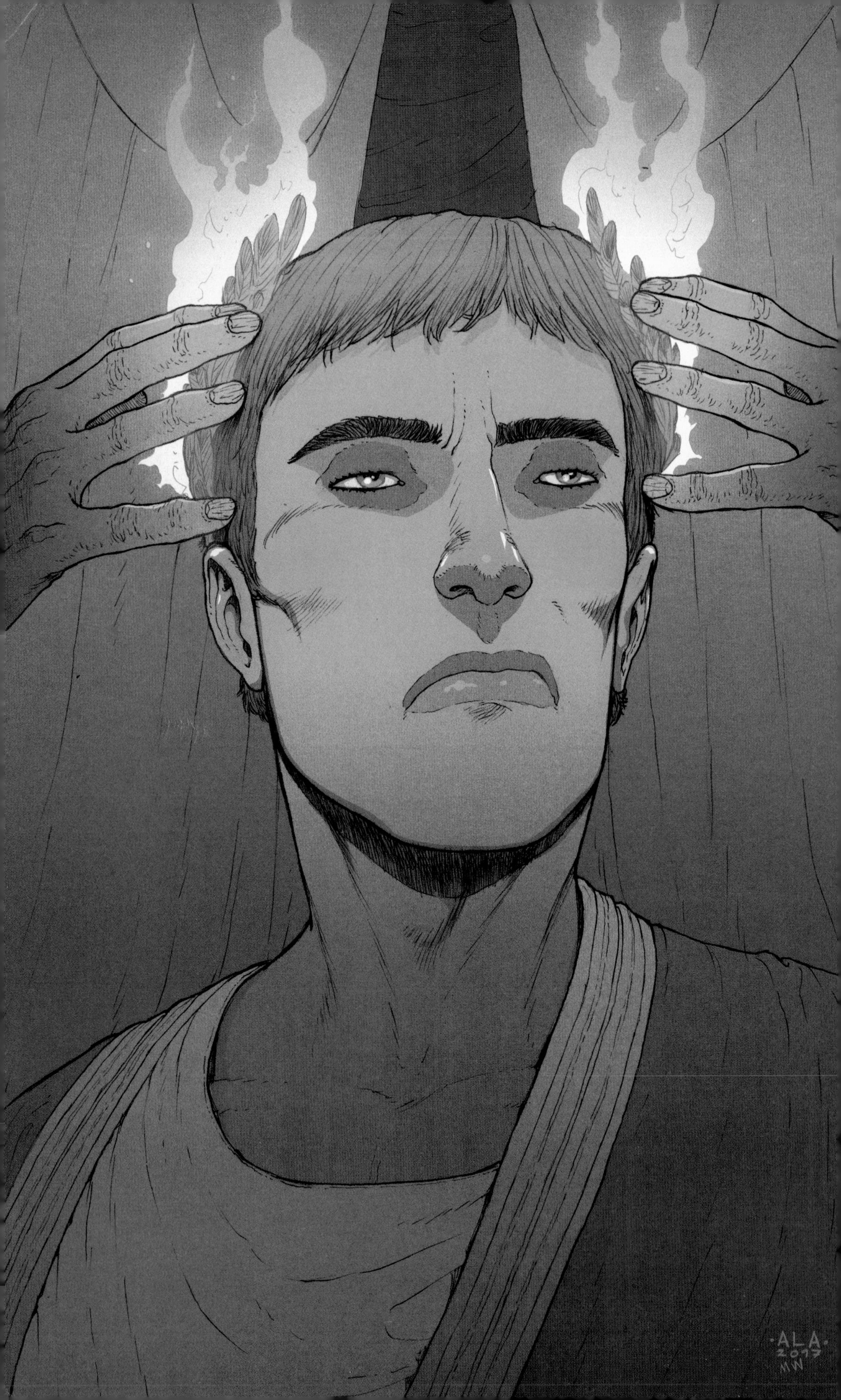
ALA
2017
MW

CHARACTER SKETCHES

While we selected each guest artist as we felt they'd capture
something essential to the historical story we were about to tell, we
also wanted Jamie to design the core cast of the book. If we're co-
creators of the series, it's important we co-create the main figures,
after all. As such, Jamie did more explicit design work for the
Specials than at any point in the rest of the series. We include some
in the following pages. It'd be rude to say all this and not, right?

Getting a chance to see Lucifers across the years is definitely part of the appeal of the project. 455's Lucifer as an actor playing Julius Caesar gave us a chance to play some games with the imagery. The burning laurel wreath was enough of a magical touch when we played with the Imperial purple — the idea that Caesar was a bit of a fashion groundbreaker also worked its way in to our vibe.

Working out the exact habit for medieval Lucifer was tricky — we did consider making her a novitiate, but couldn't get good enough reference. In the end, we settled for this — with the fantastical element of the sawn-off horns which say everything. That we included her with horns on Ryan's cover was an attempt to imply story in the spaces. Comics are juxtaposition of image, after all.

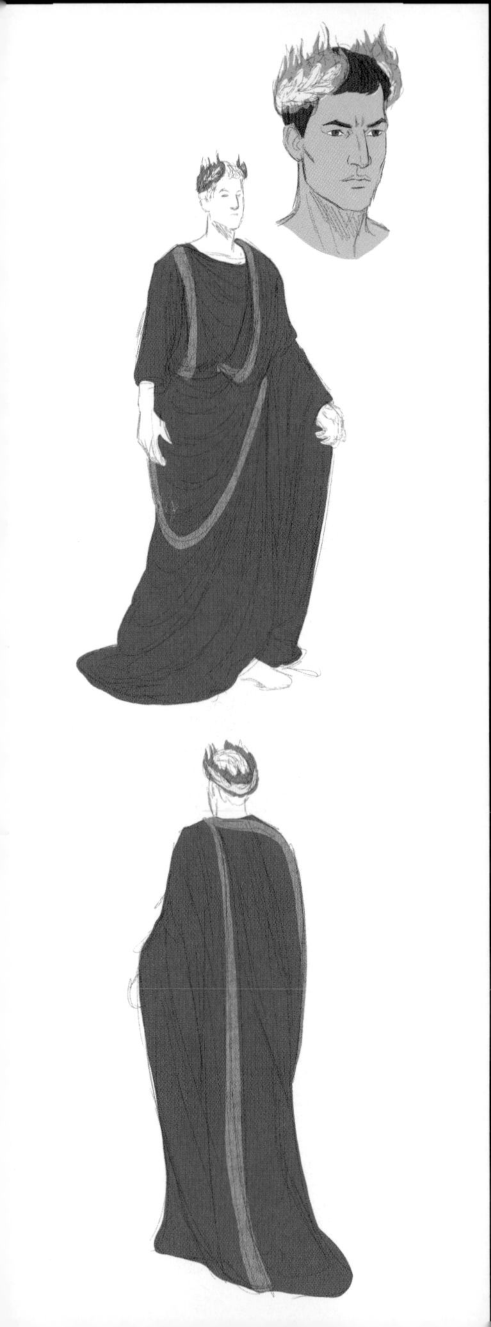

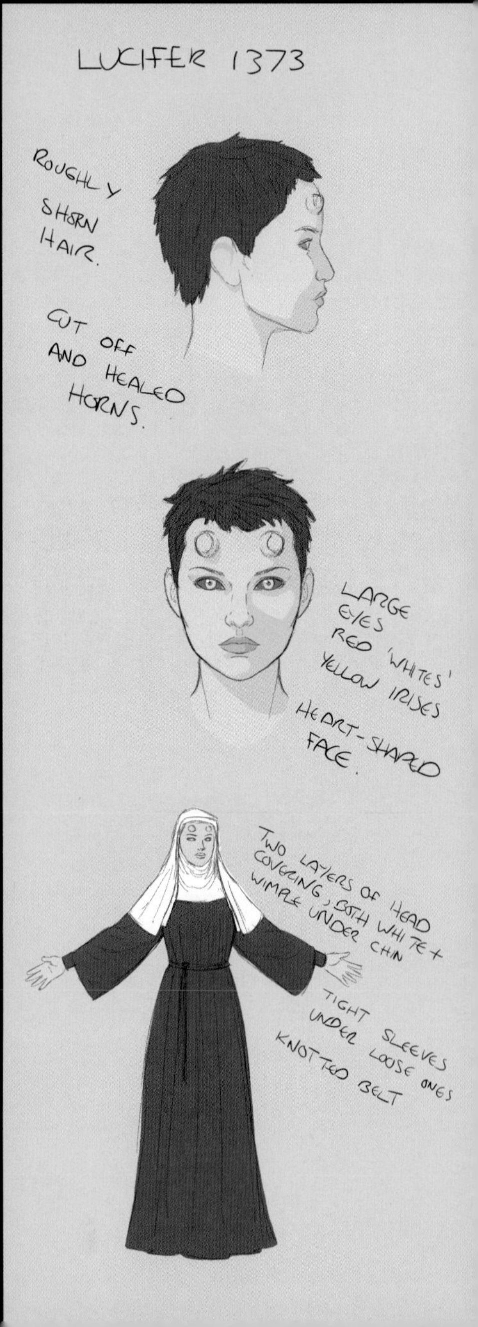
LUCIFER 1373
ROUGHLY SHORN HAIR.
CUT OFF AND HEALED HORNS.
LARGE EYES RED 'WHITES' YELLOW IRISES
HEART-SHAPED FACE.
TWO LAYERS OF HEAD COVERING, BOTH WHITE + WIMPLE UNDER CHIN
TIGHT SLEEVES UNDER LOOSE ONES
KNOTTED BELT

he first Special. Jamie had designed Lucifer and Woden when doing the actual cover, so only had to do Inanna and Morrigan here. The shifting of Morrigan's hair between the modes is a subtle element of his mercurial spirit. The trick with 1831 was to also evoke the historical figures which inspired them, as much as the 2014 pantheon evoked pop stars.

The Specials are longer than a normal issue, but that still only leaves relatively little room to explore the period. Equally, they're also serving a purpose in the larger story of *WicDiv*, focusing on the end of pantheons. They're the readers' chance to see how previous *WicDiv* pantheons have ultimately shaken down – which also means there are fewer characters in play. However, we also knew that for one Special we wanted to actually show a whole pantheon. Hence 1923, and a whole lot of work..

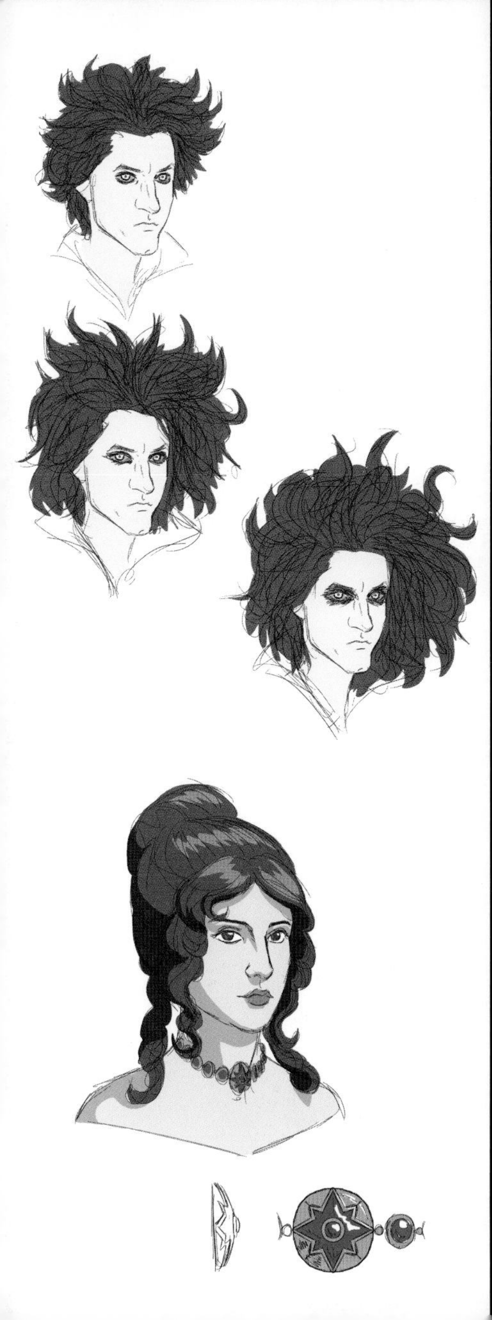

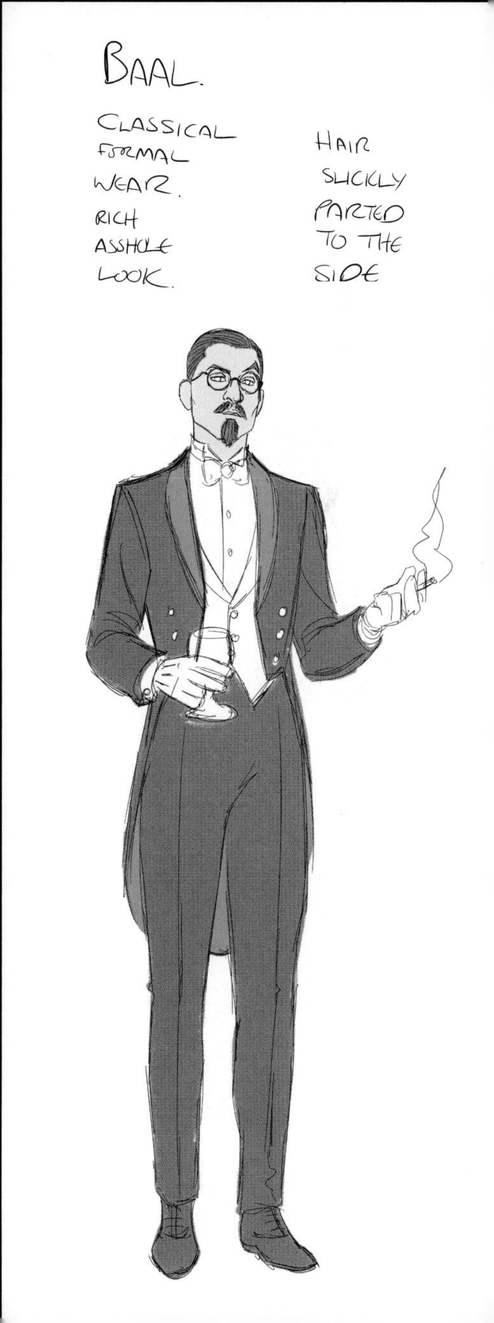
BAAL.
CLASSICAL FORMAL WEAR.
RICH ASSHOLE LOOK.
HAIR SLICKLY PARTED TO THE SIDE

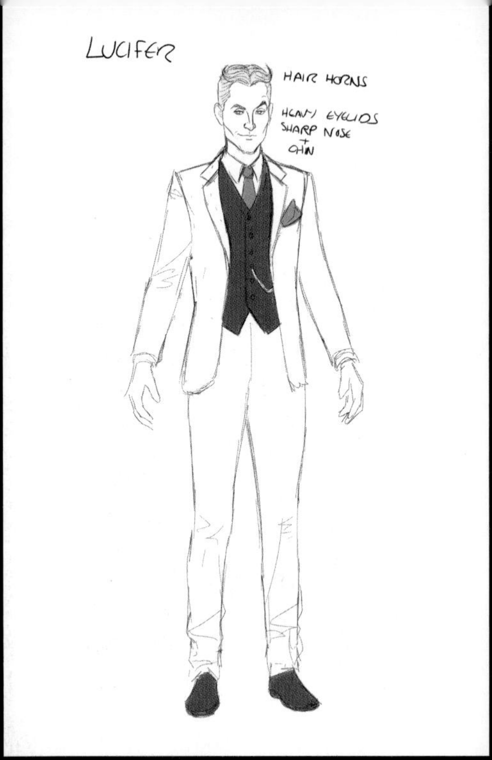
LUCIFER
HAIR HORNS
HEAVY EYELIDS
SHARP NOSE
+ CHIN

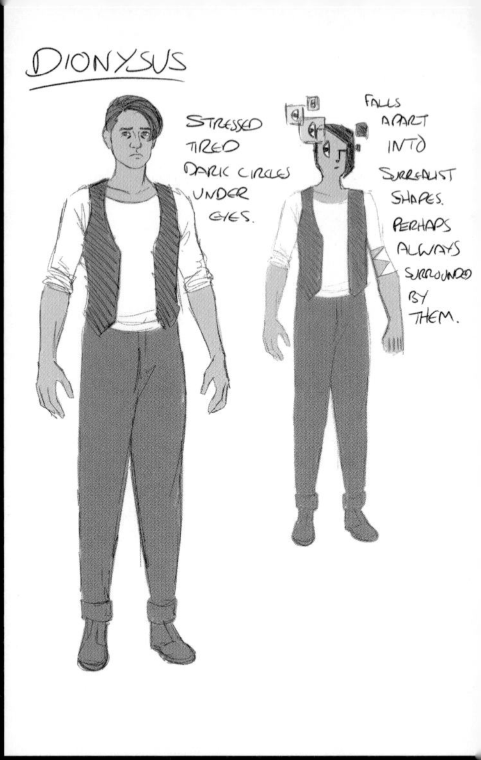
DIONYSUS
STRESSED
TIRED
DARK CIRCLES
UNDER
EYES.
FALLS
APART
INTO
SURREALIST
SHAPES.
PERHAPS
ALWAYS
SURROUNDED
BY
THEM.

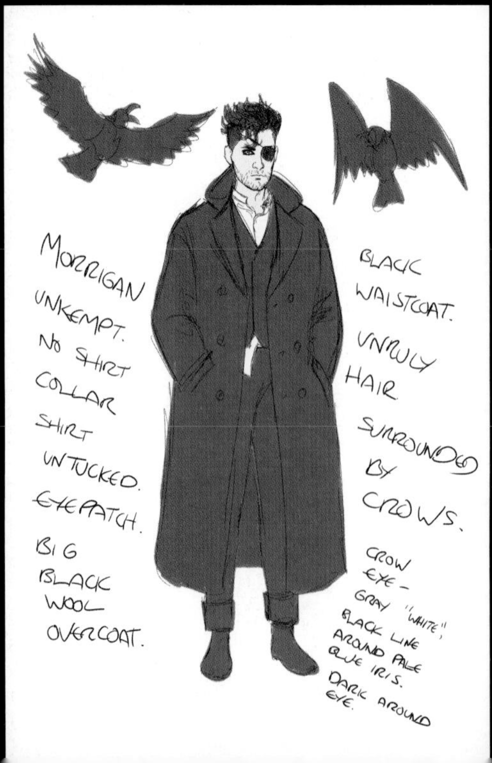
MORRIGAN
UNKEMPT.
NO SHIRT
COLLAR
SHIRT
UNTUCKED.
EYEPATCH.
BIG
BLACK
WOOL
OVERCOAT.
BLACK
WAISTCOAT.
UNRULY
HAIR
SURROUNDED
BY
CROWS.
CROW
EYE -
GRAY "WHITE",
BLACK LINE
AROUND PALE
BLUE IRIS.
DARK AROUND
EYE.

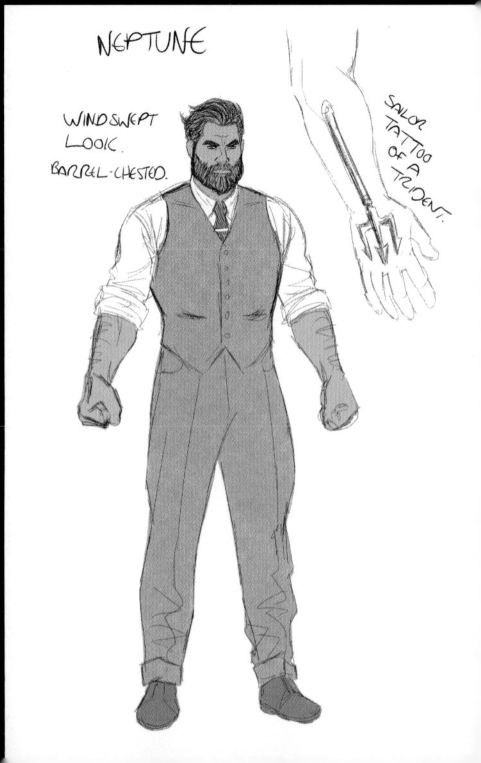
NEPTUNE
WINDSWEPT
LOOK.
BARREL-CHESTED.
SAILOR
TATTOO
OF A
TRIDENT.

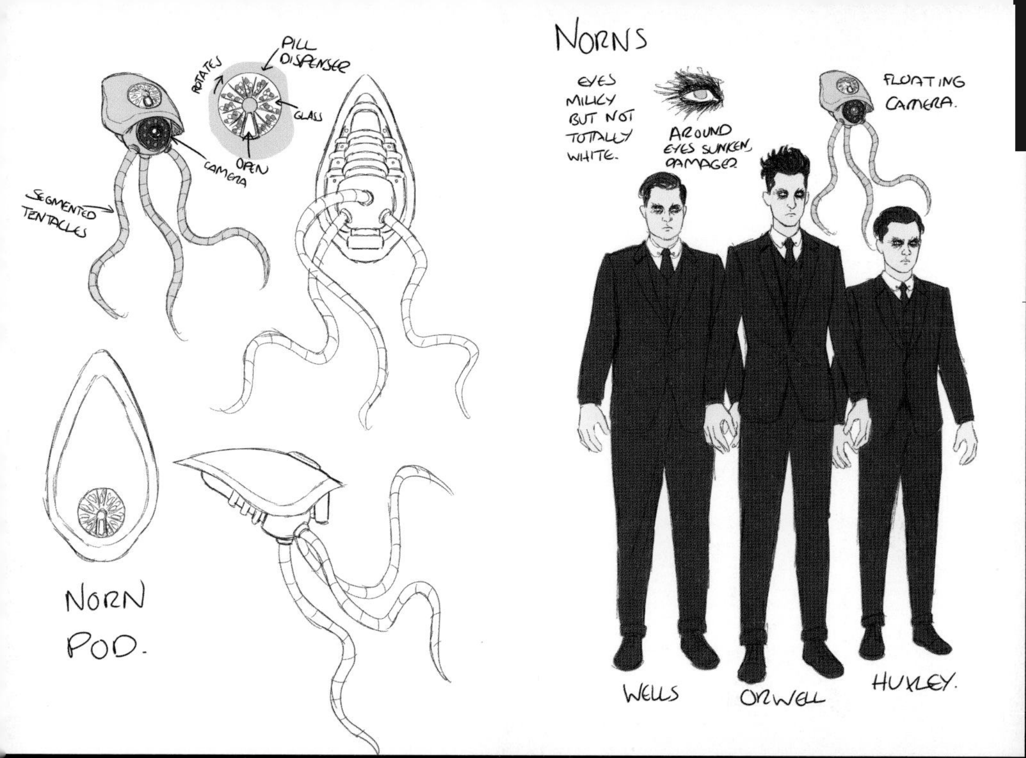
PILL DISPENSER
ROTATES
GLASS
OPEN
CAMERA
SEGMENTED TENTACLES
NORN POD.
NORNS
EYES MILKY BUT NOT TOTALLY WHITE.
AROUND EYES SUNKEN, DAMAGED
FLOATING CAMERA.
WELLS
ORWELL
HUXLEY.

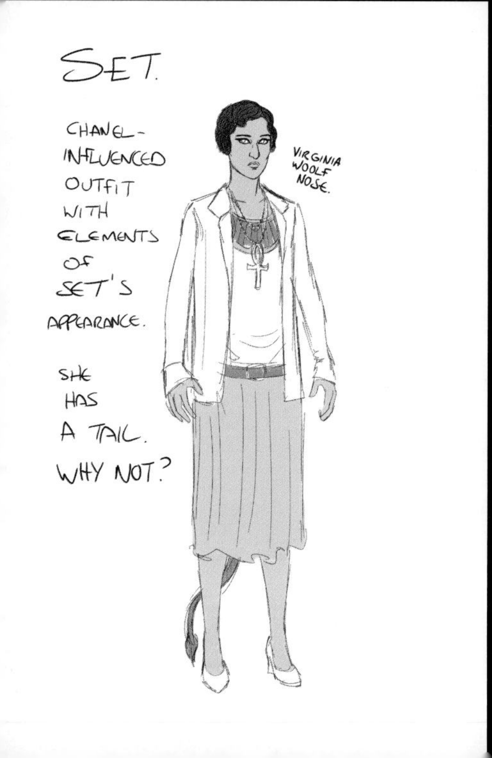
SET.
CHANEL-INFLUENCED OUTFIT WITH ELEMENTS OF SET'S APPEARANCE.
VIRGINIA WOOLF NOSE.
SHE HAS A TAIL. WHY NOT?

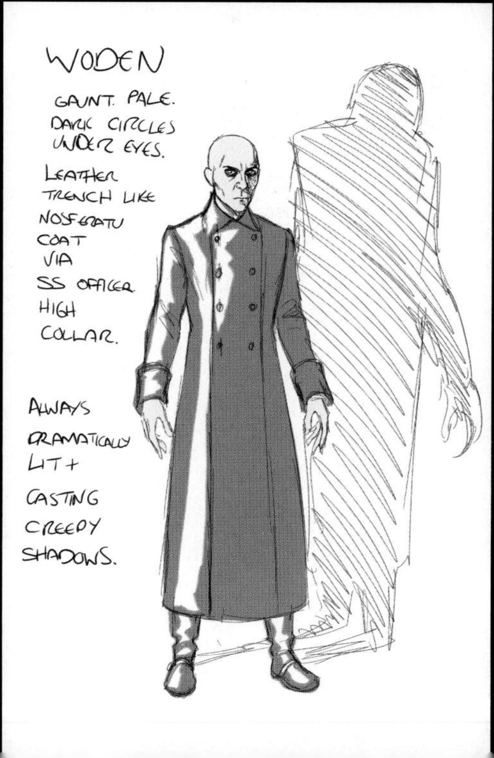
WODEN
GAUNT. PALE. DARK CIRCLES UNDER EYES.
LEATHER TRENCH LIKE NOSFERATU COAT VIA SS OFFICER. HIGH COLLAR.
ALWAYS DRAMATICALLY LIT + CASTING CREEPY SHADOWS.

ALSO BY THE CREATORS

THE WICKED + THE DIVINE

VOL. 1:
THE FAUST ACT
#1–5 COLLECTED

VOL. 2:
FANDEMONIUM
#6–11 COLLECTED

VOL. 3:
COMMERCIAL SUICIDE
#12–17 COLLECTED

VOL. 4:
RISING ACTION
#18–22 COLLECTED

GILLEN McKELVIE WILSON COWLES
THE WICKED + THE DIVINE
THE FAUST ACT

McKELVIE WILSON COWLES
FANDEMONIUM

McKELVIE WILSON COWLES
COMMERCIAL SUICIDE

McKELVIE WILSON COWLES
RISING ACTION

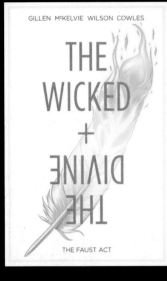

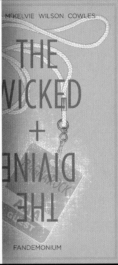

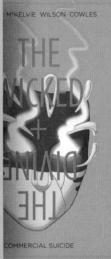

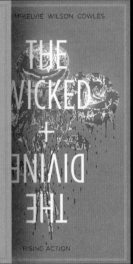

VOL. 5:
IMPERIAL PHASE 1
#23–28 COLLECTED

VOL. 6:
IMPERIAL PHASE 2
#29–33 COLLECTED

VOL. 7:
MOTHERING INVENTION
#34–39 COLLECTED

GILLEN McKELVIE WILSON COWLES
IMPERIAL PHASE PART 1

GILLEN McKELVIE WILSON COWLES
IMPERIAL PHASE PART 2

GILLEN McKELVIE WILSON COWLES
THE WICKED + THE DIVINE
MOTHERING INVENTION

www.wicdiv.com major news, new issues, merchandise
#WicDiv the hashtag on twitter for WicDiv Discussion
WicDiv the general tag on tumblr for the community
bit.ly/WicDivPlaylist the ever-updated Spotify Playlist for the series

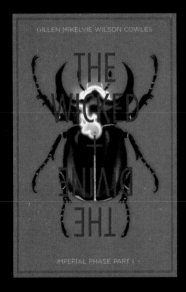

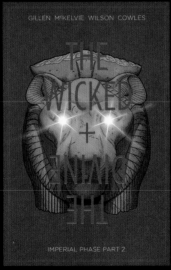

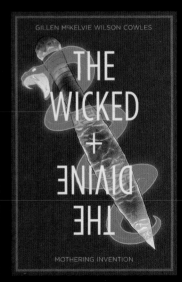

ALSO BY THE CREATORS

THE WICKED + THE DIVINE

BOOK ONE:
#1–11 COLLECTED

GILLEN McKELVIE WILSON COWLES
THE WICKED + THE DIVINE
1

BOOK TWO:
#12–22 COLLECTED

GILLEN McKELVIE WILSON COWLES
THE WICKED + THE DIVINE
2

BOOK THREE:
#23–33 COLLECTED

THE WICKED + THE DIVINE
3

THE COMPLETE
PHONOGRAM

GILLEN McKELVIE WILSON COWLES
SIDE A
THE COMPLETE
PHONOGRAM

VOL. 1:
RUE BRITANNIA

BRITANNIA
Kieron
GILLEN
Jamie
McKELVIE

VOL. 2:
THE SINGLES CLUB

SINGLES CLUB
GILLEN & JAMIE McKELVIE

VOL. 3:
THE IMMATERIAL GIRL

ONOGRAM

PHONOGRAM

THE COMPLETE PHONOGRAM COLLECTS: Vol. 1: Rue Britannia, Vol. 2: The Singles Club, Vol. 3: The Immaterial Girl, and the previously uncollected B-side stories

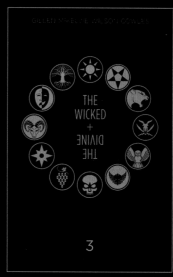

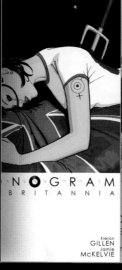

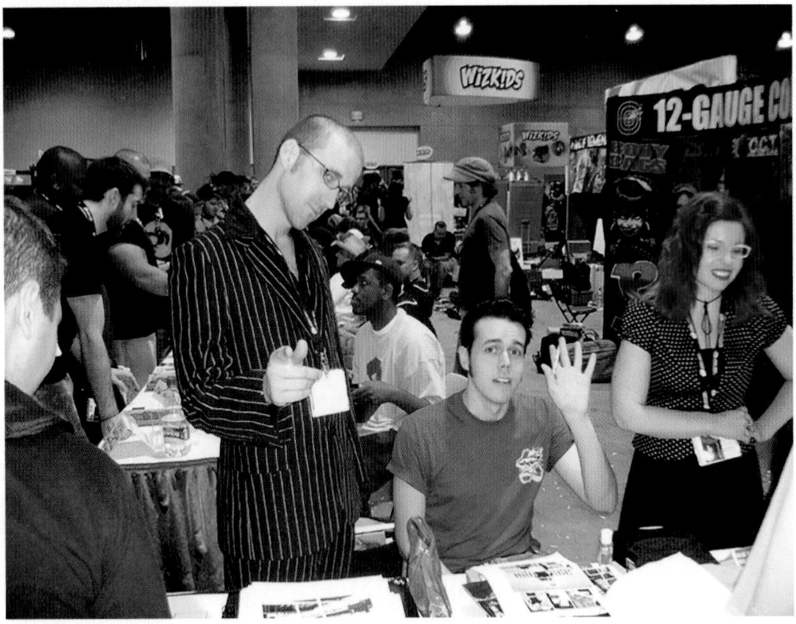
WIZKIDS
12-GAUGE CO
WIZKIDS

Kieron Gillen is a writer and this, from 2006, was his first ever San Diego.

Jamie McKelvie is an artist and this, from 2006, was not his first ever San Diego.

Matt Wilson is a colourist and this, from 2006, is not the first time we've printed a picture of Kelly Sue DeConnick rather than one of him. He should speak to his lawyer and/or never speak to us ever again.

Photograph by Rantz Hoseley